I0167919

TRIUMPH IN WARFARE

A fight for the territory of our hearts

Volume I

I have fought the good fight ...
2 Timothy 4:7

CELESTE LI, M.D.

PLUM
TREE
MINISTRIES

Triumph Series

by Celeste Li, M.D.

Book I:
Triumph Over Suffering
A Spiritual Guide to Conquering Adversity

Book II:
Triumph of Surrender
A Walk of Intimacy With Jesus

Book III:
Triumph in Warfare
A fight for the territory of our hearts
\<in two volumes\>

Serve Like Jesus
Triumph Servant Leadership Training

No profits are ever made from the sale of these books. All proceeds are given directly to the church or used to minister to the Body of Christ at large. Thank you for your love, prayers, and support. May God bless you and your family with hope and healing.

The Plum Tree Ministries Team

Dedicated to His soldiers in active service:

*May you and Jesus demolish
many strongholds together.*

**Blessed be the LORD, my rock,
Who trains my hands for war,
And my fingers for battle.**

Psalm 144:1

Lord Jesus, Yours is the Name above every other name, and at Your Name we bow our hearts before You. You are Victory, conquering all darkness by Your blood spilled at the cross and Your triumphant resurrection. You alone are our Lovingkindness and our Fortress, our Rock and our Deliverer, our Shield and our Refuge.

We know that it is not by our might nor by our power, but only by Your Spirit that battles are won and strongholds are torn down. We, Your faithful warriors, stand before You, waiting for You to equip us to join You by working in us what is pleasing in Your sight. Please, Lord, count us worthy of our calling; fulfill our hearts' desire to glorify You and our work of faith with Your power; give us courage and endurance to fight alongside You to the end. Bring forth fruit of righteous that is for the praise of Your glory.

Lord Jesus, we know that Your banner over us is love; we keep our eyes fixed on You and trust You with all our hearts. And as we take up our weapons and follow You to the battlefront, please shield us with Your canopy of Your divine love and protection. Amen.

PLUM
TREE
MINISTRIES

Jupiter, Florida
plumtreeministries@gmail.com
"The surviving remnant of the house of Judah will again take root downward and bear fruit upward." Isaiah 37:31

Triumph in Warfare
A fight for the territory of our hearts, Volume I
Copyright © 2024 by Celeste Li
Celeste.Li.Triumph@gmail.com
Visit our website: TriumphOverSuffering.com

Plum Tree Ministries
210 Jupiter Lakes Blvd., #5105, Jupiter, FL 33458 USA

ISBN-13: 978-0-9993393-2-9
Printed in United States of America
All Scripture quotations, unless otherwise indicated, are taken from the New American Standard Bible. Copyright © 1960, 1962, 1963, 1968, 1971, 1972, 1973, 1975, 1977, 1995 by The Lockman Foundation. Used by permission.
Scripture quotations marked NIV are taken from the Holy Bible, New International Version®, NIV®. Copyright © 1973, 1978, 1984, 2011 by Biblica, Inc.™ Used by permission of Zondervan. All rights reserved worldwide.
Scripture quotations marked NLT are taken from the Holy Bible: New Living Translation, copyright © 1996, 2004. Used by permission of Tyndale House Publishers, Inc., Carol Stream, Illinois 60188. All rights reserved.
Scripture quotations marked KJV are taken from the King James Study Bible, copyright ©1988 by Liberty University and Thomas Nelson, Inc.
Scripture quotations marked NKJV are taken from the New King James Version. Copyright ©1982 by Thomas Nelson, Inc. Used by permission. All rights reserved.
Scripture quotations marked AMP are taken from THE AMPLIFIED BIBLE. Old Testament Copyright ©1965, 1987 by The Zondervan Corporation. The Amplified New Testament Copyright ©1958, 1987 by The Lockman Foundation. Used by permission.
Scripture quotations marked AMPC are taken from Amplified Bible, Classic Edition AMPC, Copyright 1954 1958, 1962, 1964, 1965, 1987 by the Lockman Foundation.
Scripture quotations marked ESV are from The ESV Bible (English Standard Version), copyright © 2001, by Crossway, a publishing ministry of Good News Publishers. Used by Permission. All rights reserved.

Cover design by Alec Li
Cover photography by VitalikRadko / lightfieldstudios.net
Interior design and layout by Madie Steenkamp

If you find anything in this book helpful for yourself or your ministry – whether your ministry is a formal teaching or reaching out to a friend – without taking it out of context, you are welcome to teach it, reprint it, copy it, quote it, or reproduce it in any format, including written, visual, audio, or electronic, without my express permission. If you are using something that is footnoted, please acknowledge the original author. May the Lord bless you and others with this book.

Contents

Volume I

Part I: Battle Ready

No soldier in active service entangles himself in the affairs of everyday life, so that he may please the one who enlisted him as a soldier.
2 Timothy 2:4

Part II: Analyzing the Enemy

For our struggle is not against flesh and blood, but against the rulers, against the powers, against the world forces of this darkness, against the spiritual forces of wickedness in the heavenly places.   Ephesians 6:12

Part III: Satan Operates Out of Strongholds

For though we walk in the flesh, we do not war according to the flesh, for the weapons of our warfare are not of the flesh, but divinely powerful for the destruction of fortresses [NIV strongholds]. We are destroying speculations and every lofty thing raised up against the knowledge of God, and we are taking every thought captive to the obedience of Christ, and we are ready to punish all disobedience, whenever your obedience is complete.   2 Corinthians 10:3-6

Volume II

Part IV: Closing Doors to the Enemy

The night is almost gone, and the day is near. Therefore let us lay aside the deeds of darkness and put on the armor of light.   Romans 13:12

Part V: Dismantling Strongholds

**"THE SPIRIT OF THE LORD IS UPON ME,
BECAUSE HE ANOINTED ME TO PREACH THE GOSPEL TO THE POOR.
HE HAS SENT ME TO PROCLAIM RELEASE TO THE CAPTIVES,
AND RECOVERY OF SIGHT TO THE BLIND,
TO SET FREE THOSE WHO ARE OPPRESSED,
TO PROCLAIM THE FAVORABLE YEAR OF THE LORD."**
   Luke 4:18-19

Foreword

It is no secret that many people are struggling in life. Our culture and society clearly reflect the battles that many of us are facing, which impact our personal well-being and bleed over into our families, our friendships, and our everyday lives. What few people realize is that often these battles have a spiritual root – what Scripture calls strongholds (2Cor. 10:4): thought patterns or systems of belief that run contrary to the Word of God. So much of the pain and trials people go through are a result of these strongholds that have taken root in their lives.

Dr. Celeste Li has discerned what is actually happening in people's lives, and through *Triumph in Warfare* she not only awakens the reader to the reality that our struggles are not against flesh and blood, but she builds a pathway to break free from the strongholds and walk in the victory God has for us. This recognition, coupled with Celeste's heart to help people heal from the suffering that is a part of the fallen world in which we live, is evident to all those who know her.

Celeste and her family have made Christ Fellowship Church their home church for many years. As her pastor I have had the privilege of seeing firsthand Celeste's heart and expertise as she ministers to people, helping them heal from their past wounds, confront their current realities and step into the future God has waiting for them. Her pastoral care and patience as she walks people towards freedom has helped countless individuals experience lasting victory.

Triumph in Warfare builds off Celeste's first two books, *Triumph Over Suffering* and *Triumph of Surrender*, delving into a deeper understanding of the strategies of the enemy and how to walk in the victory and freedom Jesus made possible for us in the realm of spiritual warfare. *Triumph in Warfare* presents what can sometimes be an intimidating topic – spiritual warfare – and presents it in a way that is easy to grasp and put into action for any Christian. Celeste reminds us that spiritual warfare is not reserved for the "spiritual elite," but every Christian must prepare to engage. With a foundation on the Word of God, coupled with real life testimonies, Celeste makes this book practical and accessible for each of us.

For some, the concept of a spiritual battle taking place all around us will be a new revelation. Don't let that frighten or intimidate you. The Bible reminds us that greater is His Spirit that lives within us than he that is in the world (1 John 4:4). For others, let this serve as a timely reminder of the warfare for your lives. You have a real enemy that Jesus says has come to rob, kill and destroy (John 10:10).

As you work your way through this book, Celeste will help you to establish your identity in Christ and recognize the victory that we can all have because of Christ. You will gain a better understanding of the stratagems of your spiritual enemy, particularly around the concept of strongholds and how they take root in our lives. Then, Celeste will teach you how to proactively close the doors that allow the enemy into our lives, and how dismantle strongholds that have been set up in order to live the victorious John 10:10 life that Jesus made available to all who believe in Him.

I am particularly grateful that while Celeste addresses spiritual warfare, she helps us keep our eyes firmly fixed on Jesus, the author and finisher of our faith. He is the only One who has the power to help each of us experience the victory intended for our lives. Many of us have lived too long under the constant attack of the enemy, holding on for dear life. It's time to experience triumph over his schemes and walk in true *shalom* – the peace and wholeness that God intends for us to have.

Dr. J. Todd Mullins
Sr. Pastor, Christ Fellowship Church

Introduction
Asleep in the Light

I admit that I was once asleep in the Light. Meeting Jesus and fully surrendering my life to Him when I was 40, intently studying the Scriptures, immersing in deep Bible studies and sweet fellowship with other Christian women, I thought that demonic activity was something unique going on during Jesus' time on earth. I thought the forces of darkness had no bearing on our lives today. Yet I have learned that we have been transferred to a Kingdom that is under siege, and if we remain asleep in the Light, *we are going to get clobbered.*

"Wake up, O sleeper, rise from the dead, and Christ will shine on you." Ephesians 5:14 NIV

We may be in denial, but the enemy certainly is not. He is advancing stealthily, menacingly, and his attack is *relentless.* He has been practicing on countless opponents in innumerable arenas over many, many years. He is confident, even brash, for he is well prepared. *But are we?* As we will see in Part I,

No soldier in active service entangles himself in the affairs of everyday life, so that he may please the one who enlisted him as a soldier. 2 Timothy 2:4

Are we mesmerized by the lures of the world and asleep in the light, with no idea that we are called to be warriors? Are we living as if the war ended when we accepted Christ? Are our eyes blinded and our ears so filled with the world's noise that we can neither see nor hear the enemy approaching? Do we even *recognize* the battlefield?

"The thief comes only to steal and kill and destroy; I came that they may have life, and have it abundantly." John 10:10

As we stand by, blinded and helpless, the forces of darkness are *stealing* our privileges as children of God, *killing* our passion to live for Christ, and *destroying* our destinies. Many of God's people are carrying unhealed wounds that have caused them to believe lies, lies that are preventing them from receiving God's fathomless unconditional love. Some of God's people live aimlessly, their lives devoid of meaning, with no idea of their calling or purpose. Some live without restraint, sliding down into selfishness, pride, rebellion, jealousy, violence, pornography or other sexual sins. Others are working desperately to fill the void in their hearts with materialism, accolades, positions, workaholism, thrills, relationships, or addictions. Still others may be trapped in unforgiveness, or on a downward spiral of fear, worthlessness, depression, hopelessness, and even suicide. And for many, it seems that whatever struggles we have in our own lives suddenly appear in escalating fashion in our children. With a few well-placed swipes of his sword, the enemy has shattered our marriages, fractured our families, plundered our households, and we, blinded, have no idea what struck.

But is all this the result of spiritual warfare? Such a good question.

Although Jesus has secured everlasting triumph for us, we still live in a fallen world, bearing the brunt of sin – our ancestors' sins, the world's current sins, and our own sins. We suffer from injuries inflicted by fallen people in this broken world. We also endure the natural consequences of our own sins and irresponsible behavior. And vital to victory is *understanding* the interplay between our sinful flesh, the corrupt world, and the works of the devil.

This book can help us to discern what *is* spiritual warfare, and what *is not*. It can also help us to see how the forces of darkness can manipulate the world to tempt our weak flesh, and how those same forces of darkness can work to magnify the consequences of our sins and irresponsible behaviors. We will learn to recognize the times when we are losing the battle because we are trying to fight a spiritual battle with weapons of the flesh. We will study the difference between defensive and offensive warfare. We will learn how strongholds are created, and how to partner with Jesus to tear them down. And we will train with our spiritual weapons, applying what we are learning to our lives right now.

Spiritual warfare is as real for us today as it was in Biblical times.

But please don't read this book with a kind of morbid fascination with the demonic. I believe that God is calling us to be *educated*, but not *obsessed* (Rom 16:19).¹ Discerning, but not dangerously sucked in. Achieving His perfect balance, somewhere between fearfully hiding our heads in the sand and brazenly consumed by imagined battles (Matt 10:16, 1Cor 14:20).

This book is *not* about Satan and his demons. It is a book about our Lord and Savior Jesus Christ. We have more to learn, surely, yet battles are not won by focusing on the demonic, but on *Jesus*. For only He frees, only He saves, only He delivers. A deep abiding relationship with Him is *paramount* to victory.

This is also not a book written for super-spiritual Christians, nor is it about becoming a "deliverance minister." It is simply a book for the everyday Christian in everyday battles as a soldier in active duty. It is about how strongholds *in our own hearts* are erected – and how to pull them down. It is to train us to be victorious *in the war within our own lives and minds and hearts.* I long for you to be free indeed. And once we learn how to partner with Jesus for victory in our own hearts, we can use what we have learned to help others get free also.

This book is packed with Scripture, and we will take a deep and prayerful look at many passages. We will also read some quotes from some pastors, ministers, and Bible scholars who are listed in the *Resources* section at the back of this book. These theologians do not always agree on everything, but I think their writings mostly seem Biblical, balanced, and helpful to increase our understanding of this complex topic. **Examine everything carefully; hold fast to that which is good** (1Thess 5:21), and do not follow any teaching contrary to the Word of God (Gal 1:8).

Throughout this book, you will also come across many real life testimonies of those who have battled to victory. You will also read testimonies of those who are still in the throes of the battle. All are true testimonies, given to me by men and women I know and cherish. Almost all of these contributions are published with real names; a few have names and other details changed to protect privacy. As you read these testimonies, be alert for the Lord's freedom, deliverance, and healing.

This all may sound complex and even scary, but trust the Lord to teach you, protect you, and carry you through. He does not want you to be unprepared for the next missile strike. I want to encourage you to open your heart and engage in this study. Scattered through each chapter are opportunities to apply what you are learning to your life right now. Don't gloss over the *Ponder, Pray, and Journal* sections – become an effectual doer and invite the Lord to implant His Word deeply into your heart.

I pray that as you study this book, the Holy Spirit will open your eyes to see not only the onslaught of the enemy, but more importantly, the glory of our Commander-in-Chief. I pray that seeing Jesus with greater clarity will draw you to follow more closely after Him. I pray that seeing the assault of the enemy will drive you to Jesus, and will galvanize you to implore the Lord to train your hands for battle.

God has enlisted you, and I pray that the Scriptures packing these pages will compel you to enter the warfare. I pray you will fight alongside Jesus, standing firm in the authority He gives you. I pray you will wield your spiritual weapons with the power the Holy Spirit provides, demolishing strongholds and plundering the enemy's house. And I pray that His Words will motivate you to learn firsthand what Jesus means when He says that He came to set the captives free.

> **The Spirit of the Sovereign LORD is on me,**
> **because the LORD has anointed me**
> **to preach good news to the poor.**
> **He has sent me to bind up the brokenhearted,**
> **to proclaim freedom for the captives**
> **and release from darkness for the prisoners,**
> **to proclaim the year of the LORD's favor ...**

Isaiah 61:1-2 NIV

PART I:
BATTLE READY

No soldier in active service entangles himself in the affairs of everyday life, so that he may please the one who enlisted him as a soldier.   2 Timothy 2:4

Chapter 1
The Why Behind the Warfare

I believe that God has placed this book in your hands for the purpose of revealing something to you. Please don't turn away. Come and pray with me.

Lord Jesus Christ, You are Truth, and You have given us Your Holy Spirit to guide us into all truth. Please send Your Holy Spirit upon the men and women working through this book, speak deeply into their hearts and reveal truth to them.

I know that the enemy does not want us to know the truth of who You are and the truth of who we are in You. Satan doesn't want us to know about him or his tactics, his strategies, or his lies. But You, Jesus, do not want us to be battling blind or deaf. You love us and treasure us and do not want us to remain asleep in the light. You do not want us to remain vulnerable in our ignorance. Please remove the veil of deception that obscures the reality of the warfare. Please open our eyes to see what You see, open our ears to hear Your voice, open our minds to perceive truth, and open our hearts to deeply understand You and Your ways.

As we work through these chapters together, please give us Your protection and help us to keep our eyes fixed on You, the Author and Finisher of our faith. For You are the Blessed and Only Sovereign, the King of kings and the Lord of lords, who alone possesses immortality and dwells in unapproachable light, whom no man has seen or can

*see. Yours is the Name that is above every other name, and at Your
Name, Jesus, every knee will bow and every tongue will confess that
You, Jesus Christ, are Lord, to the glory of God the Father. To You be
all glory, honor, power, and dominion, both now and forever more.
Amen.*[1]

Deep breath. Before we enter the battlefield, let's engrave two truths
deeply into our hearts and minds.

*First Truth:
The Battle Is Already Won*

Jesus was declared the Victor by His death and resurrection:

**When you were dead in your transgressions and the
uncircumcision of your flesh, He made you alive together
with Him, having forgiven us all our transgressions, having
canceled out the certificate of debt consisting of decrees
against us, which was hostile to us; and He has taken it out of
the way, having nailed it to the cross. When He had disarmed
the rulers and authorities, He made a public display of them,
having triumphed over them through Him.** Colossians 2:13-15

**... He raised Him from the dead and seated Him at His
right hand in the heavenly places, far above all rule and
authority and power and dominion, and every name that is
named, not only in this age but also in the one to come.**
Ephesians 1:20-21

The victory was won *at the cross* and proven through His triumphant
and miraculous resurrection (Rom 1:4), and His church will not be
overcome:

**"I also say to you that you are Peter, and upon this rock
I will build My church; *and the gates of Hades will not
overpower it.*"** Matthew 16:18, emphasis added

Second Truth:
We Are On the Winning Team

For He rescued us from the domain of darkness, and transferred us to the kingdom of His beloved Son, in whom we have redemption, the forgiveness of sins.   Colossians 1:13-14

He has rescued us from the domain of Satan, made us His children (Jn 1:12), and transferred us to His Kingdom. And because we are *in Him*, we are members of His Body and are one with Him:

"The glory which You have given Me I have given to them, that they may be one, just as We are one; I in them and You in Me ... Father, I desire that they also, whom You have given Me, be with Me where I am ..."   John 17:22-24

And because we are one with Him, we are with Him where He is: seated at the right hand of the Father:

But God, being rich in mercy, because of His great love with which He loved us, even when we were dead in our transgressions, made us alive together with Christ (by grace you have been saved), and raised us up with Him, and seated us with Him in the heavenly places in Christ Jesus ...
Ephesians 2:4-6

We are seated with Him. Him in us and us in Him. Far above all rule and authority and over every name that can be named. In this world, but not of this world. Seated with Him in the heavenlies, yet still in this world to fulfill His purposes (Mk 10:37, Jn 17:15). We are one with Him, so we are victors with Him:

But thanks be to God, who always leads us in triumph in Christ.   2 Corinthians 2:14

Jesus has won, so we have won.

Now right here is where I can start to become confused. If Jesus has *already* won the victory by His death and resurrection, *why is there still warfare going on down here*? If the war ended at the cross, *why do battles continue to rage*? Let's explore.

So Why Is There Still Warfare Down Here?

Pastor and international discipleship minister Chip Ingram, in his book *The Invisible War*, gives a spectacular analogy that really opened up my understanding. His analogy relates to what happened at the end of World War II, after the nuclear bombs had been dropped on Japan, and Japan had surrendered and signed a peace treaty. Despite the end of the war ...

> ... on islands scattered throughout the region, battles raged. Though the outcome had already been determined, isolated Japanese units hadn't heard of the surrender. They continued to wage guerrilla warfare just as they had been doing during the war. The bullets were just as real, the people hiding in tunnels were still committed to killing their foes, the mortars were just as devastating, and death was just as brutal. Young men lost their lives to an enemy who had already surrendered. There was nothing at stake between the two countries anymore; the outcome was final. But the fighting wasn't over. And it was just as deadly as it had always been.
>
> That's a picture that captures exactly where we are in the invisible war. The victory is already accomplished; absolutely nothing is at stake in terms of the ultimate outcome of Satan's rebellion against God. What continues to be at stake however, is the lives of those who are still fighting. The enemy knows the war is officially over, but he wants to wreak as much havoc as possible while he still can. Demonic spirits are still intent on destroying the people of God, and their weapons are as real

as they have always been. So are the causalities. Though the victory is won, it has not yet been completely enforced.[2]

The victory is won, but it has not yet been completely enforced. Guerilla warfare abounds, and we are in the thick of it. We can see this Scripturally, in Hebrews:

But when Christ had offered for all time a single sacrifice for sins, he sat down at the right hand of God, *waiting* from that time until his enemies should be made a footstool for his feet.   Hebrews 10:12-13 ESV, emphasis added

Christ sitting down carries very significant symbolism. It indicates His work is *completed*, and that He is now **waiting** for Judgment Day, when His enemies will be vanquished.[3]

Jesus did indeed *triumph* over sin and death at the cross, but He will not *abolish* all rule, power, and authority until the end of the world:

...then comes the end, when He hands over the kingdom to the God and Father, when He has abolished all rule and all authority and power. For He must reign until He has put all His enemies under His feet. The last enemy that will be abolished is death.   1 Corinthians 15:24-26

Yes, there will be a time when even the guerilla warfare is silenced. But now, we are living in the in-between time, the time of guerilla warfare. During this time, the Lord is *waiting* for the last soul to be brought into His Kingdom:

But do not let this one fact escape your notice, beloved, that with the Lord one day is like a thousand years, and a thousand years like one day. The Lord is not slow about His promise, as some count slowness, but is patient toward you, not wishing for any to perish but for all to come to repentance. 2 Peter 3:8-9

And Jesus is *active* in the waiting. He is interceding for us (Rom 8:34). And there are also times He is *standing*. When Stephen was about to be stoned to death:

**... and he [Stephen] said, "Behold, I see the heavens opened
and the Son of Man *standing* at the right hand of God."**

Acts 7:56, emphasis added

Battles are raging, and Jesus is *standing*. He is not inactive. He is
fighting for us. **He always lives to make intercession** for us (Heb
7:25).

So just what does that mean for us right now? Pastor Chip Ingram
puts it this way:

> We do not fight *for* victory; we fight *from* victory ... That
> means that when we fight, we're not trying to win. We're
> enforcing the victory that Jesus has already secured. In His
> power, we are invincible.[4]

We do not fight for victory, we fight from victory. The war is *over*.
We have *already* won. We are only *enforcing* the victory.

Ponder, Pray, and Journal

In your own words, explain what these sentences mean:

- The war is over. We have already won. We are only *enforcing* the
victory.

- Guerilla warfare abounds, and we are in the thick of it.

- We do not fight *for* victory, we fight *from* victory.

In upcoming chapters, we will talk in more detail about how to use
the authority God has given us over all the power of the enemy, but for
now, realize that while we are here on earth, during this time of guerilla
warfare, we are empowered to *overcome* darkness with Jesus' authority
because the Holy Spirit is within us:

You are from God, little children, and have overcome them; because greater is He who is in you than he who is in the world.   1 John 4:4

And at the end of time, Jesus will completely enforce His victory:

And I saw heaven opened, and behold, a white horse, and He who sat on it is called Faithful and True, and in righteousness He judges and wages war. His eyes are a flame of fire, and on His head are many diadems; and He has a name written on Him which no one knows except Himself ... And on His robe and on His thigh He has a name written, "KING OF KINGS, AND LORD OF LORDS."   Revelation 19:11-12,16

Satan will be bound and thrown into the abyss for a thousand years, and then freed, and then ...

... the dragon, the serpent of old, who is the devil and Satan ... the devil who deceived them was thrown into the lake of fire and brimstone, where the beast and the false prophet are also; and they will be tormented day and night forever and ever.   Revelation 20:2, 10

Forever and ever. Not only is the war won, but at the end of time the victory will be *fully* enforced, and the guerilla warfare will be *completely* extinguished. Jesus will completely enforce His victory, so at the end of time, our victory will be completely enforced also.

I think I can feel your questions stirring by now. If God is infinitely powerful and unconditionally loving, if He is God and there is no other, if there is no plan that can succeed against the Lord ... then why does He not simply trounce the guerillas right now? Oh, such challenging questions.

But Why Doesn't God
Just Crush the Guerillas Right Now?

I think our little pea-brain minds would never be able to comprehend the vast complexities of His ultimate plan. But as I read through the Word and bow my heart to His sovereignty, one thing seems clear to me: warfare appears to be about our *hearts*, our *relationship* with God. All of us have been hurt by this broken sinful world, and all of us have also chosen sin. Our choices, and others' choices, continue to bring sin and destruction. Yet God is working through those free will choices *in order to drive us to Christ*. Spiritual warfare exposes the hidden depths of our hearts, and invites us to repent. Our repentance entreats Him to purify us and conform us to the image of Christ. We partner with Him in the battle when we ...

- Repent
- Forsake lies
- Obey His ways
- Submit to His control
- Surrender more and more deeply to Him

... for these steps grow us more into His image day by day.

Those the Lord loves He disciplines ... He disciplines us for our good, *so that we may share in His holiness.*

Hebrews 12:6, 10, emphasis added

I think He allows the warfare, indeed *orchestrates* it, to purify us, to expose our hearts and drive us to Him – because He loves us so deeply He wants deeper relationship with us, and desires for us the abundant life – which He knows will only happen when we are walking in His ways and connected deeply to Him. My friend Lynn is a living testimony to this.

Since childhood, Lynn was manipulated by evil, and God used the events of her life – her trauma and her sins – to drive her to Him. Today Lynn is a woman of deep peace and profound joy – but it wasn't always like this for her. I remember the terror in her eyes when I first met her as a bride of but four months, sitting before me trembling, lab reports in hand. But I'm getting ahead of the story. Let's back up a bit.

Lynn grew up with over thirty cousins who mostly lived within ten miles of her home. Minimally supervised, Lynn was catapulted into life with the older cousins because her height made her look older than she was. By the time she was fourteen, she had been introduced to cigarettes, alcohol, drugs, pornography, and older men. By eighteen she had two abortions. Her first marriage ended when her husband had an affair. I'll let Lynn pick up the story here.

I decided to follow a dream and joined the Peace Corps. In a small country far from home, God made me put on the brakes and listen to Him. Slowly, little by little, I read my Bible, got to know Jesus, and accepted Him as my Lord and Savior. When my time at the Peace Corps was completed, I went home with a plan: to get married and have babies.

I was attending church but I was not living like a Christian. I got married again, this time to a man whom I thought was a Christian, but ended up in an entanglement of lies and deception. A few years after my divorce, I married another man who claimed to be a Christian – until our honeymoon. He was verbally abusive and we divorced. I clung to God and allowed Him to heal me over the next two years.

It was then that I met a man sent by God. He is a good man, never married, and comes from a wonderful family. His parents have been married over sixty years and still love each other so much. We certainly had to learn how to be married, as he had been alone for forty-eight years and I had been in three failed marriages. But we were so happy.

Just four months after our wedding day, we had blood work for a life insurance policy, and I found out I have HIV. Life came to a screeching halt. I could not move forward. I felt my husband had to go – he didn't have HIV; how could he love someone with HIV? But he refused to leave. My husband loved me at my absolute worst. He stayed when any other man would have left.

Getting that HIV diagnosis was awful and horrible – but pivotal. I had been a Christian for a dozen years, but my heart was never fully God's. The HIV diagnosis drove me to God as nothing else in my life had. I immersed in prayer, Bible studies, classes, and church. My church family surrounded us and supported us. My husband's unconditional persevering love carried me. God is indeed at the center of our marriage, and not only did we survive, our marriage is strong, held together by the Lord. We just celebrated ten years!

Lynn
Florida

Satan meant evil against Lynn, but God meant it for good – to compel her to run to Him, to preserve her life for all eternity (Gen 50:20). The trauma of her childhood didn't drive her to God. Her three painful divorces did not propel her to fully surrender to God either. Even her marriage to a Godly man didn't compel her to put Jesus first. But her HIV diagnosis did. I am so proud of her growth in the Lord, of her God-centered marriage and her unshakable peace. Her sweet intimacy with Him announces His victory.

God created us for His pleasure and glory; what gives Him pleasure is our *relationship* with Him (Rev 4:11, 1 Thess 4:3, Jer 9:23-24). We glorify Him more brilliantly when we know Him more deeply. It seems He permits the evil that He didn't invent and doesn't approve of in order to *drive* us to Him. To make us *desperate* for Him. To show us that *we cannot live without Him*. We want more of Him, but even more so, I think He wants more of us, and seems willing to fight any battle to win us. God hand-picks our battlefields – for when we choose surrender, *He offers us more of Himself.*

Beloved, do not be surprised at the fiery ordeal among you, which comes upon you for your testing, as though some strange thing were happening to you; but *to the degree* that you share the sufferings of Christ, keep on rejoicing, so that also at the revelation of His glory you may rejoice with exultation. 1 Peter 4:12-13, emphasis added

I think the Lord is using spiritual warfare to ensure that we learn that the only safe place is *in Him*. A place of abiding, of deep intimacy, hiding under the shelter of His wings as we walk uprightly and rely on Him. I think He is using spiritual warfare to drive us to constantly seek His protection, learning from experience that the security of His shield comes when we repent and surrender fully to His will.

Ponder, Pray, and Journal

Go back over this section *But Why Doesn't God Just Crush the Guerillas Right Now?* In your own words, summarize what you have learned here.

The Purpose of Warfare: To Conform Us To the Image of Christ

Francis Frangipane is founding pastor, intercessor, and international teacher of church leaders. In his book *The Three Battlegrounds*, he explains: "Satan will be allowed to come against the area of your weakness until you realize that God's only answer is to become Christlike."[5] Without violating our free will – or Satan's – God allows the battles. His purpose for us is to be conformed to the image of Christ (Rom 8:29) – *so that* we can be in deeper intimacy with our Lord. *Pause for a moment and take that in.*

Second Chronicles Chapter 12 seems to illustrate what Francis Frangipane is teaching. Let me back up a moment and explain. As we travel together through this book, we will be studying passages in the Bible describing real life physical events. But I think that perhaps what the Bible is teaching about physical battles can be applied to spiritual ones. I think one of the reasons God included so much detail about Israel's battles in the Old Testament is to invite us to draw spiritual parallels. Let's ask the Holy Spirit to grant us deeper understanding, especially when we are in Psalms and in the Old Testament battles. Let's ask Him to show us what He wants to teach us on *spiritual* levels.

Let's read the passage from Second Chronicles that is on my mind. Solomon's son, King Rehoboam, and all Israel had forsaken the Lord, worshiping idols and building altars to foreign gods on the hilltops. Shishak, king of Egypt, was allowed to *come against* Jerusalem until Israel repented and humbled themselves. Let's read.

When the kingdom of Rehoboam was established and strong, he and all Israel with him forsook the law of the Lord. And it came about in King Rehoboam's fifth year, because they had been unfaithful to the Lord, that Shishak king of Egypt came up against Jerusalem with 1,200 chariots and 60,000 horsemen. And the people who came with him from Egypt were without number: the Lubim, the Sukkiim and the Ethiopians. He captured the fortified cities of Judah and came as far as Jerusalem. Then Shemaiah the prophet came to Rehoboam and the princes of Judah who had gathered at Jerusalem because of Shishak, and he said to them, "Thus says the Lord, 'You have forsaken Me, so I also have forsaken you to Shishak.' " So the princes of Israel and the king humbled themselves and said, "The Lord is righteous."

When the Lord saw that they humbled themselves, the word of the Lord came to Shemaiah, saying, "They have humbled themselves so I will not destroy them, but I will grant them some measure of deliverance, and My wrath shall not be poured out on Jerusalem by means of Shishak. But they will become his slaves so that they may learn the difference between My service and the service of the kingdoms of the countries." 2 Chronicles 12:1-8

Shishak was allowed to **come up against Jerusalem** until Israel repented and humbled themselves. Note, however, that although God delivered them from destruction, granting them **some measure of deliverance**, they would still bear the consequences of their unfaithfulness: they became Shishak's slaves.

In this passage in Second Chronicles, King Rehoboam and all Israel had been in complete rebellion against God. But we don't need to have completely forsaken the Lord to need a measure of sanctification. Recall our study of Job in *Triumph Over Suffering*. Job was **blameless and upright** (Job 1:8), a holy man who still had a corner of pride in his heart (Job 32:1). Although there is much we may not understand in this book, it appears that God permitted Satan's devastating – yet restricted – attack. Job's indescribable pain resulted in an incredible encounter with the Lord, bringing Job to repentance and drawing him into deeper relationship with Him (Job 42:6).[6]

Only God knows what we need for sin to be exposed and eradicated. Only God knows what we will require to be adequate and equipped and purified and healed. Only God knows what it will take for us to know Him deeply. And in His sovereignty, it seems God has chosen to work through these battles to accomplish just that.

Satan will always be God's servant, unwittingly serving the Almighty God (Gen 50:20). As my friend Jade explains it, "No matter how much Satan works to trip us up, no matter how violently he attacks, no matter how hard he tries to confound us and drive us away from God, in the end, he will only further God's plan."[7] Satan intends those attacks for evil, but God intends them for good: to conform us to the image of Christ, to drive us to be fully reliant on Him, and to further His unfathomable plan – for our lives, and for His Kingdom. We are victorious in Him when we resist temptation – and we are also victorious when we fall into temptation yet we get up, get back on His path, and grow closer to Him through it all.

Realize through every battle, in every victory, in every defeat, Jesus remains with us, in us, battling for us, and He will never, no never, fail us or forsake us.

The LORD is the one who goes ahead of you; He will be with you. He will not fail you or forsake you. Do not fear or be dismayed.   Deuteronomy 31:8

Ponder, Pray, and Journal

Explain in your own words how Satan remains ever God's servant, inadvertently furthering God's eternal plan.

Key to Victory:
Hiding in Our Strong Tower

Like physical war, spiritual warfare is both defensive and offensive, with multiple simultaneous battlefronts and diverse enemy tactics and strategies. There will be casualties and escapes, and we will celebrate victories in battles and endure defeats in battles, too. Our protection from this onslaught? Hiding in God, our only Place of safety. We hide in Him by *repenting and surrendering fully and completely*:

The name of the LORD is a strong tower;
The righteous runs into it and is safe ...
Deliver me, O LORD, from my enemies;
I take refuge in You.   Proverbs 18:10, Psalm 143:9

Surrender is the ultimate level of trust in God, acknowledging that He is all-powerful, and also trustworthy and safe. Truthfully, in our own strength, *we* can't protect anything. The enemy is on the rampage, stealing, killing, and destroying. We cannot guard our possessions, our jobs, our marriages, our loved ones, or even our own lives. We cannot control the weather or the stock market and we certainly can't control our families. We can't even bring our calling or our purposes to fruition. And when we choose to put everything in God's hands, we declare that He is *able* to guard what we have entrusted to Him – and that He *loves us enough* to do just that (2Tim 1:12, Rom 8:32).

Remember that God may allow Satan to attack us in areas we are in sin so that we realize that the only way of escape is to become conformed to the image of Christ. Satan will always be God's servant; no matter how hard he tries to drive us *away* from God, God is using him to drive us *to* God.

Spiritual warfare shows us that God is our only safe place, our only Strong Tower, our only place of protection from enemy assault. We may not yet have any training in the offensive, or even much in the defensive, but it is imperative that we know how to hide in Him by *repenting and surrendering to Him*. Through *Triumph Over Suffering* and *Triumph of Surrender*, we are well-practiced in tactics that help us to hide in Him:

- Deep Scripture immersion teaches us truths and prevents us from falling prey to Satan's beguiling lies (Jn 17:17, Ps 119:98, 160).

- Stillness, listening, and prayer work to humble us and to strengthen our connection to the reality of God, and to ward off doubts and distrust (Ps 46:10).

- Worship opens our hearts to see God as He really is, and to see ourselves as God sees us (Isa 40:12-31, Ps 19:1-4, Ps 96:1-13, Ps 100:1-3).

- Deep connection to our church family brings clarity in times of confusion and support in times of discouragement. Submitting to the authority of our pastors and leaders gives us God's protection, for they are responsible to watch over our souls (Prov 11:14, Heb 10:25, 1Cor 12:7, Heb 13:17).

- Obedience to God's commands maintains our humility, and abiding helps us to remain dependent upon Him (Jn 14:15, 15:5).

Now watch what happens in the battle when we run into our Strong Tower:

"I love You, O LORD, my strength."
The LORD is my rock and my fortress
   and my deliverer,

My God, my rock, in whom I take refuge;
My shield and the horn of my salvation,
  my stronghold.
I call upon the LORD, who is worthy to be praised,
And I am saved from my enemies ...

Psalm 18:1-3, emphasis added

When we take refuge in our Rock, He saves us from the enemy. Victory is assured when we repent and surrender, when we have died to ourselves and are fully hidden in Jesus.

For you have died and your life is hidden with Christ in God.   Colossians 3:3

Ponder, Pray, and Journal

Can you think of a time in your life when the battle suddenly ended when you surrendered to the Lord?

On Mission

Our highest *calling* is to know God and to give Him glory. And our *mission* in the war is this:

"Your kingdom come. Your will be done."   Matthew 6:10

Our mission is the advancement of God's Kingdom. His Kingdom comes, His Kingdom is advanced, when His will is done. Satan fights spiritual battles in the physical world, so whether people knowingly engage or not, warfare will affect those on earth. Jesus calls His followers to be soldiers in *active* duty, not blindsided by the war or in ignorance of it, but obeying Him as our Commander-in-Chief and engaging in the warfare in order to advance His Kingdom (2 Tim 2:4).

Surrendering to His will leads to obedience to His will, which invites Him to make His home more deeply in us (Jn 14:23).

For thus says the high and exalted One
Who lives forever, whose name is Holy,
"I dwell on a high and holy place,
And also with the contrite and lowly of spirit
In order to revive the spirit of the lowly
And to revive the heart of the contrite."   Isaiah 57:15

Those who are **contrite** are *repentant*. **Lowly** means *humbled*. The result of repentance, of humbling ourselves and surrendering to His will, is a deep abiding intimate relationship: He makes His home in us in greater and greater measure. Deeper intimacy *reveals* that a battle was won.

A deep abiding intimate relationship enables us to stand firm in our faith without wavering. It strengthens us to walk more obediently, and enables us to learn in greater measure how to deftly avoid Satan's traps as we complete the Kingdom work He has assigned us. (Eph 6:10-11, Jn 14:21, Jas 4:7, Eph 2:10, Rev 3:2.)

Scripture indicates that warfare will always be part of our lives while we walk this earth. Complete freedom from darkness will only happen in eternity (Phil 3:12, 1 Jn 1:8, 1 Jn 3:2, Rom 8:23-25).

The Word tells us that we are soldiers in active duty (2 Tim 2:4), so we might as well get that assignment settled in our hearts right now. We will continually move from one battlefront to the next. When we are victorious on one front, Satan may attack an unguarded area. And although the Lord may at times ordain for us special seasons of rest, restoration, protection, and time to celebrate Him, Satan and his demons are *relentless*. It is vital that we remain self-controlled and on the alert, that we suit up in the armor that He has provided and never remove it, that we refuse to entangle ourselves in the affairs of everyday life, and that we trust that our Commander-in-Chief knows exactly how much we can handle (1 Pt 5:7-8, Eph 6:10-20, 2 Tim 2:4, 1 Cor 10:13).

The victory will be secured at the end of the world (Rev 21:1-4), but each individual battle we engage in may result in a victory or a defeat. Realize, though, that what may appear to be defeat in the world's eyes may be victory in Jesus' eyes. Additionally, when we place a defeat into Jesus' hands, He can turn it into victory by training us, equipping us, purifying our hearts, bringing us to repentance, conforming us to His image, drawing us into deeper surrender, or revealing His glory. Remember, Jesus always has the last word.

Awake, Sleeper

And He came to the disciples and found them sleeping, and said to Peter, "So, you men could not keep watch with Me for one hour? Keep watching and praying that you may not enter into temptation; the spirit is willing, but the flesh is weak." ... Then all the disciples left Him and fled ... Then he [Peter] began to curse and swear, "I do not know the man!" And immediately a rooster crowed.   Matthew 26:40-41, 56, 74

To me, Matthew 26:56 is one of the most heartbreaking verses of the Bible: **Then all the disciples left Him and fled**. The forces of darkness are plotting against the righteous, breathing out violence, drawing their swords and bending their bows to slay the upright in heart (Ps 37:12-14). Don't fall asleep; keep self controlled and on the alert, so you do not flee when God calls you to stand, nor deny Him in the heat of the battle.

"Awake, sleeper, and arise from the dead, and Christ will shine on you" ... it is already the hour for you to awaken from sleep; for now salvation is nearer to us than when we believed. The night is almost gone, and the day is near. Therefore let us lay aside the deeds of darkness and put on the armor of light.   Ephesians 5:14, Romans 13:11-12

As we journey together through this book, we will be mastering weapons and battle tactics, understanding Satan's snares and battle strategies, and learning how to close doors to the enemy and how to pull down strongholds. To gain the victory, it is imperative that we are on the battlefield wearing the armor of light. In the next chapter, we will learn *where* the battlefield is, and *what it means* to put on the armor of light.

Chapter 2
Know Your Battlefield

*A*s we open our hearts, we can see that from Genesis to Revelation the Bible is a warfare manual across all its pages. Adam and Eve in the Garden, Joshua's conquest of the Promised Land, David's seemingly endless battles, Daniel's glimpse into the warring angels, Paul's instructions on the armor of God, and Jesus' final triumph in Revelation reveal the war underlying Kingdom advancement. Whether we recognize it or not, we are enveloped in a cosmic spiritual battle for the Kingdom. A vicious battle for the souls of men, a war over their final resting place in eternity, and for the sanctification of our hearts here on earth. And in this war, the spiritual will collide with the physical, the mental, and the emotional, for these worlds are very intertwined.

I know some of you are eager to engage in the battle. You have taken up your mission as a soldier in active duty. But where exactly is the "battlefield"? Although lots of circumstances in our lives may appear to be a battlefield, underlying the physical is where the *real* battle rages. The real battlefield is *spiritual*.

Wars in the physical are fought for *territory*, and we will adapt this concept to *spiritual territory* as part of our understanding. The New Testament alludes to this spiritual territory, commanding us to **never give place to the devil** (Eph 4:27 NKJV). The territory in dispute in these spiritual battles we will call *the battlefield*.

In a physical war, many battles can be raging on far-flung battlefields simultaneously. Armies may utilize the strategy of campaigns to concentrate forces in a particular area to gain victory in that sphere. But a *campaign* victory will not ensure an end of the war. Only when the *central core of operations* is infiltrated, crushed, and brought to surrender will the conquerors claim victory and declare the war to be over. And once the central core has submitted, then the process begins of reaching each distant area that the enemy has controlled in order to bring each of those areas under submission. As we discussed in Chapter 1, this is the process of *securing the victory*, of silencing the guerillas, of overcoming an already defeated foe.

Let's look at a spiritual parallel to physical war. In a spiritual war, Satan wars in the physical, attacking our bodies, our relationships, our finances, our jobs, our emotions, our minds, and more. He shoots flaming arrows and he lures our weak flesh to fall into temptation. Many battles can be raging on far-flung battlefields, such as in our emotions, our wills, our minds, our consciences, our bodies, our words, our actions. We can concentrate our efforts in any of these areas to try to gain victory there. But victory is declared only when the *central core of operations* surrenders to Jesus' control. And once the central core has submitted to Jesus, all those other battlefronts must be brought under submission for victory to be secured.

So what *is* our central core?

Our Central Core

Some people think the mind controls everything, but I think that the ultimate battle is won or lost *in our hearts*, for our heart **is the wellspring of life** (Prov 4:23 NIV). The heart is the core of our beliefs. The King James says **out of it are the issues of life**. The NLT says it plainly, **it affects everything you do**. And Jesus says,

"He who believes in Me, as the Scripture has said, out of his heart will flow rivers of living water." John 7:38 NKJV

I recognize that many battles are won and lost in our minds. Our minds are indeed a critical battlefield, and the connection between our hearts and our minds is undeniable. We are going to study that connection later in the chapter. But first, I'd like to pause and work through some Scriptures that seem to reveal that the *ultimate* battlefield is in our hearts, because this understanding will be important as we move through this book. To prepare us for this *Warfare* book, we did a deep study of our heart in Chapter 7 of *Triumph of Surrender*, "The Life of the Heart." Let's take another deep dive.

Look up the following Scripture verses and write out what each verse describes as under the heart's control. (I am reading in the NASB to see the Hebrew and Greek translated as "heart.")

Ponder, Pray, and Journal

Look up these verses and write in your journal what sorts of things reside in our hearts:
- Psalm 73:7
- Ecclesiastes 11:9
- Psalm 37:4
- Jeremiah 23:20
- 1 Chronicles 29:18
- Psalm 13:2

Look up these verses and write in your journal what sorts of things we do in our hearts:
- 1 Samuel 1:13
- Jeremiah 29:13
- Romans 10:9-10
- Ephesians 6:6

- Proverbs 19:3b
- Matthew 18:35

Look up these verses and write in your journal what sorts of things spill out our hearts:
- Matthew 12:34
- Matthew 15:19
- Isaiah 59:13

Summarize what you have gleaned from these passages.

Do you agree with me that the heart is the seat of control of every single aspect of our lives? **For as he thinks in his heart, so is he** (Prov 23:7 NKJV). No wonder there is fierce warfare going on for the territory of our hearts! Let's call it "Command Central."

Command Central

We belong to the Lord Jesus Christ, and He lives inside of our hearts (Eph 3:17). We are His own possession (2Pet 2:9). The Holy Spirit lives inside of our hearts (2Cor 1:22), and as we are led by the Spirit, we invite Him to influence the outflows from His seat of reign in our hearts. But although God completely *owns* us as His possession, the Holy Spirit *can only lead* the portions of our hearts that we *surrender* to His control.

Although we have been rescued from Satan's domain and transferred to Jesus' kingdom (Col 1:13), we have free will to *give* our obedience to Jesus, or to *withhold* our obedience. We can obey God, or let sin reign and obey its lusts (Rom 6:12). Heed this warning *to the brethren*:

Take care, brethren, that there not be in any one of you an evil, unbelieving heart that falls away from the living God.

Hebrews 3:12

We have received the Holy Spirit, and it is our lifelong journey to increasingly *submit* our hearts to His rule.

When you believed, you were marked in him with a seal, the promised Holy Spirit, who is a *deposit* guaranteeing our inheritance until the redemption of those who are God's own possession.

Ephesians 1:13-14, emphasis added

A **deposit** is a part of the whole. It *guarantees* the whole will be ours. In Jesus, the **fullness of God** dwells (Col 1:19, 2:9). God has given all things into Jesus' hands, and Jesus speaks the very words of God because God has given Him **the Spirit without measure** (Jn 3:34-35). But we only have a *portion* of the Holy Spirit, a *deposit*:

By this we know that we abide in Him and He in us, because He has given us of His Spirit.

1 John 4:13

He has given us *of* His Spirit. This word "of" is an important word in the Greek; my *Greek Word Study* says in this passage the word "of" means that the Spirit of God originates from God and a portion comes out of God to us.[1] Upon our salvation, we received a **deposit** of the Holy Spirit, a *portion* of the *fullness* we will one day receive:

... so that Christ may dwell in your hearts through faith ... that you may be filled up to *all the fullness of God*.

Ephesians 3:17,19, emphasis added

Read this passage in the Amplified slowly and carefully:

May Christ through your faith [actually] dwell (settle down, abide, make His permanent home) in your hearts! ... that you may be filled [through all your being] *unto all the fullness of God* [may have the richest measure of the divine Presence, and become a body wholly filled and flooded with God Himself]!

Ephesians 3:17,19 AMPC, emphasis added

As we mature, we walk less in the flesh and more in the Spirit as we grow into the fullness of Christ (Eph 4:13, 1Cor 3:1), and in eternity we will be filled with **all the fullness of God**. But during this time on earth, we are on a journey of increasing fullness. Recall the disciples being **filled with the Holy Spirit** at Pentecost (Acts 2:4). Not long afterwards, after a time of persecution, they gathered and prayed and were **filled with the Holy Spirit** again (Acts 4:31). Remember our analogy from *Triumph of Surrender*, the rocks in our jars of water representing our sins impeding the flow of the Holy Spirit. The more we repent and surrender, the more rocks we release to Him, the greater His Holy Spirit can fill us and operate in us and through us.

Ponder, Pray, and Journal

Going back to the passage from Ephesians 1:13-14, I want to focus on the word **inheritance**, our share in His Kingdom, our share in His Holy Spirit. Inheritance is an important Old Testament word which indicated *territory* in the Promised Land. In a spiritual parallel, I see our hearts as the battlefield, our intended *inheritance*, the spiritual territory Jesus is warring for.

Read 1 Peter 1:1-9. Focus on the words inheritance and salvation.

Our inheritance is **imperishable and undefiled and will not fade away, reserved in heaven for you** (1Pet 1:4). We are commanded to purify ourselves (1Jn 3:3), and Peter reminds us that we are only able to obey Jesus Christ by the sanctifying work of the Holy Spirit (1Pet 1:2). While we are here on earth, in mid-process of this sanctification, God's power protects us though our faith all the way until eternity, when His sanctifying work will be complete (1Pet 1:5).

I think our inheritance may include our sanctified hearts, an inheritance we are receiving by incremental deposits on earth, and will receive fully in heaven. The deposit guarantees the whole: our full inheritance, our hearts fully sanctified, completely surrendered to Jesus, and filled up to all the fullness of God upon our final redemption.

Additionally, although the war for *ownership* of our hearts was won at our salvation, Satan and his armies are still fighting guerilla warfare for *influence* of our hearts. Hebrews teaches us that we are sanctified and being sanctified all at the same time (Heb 3:14 – the ESV and NKJV seem to translate these verb tenses most clearly). We are made righteous in Jesus at salvation; and our sanctification, our process of incremental surrender to the Lord, then becomes our ongoing lifelong journey. A portion of our inheritance, a deposit of the territory of our hearts, has been sanctified and secured in Jesus because it is surrendered to Him. While on earth, we continue to battle alongside Jesus to secure more territory in our hearts, territory submitted to His rulership, surrendered to Him, filled with His Spirit and led by Him. Of course our goal is *full surrender* to the Holy Spirit's leading. It is our ongoing lifelong battle to fight against our flesh, the world, and Satan in order to submit our "Command Central" *completely* to the leading of the Holy Spirit.

We can see from our study of the passages about the heart that the power that has the greatest influence in our hearts – whether the Holy Spirit, or our flesh, or the world, or Satan – will also have the greatest influence over *all the outflows* of our heart as well: our words and behaviors, our mind and our thoughts, our desires and emotions, our intentions and plans and will, our conscience and moral compass, and our beliefs. Whoever has the greatest influence in a particular *territory* of our heart will have the greatest influence over all the outflows *related to that part*. These outflows I call *the spoils of war*. The plunder. When it comes to Command Central, *we cannot afford defeat on this battlefield*.

Choosing Who Influences Command Central

God has given us free will. We *choose* the victor. We *choose* whether a certain area of our hearts will be led by the Spirit, or led by our flesh. We choose whether we will walk in obedience to the Lord, or walk in disobedience. We have been freed from sin and enslaved to God (Rom 6:22), but we must daily walk out that freedom by no longer allowing our bodies to be instruments of unrighteousness (Rom 6:12-14). Romans details our lifelong guerilla warfare, our spirit battling with our flesh, and shows us that victory is only possible through Jesus, by the grace and strength His Spirit provides (Rom 6:14, 7:24-25, 8:3-4, 11, 37).

Romans Chapter 8 describes what it means for the flesh to rule:

For the mind set on the flesh is death, but the mind set on the Spirit is life and peace, because the mind set on the flesh is hostile toward God; for it does not subject itself to the law of God, for it is not even able to do so, and those who are in the flesh cannot please God.   Romans 8:7-8

But hear this encouragement:

However, you are not in the flesh but in the Spirit, if indeed the Spirit of God dwells in you.   Romans 8:9

Yet heed this warning:

So then, brethren, we are under obligation, not to the flesh, to live according to the flesh – for if you are living according to the flesh you must die; but if by the Spirit you are putting to death the deeds of the body, you will live.
      Romans 8:12-13

So we see that the choice is ours. We can live according to the flesh, or we can put to death the deeds of the flesh. We can allow our flesh to lead, or we can surrender and submit our hearts to the Holy Spirit's leading. The flesh and the Spirit are in opposition to each other (Gal 5:17). Evil is present in us, and nothing good dwells in our flesh (Rom 7:18-21).

What does it mean to live according to the flesh? Read Romans 8:7-8 again (above). We can see in this passage that the flesh is hostile towards God and is rebelling against God. *Those are the hallmarks of Satan*: Satan is the spirit at work in the sons of disobedience (Eph 2:2), and those who make a practice of sinning are slaves of sin and are of the devil (Jn 8:34, 1Jn 3:8). Making a practice of sinning means repetitive, continued, unrepented sin. We are going to study in Chapter 6 how Satan can amp up the temptations of our flesh and the world as he capitalizes on their corruption. When we succumb to those temptations, particularly when we make a *practice* of sinning, *we are inviting Satan's influence in our hearts and lives.*

What about being led by the world? Realize that the world is enslaved to corruption, Satan is the god of this world, and the whole world lies in his power (Rom 8:21, 2Cor 4:4, 1Jn 5:19). So if we are being influenced by the world, that means we are *ultimately still being influenced by Satan.*

Any area where our hearts are in obedience to God and we are surrendered to His will, we are positioned to be led by His Spirit. But any area where we are not in obedience to God or our hearts are fighting His will, we are open to the influences of our flesh, the world, or demonic forces.

Ponder, Pray, and Journal

Romans 6:17-18 emphasizes that our obedience must be **from the heart ... having been freed from sin, you became slaves of righteousness**. The word **slave** in this passage is *doulos*:

> ... which means "servant by choice" ... a slave who had been granted freedom from his master but who loved his master so deeply that he voluntarily chose to continue on as that master's servant.[2]

Ponder that definition. We are *servants by choice.* The choice to obey or disobey, to be led by the Spirit or led by the flesh, is ours. When it comes to who influences Command Central, we *choose* the victor.

In the battle for influence of our hearts, our minds become a hotly contested battleground. The heart and the mind are very interconnected, and at times it can be hard to separate the two. A good understanding here will be critical in warfare, so we are going to spend some time discerning the difference and recognizing the connection, and then we will wrap up this chapter putting on the armor of light as we train with two vital strategies of warfare: renewing our mind, and rejecting lies and choosing truth. Both of these strategies require the Word of God

The Heart-Mind Connection

Sometimes, what our heads know and what our hearts believe don't match up. Let's take a look at the difference.

Head knowledge is what our minds know the answer is supposed to be. It's what our mouths would say because we've memorized it. It's the answer on the test that would earn us an A. Head knowledge is quite persuasive. Unless put to the test, we *really do believe* that what is in our head *is* what we really believe in our heart.

It is when we are tested that our true *heart beliefs* are often exposed. For example, we may say we trust God fully (head knowledge), but when someone we love is suddenly facing death, what may suddenly surface is our distrust of God's love and His perfect plan (heart belief). We may say that we believe God is always working for our good (head knowledge), but when we lose a job or receive a cancer diagnosis or our children abandon their faith, we may suddenly doubt that He really *is* working things for our good (heart belief).

Because our hearts are "Command Central," we live out our *heart beliefs*, not our head knowledge. Our hearts rule – even when we think our minds are ruling. When put to the test, all the outflows of the heart, including the mind, will follow the heart's rule.

Let's study some passages that demonstrate how our hearts and minds become darkened, how our *minds* are enlightened when light enters *our heart*, and how we can partner with the Lord to invite His light to enter our hearts and unblind our minds.

Ponder, Pray, and Journal

Read Romans 1:18-32 to see how minds can become confused and hearts darkened. This passage is describing those who are unsaved. Read it carefully, take notes if that would help you. Meet me back here when you are finished.

Confused Minds and Darkened Hearts

Note the *deliberateness* of the sin described in Romans 1: these are people who **suppress the truth in unrighteousness**, who **exchanged the truth of God for a lie** (Rom 1:18,25). They *know* the truth, but they *refuse to obey it*. Watch the result:

For even though they knew God, they did not honor Him as God or give thanks, but they became futile in their speculations, and their foolish heart was darkened.

Romans 1:21

Notice the progression. These people *chose* rebellion against God's ways, deliberately exchanging truth for lies, refusing to honor or thank God, and living in unrighteousness. This led to hearts that were **darkened**. A darkened heart is a heart under Satan's rule. It is deprived of light and truth, and operating in the ignorance of darkness and lies. Since the heart is Command Central, this darkened heart affects the outflows, including the mind, the conscience, and behaviors:

- Their minds: Their thinking became useless, devoid of meaning or purpose. As the NLT translates, **their minds became dark and confused** (Rom 1:21). Confusion is a hallmark of entrenched lies. Then, as the darkness progressed, their minds became depraved (Rom 1:28).

- Their consciences: A dark heart causes evil speech (Lk 6:45). Speaking lies, living lies, believing lies causes consciences to become insensitive, hardened, dead (1 Tim 4:2). Moral compasses spin in the wrong direction. People begin to believe that what is sinful, is *acceptable* (Isa 5:20).

- Their behavior: God gave them over to depravity, including impurity and degrading passions (Rom 1:24,26, 28), and a host of other things that are **not proper** listed in Romans 1:28-32.

This phrase **gave them over** is used three times in Romans 1. *Paradidomi* in the Greek *means* "to deliver over or up to the power of someone."[3] God took His hands off these people because of their willful rejection of Him. He released them to Satan, allowing them to do and to be what humans are without God: utterly depraved.

This passage in Romans is describing those who are unsaved, who do not belong to Jesus, but it seems that those who belong to Jesus can struggle with areas of darkness also. Jesus, in the Sermon on the Mount, cautions, **"If then the light that is in you is darkness, how great is the darkness!"** (Matt 7:23). And Ephesians teaches us to ...

walk no longer just as the Gentiles also walk, in the futility of their mind, being darkened in their understanding ...

Ephesians 4:17-18

Although we were formerly darkness and now are light in the Lord, we still have a choice: we can walk in futility of mind with darkened understanding, or we can walk as children of the Light (Eph 5:8).

Ponder, Pray, and Journal

- Go back to the three bullets in the above section. Realizing that believers can also have areas of darkness, ponder how the effects of darkness described in Romans 1 could also impact a believer.

- When light enters our hearts, our *minds* will also be enlightened. Read about this process in 2 Corinthians 3:7 – 4:6. Meet me back here when you are finished, and we will focus on a few key verses to see how our *minds* are enlightened when Light enters our *hearts*.

Light in Our Hearts Unblinds Our Minds

In this passage, Paul is speaking of unbelievers, describing how **their minds were hardened** (2Cor 3:14). He writes that the gospel is **veiled to those who are perishing, in whose case the god of this world has blinded the minds of the unbelieving so that they might not see the light of the gospel of the glory of Christ** (2Cor 4:3-4). Their *minds* are blinded. Now watch this. Paul explains *where* the veil is, and *how* the veil is removed.

... the same veil remains unlifted, because it is removed in Christ ... a veil lies *over their heart*; but whenever a person turns to the Lord, the veil is taken away.

2 Corinthians 3:15-16, emphasis added

Minds are blinded by a veil *over the heart*; the veil is removed when someone **turns to the Lord** – that is, when they repent and surrender. Paul explains how this happened to us, and explains further how what goes on in *hearts* opens *minds*:

> **For God, who said, "Light shall shine out of darkness," is the One who has shone *in our hearts* to give the Light of the knowledge of the glory of God in the face of Christ.**
>
> 2 Corinthians 4:6, emphasis added

God shining *in our hearts* gives us the Light of knowledge of Jesus, *unblinding our minds*. Light shines in the darkness, and darkness cannot overpower it (Jn 1:4).

One more crucial point here. Paul has begun this passage talking about unbelievers, and ended it with a description of our salvation. But in the midst of the passage Paul describes our process of sanctification, being transformed from glory to glory:

> **But we all, with unveiled face, beholding as in a mirror the glory of the Lord, are being transformed into the same image from glory to glory, just as from the Lord, the Spirit.**
>
> 2 Corinthians 3:18

We all. I think this indicates that as believers, we *also* may have times of blinded minds and areas of veiled hearts. **From glory to glory**. It is our ongoing process of sanctification. More veils removed, more unblinding of our minds. Our journey of transformation from glory to glory. **Not that I have already obtained it** ... (Phil 3:12).

Is transformation God's job, or our job? Back to Romans for that answer.

Be Transformed by the Renewing of Your Mind

Transformation occurs *in our hearts*. Transformation in the Greek is *metamorphoo*,[4] a word we studied in *Triumph Over Suffering*.[5]

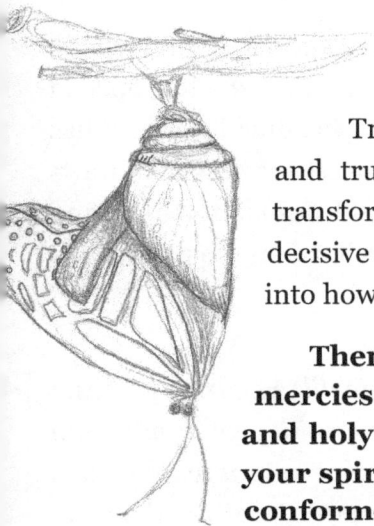

Transformation is a sudden radical change, a metamorphosis, caterpillar to butterfly. Transformation is a lie broken in our hearts and truth implanted. Transformation is freedom; transformation is deliverance. Transformation is a decisive victory in warfare. Romans gives us a glimpse into how transformation occurs:

Therefore I urge you, brethren, by the mercies of God, to present your bodies a living and holy sacrifice, acceptable to God, which is your spiritual service of worship. And do not be conformed to this world, but *be transformed by the renewing of your mind*, so that you may prove what the will of God is, that which is good and acceptable and perfect. Romans 12:1-2, emphasis added

First, note the passive tense: **be transformed**. We do not accomplish the transforming. Transformation is completely a miraculous work of the Lord in our hearts. But note also the way we partner with the Lord in this transformational process: be transformed *by the renewing of your mind*.

We renew *our minds*, but transformation occurs *in our hearts*. We *position* ourselves to receive His transformation by renewing our minds. Only God can transform a heart, but our minds are our responsibility. We must *work out our salvation* (Phil 2:12). We are commanded to take every thought captive, to force our minds to run God's way – and that is important work – but when Jesus steps in and *transformation* occurs, our minds will naturally run in God's direction. Repentance, surrender, and identifying lies and renouncing them are all key pathways that lead to transformation.

I'd like to invite my friend Janet to share her testimony so you can see an example of how this may play out in our lives. In the few years I've known Janet, she has been on a skyrocketing growth path, renewing her mind through *Triumph* classes. Through classes she is on a challenging journey of bold honesty, repentance, and forgiveness, as the Lord exposed lies and she embraced truth. As she has opened the painful parts of her heart to the Lord, layer after layer, He has taken her from a life of stuffed emotions to a sweet softness that draws people to the Light within her. And just last night, Jesus showed up and transformed her heart, enabling her to comprehend and to receive His love as never before. Let's listen in.

I spent my teenage years looking for love in all the wrong places. I chased after guys, trying to get them to love me with promiscuity and too much partying. At nineteen, I found myself pregnant with no idea who the father was. I thought my only option was to seek an abortion.

The clinic told me I was too far along for an abortion that day. I would have to come back the following week and it would cost more money. I didn't have more money. So I went home to tell my parents. With their support, I raised my daughter, and I grew up alongside her.

Thirty-one years later, when someone was commending me for making the right choice and choosing life, I was silently berating myself. I was ashamed to admit that if I had enough money, I would have gone through with the abortion. At that very moment, God told me it wasn't because I didn't have enough money that I didn't have the abortion. It was because He stepped in at the right moment to save me. To save me from possibly the biggest mistake I could have ever made, and to save my daughter.

I had known that God loves me. I believed it in my head – but my heart didn't truly know it until the day that He showed me how He had stepped in. I never fully understood what it meant for God to take His right hand and place it on my head, and His left hand on Jesus: to give me the blessings, and to send Jesus to hang on the cross (Gen 48:8-20). I am eternally grateful. Now I <u>know</u> that the only love I need is God's love.

Janet Crider
Jupiter, Florida

With this incredible encounter, God has not only cracked open her heart, but also began to pour His tender love into it. Through this encounter with the Lord, and pressing into Him for further revelation, Janet has come to realize that one of the reasons that her heart didn't truly know God's love was because she had been trapped in people-pleasing. She had been seeking approval, acceptance, and love from people. But over the past few years, as she has done hard spiritual growth work, renewing her mind by immersing in the Word and repenting and surrendering as the Holy Spirit led, her heart has moved step by step from finding out what pleases people, to finding out what pleases the Lord (Gal 1:10, Eph 5:10).

I believe the spiritual work she has done with the Lord is what positioned her to receive this beautiful healing time with the Lord. She has been **transformed by the renewing of her mind**. As He spoke His truth deeply into her heart, lies were demolished and the stronghold of people pleasing has come crashing down. *"Now I know that the only love I need is God's love."*

Sometimes, when we are blinded, the lies may *feel* more true than the truth. The reality of our circumstances may be speaking louder than the voice of the Lord. The many voices that have spoken lies over us for years may be overwhelming the still small whispers of God. The lies may be so entrenched in our hearts and minds that they have become part of us, and we may even think that *they are our own thoughts*. We may not recognize them as coming from the father of lies. These lies can even sound as if they are in the first person, manifesting as thoughts such as, "God won't use me. I'm not enough ... so insignificant ... sinful ... worthless ... ill-equipped ... stupid ... I'm a failure ... If I lose my job I am worth nothing ... I might as well just give up ..." And sometimes, the lies are not an isolated sentence or phrase, but such a complete mindset that it may be very hard to recognize any of the individual lies.

Renewing our minds is a deep and often lengthy journey that will involve forcing our unwilling minds to run in thought processes that are unfamiliar and seem unbelievable, yet are truth. This will involve difficult spiritual work, requiring us to *choose* to believe truths that feel anything but true. It sort of reminds me of jeeping.

Lessons from Jeeping

My son's friend loves to go jeeping. I actually had never heard of "jeeping" before, and was quite interested to hear of his escapades. He told us that when he was climbing up nearly vertical inclines in his jeep, he was forced to drive in the deep ruts that were already worn into the mountainside. He described the great difficulty of trying to maneuver his jeep out of those deep ruts and onto a different path – and how he might have a rollover accident if he was forcing his jeep to climb out of a particularly deep rut.

I think that our minds are sort of like jeeps. They naturally run in the old ruts that are there. Whatever we have learned throughout our lives – whether lies or truths – will be the rut that our mind runs in. Now if a particular rut of our mind is a deep truth of the Lord, we certainly want our mind to keep running in it. But what if it is a rut of deception? A lie of the enemy? What if it is a rut that deceives us, even convincing us that the lie we are believing *is* truth? How will we get out of it?

God's wording for forcing your mind to run in a new rut is **renewing your mind**. And just as driving a jeep out of a rut will be difficult, forcing your mind to run in a new rut can be difficult – and will require the power and strength of the Holy Spirit (Titus 3:5).

I am going to take us medical here for some deeper understanding on how a mind is renewed. The mind is not physical, but the brain is physical, and the physical and spiritual are very intertwined. I'm going to share with you some information about neuroplasticity, which is the capacity of the brain to develop new nerve connections – or create new "ruts."

Neuroplasticity

A young child's brain is more malleable and can learn new things faster than an older person's brain. Also, it will take much longer for a person to unlearn something that he has been doing for many years than for someone who has been doing that same thing for a short time. This is due to *neuroplasticity*.

There is a wild YouTube video by *Smarter Every Day* that demonstrates this magnificently.[6] Destin Sandlin reconstructed his bicycle so turning the handlebars to the left caused the bike to go to the right, and turning the handlebars to the right caused it to go to the left. He practiced on the new bike five minutes a day for *eight months*, with no success and many falls – and then suddenly his brain "leapt" into the new rut, and he could ride the bike with ease. His young son, who had been biking for three years, tried the backwards bicycle also – and in just two weeks had mastered it.

Let's see what this means spiritually. When it comes to lies of the enemy, there is indeed a spiritual battle raging. But although we are not of this world, we are living in this world, so our spiritual battles often involve the physical also – and that may mean neuroplasticity is involved; changes we can effect in the brain can impact the mind.

In one of my own battles, I was believing lies since my childhood that I was worthless and insignificant. I was about forty-five when I began my renewal process – I was about five years old in the Lord. It took me many hours of renewing my mind over many, many months before the Holy Spirit's transformation happened. Of course God is limitless and may transform in an instant if He pleases, but often He invites us into the process. And if He invites us to partner with Him, someone who is battling lies entrenched for a shorter period may uproot those lies much more quickly than someone who is battling lies rooted since childhood.

One more piece to Destin Sandlin's story. After a period of time, he tried to return to a normal bicycle. He was completely unable to ride it – for twenty minutes. Then, his brain "leapt" back into the original neural pathway and he was able to ride a normal bicycle again.

Now don't miss this: just as Destin Sandlin was able to revert to his original neural pathway with minimal effort, it may also be easy for us to revert to our old belief systems. Once we have received the Lord's transformation, we must keep our guard up. It is critical to renew our minds daily by immersing in the Word and other spiritual disciplines, making the new rut deeper and deeper, and allowing the old rut to shrivel from disuse. The Lord will begin His healing process, and begin to fill the old rut in with Himself. Throughout this transformation process, if we fall back into the old rut, we must repent and get into the new rut again. Satan would like to shame us and drive us into overwhelming guilt, but the Holy Spirit only desires to lovingly convict us, lift us up, and help us get back into the new rut of truth. And finally, when the Lord fully heals us, He will fill in the old rut completely, so there will be no old rut to revert back to. Sometimes He grants us that full healing here on this earth; other times our healing may be partial on earth and completed in eternity.

Realize also that the process of transformation may be a more gradual conforming than a sudden "leap" into the new rut as J.C. experienced. Spending more time in the new rut and less time in the old rut is progress. Additionally, if we fall back into the old rut but our "turn-around time" is quicker, that is important progress too.

If you are struggling with a false belief system, persevere and don't stop forcing your brain into that new rut. Because one day – we don't know when – Jesus will bring transformation. He will destroy a lie or bring healing or tear down a stronghold, and seemingly suddenly, your thoughts will run in that new rut of truth.

Will we forever need to keep our guard up, fearful that we may fall again into the old rut? We are going to explore this question in a later chapter, but for now, understand two things:

- Put on and keep on the armor of light (Rom 13:12), because the war will not be over until Jesus returns.

- We have no need to fear. Be alert, yes, but fear not, because the battle is the Lord's, and as we stay close to Him, He will bring victories.

As we move into studying some ways we can renew our minds, do realize that transformation is ultimately a work of the Holy Spirit. It is all Him and only Him – and yet He calls us to *partner* with Him. To *co-labor* with Him. We work out, and He works in (Phil 2:12-13). We do our part, immersing in the living and active Word, refusing to dwell on lies, changing our words and our behaviors as best we can – and He causes His Word to wear a new rut in our mind, ultimately freeing us, healing us, delivering us, and transforming us from glory to glory.

Some Ways To Renew Your Mind

You will find renewing your mind to be an essential part of the armor of light. Renewing our minds is relying upon truth of His Word, replacing lies with truth. Let's briefly discuss some ways to do that.

The most important way we renew our minds is by studying the Word under the power of the Holy Spirit. The Holy Spirit will use this time as a means of alignment, to prevent lies from taking root as He cements His truths into our hearts. We must *choose* to believe the truth of the Word, whether or not we feel it, whether or not we sense it.

We renew our minds when we have courage to enter His throne room in prayer, trusting He will grant us mercy and grace, and drive out shame and false guilt (Heb 4:16, Rom 8:32).

We renew our minds when we praise, thank, and worship Him. When we meditate on His Word, His beauty, and His wonderful works (Josh 1:8, Ps 119:147-148, 27:4, 145:5).

We renew our minds when we rest in solitude of His Presence, soaking in worshipful music, or silent and listening, *focused on Him*. When we are still enough to know that He is Lord and we are not (Ps 46:10, 100:3).

Renewing our minds opens us to receive truth and positions us to receive the Holy Spirit's revelation that we are ensnared in a lie. What do we do when lies are exposed? The Word gives us a plan.

When Lies Are Exposed

When the Holy Spirit has revealed to us a rut of deception, it is time to rejoice! He is in the process of a mighty work in our hearts. At that moment, we have a choice: we can continue to believe that lie, rebelling against the truth, rebelling against God. Or, *we can choose obedience*. Choosing obedience means aligning our behaviors, words, and thoughts with His truth – *whether our feelings match up with the truth or not.*

Satan is **a liar and the father of lies** (Jn 8:44); every lie, every deception, every delusion *originates* in him. He is the source, the root, of every lie. Forsaking lies and choosing truth will be one of our most crucial weapons in warfare, so let's learn how to wield it proficiently. Because this is not as easy as it sounds, I have outlined four steps to help us exchange lies for truth:

1) Confessing, repenting, and renouncing.

2) Declaring Scriptural truths.

3) Asking for filling of the Holy Spirit.

4) Walking it out.

Let's look at each step.

Confessing, Repenting, and Renouncing

Confessing is acknowledging that we have been believing a lie, and admitting that it is a *sin* to believe something that is not in alignment with God's Word (1Jn 1:5-10). Truly there may be many circumstances outside of our control that led us to believe this lie, such as woundings from the world, or untruths that we have been taught as children. These issues require attention, and we will address them later in this study. But for right now, if the Holy Spirit has exposed a lie, confessing is the first step to freedom from this lie.

We studied *repentance* deeply in *Triumph of Surrender*, and we know that flippantly telling God "I'm sorry" is not real repentance. Repentance is an about-face, a deep heart commitment to live according to God's commands. Repentance is not a perfect change in behavior, but a *heart* change. It is an acknowledgment of how our sins have wounded God's heart and have wounded others, and a deep desire to change and to live according to God's ways. A change in actions and behavior that follows proves our repentance to be genuine.[7]

Renouncing the lie seems most effective when we proclaim, out loud, our rejection of the lie, our refusal to continue to believe it or walk in it, and our declaration of truth. We can certainly pray in our hearts, but somehow it appears that declaring out loud is going on the offensive and seems to carry a greater power.[8]

Declaring Scriptural Truths

If we are casting down a lie, we need to take renewing our minds up a level. Carefully select verses that speak truths which counteract that lie. If the lie is relating to deception, flood your mind with verses of purity, integrity, and fear of the Lord. If the lie is relating to depression and heaviness, focus on verses of praise, joy, and hope. If it's disobedience, hone in on surrender, submission, and fear of the Lord.

Proclaim the Word out loud, with deep conviction and authority that refuses to be quashed by the enemy. This is no mealy-mouthed mumbling of Scripture! If we want the enemy to flee, we must go on the offensive, declaring out loud with boldness and Godly confidence, or, as some would say, "God-fidence" - that deep heart knowing, trusting, that God is in control. As we learned in *Triumph Over Suffering*, Philippians 4-8 it!

Finally, brothers and sisters, whatever is true, whatever is noble, whatever is right, whatever is pure, whatever is lovely, whatever is admirable – if anything is excellent or praiseworthy – think about such things.   Philippians 4:8 NIV

Drench yourself in these new truths, again and again throughout the day, day after day, week after week, month after month, until your mind starts to naturally run in these new ruts of truth, and *in your heart are the highways to Zion* (Ps 84:5). This may be a long process, even longer if there is much pain in your life that drove you to that rut of lies in the first place. But when His transformation appears, you will know it was worth every tear.

Asking for Filling of the Holy Spirit

We can humbly ask the Father to fill us with the Holy Spirit (Lk 11:13), and pray for the Holy Spirit to fill us with His fruit that is the "glorious opposite"[9] of whatever we are battling (Gal 5:22-23). If the lie is rooted in impatience, I ask for patience. If it's rooted in fear, I ask for trust and peace. If it's self-hatred, I ask for the ability to receive His love. If I am dealing with pride, I ask for humility and fear of the Lord. If I'm battling rebellion, I ask for obedience, surrender, and submission. If I'm caught up in distrust, I ask for faith and trust. If jealousy, I ask for contentment and intimacy with Him.

Walking It Out

Throughout this book, you will hear me often use this phrase, "walking it out" (Eph 5:8-10, Gal 5:16, 1Jn 1:6-7). Walking it out involves making the spiritual a physical reality. We are not of this world, yet we are living in this world, and we must connect the spiritual with the physical. For example, if we choose to forgive, God may call us to work to restore a relationship. If we repent of a lie, God may call us to confess to the person we lied to. If the Holy Spirit convicts us of an impure relationship, God may call us to set Godly boundaries, or to flee, or to sever ties.

Walking it out means *obeying*. We must make active choices in the physical to walk out what we prayed in the spiritual in order to align our lives and thoughts according to His truth. I find that in this season of exchanging a lie for His truth, He often orchestrates tests to give me an opportunity to *choose* His way as a means of deep repentance and to strengthen the truth in my heart.

Let's watch these four steps put into practice. I will give you an example from my own life of a battle to gain freedom from an entanglement of lies. You will see how these steps are actually battle strategies, and how the Lord brought victory as I used these strategies, partnering with Him in the battle.

The Lord had given me a calling, to write and teach. After years of walking in that calling, following the Lord as best I could understand, I hit a season when I was stymied, paralyzed with perfectionism and fear of failure. I was unable to continue to write and teach. I was confused, caught in a labyrinth of lies, and I could not see the way out.

I spent time in the Word, in solitude, prayer, fasting. When the Holy Spirit exposed the lies that were ensnaring me, lies that I was worthless and insignificant, He also showed me how those lies were driving me to try to earn His love and acceptance. The veil was pulled back, and with great clarity I was able to see how I was entrapped. As I repented and desired to align my beliefs with His truth, my initial prayer sounded something like this:

Lord, I have been believing lies that I am too sinful and insignificant, that I am worthless and not enough, and that You have no purpose for me. I am sorry for rejecting Your profound workmanship in the way You created me. I am sorry for believing these lies, for aligning myself with Satan, for not relying on Your death as payment for my sins. I am sorry for harboring the fear that I will lose your love, and for striving to earn Your love and acceptance, which You have freely given me.

I reject the lies that I am worthless and not enough, and I choose to believe the truth, that You love me fully and accept me unconditionally, and that You have a unique plan to fit me into Your Kingdom design. I choose to believe that You call me a child of God, that nothing can separate me from Your love, and that You have called me according to Your purposes. I choose to believe that I am Your workmanship, created in Christ Jesus to do good works, which You have planned in advance for me.

Please Heavenly Father, fill me with Your Spirit. Grow my intimacy with You. Please, Holy Spirit, please fill me with Your peace and Your love, and with a heart that trusts in You and in Your love for me. Amen.

I then dove into Scripture for truths to declare. The Holy Spirit led me to verses that countered these lies: 1 John 3:1, Romans 8:38-39, Romans 8:28, and Ephesians 2:10. These verses and others were the ones I meditated on, memorized, and proclaimed many times a day over many, many months.

I also spent much time over many months soaking in Him, listening in stillness to quiet worshipful music, resting in His presence as I meditated on His Word, allowing Him to speak truth to my heart. It was during these times that He began to wear new ruts of truth into my mind and heart.

And I walked it out by beginning to pay attention to my thoughts, and when I found myself falling back into those same sinful thought patterns, I would take every thought captive and choose to think God's truths, even if at first I didn't really believe it. I stopped speaking words that lined up with lies, and instead began to speak His truths. And I stepped back into the calling He had assigned me, writing and teaching, without holding back any longer in fear. I knew I was imperfect and would not always get it right, but that His grace would cover my failures and His power would be perfected in my weakness.

And finally, miraculously, the Holy Spirit uprooted Satan's lies and rooted His truths in my heart. I truly don't know exactly how or when it happened. It seemed to happen gradually, without fanfare or earthquakes. One day, I simply noticed that I truly believed the truths I was declaring. It was no longer a battle to choose to believe those truths – I seemed to just naturally believe them. My smile broke into a refrain of rejoicing, knowing that, somehow, in a way I could barely understand, He had stepped in and transformed my heart.

Celeste Li
Jupiter, Florida

Go back to my prayer and mark the parts that cover confessing, repenting, renouncing, declaring truths, and asking for filling. Note also how I utilized Scripture and stillness to renew my mind, and how I walked it out.

I have been privileged to join forces with many people in similar battles. I have asked my friend Sally to share how she also used these four steps as she fought to triumph. This precious woman had been under a tormenting enemy attack night after night for many months – let's watch her pathway to victory.

It had been over a year since my divorce. I was still being awakened every night at 3 AM by the same thoughts going over and over in my mind, kind of like a loop recorder that would never end. Cruel things that had been done to me, and cruel words spoken over me, awakened me from my sound sleep. I dreaded getting into bed, knowing that there was going to be a repeat performance that would last many hours. Why, God, couldn't I put my past to rest? I had forgiven my ex, not only because God commands it, but because my life demanded it to move forward. Still, the nightly torment persisted.

I realized there was a stronghold in my mind, and Satan was trying to control my heart and mind through this stronghold. There was a battle going on, and it was spiritual warfare. I was learning that my spiritual weapon to combat this ongoing war was to replace Satan's lies with God's Truths. I decided to try it. So each night, when I was under attack, I started speaking out loud: "I am a child of God! I am a saint! Jesus loves me! If God is for me, who can be against me? Jesus loves me, and I can do all things through Christ who strengthens me!" I would keep repeating these truths over and over until I fell peacefully asleep. Within a few nights, the frequency of these attacks decreased markedly, and now I often sleep through the entire night without being awakened by these attacks.

Sally Klinginsmith
Jupiter, Florida

When Sally entered the battle, her heart didn't quite believe those truths. But she *chose* to believe the truth of the Word *even though her feelings didn't match up with those truths.* She then went on the offensive by *proclaiming* those truths night after night in the midst of these attacks. This was no wimpy recitation of truths! Victory in Jesus was imminent for her as she proclaimed these truths out loud with "God-fident" authority. Sally moved from torment, to peace. She has been freed. As she rests in contentment, I can now see the Lord's peace reflected deeply in her eyes.

Heart beliefs that don't align with the Word of God are Satan's lies. When our hearts believe lies, our minds can become dark and confused, as we have seen in this chapter. Demolition of lies will be paramount for victory.

As we work our way through this study, we will constantly utilize the weapons and strategies we trained with in this chapter. But before we go any further into battle training, we are going to focus in the next chapter on what is *truly foundational* in warfare: knowing God deeply.

Chapter 3
Know Your Victor

*I*n Chapter 1, we learned that the battle is already won, and that we are on the winning team. We now understand that the ultimate purpose of warfare is to conform us to the image of Christ, and that the key to victory is our surrender. In Chapter 2, we learned that the true battlefield is in our hearts, and we trained with some essential weapons and strategies as we learned how to renounce lies and renew our minds.

In upcoming chapters we will study spiritual weapons in greater depth, but realize that even more important than training with our weapons is learning to be led by the Spirit. For if we have become strong enough to heft a sword, but just wildly slash through the air, this weapon will be useless. If we have sharpened our sword but don't know when to lunge and when to sheath, we may miss the call to battle – or we may exhaust ourselves fighting the wrong battle at the wrong time. We will only know God's strategy and His timing if we have a very close connection with our Commander-in-Chief – and we will be able to handle our weapons with authority and power when we are *obedient* to that strategy. In this chapter, we will lay the most important foundation for victory: growing deeper in our knowing of God.

Focusing on knowing God may feel like a detour, but that could not be further from the truth. Battles are not won by focusing on darkness, but by coming to know the Lord more deeply. This is God's plan for our victory. For knowing our Victor, knowing His irrefutable truth, knowing His righteousness and holiness, knowing *His Name*, trusting the depth of His character, the beauty of His heart, and the fathomlessness of His love for us – as well as who *He says* we are – is our protection from enemy assault and our strength in the battle.

> **The steadfast of mind You will keep in perfect peace,**
> **Because he trusts in You.**
> **Trust in the LORD forever,**
> **For in GOD the LORD, we have an everlasting Rock.**
>
> Isaiah 26:3-4

The Lord spoke through the prophet Hosea that the Israelites were destroyed because they did not *know* God.

> **... there is no faithfulness or kindness**
> **Or knowledge of God in the land ...**
> **My people are destroyed for lack of knowledge.**   Hosea 4:1,6

God's people did not *know* Him, and that lack of intimate knowledge of their God led to their downfall.

The Word also tells us that those *who know their God* will display strength and take action – indeed will do *great exploits* (Dan 11:32 NASB, NKJV). Remember the handsome ruddy youth who carried out great exploits? In the time of Philistine oppression, the Israelites focused on Goliath and were terrified (1Sam 17:11). But David focused on the God he knew deeply, recognizing that God had prepared and equipped him for this moment, and concluded that the battle was the Lord's and that the Lord would deliver him.

Then David said to the Philistine, "You come to me with a sword, a spear, and a javelin, but I come to you in the name of the LORD of hosts, the God of the armies of Israel, whom you have taunted. This day the LORD will deliver you up into my hands, and I will strike you down and remove your head from you. And I will give the dead bodies of the army of the Philistines this day to the birds of the sky and the wild beasts

of the earth, that all the earth may know that there is a God in Israel, and that all this assembly may know that the LORD does not deliver by sword or by spear; for the battle is the LORD's and He will give you into our hands."

1 Samuel 17:45-47, emphasis added

"I come to you in the name of the LORD of hosts." David knew not merely the *name* of the Lord of hosts, but also *what that name revealed*: when we are in the center of his will and circumstances are desperate, when there is no human way out, when our own resources are completely inadequate, *and we turn to the only One who can rescue us*, the Commander of the Host of Heavenly Angels delivers His victory. A victory wrought not by human means (swords, spears, and javelins), but through anointed slingshots and angelic hosts. When we know our Savior that deeply, it will inspire us to face the enemy as David did instead of turning tail and running.

I think David knew God by the name "Lord of hosts" because he had personally experienced God in this way. I can imagine him crying out to the Lord of hosts in desperation when he faced the terrifying lion and formidable bear. David *knew* the name of his God and God positioned him in the center of His will, and thus David did great exploits as God ushered in His victory.

What's In a Name?

Names in Biblical times were very significant, revealing the essential nature and character of a person.[1] I believe that knowing the Lord's name – not just the name itself, but the depth of *what that name means* – will enable us to trust Him in greater measure:

And those who know Your name
will put their trust in You,
For You, O LORD, have not forsaken those who seek You.

Psalm 9:10

And trusting Him helps us to release to His control, and invites Him to move on our behalf:

Commit your way to the LORD;
Trust in him and he will do this:
He will make your righteous reward shine like the dawn,
Your vindication like the noonday sun.   Psalm 37:5-6 NIV

Deliverance comes to those who love Him and know His name:

"Because he has loved Me,
Therefore I will deliver him;
I will set him securely on high,
Because he has known My name.
He will call upon Me, and I will answer him;
I will be with him in trouble;
I will rescue him and honor him.
With a long life I will satisfy him
And let him see My salvation."   Psalm 91:14-16, emphasis added

We see two keys to receiving the Lord's deliverance listed here: we must love God, and we must know His name.

- *Love God*: Jesus tells us that loving God means *obedience* (Jn 14:15). We have practiced a deep walk of obedience from the heart as we have journeyed through *Triumph Over Suffering* and *Triumph of Surrender*; through this book we will build on those foundations as we seek more layers of sanctification, deeper surrender, and greater obedience.

- *Know His name*: In this chapter, we will explore some of the Hebrew names of God, and some of the names of Jesus and of the Holy Spirit used in the New Testament. Through our study of His names we will come to know Him more, for His names reveal His will and His ways and how He relates to His people. His names show us what pleases Him and how we can glorify Him. His names also draw us into intimacy, as they illustrate many different facets of His character, features of His personality, intricacies of His nature, and hidden corners of His heart.

God Reveals Himself Through His Names

Think about the various names you may call a particular loved one. You may use different names in different circumstances. When you ponder how a name developed, it reminds you of a special time and is a treasure of your love for each other. The uniqueness of those names speaks of a delightful intimacy between you.

Similarly, in profound moments of history, God has revealed to mankind some of His names. In this chapter, we are going to learn some names He has given us in His Word in order to come to understand Him more and to know Him more deeply. Our study will only skim the surface and touch on some nuances; if you want to delve deeper, there are some books listed in the *Resource* section.

It seems to me a great tenderness that God has given us *His names*. Ponder the intimacy of this gift – He is unveiling Himself to us! He *wants* us to know Him! And as we come to know His character and nature and ways through this study of His names, when we are in the midst of a battle, and we recall His work, His strength, His power, His love, His mercy represented in these names, it will grow our trust in Him and give us the fortitude we need to persevere to victory.

Ann Spangler, in *Praying the Names of God*, shares this:

> As I studied and prayed, God worked these names into my own life, like kneading yeast into bread. I felt challenged by names that revealed God's holiness. They exposed my own imperfections. I felt comforted by ones that revealed him as healer and provider. They satisfied my need.[2]

I believe as we study these names, the Name of the Lord will become increasingly sacred to us; we will realize that it is *His enemies* who take His name in vain (Ps 139:20).

As you study these names, I encourage you to use them in your private prayer time with the Lord to invite Him to work these names into your own walk with Him. Knowing His Names will also grow our trust in Him (Ps 9:10). I have added pronunciations to the Hebrew names to facilitate making them part of your comfortable vocabulary. Although there can be various spellings as these names are translated into English, and various suggested pronunciations, I have used the pronunciations from Ann Spangler's book throughout this chapter for consistency.

Abba – and also Adonai
[AB-ba and a-do-NAI]

A number of years ago, my family traveled to Israel. As we walked the streets of Jerusalem, I was shocked to hear so many children running around calling out, *"Abba! Abba!"* I watched these Israeli fathers as they responded to those cries. I witnessed their tenderness as they picked up their children, their attentiveness as they listened ever so carefully, their obvious love as they stroked heads or wiped tears – and suddenly God gave me a new depth of understanding of His name, *Abba*.

Because you are sons, God has sent forth the Spirit of His Son into our hearts, crying, "Abba! Father!" Galatians 4:6

"Or what man is there among you who, when his son asks for a loaf, will give him a stone? Or if he asks for a fish, he will not give him a snake, will he? If you then, being evil, know how to give good gifts to your children, how much more will your Father who is in heaven give what is good to those who ask Him!" Matthew 7:9-11

In *Triumph of Suffering* and *Triumph of Surrender*, we joined that tender knowing of Him as *Abba*, Father, Daddy, to the awe-inspiring knowing of Him as *Adonai*, Lord, Master. *Adonai* signifies sovereignty and ownership, and indicates God as our Master and Owner of all.

O LORD, our Lord [*Adonai*],
How majestic is Your name in all the earth,
Who have displayed Your splendor above the heavens!

Psalm 8:1

As Isaiah did in the temple, when we use the name *Adonai*, it indicates our surrender to Him as Master of everything, Master of all we own, Master of even ourselves.

In the year of King Uzziah's death I saw the Lord [*Adonai*]
sitting on a throne, lofty and exalted, with the train of His
robe filling the temple ... Then I heard the voice of the Lord
[*Adonai*], saying, "Whom shall I send, and who will go for Us?"
Then I said, "Here am I. Send me!"   Isaiah 6:1,8

In calling Him *Adonai*, we not only recognize Him as Lord, but ourselves as His bondservants. We rely on His protection, we acknowledge He has a right to our very lives, and we give Him our complete obedience, from the heart (Rom 6:17).

Ponder, Pray, and Journal

We are not our own. We have been bought with a price (1Cor 6:19-20). We are summoned to service, promised protection, and given all the grace necessary to fulfill His assignment.

To me, being the bondservant of *Adonai* is just as tender as being a child of *Abba*. Journal your thoughts.

The concept of *Abba* and *Adonai* simultaneously is indeed a great mystery, yet grasping this on some level is crucial for victory. If you don't confidently know the Lord as both *Abba* and *Adonai*, if your heart seems to focus on one without the other, I recommend you go back through the *Triumph* books, because this deep heart knowing and profound intimacy is foundational for warfare. In these next sections, we will build on that groundwork by studying further some of His names that will be particularly important on the battlefront.

God Unveils His Names To Us:
Elohim and Yahweh
[e-lo-HEEM and yah-WEH]

In the beginning God [*Elohim*] created the heavens and the earth. The earth was formless and void, and darkness was over the surface of the deep, and the Spirit of God was moving over the surface of the waters. Genesis 1:1-2

The very first verse of the Bible contains this name, *Elohim*. God created everything *out of nothing*. He spoke, and called into being *that which did not exist* (Rom 4:17, Heb 11:3). Omnipotence, creative power, and might beyond comprehension are expressed in the name *Elohim*. He is the all-powerful Creator and the matchless Ruler; He created all, and all belongs to Him (Deut 10:14, Ex 9:29, 1Chr 29:11-12, Ps 24:1). His creation reveals His glory, His invisible attributes, His eternal power, His divine nature (Rom 1:20). *Elohim* is God completely *other* than us. As I stand in awe of a breathtaking sunrise, and the name *Elohim* is on my lips, this reminds me that **it is He who has made us, and not we ourselves** (Ps 100:3).

Elohim is in the plural, seeming to foreshadow God's unveiling of Himself as Trinity. This is further emphasized later in the chapter: **Then God [*Elohim*] said, "Let Us make man in Our image, according to Our likeness"** (Gen 1:26). Indeed we see the Spirit of God was moving over the surface of the waters (Gen 1:20), and we know that all things were created by Jesus, through Jesus, for Jesus (Col 1:15-16, Jn 1:3, Heb 1:2).

Then, in the second chapter of the Bible, we meet God as *Yahweh*, often translated as LORD in capital letters.

Ponder

This name in the Hebrew is YHWH, known as the Tetragrammaton, or "four-lettered name."[3] The Jewish people revered YHWH as such a sacred name that they were afraid of profaning it, and eventually it was spoken aloud only by the priests worshiping in the Jerusalem temple. After the temple was destroyed by the Romans in AD 70, the Jewish people no longer pronounced YHWH. *Adonai* (which means Lord) was substituted in their biblical text;[4] "The Great And Terrible Name" or "The Unutterable Name"[5] was also used for YHWH.

In the tenth century, Jewish scholars began supplying vowels to Hebrew words which had vowels that were pronounced but not written. The vowels from the Hebrew word *Adonai* were at that time inserted into YHWH as YoHoWaH. YHWH was JHVH in German, so the word "Jehovah" resulted. In the King James translation, which uses LORD for YHWH, Jehovah was substituted for LORD in some passages.[6]

As we study God's names together, we will use *Yahweh* since it is closer to the original Hebrew word. Most scholars think the correct pronunciation is yah-WEH.[7]

YHWH is derived from the Hebrew word *havah*, which means "to be," and is almost exactly like the Hebrew word *chavah*, which means "life."[8] It seems there are multiple facets of who He is that God has wrapped up in this name.

At creation, *Yahweh Elohim* formed man from the dust of the ground and breathed into him the breath of life (Gen 2:7). The name *Yahweh* speaks of God as eternal, unchangeable, absolutely self-existent, and the source of all life,[9] and to me also reveals a sweet gentleness, His hands shaping Adam from clay. The name *Yahweh* also seems to reveal a loving tenderness for His creation, as it is *Yahweh Elohim* who searched for Adam and Eve after the fall (Gen 3:9).

You know the translation as **"I AM WHO I AM"** (Ex 3:14) when God gave Moses His name as *Yahweh* at the burning bush. The Great I AM. Eternally self existent – but also the God of *relationships*: **"I am the God of your father, the God of Abraham, the God of Isaac, and the God of Jacob"** (Ex 3:6).

Then, as He invaded earth to redeem His people from slavery in Egypt, *Yahweh* demonstrated how He is *intimately involved* in the lives of His people, and delights in *every detail* of their lives (Ps 37:23 NLT). My friend Carol explains, "Knowing that He is a personal God who keeps His promises to be with us, who loves and cares and directs everything according to His purposes, affects all parts of my daily walk with Him." I've asked her to describe how knowing Him as *Yahweh* enabled her to trust Him in a difficult time.

Recently, my husband and I did not understand God's hand in our circumstances, and we were questioning His ways. My 97 year-old father-in-law had moved into our home. He was a faithful pastor who served the Lord most of his life, and now he was suffering with dementia and the loss of his dignity. It was very painful to witness, and caused division within the family. We could not understand why God would allow this for such a Godly man.

Knowing God as Yahweh gave me strength in the middle of the storm. I kept telling my husband that God loves his father so much more than we can, and He is forever faithful to those who serve Him well. But it was the miracles that happened in the last week of his life that caused this knowledge to grow and be implanted deeper into my heart.

A terminal infection caused my father-in-law's physical body to begin to shut down. Estranged family members came from near and far to see him in his last days. In the last week of his life, we were utterly amazed to witness miraculous forgiveness and restoration of unity within the divided family. God's love, mercy, and grace within each heart was clearly evident.

We can now see that God was orchestrating every detail. I have come out of this season with an even greater trust in God's heart for His children. No matter what the surface appearance of a situation appears to be, I know that God is working behind the scenes for the good of all who love and serve Him. That is Yahweh!

Carol Virelles
Triumph Servant Leader
Wellington, Florida

I recall those final heartbreaking months of the life of this beloved pastor and prayer warrior, known to us who loved him as *"Abu."* If he could have had an awareness during that final time, I think he may have realized that God was answering his prayers to the very end, for his only desire was for Christ to be exalted in his body, whether by life or by death (Phil 1:20). Who could have anticipated the glories to be revealed in the final week of his life? What became so real to Carol during this trial was the dual-nature revealed in the name of *Yahweh*: the sovereign God who is orchestrating everything according to His eternal purposes, and yet is also ever-present and personally and intimately involved in our lives.

As we read further into the Word, I see yet another layer of meaning wrapped up in this name. The Lord speaks as *Yahweh* when emphasizing His righteousness, holiness, and justice, requiring righteousness in His people. It is *Yahweh* who declares we shall be holy for He is holy (Lev 19:1-2). But not only does He require righteousness, it is *Yahweh* in His great mercy and lovingkindness who promises that He will give us His righteousness, will make with us a new covenant, writing His law on our hearts, forgiving our iniquities, and remembering our sin no more (Jer 31:31-34).[10] **He made Him who knew no sin to be sin on our behalf, so that we might become the righteousness of God in Him** (1Cor 5:21).

Although I did not know these Hebrew names of God when I first came to Christ, at that weighty, mysterious, and penetrating moment I did indeed meet Him as *Yahweh Elohim*. I saw the enormity of my many sins, large and small ones, contrasted to His holiness, and all that was required to forgive me and put me in right relationship with Him: Jesus' torturous death in my place. I experienced His *mercy*, and at the moment I received His forgiveness, He enabled me to forgive. And I discovered *relationship* with Him, as I experienced His love, so overwhelming and personal, and heard His voice for the very first time.

Ponder, Pray, and Journal

Yahweh. Redemption, relationship, and special revelation. Righteousness, justice, and holiness – yet lovingkindness, mercy, and grace. Do you at times focus on His justice and forget His grace? Or focus on His mercy and forget His holiness?

Surrender Leads to Dependence:
El Elyon and El Shaddai
[EL el-YOHN and EL shad-DAI]

He who dwells in the shelter of the Most High [*El Elyon*]
Will abide in the shadow of the Almighty [*El Shaddai*].

Psalm 91:1

These names are very tied together. Let's explore.

The name *Elyon* means "Highest" or "Exalted One."[11] *El Elyon* indicates God's supreme sovereignty, His utter control, His undefeated rule.

El Shaddai is often translated God Almighty. The actual derivations and meaning of this name are uncertain, but some theologians believe it is derived from a similar word *shad* that means "breast" or "breasted." This signifies "one who nourishes, supplies, satisfies," shedding forth and pouring out blessings as all-sufficient and all-bountiful God (Gen 49:25).[12]

In Genesis 17, Abram had been waiting for many years for God to fulfill His promise of a son and descendants as numerous as the stars. Here is where we first encounter the name *El Shaddai*, as God seals his promise with the covenant of circumcision and reveals the name, Isaac. When we consider the fulfillment of this promise, it seems God required Abraham and Sarah to finally come to an end of their own human efforts. He waited until their bodies were as good as dead (Rom 4:19), and until their faith was alive and strong (Rom 4:18-21, Heb 11:11). It seems He waited for full dependence upon Him, as a baby is fully dependent upon the breast.

Ponder, Pray, and Journal

All these blessings will come upon you and overtake you if you obey the LORD your God (Deut 28:2). Often, it seems God requires that we align our lives with His commands before He sheds forth His blessings.

Read Psalm 91:1 again. When we bow our hearts in submission to the sovereign plan of *El Elyon*, it is then that we will abide in the shadow of protection, sustenance, blessings, fruitfulness, and grace of *El Shaddai*. Journal your thoughts.

Sometimes, maybe even often, we work in our own strength. We thwart the release of God's bountiful blessings because of our own self-sufficiency. It seems we must completely die to ourselves to position ourselves for a move of God.

Think of prayers you are waiting on the Lord to answer. Are you working for solutions by your own control? A baby at the breast is totally and fully dependent upon the mother to sustain him. It is a place of complete trust. From that place of total dependence upon and trust in the Lord, cry out to Him as *El Shaddai*.

The Healing Touch of Yahweh Rophe
[yah-WEH ro-FEH]

Praise the LORD, my soul,
And forget not all his benefits –
Who forgives all your sins
And heals all your diseases.   Psalm 103:2-3 NIV

Note the order here: forgives, then heals. When we confess and repent, He forgives and cleanses (1Jn 1:9). Forgiveness first, then healing.

Jesus' ministry was anointed with so many physical healings, but His true goal was to draw people to repentance and into right relationship with God (Mk 1:15, Lk 4:43). To the paralyzed man lowered through the roof He said, **"Your sins are forgiven"** (Mk 2:5), and then He healed him. Jesus had not come for the purpose of performing miracles, but to bring people into right relationship with God, to proclaim the good news, to heal the brokenhearted, to proclaim freedom to captives (Isa 61:1). The miracles simply announced that He came from God (Jn 10:25).

When we are in need of healing, whether it is physical, mental, emotional, spiritual, or any combination, it is good to ask God to search our heart. Our own personal sin may or may not be the *cause* of our sickness or pain, but if we have sins blocking His healing, repentance can open us to *receive* His healing (Jas 5:16). We can ask *Yahweh Rophe* to reveal the diagnosis or uncover the roots. We can ask Him how He wants us to partner with Him in the healing process, always keeping in mind the price He paid for our healing: **by His stripes we are healed** (Isa 53:5 NKJV).

I recall the season when I met the Lord as *Yahweh Rophe*. It was about nine years ago, when God was calling me to allow Him into the most profound wounds of my heart. Although I had repented of these sins from the deepest part of my heart, and these sins were what drove me to Jesus for salvation ten years earlier, this region of my heart was an area that I had barricaded off fully. I had never allowed His healing power to penetrate. But now, He showed me it was time.

I next spent two long painful years processing through this pain in healing classes and Christian counseling, doing the hard work of revisiting these sins. With great trepidation, I gradually opened my heart to Him, and met His grace and forgiveness so deep and intimate and powerful and infinite as He reached into the depth of my wounds and brought His miraculous healing. I cannot even put my transformation into words as *Yahweh Rophe* took my shattered heart into His hands and made it whole again.

Because I *know* Him as *Yahweh Rophe*, I can be a beacon of Light pointing to Jesus those who are devastated, despairing, or drowning in pain. *Because I know my Savior*, I have the deepest of faith and utter confidence that whatever pain they are enduring, He is *fully* able to heal.

My friend Kolleen knows *Yahweh Rophe* deeply also. I have asked her to share how knowing God as *Yahweh Rophe* helps her to walk through painful times in her life.

I began my journey of emotional healing with God seven years ago during my painful divorce. Over time God proved to be faithful *and did bring healing to my broken heart as He promises in Psalm 147:3. However, what I didn't expect was that healing happens over time and as we grow in our spiritual walk, God takes us to deeper and deeper levels of healing. It is in those times of facing another layer of healing that I cry out to God by His name <u>Yahweh Rophe</u>, the God of Healing. God doesn't need to hear me call Him by that name, but calling out to <u>Yahweh Rophe</u> reminds me that God the Healer is present to heal my emotional pain. By crying out to <u>Yahweh Rophe</u> in my time of emotional pain I am attaching my faith to the name that reminds me of God's nature to heal my broken heart.*

Kolleen Bannon
Jupiter, Florida

This is key: God doesn't need us to pray to Him by these names, but knowing Him in this way can give us hope and strength to cling to Him and wait on Him.

The Piercing Gaze of El Roi
[EL raw-EE]

This name of God is used only once in the Bible, in Genesis 16:13. Read Genesis 16:1-16, and meet me back here when you are finished.

This name of God, *El Roi*, reminds me that He knows every word before I speak it, He has counted every hair on my head, and a sparrow does not fall to the ground apart from Him. He never slumbers and never sleeps, He knows my going out and my coming in, He searches my heart, He sees the end from the beginning, and no creature is hidden from His sight. (Ps 139, Lk 12:7, Matt 10:29, Ps 121:3-4, Jer 17:10, Isa 46:10, Heb 4:13.)

My friend Ann Marie is a treasure. It's not unusual to see her eyes brimming with tears because her heart is going out to someone in their pain, or because she was just overwhelmed once again by the depth of her Savior's love. Her own life challenges and her deep knowing of the Lord equips her so beautifully as a *Triumph* leader. I've asked her to share her journey of coming to know *El Roi*.

So much of my youth, I felt like an outcast. My parents uprooted me from everything I knew as a teenager when they decided to move us to Florida. Leaving everyone I loved dearly was so very hard for me. I found it very difficult to make friends, often feeling judged and rejected. I spent so much of my time alone in my bedroom, crying myself to sleep. But <u>El Roi</u> was there. I know this, because although I felt sad and at times hopeless, I had a peace and confidence that was not of me. I could rest knowing that God was never unaware of what I was going through. The Lord was watching over me, protecting me and strengthening me.

In my twenties I was in a very unhealthy marriage, partly due to choices I had made. There in the wilderness of my own making, I was again feeling very alone. I was riddled with guilt and sadness.

I knew that this was not an ideal situation for my two young children to be in and wanted so desperately to leave. Without going into details, my husband was removed from our home. This allowed me the time and space I needed to make arrangements to move out and protect my children. Once again, God was there. Once again, He saw me. He was so tender and loving to me and gave me the strength I needed to move forward. It was during this very difficult time that a friend of mine spoke a Scripture over me that I know was directly from the Lord. This Scripture changed the trajectory of my life:

The LORD watches over you —
the LORD is your shade at your right hand;
the sun will not harm you by day,
nor the moon by night.
The LORD will keep you from all harm —

he will watch over your life;
the LORD will watch over your coming and going
both now and forevermore.   *Psalm 121:5-8 NIV*

So powerful!

My current marriage has not been without heartache. My husband was unfaithful. I was heartbroken, yet once again the Lord saw me. The God Who Sees was with me in my prayer closet as I cried and screamed from the pain in my heart. Each time, He so tenderly comforted me there and brought me to the exact Scripture that would speak over me as a loving Father would. <u>El Roi</u> saw my mistreatment, and I learned to trust His instructions since He sees the bigger picture. The Lord gave me the strength to continue in my marriage, and today, my marriage is everything I could have ever hoped for. I am eternally grateful.

I understand Hagar's urge to run away. I have felt it many times in my life. But through the name <u>El Roi</u>, I discovered that in my lowest moments, Someone sees me. God sees my pain. He hears my cries. The God Who Sees, <u>El Roi</u>, has always been with me.

Ann Marie
Triumph Servant Leader
West Palm Beach, Florida

With those dewdrops in her eyes again, Ann Marie sums it up this way: "I never really realized it at the time, but when I look back over my life, the God Who Sees, *El Roi*, has been with me all along. Because He cares for and loves me so deeply, He sees *me*. Imagine that! The same God that created the oceans and the mountains – *sees me!!* This overwhelms my soul!" I believe her heart positioned so close to Him gives Him great joy.

El Roi healed Ann Marie with His presence and led her to perfect Scriptures that transformed her heart. He saw the wounds inflicted upon her, and her own sin – and loved her enough to rescue her and give her calling and purpose. God had beautiful plans for Ann Marie, including a clan of children and grandchildren, an exploding restaurant for her and her husband (that many say is more about ministry than eating), and Kingdom work reaching hurting women as *Triumph* leader. But in order to fulfill those plans, He required her to leave her first marriage – and to leave the guilt and shame behind. And He required her to stay in her second marriage, to forgive, to rebuild trust, and open her heart to His healing.

My friend Ashley is also overwhelmed with The God Who Sees. Ashley is like a fountain, always moving, always flowing, gushing forth excitement and laughter in wide-eyed wonder at the awesomeness of her God. Serving as youth pastor for over a decade, she has a passion for youth and a deep compassion for hurting students. I have asked her to share her own rocky journey to healing as she came to know God as *El Roi*, The God Who Sees.

I was adopted. It was a closed adoption, which meant there would be no contact with my birth parents. Yet I wanted to know my mother so desperately that I spent many years of my life futilely searching for her.

When I was twenty-four, the adoption agency sent me a letter that gave me a few more details about my adoption. I wrote back to them to ask my mother's name. Their answer brought my search to a screeching halt: my mother did not want to be found.

This response sent me into a tailspin of despair and hopelessness. I was a believer, I was serving in church, I had been on mission trips. Why, God, why? I did not choose this. I did not deserve this. This was my one and only request, to find my mother. Why are You not giving me this?

I stumbled outside and sat on the seawall nearby and sobbed and sobbed. I had no control over what was happening to me. Seeing God through my pain and shame, all I could see was His betrayal, rejection, and abandonment. What had happened to me dictated what I believed about myself. I wanted to run away. Just like Hagar.

Genesis 16 outlines Hagar's horrific story of how events outside of her control impacted and shaped her life. Since Sarai was barren and there was no heir, this slave of Abram and Sarai was forced to bear Abram's child. Hagar was then abused, rejected, and hated by Sarai. In a moment of despair, feeling God had turned His back on her, Hagar ran away. I could totally relate.

But God saw Hagar in her brokenness. He found her in the wilderness, and promised her that her son, still in the womb, would have innumerable descendants and would be a great nation. Suddenly, Hagar stopped looking at what had happened to her, and started looking at Who deeply loved her. Out of that tender moment was birthed from Hagar's lips this name of God: <u>El Roi</u>, The God Who Sees. Hagar is the only person in Scripture with the honor of giving God a name.

When I thought that no one saw me in that moment, I realized God saw me in my brokenness, and gave me the strength to go on. But I never relinquished the desire to find my mother. On my thirtieth birthday, my husband gave me a DNA test, thinking it would be helpful to find my birth mom, but it led nowhere. A few years later, I was diagnosed with mild borderline personality disorder, which can be triggered by abandonment and fear of rejection. It was the devastation of this diagnosis that drove me to pray, "God, either do something to help me find my mother, or help me to let this go. I choose healing, however You will to heal me."

Six months later I received an email, "I think I can help you find your birth family." I thought it was a scam. Hesitantly, I responded, so much hope and fear overwhelming me – and was soon talking to my half-brother! Although my half-brother was willing to connect with me, he told me that my birth mother wanted nothing to do with me. Spiraling down, I felt like Hagar when she was abandoned a second time, when she and Ishmael were rejected by Abraham and sent away into the desert (Gen 21).

But once again, God saw Hagar. His angel called to her from heaven, and reminded her of His promise that Ishmael would be a great nation – and then her eyes were opened to see a well of water. She was once again able to define herself not by what had been done to her, but by Who would take care of her.

God would now do the same for me. Once again, He saw me in my brokenness. This time I was willing, and He led me to a place of healing.

Healing and freedom required me to go through many months of counseling. To look into the mirror in order to face my pain, accept it, and process it. To sit with what had happened to me and how I had responded to it. I needed to own the pieces of my story that I was afraid to address: how, in my pain, I had hurt others. This was not an easy journey, and it is a path I avoided for many years, but God did not call me on this healing journey until I was ready for it. Additionally, God also used the birth of my first child in His healing process, enabling me to see His heart and not my hurt. My story did not change, but the way I saw myself did. This verse captured my heart:

... for you are a chosen people. You are royal priests, a holy nation, God's very own possession. As a result, you can show others the goodness of God, for he called you out of the darkness into his wonderful light.   1 Peter 2:9 NLT

God didn't change my story; He changed me in it. When I came to God and saw Him as El Roi, The God Who Sees Me, and accepted what He saw in me, then how I saw myself changed.

I did not choose this story; I did not plan it; all that happened to me was utterly outside of my control. For many years, the pain of rejection as well as my shame blurred out God's care and love. But I learned that the times I thought God turned His back on me were actually the times His promises were solidified into my story. I finally realized that my story would not change – and neither would God's love. I merely got to choose which one I wanted to look at for the rest of my life.

Ashley Murphy
Stuart, Florida

"God didn't change my story; He changed me in it." I bear testimony to that statement! Ashley's transformation is unmistakable. She has always had eyes that are deep pools of water. In earlier years, they were pools of pain, but now they are pools of His bottomless love.

I love knowing that *El Roi*, The God Who Sees, is actually the only one who knows *all* about us – *and He accepts us and loves us completely*. That is so very precious. And yet, I think what we see in Genesis 16 is even more so.

Theologians believe that as an Egyptian woman, as Sarai's maid, most likely a slave, Hagar probably had no choice in this matter. But note that though she was given what was thought to be a great honor of those times, to bear a wealthy man's son, she treated Sarai *with contempt*. She *despised* her. And when the consequences of Hagar's sin rolled forth, she fled. She ran from her assignment.

Sometimes, I focus on the fact that God sees and knows *all my pain*, but I forget that He also sees all my sins, faults, failures, and the blackness of my heart.

Now this is very important as we study this name: Hagar ran into the wilderness (some translations say desert), and ended up *by a spring*.

This name, *El Roi*, reminds us that God sees us in our pain, our trials, our moments of helplessness and desperation – *and* He knows our sins – and He *still* takes care of us anyway! In the midst of this trial that was mostly out of her control and partly of her own making, God led Hagar to a *spring in the desert*. God saw the wounds inflicted upon her, and her own heart sins – and loved her enough to rescue her from a desperate and perilous place and give her purpose.

Similarly, in the midst of Ashley's trials that were mostly completely out of her control and partly of her own making, God showed up in dramatic ways. He led her to places of healing, both with counseling and the birth of her daughter. He saw the wounds inflicted upon her, and her own heart sins – and loved her enough to rescue her from a desperate and perilous place and give her calling and purpose.

Though we may fear that we will be completely seen, fully judged, and totally rejected, realize that *El Roi* completely sees us, fully loves us, and totally accepts us. *El Roi* sees all our wounds and our shame – and *still* does not reject us, but embraces us with His acceptance and tenderness. And *El Roi* sees all our sinfulness and our failures – and *still* does not reject us, but welcomes us with His forgiveness and love.

God had beautiful plans for Hagar and her son – but in order to fulfill those plans, He required her to leave her sin. To return to Sarai and submit to her authority. I think that submitting to her authority would entail treating her with respect and not contempt.

God had beautiful plans for Ashley too, including positions as youth pastor in multiple churches, and three precious children to raise. But in order to fulfill those plans, He required her to leave her sin. To accept His sovereign plan, to take responsibility for how she had hurt others, to open her heart to His healing, and to embrace what *He* says about her.

The Lord loves us so much He won't leave us in a desperate wilderness place – or in a place of sin. As He rescued Hagar and then sent her back to Sarai, as He healed Ashley and called her to repentance, He disciplines us for our good – so we can share in His holiness (Heb 12:10).

From His Hand We Give Back to Him: Yahweh Yireh
[yah-WEH yir-EH]

"... take now your son, your only son, whom you love, Isaac, and go to the land of Moriah, and offer him there as a burnt offering." Genesis 22:2

God gave Abraham the free will to obey, or refuse. Abraham chose obedience and surrender, and met God as *Yahweh Yireh*:

Abraham said, "God [*Elohim*] will provide for Himself the lamb for the burnt offering, my son."

... He said, "Do not stretch out your hand against the lad, and do nothing to him; for now I know that you fear God, since you have not withheld your son, your only son, from Me." Then Abraham raised his eyes and looked, and behold, behind him a ram caught in the thicket by his horns; and Abraham went and took the ram and offered him up for a burnt offering in the place of his son. Abraham called the name of that place The LORD Will Provide [*Yahweh Yireh*], as it is said to this day, "In the mount of the LORD [*Yahweh*] it will be provided."

Genesis 22:8,12-14

At times, I may forget that all things come from God's hand, and it is only from His hand that I give back to Him (1Chr 29:14). But when I utterly surrender to *Elohim Adonai* what is already His, whether it be someone I love or something I treasure or a plan or a calling He has on my life, if He returns it to me, on a much deeper level I can comprehend that I am merely a *steward* of His gift. I can come to know Him as *Yahweh Yireh*, as Provider. Surrender is the way I learn that He is God, and I am not.[13] *This is worship.*

The Temple of Solomon was built on Mount Moriah (2Chr 3:1), and it is believed that only a quarter of a mile away is where God sacrificed His Son, His only beloved Son.[14] **He did not spare His own Son, but delivered Him over for us all** (Rom 8:32). *Yahweh Yireh* provided the last and perfect sacrifice for sin, the only Way to Himself: His Son, the Lamb of God who takes away the sin of the world (Jn 1:29). I believe that is truly the depth of God's heart when He introduces Himself to us as *Yahweh Yireh*.

I would like to introduce you to some friends of my husband and mine, Rob and his wife Lori. As you read this testimony, watch how *Yahweh* worked so personally in their lives, and how no one could foil the ultimate plans of *El Elyon*. Note their dependence on *El Shaddai*, and how *Yahweh Yireh* provided every step of the way.

We felt God's leading to adopt a little girl from Guatemala, and were waiting and waiting for the adoption paperwork to be completed by the Guatemalan government. I became strongly convicted in my heart that we just needed to go to Guatemala regardless of the status of the paperwork, to step out in faith that God would take care of things … we just needed to get down there to hold our little girl and bring her home. And so, against the advice of the adoption agency, we went.

We met another couple who was there to adopt a child. They had been there for nine months dealing with the corruption and bureaucracy, trying to get home with their child. Apparently, this was a very common experience, and so heartbreaking to hear about.

By God's grace, when we went to the foster home the day after our arrival, little Grace was placed right in our arms, and we fell in love with her instantly. God was watching over us, and provided an appointment to finalize the paperwork at the U.S. Embassy 24 hours earlier than normal, and the day just before our scheduled flight home.

At the airport checkpoint was an ominous looking guard who held us up while he questioned our status. Our lawyer made an exasperated face, pulled out a one inch thick file folder full of the official paperwork, opened it and in Spanish started going through each page one by one, explaining as she went. After about page four the guard relented and let us through. We knew without question our steps had been directed by God.

Two days after we returned with Grace, we learned that adoptions were shut down in Guatemala, and it stayed that way for well over two years. God had worked mightily in our lives and the lives of others to bring this precious child into our family and to bless us in so many ways.

Major General (Ret) Robert M. Worley II
Dr. Lori E. Worley
Houston, Texas

Ponder, Pray, and Journal

Read through this testimony again, and in the margin, write the names of God that you see manifested in various parts of their story. Here is a quick summary of the names we studied in this chapter:

Abba (Father)
Adonai (Lord)
Elohim (Creator, Ruler)
Yahweh (I AM, redemption, relationship and holiness)
El Elyon (God Most High)
El Shaddai (God Almighty, nourishes and satisfies)
Yahweh Rophe (Healer)
El Roi (The God Who Sees)
Yahweh Yireh (Provider)

Rob and Lori had held fast to their faith throughout hard times in the military and through difficulties in this adoption process, and twenty-one years later, they were challenged to trust in God's love and sovereignty through the deepest of heart pains.

Exactly twenty-one years from the day we first held Grace in our arms, she was accidentally shot in the head and killed instantly while her husband was playing around with a pistol. Grace was a young believer, and we hold peace in our hearts, yet it was the most horrific night of our lives.

Major General (Ret) Robert M. Worley II
Dr. Lori E. Worley
Houston, Texas

Somehow, they surrendered to their Lord and Master *Adonai*, acknowledging that Grace had come from Him, and from His hand they gave her back to Him (1Chr 29:14). Somehow, through their deep faith and trust that the plans *of His heart* would stand (Ps 33:11), they were able to forgive Grace's husband. Somehow, though *Yahweh* gave and *Yahweh* took away, they were able to say, **"Blessed be the name of the Lord"** (Job 1:21), and turn their focus to the young son Grace left behind.

Despite our forgiveness and desire to help Grace's husband raise their thirteen-month old son, he chose a most destructive and counterproductive path. He did not have the strength of character, faith, or desire to take responsibility for raising his child, and soon moved out of state and out of contact. God laid it on our hearts to legally adopt little David, yet his father would not relinquish his parental rights. But one day, after hearing nothing from him for many, many months, and having no way to contact him, he showed up and signed the paperwork, and we have not heard from him since.

The whole process of adopting David, which could likely have taken months or years, had occurred in the absolute <u>minimum amount of time legally possible</u>. God answered our prayers, and when we had no idea where Grace's husband was or how to contact him, God delivered him to us from as far away as one can get within the continental United States. God allowed us to get the papers we needed, and then moved him safely away. All this in a matter of three days, and at exactly the perfect timing. The judge signed the decree making us David's legal parents exactly twenty-three years from when we first held Grace, and exactly two years after her death.

Major General (Ret) Robert M. Worley II
Dr. Lori E. Worley
Houston, Texas

Rob sums it up this way, "We are so thankful we had Grace for those twenty-one years. The story of her adoption and our ultimate loss of

Grace is a story of the hand of God working mightily in our lives. He is a mighty, powerful and loving God, to whom we are *so* thankful for blessing us with David and equipping us to raise him."

Floyd McClung in *The Father Heart of God* writes this: "How we deal with disappointment and respond to what God wants to do in our lives reveals, perhaps more clearly than anything else, how secure we feel in His love and how close we are to His Father heart."[15] Indeed. Rob and Lori are a couple who are secure in *El Elyon's* love and trusting of *Abba's* heart. And from that secure place they have experienced His righteous right arm gain the victory for them – and for Him.

Ponder, Pray, and Journal

As you read Rob and Lori's testimony, the Holy Spirit may have been stirring in your own heart a testimony of your own. Spend some time in stillness with the Lord, remembering miracles He has wrought for you, and ask Him to reveal to you how He is unveiling His names to you through His work in your own life.

Then, with a renewed depth of understanding of one or more of His names, apply that understanding of who He is to a struggle or an unanswered prayer right now. Allow the Holy Spirit to bring you to new layers of surrender, trust, and peace.

Our Messiah, Our Redeemer, The Christ

The woman said to Him, "I know that Messiah is coming (He who is called Christ); when that One comes, He will declare all things to us." Jesus said to her, "I who speak to you am He."
John 4:25-26

Jesus is the Christ, the long-awaited Messiah (Matt 16:16, Lk 4:17-21). In the Hebrew and in the Greek this word means the Anointed One.[16] Son of God and Son of Man, fully God and fully man, our Savior, Deliver, the Way, the Truth, and the Life, and the only way to the Father. At the end of time, He will secure His victory and cast Satan into the lake of fire (Rev 19 and 20).

And I saw heaven opened, and behold, a white horse, and He who sat on it is called Faithful and True, and in righteousness He judges and wages war. His eyes are a flame of fire, and on His head are many diadems; and He has a name written on Him which no one knows except Himself. He is clothed with a robe dipped in blood, and His name is called The Word of God. And the armies which are in heaven, clothed in fine linen, white and clean, were following Him on white horses. From His mouth comes a sharp sword, so that with it He may strike down the nations, and He will rule them with a rod of iron; and He treads the wine press of the fierce wrath of God, the Almighty. And on His robe and on His thigh He has a name written, "KING OF KINGS, AND LORD OF LORDS."   Revelation 19:11-16

Ponder, Pray, and Journal

Circle the names of our Messiah given in this passage from Revelation. As you look up the following verses that amplify these names, ponder why Jesus was given each of these names.

- Faithful: 2 Thessalonians 3:3, Lamentations 3:22-23, 1 Corinthians 10:13, 2 Timothy 2:11-13

- True: John 14:6, John 17:17, 1 John 5:20, John 18:37-38

- The Word of God: John 1:1-5, 14

- King of kings and Lord of lords: 1 Timothy 6:15-16, Revelation 1:5, 17:14, Deuteronomy 10:16-17, Psalm 136:3

The Messiah, the Lion of Judah, is the One who redeems us from our sins, who opens the gates of heaven and paves the way for us to come boldly into the Father's throne room. By His blood poured out on the cross and His triumphant resurrection, the Lamb of God has torn the veil in two and given us access to the Father. (Matt 1:21, Eph 1:7-8, Heb 4:16, 10:19-20.)

Jesus Christ is the faithful witness, the firstborn of the dead, and the ruler of the kings of the earth. He loves us and released us from our sins by His blood. The Alpha and the Omega, who is and was and is to come, the Almighty, has eyes like a flame of fire and a voice like the sound of many waters. (Rev 1:5,8,14,15.)

And He placed His right hand on me, saying, "Do not be afraid; I am the first and the last, and the living One; and I was dead, and behold, I am alive forevermore, and I have the keys of death and of Hades."   Revelation 1:17-18

The Name of Jesus

Have this attitude in yourselves which was also in Christ Jesus, who, although He existed in the form of God, did not regard equality with God a thing to be grasped, but emptied Himself, taking the form of a bond-servant, and being made in the likeness of men. Being found in appearance as a man, He humbled Himself by becoming obedient to the point of death, even death on a cross. For this reason also, God highly exalted Him, and bestowed on Him the name which is above every name, so that at the name of Jesus EVERY KNEE WILL BOW, of those who are in heaven and on earth and under the earth, and that every tongue will confess that Jesus Christ is Lord, to the glory of God the Father.   Philippians 2:5-11

Ponder, Pray, and Journal

Jesus. The name means "Savior." The name above every other name, bestowed because He humbled Himself by His obedience to death on the cross. Ponder His timelessness, and bow your knee in worship of Him.

Look up these verses, in awe that He *gives* us His name for these purposes.

- Romans 10:13
- Acts 4:12
- John 14:13-14, 15:16, 16:23-24

Consider also Exodus 20:7.

Wonderful Counselor, Mighty God, Eternal Father, Prince of Peace

**For a child will be born to us, a son will be given to us;
And the government will rest on His shoulders;
And His name will be called
Wonderful Counselor, Mighty God,
Eternal Father, Prince of Peace.** Isaiah 9:6

Wonderful Counselor. Jesus **became to us wisdom from God** (1Cor 1:30), and through His Holy Spirit guides us into all truth, teaches us what to say, and directs our lives – and His plans will never fail (Jn 16:13, 1Cor 2:13, Rom 8:14, Isa 14:24). His counsel is *wonderful*, meaning "a wonder, a miracle, a marvel ... something unusual or extraordinary."[17]

Mighty God. Jesus is our all-powerful Champion, our ultimate Victor; it is impossible for Him to lose a battle (Col 2:15, Lk 1:37, Matt 19:26, Prov 19:21, Dan 4:35).

Eternal Father. Jesus is the Alpha and Omega, the Beginning and the End, the timeless, changeless, infinite Source of all life (Rev 1:8, Heb 13:8, Jn 1:4, 14:6). "I and the Father are one" (Jn 10:30).

Prince of Peace. True, deep, everlasting peace only comes from being in right relationship with God. Jesus is the only One who can provide that kind of peace, our sins forgiven through His death on the cross (Isa 53:5, Jn 14:27).

Lion Lamb

You may be wondering about the juxtaposition of these names. Seems an oxymoron![18] Read Revelation 5:1-10. Meet me back here when you are finished.

"*The Lion that is from the tribe of Judah*, the Root of David, has overcome so as to open the book and its seven seals." And I saw between the throne (with the four living creatures) and the elders *a Lamb standing, as if slain ...*
"Worthy are You to take the book and to break its seals; for You were slain, and purchased for God with Your blood men from every tribe and tongue and people and nation."

Revelation 5:5-6, 9, emphasis added

Jesus is the Lion of Judah, our invincible King. He is majesty and royalty, authority and might, strength and power, victory and rule.

As the Passover lamb was to be without blemish, the Lamb of

God is perfect, sinless, holy. Our King, the Lion of Judah, overcame by becoming the sacrificial Lamb. The Lion of Judah conquered by humbling Himself to become obedient to the point of death, even death on a cross. (Ex 12:5, Jn 1:29, 2Cor 5:21, Heb 4:15, 1Cor 5:7, Phil 2:8.)

And it is through this perfect sacrifice of the Lion Lamb that we are redeemed, made clean, and welcomed into the very presence of God, for the Lion Lamb released us from our sins by His blood (Rev 1:5).

... knowing that you were not redeemed with perishable things like silver or gold from your futile way of life inherited from your forefathers, but with the precious blood, as of a lamb unblemished and spotless, the blood of Christ.
1 Peter 1:18-19

Saint Augustine comprehended how the Lion and the Lamb co-existed in one Being, and how both the Lion and the Lamb were active in His death as well as in His resurrection:

Who is this, both lamb and lion? He endured death as a lamb, he devoured it as a lion ... the prey of death, the predator of death ... silent when he was being judged, roaring when he comes to judge ...

Why a lamb in his passion? Because he underwent death without being guilty of any iniquity. Why a lion in his passion? Because in being slain he slew death.

Why a lamb in his resurrection? Because his innocence is everlasting. Why a lion in his resurrection? Because everlasting is also his might.[19]

"These will wage war against the Lamb, and the Lamb will overcome them, because He is the Lord of lords and the King of kings, and those who are with Him are the called and chosen and faithful."
Revelation 17:14

Paraclete

The Holy Spirit is called the Spirit of God, the Spirit of Christ, the Spirit of Truth, the Spirit of Holiness – and my personal favorite, *Paraclete*.

Paraclete is an English transliteration of the Greek word *Paracletos* (Jn 14:16). This word means to comfort, encourage, exhort, advocate, or aid. It is actually a legal term, referring to a legal advisor or an advocate in a court of law, who comes forward on behalf of another.[50] *Paracletos* is translated as **Helper** (NASB, ESV, NKJV), **Advocate** (NIV and NLT), and **Comforter** (KJV). The Amplified combines them all: **Helper (Comforter, Advocate, Intercessor – Counselor, Strengthener, Standby)**.

Grasping the Holy Spirit as our *Paraclete* will be very important when we discuss Satan's legalistic tactics in upcoming chapters.

In the Thick of the Battle

Knowing God's names can bring another level of understanding and revelation as we draw nearer to know our infinite God. And when the fighting is the fiercest, we will be able to stand firm if we know deeply the great and awesome *Elohim*, and that the plans of *El Elyon* will succeed (Dan 4:35). We will stay connected to Him for victory if we recognize that the sovereignty of *Adonai* will determine the strategy and the outcome of each battle (Prov 19:21) and if we rely on *El Shaddai* in utter dependence (1Sam 17:47). When the enemy hurls lies to wound our hearts, we must know that *Yahweh* is with us and will never no never leave or forsake us (Heb 13:5), and that *Yahweh Rophe* will be our one and only Healer (Ex 15:26). When the stakes are high and the battle seems hopeless, we must know that *Abba* is always working for our good and that *Yahweh Yireh* will provide everything necessary for victory (Phil 4:19). When we have stumbled and the enemy is crushing us with shame, guilt, and regret, he will be silenced if we know that *El Roi* sees us and that *Yahweh Yireh* has made a way for us to become the righteousness of God in Jesus (2Cor 5:21). I have found that knowing His names will help us know Him and trust His works (Ps 37:5). Our faith in our Messiah, Jesus, the Name above all names, the Lion Lamb who conquered sin, death, and the grave, will enable us to count on Him to do whatever we ask in His name. As we rely on the strength and grace of *Paracletos*, we will trust that in every place in our lives He will manifest the sweet aroma of the knowledge of Him, leading us in triumph in Him (Jn 14:13, 2Cor 2:14).

Both the Old and New Testaments contain many more names of God. I have provided some books in the *Resource* section in the Appendix that take a deep dive into the some of the names of God. These books show how God gradually revealed Himself to mankind over thousands of years, and how Jesus Christ fulfills and embodies all the names of God. I encourage you to explore more on your own, for knowing Him more opens our hearts to walk in greater victory.

In the next chapter, we will tackle another area critical in warfare: our identity. I call knowing God and knowing our identity *foundational* because if either of these areas are rife with lies, we will be standing on a ruptured foundation, easily toppled by even minor enemy attacks. Put on your armor of light, because we will be entering enemy territory as we work to demolish lies about our identity.

Chapter 4
Know Your Identity

Undoubtedly the foundational weapon in the battle is believing deeply within our hearts the truth according to the Word of *who God is*. And a weapon of parallel importance is knowing deeply within our hearts the truth according to the Word of *who we are*. It seems to me that these are two areas the enemy repeatedly attacks, and if our heart-knowing is not ingrained here, we will be open to fall into Satan's snares.

As we discussed in Chapter 2, we are not talking about head knowledge here. We are talking heart belief of who *God* says we are. How *He* defines us. What *He* says our identity is. What *He* has to say about us *in His Word*. What it means to be in Christ. Who we are in Him. *Our true identity.*

We want to believe so deeply that we *live* like we believe it. When we believe *that* deeply, our actions, thoughts, words, and decisions will demonstrate that we trust and rely on who we really are in Him.

Remember what we learned in Chapter 1: God will allow Satan to come against any areas that are not aligned with God – areas of sin or weakness or false beliefs – until we realize that the victory will only come when we are willing to be conformed to the image of Christ, willing to walk in His ways and believe His truths. *This means war.* This is the process of our sanctification.

"Sanctify them in the truth; Your word is truth."

John 17:17

I have invited my friend Darla to share with us how she has battled to victory here. Darla's identity was fractured by the pain of her past, and over the years, Satan thrust those lies deeper, demolished her identity, and drove her into darkness. She simply did not know her true identity. But God was about to change that.

Just four short years ago, I walked into my first <u>Triumph</u> *Class. I was full of shame, guilt, fear, self-loathing, and pain. I had already completed ten years of therapy, both group and individual. Through a twelve-step program, I had been clean from drugs for thirty-five years. I read all the books, I meditated on the Lord, I attended church regularly. So why was I still suffering? Would I always be the victim? If God is sovereign, why did others get free, while I was still trapped?*

The pain was so great that I contemplated not living anymore. I was broken emotionally, spiritually and physically. I walked around projectile vomiting my feelings on everything and everyone.

I prayed to God, and I asked Him to seek me out, to heal my hurts, to use me for His purpose and to never let go. Thus began the most amazing transformation that became so complete and so deep no words can do it justice. Suffering turned to hunger for the Lord. I started running a different race, one that was full of prayer, and reading, and writing. It was full of women who ran beside me and prayed for me and with me. I know now that it is all about Calvary, and what <u>He</u> <u>did for</u> <u>me</u>. At this time, my life is all about His character, His sovereignty, His plans and purpose, and my obedience and trust. It is not about me, or what was done to me. I am known by Him. I am who He says I am!

We are promised that there will be storms, there will be trials, and there will be mourning. We live in a fallen world. Sometimes, I fail miserably at being content in all situations. However, I have learned to fight my battles down on my knees. For my battles are not of flesh and blood, but of the Spirit. The Lord says that no weapon formed against me shall prevail, and no temptation shall not have a way out. If God is for me, then who can be against me?

"I am a daughter of the King!" Those words actually flowed from my lips as I stood there with the ladies after church. For the very first time it was not a slogan on a mug, or some ungraspable concept in my head. It was not just words on paper. No, these words came from the deepest part of my being. Words of truth, louder than the lies. Our mighty God will always make a way, and this "daughter of the King" is no longer afraid! Jesus, my Savior, King of all kings, our sovereign God of miracles and faithfulness, from everlasting to everlasting, has healed me and set me free!

Darla
Jupiter, Florida

Victim mentality was Darla's identity. She needed God to imprint on her heart who she really is, His chosen and adopted daughter, a daughter of the King. Through *Triumph* classes, Darla learned how to renounce lies about her identity, to accept truth, and to renew her mind. She learned the depth of who God is, and who He says she is. She has traveled a breath-taking journey of sanctification as she has moved from lies to truth.

Darla positioned herself for this transformation through deep Bible study, praying, reading, journaling, and connecting into her church family. As she fully immersed in the truth of the Word, embracing its truths even when the lies of the world, her mind, her past, and her experiences were shouting ever so much louder, God has delivered her from fear and shame and filled her with peace and joy. Her selfish thoughts fell away, and her focus turned to her Lord. And then suddenly, surprisingly, her heart grasped her true identity.

"The mouth speaks out of that which fills the heart" (Matt 12:34). The words that tumbled from her mouth unexpectedly, uncontrollably, "I am a daughter of the King!" are evidence of the transformation of her heart. As Darla has welcomed her identity as

written in His Word, she has truly received from the Lord her title.
Chains have been broken and she has been set free.

I have watched Darla's amazing transformation. She has moved
from being served to serving. She has moved from projectile vomiting
her emotions to listening to others in pain and praying for them. As
she has been transformed, she is now positioned to walk forth in the
Kingdom work He has planned for her:

**Now the God of peace, who brought up from the dead the
great Shepherd of the sheep through the blood of the eternal
covenant, even Jesus our Lord, *equip* you in every good thing
to do His will, *working in us that which is pleasing in His
sight*, through Jesus Christ, to whom be the glory forever
and ever. Amen.**   Hebrews 13:20-21, emphasis added

Equipping us to do His will entails **working in us that which
is pleasing in His sight**. Darla's view of herself as a victim was not
pleasing in His sight, and with that as her identity, she was not ready for
the purposes He has for her. God has now equipped her by sanctifying
her. Equipping is conforming us to the image of Christ. Equipping
is demolishing lies and being sanctified in truth. Equipping includes
walking in our true identity.

Realize that Satan is constantly working to engrave on our hearts
his lies of who *he* says we are. He attempts to use the world and culture
to define us. He strives to use people – with good intentions or evil
intentions – possibly even family, friends, church members, even
people we have never met – to define us. He taps into the pride of our
hearts to define us. He endeavors to use the experiences and traumas
of our life to give us definition. And he may even twist and pervert our
thinking so severely to try to lure us into defining ourselves. But the
only truth of who we are is *how God defines us* – and that truth is found
in the Word of God.

Ponder, Pray, and Journal

Spend some time with the Lord, asking Him to reveal how Satan has worked throughout your life, especially your childhood, to warp your identity.

We will learn more about the Lord's healing in upcoming chapters. For now, if the Holy Spirit has revealed wounds to you, ask Him to reveal lies that grew out of those wounds, and ask Him to touch and heal you.

I believe God wants to seal in our hearts His truth of who we are. It seems to me that often that sealing of our identity occurs through a lengthy stepwise process, with breakthroughs of great suddenness as Darla shared. My friend Tamar has a parallel testimony. Tamar has spent countless hours growing in the Lord, and her identity was suddenly sealed into her heart during an unexpected visit by her Heavenly Father.

Tamar is a powerhouse of an intercessor, her prayers birthed out of her constant deep times of worship, sweet times when Jesus simply scoops her up into His holy presence. Come with me as we hear how, in a moment, the Lord uncovered the truth, then demolished Satan's lies, and finally engraved on her heart who *He* really is – *as well as her identity in Him.*

As a little girl, I used to spend a lot of time in my room to escape my situation. When I wasn't reading, I would daydream and fantasize about my <u>real</u> daddy coming to rescue me. I was so sure my dad wasn't my real dad. He was so mean and he clearly hated me. In fact, he told me often how much he hated me. I don't ever remember a time as a child when he told me that he loved me.

When I was about nine, I found a letter that he had written to my mom when she was sixteen and pregnant with me. He was asking if she was sure I was his baby, and even said something about what about so and so? Couldn't I be his baby? This only confirmed what I already knew: He wasn't my real dad.

Over the years, this secret world I created grew with greater and greater details. He, my <u>real</u> daddy, would come. I knew he was out there looking for me.

He would rush in and grab me and hug me and kiss me and tell me I was his daughter and how he had never stopped looking for me. He'd tell me how much he loved me. He would be <u>furious</u> for all the abuse I had endured, and he would cry with me, knowing the pain I felt.

He would take me away from this dark place and protect me. He'd rescue me. His house would be a big mansion with a big yard and my room would be filled with all things pretty, just for me.

He'd buy me nice clothes and treat me like a princess. He would let me sit on his lap, and he'd call me "daddy's little girl," like I'd only seen in the movies. He would stroke my hair and tell me I was beautiful, and I would finally feel loved. I'd be cherished. He would be so proud of me. He would put his strong arms around me and assure me that I would never again have to worry. I'd never ever be without him or his protection.

I could finally rest. I finally had peace. Everything was going to be okay.

Although I came to know the Lord in high school, I fully surrendered my life to the Him and began walking with Him about a dozen years ago. Scripture study, prayer, and worship became part of my everyday life. Little by little, as I came to know Him more, He healed me and freed me.

One morning, while I was worshiping and praising and thanking Him for His goodness and mercy, the Holy Spirit arrived and gave me a sudden revelation. He reminded me of everything I had hoped and dreamed and wished, and then He showed me that it wasn't a dream, it is – and always was – <u>a reality</u>. He was always holding me and always calling me "Daddy's little girl." He was always stroking my hair and telling me I was beautiful and that He was so proud of me.

He was always loving me, cherishing me, protecting me. It felt like a veil had been torn away. Daddy was always there, I just couldn't see that until now.

My real Daddy did come and rescue me. He never stopped pursuing me and He left 99 others to save me. He loved me so much that He willingly died a painful death for me. Every tear I ever cried, He was there. He was collecting each one in a bottle. To him, I am beautiful and He loves to shower me with good gifts. He has never left me or forsaken me. He has given me beauty for ashes and has turned my mourning into joy. He still holds me in His strong hands and He protects me each and every day. He is preparing a mansion just for me, with all things pretty. I am indeed rescued. And I am loved.

Tamar

You can see how a deep encounter with her Heavenly Father exposed the lies and toppled Tamar's false identity stronghold. Nothing but a profound encounter too deep for words could have brought her such healing and freedom. And this transformation brought her to new levels of worship and connection to Him. As she explains, "I thank God for reminding me that I need Jesus, I need His death for me. I now understand that condemning voices are not from God. Demands for perfectionism are not from God. These voices are from the enemy, and the more he harasses me, the more I worship."

The more he attacks, the more she worships. Satan now loses that battle every time.

Sometimes, as in Tamar's and Darla's testimonies, worthlessness can become our identity. Our traumas and wounds can become our identity. Lies that we have been told, perhaps that we are worthless or unlovable or not enough, or that we will never find a spouse or will never amount to anything, can also become our identity.

And there are many other things that can become our identity too. Our *successes and accomplishments* can become our identity. We may find our identity in our titles, our degrees, or our positions at work, at home, at church, or in the community. This sort of identity struggle may be very subtle. Those looking on may only see an accomplished lawyer, CEO, mechanic, teacher, pastor, businessman, spouse, parent. My husband John is a reputable Ear, Nose, and Throat surgeon, a successful CEO of an aeronautical business, a Lieutenant Colonel in the Air National Guard and trusted flight surgeon. He recently admitted to me, "I'm afraid of that day when I no longer hold these positions." We pray together for his identity to be sealed in the Lord.

Is Your Identity Sealed?

Knowing our true identity and walking forth in it is paramount to victory on the battlefield, so although we have done identity work throughout the *Triumph* books, we are going to spend this chapter strengthening our identity in Him. I know you are a student of the Word, and you know the truth, so you may be tempted to skate through this section. But don't. We want to be sure that we believe truth in our hearts and not just our minds.

Come to the Lord in bold honesty, as my husband has about his identity. Rely on the Holy Spirit to reveal what your heart truly believes. We'll ask ourselves some tough questions, and then we will soak in Scriptures about our true identity.

Ponder, Pray, and Journal

The first set of questions about identity may help to expose if *status* has become your identity. Accomplishments, material things, positions, titles. The second set of questions may help to expose if *your past* has become your identity. Wounds, sins, worthlessness, not-enoughness, pain of your past, lies spoken over you. Pray first, then allow the Holy Spirit to search your heart. Don't just hone in on one section. Be sure you ponder all the questions.

Has status become your identity?

- What if you lost it all? What would happen if you lost all your accomplishments, positions, titles, degrees? Who are you then?
- What will you do when you retire?
- Do your kids' accomplishments define you?
- Are you transparent and vulnerable with others? Do you hide behind your degrees?
- Do you think you are indispensable? Do you think you are more important than you really are?
- Do you always get what you want?
- Do you have trouble admitting you are wrong, or taking responsibility for your mistakes?
- How do you want people to remember you?
- Do you feel you have lots of purpose on earth, but wonder if you have any *Kingdom* purpose?
- What about your priorities? Have you put your relationship with God and His Kingdom plan in *first priority*?
- Are your accomplishments or titles part of your introduction to others?
- Have you forgotten that even the **power to make wealth** has come from God (Deut 8:18)?

Has the pain of your past become your identity?

- Do you feel unwanted, unplanned, unloved, or unlovable? Do you think you are a mistake?
- Do you think of yourself as worthless, useless, stupid, good for nothing, or disposable?

- Do you think your contributions are inadequate, not valuable, and insignificant?

- Do you feel you are not accepted, that you do not belong? Do you feel abandoned, rejected, or alone?

- Do you feel no one understands you?

- Do you feel you have no purpose in life, that God has forgotten you or does not see you?

- Do you feel insecure? Not enough?

- Are you ashamed, do you believe your sin is too great to forgive?

- Do you think of yourself as defective or flawed, impossible to heal / fix / change?

- Are you having trouble forgiving those who have hurt you?

- Is your past part of your introduction to others?

And one more set of questions:

- Do you feel you need to earn God's love, attention, or acceptance?

- Do you feel God will abandon you if you fail?

- When you make a mistake, do you feel you are a failure? That you are not a "good" parent / spouse / employee / friend?

- How do you respond to disappointment?

- To whom or to what or where do you run when you fail?

That may have been a hard exercise for some of you. I understand. As I shared in Chapter 2, there was a time my heart believed all sorts of lies, and accomplishments were my identity while I simultaneously believed I was worthless. We are going to spend the rest of this chapter uprooting lies and replacing them with truth, but before we begin, I will share personally in order to impress upon your hearts what it means to remain ensnared in these lies about your identity.

When accomplishments defined me, I was mired in pride, self-idolatry, and people-pleasing. And as far as worthlessness was concerned, I thought it was not such a big deal to believe these lies. This was just my own personal issue – or so I thought. I didn't think God really cared about what I thought about myself. I just thought that was who I was, that was who I would always be, and there was nothing I could do to change that. But Psalm 107 has something to say about those thoughts:

> **There were those who dwelt in darkness**
> **and in the shadow of death,**
> **Prisoners in misery and chains,**
> **Because they had *rebelled against the words of God***
> **And spurned the counsel of the Most High.**
>
> Psalm 107:10-11, emphasis added

As the Holy Spirit revealed, it suddenly struck me that when I refuse to believe God's Word, I am *rebelling against God*. I was aligning myself with Satan! Although I was still God's child, I had forsaken Him and allied myself with the enemy! I was indeed fighting a battle – *but on the wrong side!*

I began also to see how I was grieving God's heart by rejecting the identity He was offering to me. This was an affront to God and all Jesus had done on the cross to secure my forgiveness, my adoption as God's child, my calling and purpose on earth, and my place in eternity with Him.

In Chapter 2, we learned how to reject lies and *choose* to believe truth about who God is, whether we can feel it or not. We will follow this pattern regarding our identity, and renew our minds until God transforms our hearts to believe it. We will ask our Heavenly Father to establish us in Christ and to seal in our identity.

> **Now He who establishes us with you in Christ and anointed**
> **us is God, who also sealed us and gave us the Spirit in our**
> **hearts as a pledge.** 2 Corinthians 1:21-22

Nevertheless, the firm foundation of God stands, having this seal, "The Lord knows those who are His."   2 Timothy 2:19

Yes, He knows those who are His, and He wants those who are His to know who He says we are. In the next section, we are going to take another deep dive into Scripture. Saturate yourself with these verses. Highlight the ones that speak the truth specifically related to what the Holy Spirit has revealed as you worked through those questions. In areas you need more work, look up the additional Scriptures referenced.

Recognize the entrenched lies. Then, just as we did in Chapter 2, confess, repent, renounce; declare Scriptural truths; ask for filling — and purpose to walk it out. Make a choice, in faith, to *believe* truth, even if you don't *feel* it. Select the Scriptures that counteract lies that are ensnaring you, meditate on them, and speak them out loud over yourself every morning and every night and every moment in between. You may need to proclaim these truths over many days in order to implant God's Word in your heart.

My friend Sophia, one year old in the Lord and just completing her freshman year in college, concludes this: "My identity and worth don't come from what I accomplish or what I strive to do or be; it comes from the love Christ has for me. I am not a student – I am a Christian who studies. I am not a rower – I am a Christian who rows. I am not defined by the world – I am defined by His Word." May we all be inspired to declare the same.

I Am a Child of God

See how great a love the Father has bestowed on us, that we would be called children of God; and such we are.

1 John 3:1

Abba, Father, Papa, Daddy, has *chosen us* as His children, and made us co-heirs with His Son. Deeply grasping the truth of this irrevocable position casts out fear. (Rom 8:1, 1Jn 4:18.)

I Am Adopted by God

For you have not received a spirit of slavery leading to fear again, but you have received a spirit of adoption as sons by which we cry out, "Abba! Father!"   Romans 8:15

He has adopted us and given us His name. No matter how far we think we are from Him, He is right there next to us, seeking us, calling our name, eager to embrace us and remind us of His eternal love. (Ps 139:7-10, Lk 15:11-32.)

I Am Loved by God

"As the Father has loved me, so have I loved you."
                    John 15:9 NIV

He loves us so much He went to the cross to secure a place in eternity for us. And not only does He want us in eternity with Him, He wants us in deep relationship with Him *right now*, One with Him and loved by Him. (Rom 5:8, 8:32, Jn 17:21.)

I Am Purchased with Jesus' Blood

For you have been bought with a price ...   1 Corinthians 6:20

God emptied the treasure trove of heaven to purchase our redemption. No other purchase price would do. I have no worth of my own, but He gives me worth. He deemed it worth His death to pay for me (Eph 1:7).

My Sins Are Forgiven

In Him we have redemption through His blood, the forgiveness of our trespasses, according to the riches of His grace which He lavished on us.   Ephesians 1:7-8

He has put our sins as far away from us as the east is from the west. Though our sins were scarlet, He has made them white as snow. He mercifully remembers our sins no more. (Ps 103:12, Isa 1:18, Heb 8:12.)

I Am Not Condemned

Therefore there is now no condemnation for those who are in Christ Jesus.   Romans 8:1

Jesus has come full of grace and truth. Who dares accuse those whom God has chosen for His own? And if God is for us, who can ever be against us? (Jn 1:14, Rom 8:33 NLT, Rom 8:31.)

I Am Chosen to be Holy and Blameless

For he chose us in him before the creation of the world to be holy and blameless in his sight.   Ephesians 1:4 NIV

We are set apart for His divine purposes. We are not without sin, but when we are repentant we are forgiven when we fall. When we stumble,

He holds our hand so we are not hurled headlong. He is the only One able to keep us from stumbling and make us stand blameless in His presence. (Ps 37:24, Jude 1:24.)

I Am Never Abandoned

"Never will I leave you; never will I forsake you."

Hebrews 13:5 NIV

I have heard it said about this verse in the Greek that because of the many negatives piled on top of each other, it is better translated, "I will never, no never, leave you or forsake you." The Amplified translates it this way:

... for He [God] Himself has said, I will not in any way fail you nor give you up nor leave you without support. [I will] not, [I will] not in any degree leave you helpless nor forsake nor let [you] down (relax My hold on you)! [Assuredly not!]

Hebrews 13:5 AMPC

Our family and our friends may have deserted us, but God never will. Never, no never, will He desert us. We can be strong and courageous because He lives inside of us. (Ps 27:10, Josh 1:9, Rom 8:9.)

Jesus Has Prepared a Place for Me in Heaven

"Do not let your hearts be troubled. Trust in God; trust also in me. In my Father's house are many rooms; if it were not so, I would have told you. I am going there to prepare a place for you." John 14:1-2 NIV

No matter what we do or don't do, no matter what is done to us or not done for us, He is preparing a place for His followers to be with Him in heaven. A place full of riches that will never rot away or be snatched away by the enemy. A place of indescribable peace and joy with God Himself. (Mt 6:19-20, 2Cor 12:4.)

I Am the Righteousness of God

He made Him who knew no sin to be sin on our behalf, so that we might become the righteousness of God in Him.

2 Corinthians 5:21

We don't simply *wear* His righteousness, we *become* His righteousness.

I Am a Partaker of His Divine Nature

For by these He has granted to us His precious and magnificent promises, so that by them you may become partakers of the divine nature, having escaped the corruption that is in the world by lust.   2 Peter 1:4

We no longer need to walk according to the flesh, but can walk by the Spirit, because we are partakers in His divine nature. He disciplines us for our good, so we can share in His holiness. (Gal 5:16, Heb 12:10.)

I Am Granted Unshakable Peace

"Peace I leave with you; My peace I give to you; not as the world gives do I give to you. Do not let your heart be troubled, nor let it be fearful."

John 14:27

Our peace does not depend upon our circumstances, but upon our relationship with Jesus. We walk in His peace, and as we surrender to Him, we grow in it, and that unsurpassable peace penetrates our hearts in greater and greater measure. And though the mountains may be shaken and all the circumstances of our lives collapse, His unfailing love for us will never be shaken, and His peace will never falter. (Phil 4:6-7, Isa 54:10.)

I Am Infinitely Valuable to God

"Are not two sparrows sold for a cent? And yet not one of them will fall to the ground apart from your Father. But the very hairs of your head are all numbered. So do not fear; you are more valuable than many sparrows." Matthew 10:29-31

And those sparrows, who don't fall to the ground without our Father noticing, don't sow or reap or gather into barns – and yet our Heavenly Father feeds them. He promises that when we seek first His Kingdom and right relationship with Him, He will fully provide for our needs. (Mt 6:26, 33.)

I Am a New Person Altogether

Therefore, if anyone is in Christ, he is a new creation; the old has gone, the new has come! 2 Corinthians 5:17 NIV

He has made streams in our deserts and paths in our wilderness. He has transferred us to His Kingdom and is conforming us to the image of Christ. (Isa 43:19, Col 1:13, Rom 8:29.)

I Am God's Workmanship

For we are God's workmanship, created in Christ Jesus to do good works, which God prepared in advance for us to do.

Ephesians 2:10 NIV

We are His uniquely crafted work of art, created perfectly for His enjoyment. He planned our purposes before the beginning of time, and shaped us just so to enable us to fulfill them. Although His Kingdom and His overarching plan will come with or without us, no one else can uniquely reflect His heart and character as He designed us to do (2Tim 1:9, Rev 4:11 KJV).

I Am Christ's Ambassador

Therefore, we are ambassadors for Christ, as though God were making an appeal through us ...   2 Corinthians 5:20

He has approved us and entrusted us with representing Him on this earth. Walk worthy of that trust (1Th 2:4, Eph 4:1, Col 1:10-12).

I Am On the Winning Team

What can we say about such wonderful things as these? If God is for us, who can ever be against us?   Romans 8:31 NLT

The Captain of the Host of the Lord is for us, but He is not on *our* side. We are on *His* side (Josh 5:13-15).[1] And that means that no matter how much we mess up, we are still on the winning team, for the battle is the Lord's (1Sam 17:47).

Ponder, Pray, and Journal

These two chapters, *Know Your Victor* and *Know Your Identity*, are foundational for battle victory. Before we move into further weapons training, let's ask the Lord to cement into our hearts some of His key promises.

Pray for the Holy Spirit to search your heart, then read the bullet points and look up the verses that He is nudging you to ponder.

- He promises to never no never leave us or forsake us, and that nothing can separate us from His love (Deut 31:8, Rom 8:38-39).

- He promises to bring beauty from ashes when we surrender the ashes to Him (Isa 45:2-3).

- He promises to grant us purpose in Him – and fulfill that purpose (Isa 64:4, Jer 29:11-14, 1 Thess 5:24 AMPC).

- He promises to make a way when there seems to be no way (Isa 43:19, 1Cor 10:13).

- He promises to flood us with His peace when we put everything in His hands (Phil 4:6-7).

- He promises that in Jesus, we will never be put to shame (1 Pet 2:6, Ps 34:5).

- He promises He will fight our battles (Josh 23:10, Ex 14:14).

In these first few chapters, we have laid crucial groundwork for warfare, but we have even more groundwork to lay before we rush into the battlefield. In the next chapter, we are going to learn God's battle strategy, and train with our spiritual weapons in order to learn to wield them with strength, skill, and proficiency.

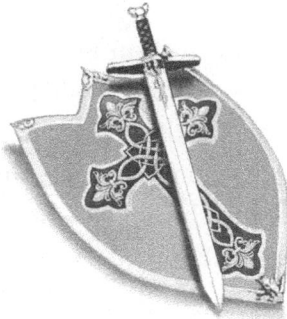

Chapter 5
Divinely Powerful Weapons

trategy and training will be the key notes in this chapter. For no matter how anointed our weapons may be, we will need more than mere *possession* of them. A sword in a glass case or a shield gathering dust in the closet will be useless when combat strikes. We must train with our weapons and be comfortable fighting with them – and we must know how to hear the Lord's strategy and battle plan in order to wield them with effectiveness.

Remember: our mission in this war is for God's Kingdom to come. It is *not* to advance our own little agendas or to get prayers answered the way we want them to be answered. The goal of each battle is *the glory of God and the advancement of His Kingdom.*

Ponder, Pray, and Journal

Re-read that last paragraph. Be still before the Lord, asking the Holy Spirit to search your heart. Are you advancing *your* kingdom, or God's Kingdom? Are you seeking *your* glory, or God's glory?

Ponder, Pray, and Journal

Go back to Chapter 1 to the section near the end, *Key to Victory: Hiding in Our Strong Tower*. Hone in on the all-important tactics listed in the bullet points. Realize that these tactics function much like an armor of protection from enemy attacks, and also as weapons to advance the Kingdom in our own hearts. Re-read this section, and meet me back here when you are finished.

I consider something a weapon or tactic if the Word demonstrates the power it has to advance the Kingdom and defeat the enemy. Our most basic weapons are not flashy. Scripture immersion, prayer, worship, our church family. These weapons require repentance, obedience, discipline, and humility, and they lead to surrender. We may prefer to avoid them and instead try to seek out something easier and more exciting. But that would be inviting defeat.

If you are not confident in handling these most basic weapons, I recommend you pause your work in this book, and go back and work through *Triumph Over Suffering* and *Triumph of Surrender* again in order to gain proficiency.

Suiting Up

I know you are very familiar with the Armor of God passage in Ephesians 6. But this is not a passage to blithely memorize and rattle off like some type of rote prayer. This passage in Ephesians requires a depth of understanding in order to apply it to our everyday battles, so let's jump into the deep waters.

Ponder, Pray, and Journal

Read through Ephesians 6:10-18. Take it apart, and ponder each phrase. For example, what does it mean to *put on?* And what does it mean to put on the *full armor?* And what does it mean that it is the armor *of God?* Work your way slowly through this passage, and journal what the Holy Spirit is showing you.

Our ability to stand firm, *histemi*,[1] comes completely and totally from Jesus. **Be strong *in the Lord* and *in His mighty power*.** Note that we are *commanded* to hold this crucial position in battle, and we hold it by taking a stance of humility and reliance upon the Spirit. From this place of dependence, let's take a look at each piece of the armor listed here. If you want to go even deeper, look up the Scriptures referenced.

The Belt of Truth

Jesus is Truth; His Word is truth (Jn 14:4, 17:17). All Scripture is divinely inspired, God-breathed (2Tim 3:16), and entirely trustworthy. In all matters of faith and conduct, the Bible is inerrant and infallible; it is the supreme authority – and it is relevant to our everyday lives. Pastor Ryan McDermott of Christ Fellowship explains, "We cannot add to the Word of God, but we *can* add to our understanding."[2] We grow up in our salvation by the pure milk of the Word (1Pet 2:2). We study the whole counsel of the Bible, for **the sum of Your word is truth** (Ps 119:160). The truth of His Word is our protection, but it is of no value to us if we do not understand it, believe it, trust it, abide in it, and apply it to our lives. We must study it deeply to grasp the whole counsel of the Bible.

We wear the belt of truth when we hide the truths of Scripture in our hearts so that we will not be ensnared in Satan's web of deception (Ps 119:11). We buckle on the belt of truth when we *choose* to renounce lies and to believe the truths of His Word. We secure it in place when we *align* our lives with those truths, and when we walk in integrity, by the power of the Holy Spirit seeking to ensure that our behavior matches what we profess to believe (1Jn 1:6-10, Eph 4:25-27). We are also putting on this belt when we are truthful with God about what is in our hearts, not only our sins and our pain, but also our deep heart passions and desires (Ps 139:23-24, Lk 8:17, Ps 37:4).

The Breastplate of Righteousness

Satan may try to fill us with shame because of our sins and failures, trying to convince us that we cannot possibly achieve victory because we are too sinful, not worthy, or have failed too many times. Or, he may work to draw us into a place of striving as we try to *earn* our right standing with God. When we wear the **breastplate of righteousness**, we know that we have no righteousness of ourselves; our right standing with God does not depend on what we think *we* can do for God, but on what *Jesus* has already done for us (2Cor 5:21, Phil 3:9) – and it is that deep heart-knowing which protects our hearts.

> **"Be still and know that I am God;**
> **I will be exalted among the nations,**
> **I will be exalted in the earth."**   Psalm 46:10 NIV

Be still. Cease striving. This ability to rest in what He has done shields our hearts from enemy condemnation.

When we wear the breastplate of righteousness, we also *live righteously*. We choose to be in right standing with God and with man, and we **find out what pleases the Lord** (Eph 5:10). He commands, **"Walk before Me, and be blameless"** (Gen 17:1) – and only His Spirit enables us to do that (Gal 5:16, Col 1:29).

The Shoes of Peace

If our peace is the world's peace, it will be dependent upon our circumstances (Jn 14:27, 16:33). Satan can easily rob us of that false peace by attacking us with trials, sufferings, and tribulations. Our feet will be on sinking sand (Mt 7:24-27).

But when we know that the *only true peace* – for ourselves and others – is the gospel of salvation of our Lord Jesus Christ, we will stand on the sure foundation of Jesus. Trials will not rob us of our peace. And resting in His peace helps us prioritize and avoid getting sucked into distracting, worthless, exhausting activities (Isa 28:16, Rom 9:33, Jn 14:27, Matt 6:25-33).

The **gospel of peace** tells us that there are no barriers between us and God's love because of Jesus' blood (Rom 8:38-39). God's peace transcends our circumstances because our salvation is secure, completely dependent on Jesus. Surrendering to Jesus is the *only* path to true deep everlasting *shalom* peace.

The Shield of Faith

Fear is a major weapon in Satan's stockpile, and he couples it with doubt, unbelief, and confusion. He aims arrows carefully at the vulnerable areas of our hearts and minds. One of his greatest ploys is to tempt us to question with a hard heart, instead of with openness (Lk 1:18-20, 34-35). Hardening our hearts may lead to unbelief and even falling away (Heb 3:7-12).

Satan may try to cause us to doubt God's love for us and our position as His child. He may even cast doubt upon our initial salvation or on our lifelong sanctification process. He may try to cause us to question if we are making any progress in our spiritual growth or to wonder if God even wants to bother with our sanctification.

Remember faith is *pistis*, also translated trust.[3] Trust in God is the **shield of faith** that drives out fear. When we surrender, we choose to trust Him, and this gives us security, assurance, and God-fidence, for our adequacy is in Him alone (2Cor 3:4-6). It is trust that shields us from the arrows of fear, doubt, unbelief, distrust, and confusion that the enemy is aiming at our hearts (Heb 11:6).

The Helmet of Salvation

Put on the **helmet of salvation** by receiving the mind of Christ so that your identity in Christ is secure and immovable. Don't let the enemy take you captive by empty deception. Remember that your salvation is eternal and no one can snatch you from His hands. Be all the more diligent to make certain of His calling and choosing of you. Allow the Spirit to testify with your spirit that you are His child. Hold fast to your hope, and draw near with a sincere heart and full assurance of faith. Settle in your mind right now that because you are His child, God is conforming you to the image of His Son, and He will not abandon the good work He has started in you, but will carry it through to completion. You are chosen for unique Kingdom work, anointed and equipped for that work, and sealed forever with His Holy Spirit. (1Cor 2:16, 1Jn 5:11, Jn 10:28, 2Pet 1:10, Rom 8:16, Heb 10:22-23, Rom 8:29, Phil 1:6, Eph 1:4-14.)

The Sword of the Spirit, The Word of God

The Word is a weapon, a *sword*, because it is piercing (Heb 4:12). But why is it the sword *of the Spirit*?

It is the Holy Spirit's sword because *He forged it*. **All Scripture is God-breathed** (2Tim 3:16 NIV). Somehow, in some unfathomable way, He spoke into the hearts of the authors and caused them to write according to His will.

It is the Holy Spirit's sword because *He is our Teacher*, training us how to use His sword against the forces of darkness (Jn 14:26, 16:13, Lk 12:11-12, 1Jn 2:27), both on the battlefield of our own hearts, and on the battlefields of others' hearts as we help them fight the enemy to victory.

It is the Holy Spirit's sword because *He anoints it with His power*. He works through it, to touch, change, transform, convict, comfort, heal, reveal. The Word without the Holy Spirit is useless and powerless, because it is the **Spirit of truth** who will **guide you into all the truth** (Jn 16:13). Studying the Word without the Holy Spirit can even lead us into traps of spiritual pride and legalism, and a form of powerless godliness (2Tim 3:5). Spending time first in praise, worship, and gratitude can open our hearts to be more focused and receiving when we read the Word.

I recall the season when I was attending Christ Fellowship Church before I came to Christ. Because Pastor Tom Mullins repeatedly taught that we must read the Bible, I bought my first Bible and began to read it. For many months I read it every day, although I did not understand a word of it. I was reading Romans the day I surrendered to Christ; the Holy Spirit came to live inside my heart, and suddenly, I was able to understand what I was reading! That was twenty years ago; even today, as I read the Word every day, I ask the Holy Spirit to speak to me whatever He wants to say.

Hypocrites and liars deluded by deceiving spirits can distort the Word legalistically, twist it to destroy its true meaning, and pervert it to tell us what we want to hear (1Tim 4: 1-5, 2Tim 4:3). Reading the Word with an open heart under the power of the Holy Spirit and learning how to apply it to our own personal lives is our protection from these attacks.

As on the day of Pentecost, when three thousand were **pierced to the heart** (Acts 2:37), the Holy Spirit desires to use His sharp living and active sword to sanctify *our own* hearts. To expose our motives, to reveal when our thoughts don't align with His truth or when our behaviors are not obedient to His Word.

For the word of God is living and active and sharper than any two-edged sword, and piercing as far as the division of soul and spirit, of both joints and marrow, and able to judge the thoughts and intentions of the heart.   Hebrews 4:12

Today, I know I can read His Word under the anointing of the Holy Spirit, with my heart open to Him, receiving from Him, asking Him to open my mind to understand the Scriptures (Lk 24:45), or, I can read with a closed heart. If my mind is on other things, if I am worrying or burdened with cares of the world or too busy to focus on Him, if I have erected an idol, if He has revealed sin that I have not repented of and dealt with or if I haven't obeyed something He has told me to do, I have found that my heart will be closed to Him and He will not anoint His Word. I will not be able to understand the Word, and I am open to deluding influences.

The sword of the Spirit, the word of God. Word in this verse is not the Greek word *logos*, the Word of God in totality, the whole counsel of the Word of God (as used, for example in Jn 1:1, 1Cor 1:18, 2Cor 4:2). But word as used here in Ephesians 6:17 is *rhema*, which is a *precise* word, a verse or promise or precept from Scripture that is for a very *specific* situation.[4]

It is the Holy Spirit's sword because it is the Holy Spirit who gives us His *rhema* word that is needed in the battle. We must be very attuned to His still small voice to hear that *rhema*, and our hearts must be open to **take** that *rhema*, whether it is for the sanctification of our own hearts, or for a defensive battle, or for advancement of the Kingdom. **Take ... the sword of the Spirit.** In this verse the word **take** is *dechomai*, which means "to accept an offer deliberately and readily. To take to oneself what is presented or brought by another."[5]

Let's learn from Scripture how Jesus used the *rhema* sword of the Spirit with deftness to defend Himself and to vanquish Satan.

Ponder, Pray, and Journal

Read about the wilderness temptations in both Matthew 4:1-11 and Luke 4:1-14. Look up the verses Jesus quoted, Deuteronomy 8:3, 6:16, and 6:13, and also the verses Satan quoted, Psalm 91:11-12. Journal your thoughts.

The Sword of the Spirit

First, note that Jesus was **full of the Holy Spirit** (Lk 4:1). It is the Word of God *anointed by the Holy Spirit* that overcomes the enemy. Jesus was wielding the **sword *of the Spirit.*** He understood the true meaning of the verses He quoted, He did not misapply them, and He spoke with authority and with the anointing of the Holy Spirit.

Satan launched an attack on Jesus' identity (**"If You are the Son of God ..."**). But notice that Jesus did not argue with him. He did not try to defend Himself or prove His identity. He very simply spoke specific verses from the Word, *rhema* verses selected carefully to counter Satan's temptations (**"It is written ..."**). We must do likewise. We must know the Word of God, understand it in context, memorize it, hide it in our hearts, and rely on the Holy Spirit so we can wield this sword of the Spirit under His anointing with expertise and confidence.

Now this is really important. As we see in these passages, *Satan knows Scripture*, and may use it to attack and tempt. He has had thousands of years to memorize it, so he has a head start on us. He has certainly confused me at times as he quoted Scripture; since it is God's Word, my first thought is that it must be God speaking to me. Satan will try to use the Word also – but since lying is his native language he will use it distorted, perverted, twisted, or misapplied. He may use it to justify our sin, or to tickle our ears and tell us what we want to hear. He may take it out of context, or omit a critical part of it, or add something to it that twists it, even just a little bit. The more time we spend with God in His Word, the more we will learn to recognize when what we are hearing from the Word is God's voice, and when it is Satan's forgery.

We can see that we must not only *know* the Word of God, we must also *understand its meaning*. We must study it under the power of the Holy Spirit to gain this understanding and discernment, so that we will be able to detect when it is being misapplied, perverted, or used out of context. Remember that our weapon is the sword *of the Spirit,* so that although we may not have memorized the entire Bible, the Holy Spirit is at our side to bring to mind the verses we have hidden in our hearts when we need a specific *rhema* in the heat of the battle.

Reading Charles Spurgeon's sermons in *Spiritual Warfare in a Believer's Life* opened my eyes to understand in greater measure the sword of the Spirit, and to see just how Satan perverted Scripture in these wilderness temptations. I'd like to share some things I have learned.

First, let's look at how Satan omitted part of the verse he was quoting. Here are those verses in their entirety from Psalm 91. I am using KJV since Satan's perversion comes through most clearly in the KJV:

For he shall give his angels charge over thee,
To keep thee in all thy ways.
They shall bear thee up in their hands,
Lest thou dash thy foot against a stone.   Psalm 91:11-12 KJV

Go back to the passages in Matthew and Luke to see if you can spot what he omitted.

Satan omitted "To keep thee in all thy ways." In all *Thy* ways. In all of *God's* ways. Not in any way we feel like going. God will protect us when we are on *His* path. Charles Spurgeon explains it this way:

Notice he knocks out the words "in all thy ways," which limits the protection promised. The Lord never promises to keep us in ways of our own choosing. Every duty that is required of us and every path that is mapped out by Providence shall have divine protection accorded to its travellers, but if we go our own road, we have no promise that we will be cared for.[6]

Notice also that not only has Satan omitted a portion of the verse that is important for its meaning, Satan has also taken this verse out of context. The very first verse of Psalm 91 teaches us that if we bow our hearts to His sovereign plan, *then* we will rest in His protection. Verse 14 of Psalm 91 teaches that God will deliver and protect those who love Him and know His name. (We discussed both of these promises in Chapter 3.) Many other passages in the Word teach this principle also. The whole counsel of the Bible tells us that we are under God's protection *when we are walking in His ways* (Isa 59:8, Ps 1, Prov 4:18-19, Ps 25:10, 12, 13).

Of course we know through our deep studies of the sovereignty of God in *Triumph Over Suffering* and *Triumph of Surrender* that we cannot *earn* God's protection by our obedience, but we can *trust* that He is always working for our good. In this world we will have trouble, but it seems when we are walking on His paths, He shields us in special ways, not allowing anything into our lives that is not for our good and His glory. (Rom 8:28-29, Jn 16:33.)

Satan, however, is perverting the interpretation of verses 11 and 12 in Psalm 91 to mean, "He sends His angels to guard you, no matter what you do." When we stray, we put ourselves in a vulnerable place, open to be attacked by the enemy. In His sovereignty and His graciousness, God may choose to protect us, but we are presuming on His protection if we abandon His paths. Yet remember also that when we repent and put our sins and failures in His hands, although we may not escape the consequences of our sins, it remains His specialty to bring beauty from ashes. (Prov 11:8, 18:10, Ps 1:6, 34:15-22, Heb 12:28-29, Isa 61:3.)

Charles Spurgeon also points out exactly what Satan added. Now this is very subtle, so stick with me here. We will use the KJV since what Satan added is most clear in this translation. Psalm 91 reads, **Lest thou dash thy foot against a stone.** But Satan quotes it **"Lest at any time thou dash thy foot against a stone"** (Matt 4:6 KJV). The word Satan added is *mepote*, which does indeed mean "lest at any time ... that not ever, that never, lest ever."[7] Spurgeon explains that Satan's goal "was to break down the text's hedges and to remove its landmarks."[8] To tempt Jesus to believe that no matter what He did, He would not ever be injured. Jesus did not fall for Satan's traps.

This is heavy. We can see that training with our sword does not mean that we just read a devotional in the morning and head out the door to go about our day. It does not mean we read a quick verse or race through a chapter and think we have girded on our sword. We will need to immerse in it, study it, and ponder it under the anointing of the Holy Spirit. When the Word of God **abides** in us, we are empowered to overcome the evil one (1Jn 2:14). There are many anointed books, but there is only one *God-breathed* book. The Word of God is *alive* because the Word *is* Jesus (2Tim 3:16, Jn 1:1, Heb 4:12).

All Scripture is God-breathed and is useful for teaching, rebuking, correcting and training in righteousness, so that the servant of God may be thoroughly equipped for every good work. 2 Timothy 3:16-17 NIV

We must also trust that God will use Scripture to thoroughly equip us for every good work. The Greek here means the Word is useful to make us adequate, complete, competent, sufficient, and completely qualified. The Word furnishes us with necessary skills and tools needed to complete the purposes for which God has destined us.[9]

It seems to me that the Word of God is the weapon that will require the most training to develop expertise. The Bible *must be* our number one priority. It is *His Word*, and the primary way He speaks to us. We are to receive the Word implanted *with humility*, and pay close attention to it so we don't drift away. The Word convicts us of sin and directs us to His sanctification. It our source of wisdom and guidance, our font of illumination and revelation, our wellspring of peace, comfort and refreshment, and our protection against enemy attacks. Other books or teachings can be helpful to increase understanding, but they are peripheral to the Word, and we must exercise discernment and not follow teachers who are teaching contrary to the Word of God. (Jas 1:21, Heb 2:1-4, 2Tim 3:16-17, Ps 119:24, 50, 76, 93, 97-100, 104-105, 130, 165, Gal 1:8-9.)

Let's go back to these wilderness attacks and look at how Jesus handled the Word as His weapon. Jesus did use parts of verses, yet He did not pervert their meaning. And Charles Spurgeon points out that Jesus slightly altered one of the verses. This doesn't come through in the English, but in the original verse from Deuteronomy 6:16 "You shall not put the LORD your God to the test," the word "you" is plural, and when Jesus quoted it, He used the singular. Spurgeon explains that this is how we apply Scripture to ourselves and our situations, how we "appropriate" Scripture and "learn so to use Scripture that you take home to yourself all its teachings, all its precepts, all its promises, all its doctrines."[10] Jesus did not pervert Scripture or misapply it by altering it; He kept its meaning and applied it to Himself and the situation at hand. Likewise, as Jesus did, we can personalize Scripture if we are careful not to misapply it or distort its meaning.

We don't need to understand every word of the Bible for the Lord to begin to use it as a weapon in our hands. He can use even one verse that we know and understand. Yet when we are *steeped* in the Word of God, when we have studied it, pondered it, memorized it, understood it, received His revelation through it, and hidden it in our hearts, when we have applied it to our lives and become effectual doers instead of forgetful hearers (Jas 1:25), *then* we will more effectively be able to use this weapon both defensively and offensively. Defensively, we will be able to counter Satan's lies and attacks and flaming arrows with a *specific* Scripture, *rhema*, declaring, as Jesus did, "It is written ..."

When Satan tries to persuade us that God has forsaken us, we can silence him with Deuteronomy 31:6: "It is written, 'The Lord my God will never fail me or forsake me.' "

When Satan heaps on the false guilt and shame for past sins that we have already repented of, we can squash that attack with Psalm 103:12: "It is written, 'As far as the east is from the west, so far has He removed my transgressions from me.' "

If Satan shoots an arrow at our heart to tell us that we are unwanted, we can counter that missile with Ephesians 1:5: "It is written, 'He has adopted me as His child through Jesus Christ to Himself.' "

And offensively, we can pray specific Scriptures over seemingly hopeless situations, inviting God's power into these circumstances. We will practice this tactic later in this chapter.

I have asked my friend Angelique to describe how she wielded the Word of God with the Holy Spirit's power. Angelique has such a tender relationship with the Lord. A passionate worshiper with a glorious voice, she has served as my "worship pastor" throughout many of my *Triumph* classes, selecting the music and leading us in worship. But for many years I did not know about the demons that tormented her.

I initially didn't know what it was, but I was depressed since I was a kid. I'd been through childhood sexual trauma, but I never realized the connection to the dark black cloud that hung over me 24/7 through so many decades of my life. I had been to counseling since high school, and on and off different medications; I was officially diagnosed "clinically depressed" in college.

I had thoughts of suicide as early as junior high. I had a lot of self-hatred and shame and was very hard on myself. I thought if I committed suicide, the pain would stop, and life would be better without me in it. I had been a Christian since I was about ten years old, so leaving this life behind and being with Jesus was something I looked forward to. But somehow, I knew these thoughts were from that dark cloud.

My first marriage was ending due to physical and sexual abuse, and I was at my lowest point in my adult life. The wounds of my childhood were re-opened by the betrayal by the one person I had risked to trust more than any other. Add to that the failure I was feeling at the prospect of divorce, and my mind began flirting once again with how life would be so much better if I didn't have to be in it. In that moment of desperation, the Lord led me to His Word. I literally randomly opened the Bible to this verse:

But if I live, I can do more fruitful work for Christ ... I long to go and be with Christ, which would be far better for me. But for your sakes, it is better that I continue to live. Knowing this, I am convinced that I will remain alive so I can continue to help all of you grow and experience the joy of your faith. *Philippians 1:22-25 NLT*

Hallelujah! In that miraculous moment, God's Word freed me permanently from the mental anguish of suicidal thoughts!

Angelique
Palm Beach Gardens, Florida

Although this freedom happened in an instant, it was Angelique's many years of growing in Him that prepared her for this final battle victory. And although at this moment she "randomly" opened her Bible, on a day-to-day basis she was *immersed* in the Word and *maturing* in Him, open to receiving from the Word of God. For her, the Word is living and active; the sword of the Spirit piercingly judging the intentions of her heart and laying her heart bare before God (Heb 4:12-13). Because she is truly His disciple, when the Lord spoke to her through His *rhema* Word, she immediately *received* His truth, and that is what set her free (Jn 8:31-32).

Before we leave this passage of the armor in Ephesians, there is a critical command that we will focus on. Although it doesn't have a parallel piece of the armor, it is clearly a crucial weapon in our battle against the enemy.

Pray In the Spirit

I have heard it said many times that prayer is not to change God's mind; it's to change *us*. I find that as I continue to pray over an unresolved situation or an unanswered prayer, my prayers often change as He aligns my prayers with *His* will. I have also discovered that prayerful rest and solitude with Him in meditation of His Word gives Him the opportunity to flood me with His love and strength, to realign my heart with His, to reveal deep mysteries of Himself. Being still before Him opens my heart to receive the Spirit's clarity, discernment, and fortitude. Requesting and supplicating develops my humility, dependence upon Him, and a deep acceptance of His sovereignty.

Ephesians 6 commands us to **pray in the Spirit**. Just what does that mean?

I think this phrase indicates the spiritual gift of praying in tongues (Jude 1:20, 1Cor 14:2, 14-15). Yet I think it may also mean that we stop and ask the Holy Spirit to lead our prayers before we just leap in. I think it may mean we worship in spirit and in truth, not with lip service, and not with deception about the sinful states of our hearts, but open to hear from Him. I think it may also mean that we trust that the Holy Spirit is interceding for us, interceding in such a fashion that somehow, in some unfathomable way, as He is en route to the Father with our prayers, He will transform those prayers so that they arrive as prayers prayed according to His will (Rom 8:26-27).

Prayer strengthens us for the battle by reminding us of God's infinite power and His bottomless love for us. Prayer enables us to stand firm because we know who God is, who we are in Him, and what our position is as His child in His Kingdom. Remaining deeply connected to Him throughout the day in prayer, consciously bringing Jesus into each conversation and activity, invites Him to step in as our Mighty Man and take over each situation and each battle (Isa 42:13).

Pray in the Spirit *on all occasions*. Pray before the battle for equipping and to receive the battle strategy. Pray in the midst of the battle to maintain our connection to the Spirit, so that we can follow His leading, not running ahead or falling behind. Pray after the battle, rejoicing and thanking, no matter what we *perceive* the outcome to be.

On *all* occasions. From a human perspective we may think these situations are "good" or "bad," yet we are to **rejoice always, pray without ceasing,** and **in everything give thanks** (1Thess 5:16-18).

Notice that we are to pray not only for ourselves but also **for all the saints.** When we pray for others, it moves our prayers out of the selfish arena. It takes the focus off of ourselves, and helps us to see the needs of others and to see God's heart.

Putting on the Full Armor of God

Angelique's freedom from suicidal thoughts was a decisive victory and a tremendous deliverance, yet her depression remained. She refers to this as "the black cloud of depression." Perhaps this is the **spirit of heaviness** or **spirit of despair** that Scripture describes (Isa 61:3 NKJV, NIV).

Angelique was about to enter another battle. I think that because of her victory with Jesus over suicidal thoughts, she entered this battle **in the power of the Spirit.** Come hear the next part of her deliverance testimony: grave clothes unbound by the sword of the Spirit, wielded with proficiency as she followed the Lord's strategy.

Not long after this deliverance, I started a new job that I really felt was straight from the Lord. However, this was one of the most trying, insecure, faltering, attempts of my life, and the black cloud of depression became deeper than ever. I had worked since I was a teenager while most kids were partying. I had great confidence in my abilities and had always been successful in my work life, but this time I was failing miserably.

The hardest thing to do was just to get out of bed to go to work in the morning. So, despite everything, believing this job was what God had called me to, I persevered. God led me to pray the "Armor of God" over myself before my feet even hit the floor in the morning. I would put on each piece of Ephesians hardware one at a time, meditating on what each piece meant for me spiritually, and physically mimicking the movement as though I was a soldier actually preparing for war. The Lord would speak to me personally about each piece as I put it on. I did this every morning, week after week. Every day was still as hard as the last, but I would cling to the promise that the Armor I was wearing was <u>The Lord's Himself</u>. I was trusting that I might be losing the everyday battle, but He had won this war ... whatever this war was. At the time, I couldn't understand why this job was such a war. Why was I being attacked? Why did the devil feel that it was worth his time and effort to mess with me? And why was this failure so profound?

At church on Sunday, the pastor felt led to pray for me. Without me saying a word, he started praying for this tough experience I was going through. Then he also began praying against the oppressive spirit that had been holding me back my whole life.

That week, I was fired. I felt it was God's provision to relieve me of this suffering. Yes, it was a failure, but it was also a relief. And there was more relief in store.

As the next month went by, I started noticing something different about me. Things that would normally send me into a tailspin of depression didn't anymore. Hurts that would keep me in bed for the day, I was now able to overcome and stay engaged in life. Insecurities about my acceptance in God that had been a constant struggle for me weren't really there anymore. And most noticeably, in my "time of the month," when I had always been my most emotionally unstable ... I wasn't. And it was then that I realized that the cloud was gone! I did still have emotional moments, but they were in reaction to actual *current situations or interactions instead of for no reason. And I no longer spiraled down into shame. When I asked the Lord about this, I heard Him say, "I took it away. You are delivered from depression. It's over. This is not your thorn. You are not meant to live like this!"*

I realized that during one of my hardest sufferings, I turned to the Lord for protection, and obeyed Him to put on His Armor every day. I now realize this was a great catalyst for this life-changing miracle! I was putting on Armor for the everyday fight, and little did I know it was Armor for the fight of my life.

I am now married to a wonderful Godly man and spiritual leader, and I am living a redeemed life unhindered by crippling depression. It was the answer to a prayer I didn't even pray. The evil one didn't want freedom for me and he knew God did, so he pulled out all the stops, but **"… if God is behind it, you cannot stop it anyway, unless you want to fight against God"** *(Acts 5:39 CEV[11]). It is sealed. It cannot be taken from me by the evil one, his demons, or any other creature.*

I stand here now to proclaim that no force, no matter how long it has held us down, and no matter how powerful it seems, is greater than our God. He is stronger, and a lifetime is just a moment to Him, redeemable at anytime, anywhere, and for anyone who calls on His Almighty Name!

Angelique
Palm Beach Gardens, Florida

This was no rote repetition of Scripture! Angelique was following the Holy Spirit's selected strategy, wielding the sword of the Spirit with the anointing of the Spirit. She was meditating on the depth of truth each piece of the armor represented: that she is righteous in Christ, that her salvation is secure, that her source of peace is only through the cross. Yes, God gives us *His* armor (Isa 59:17). But *we* must put it on (Eph 6:11). Each morning, as Angelique was washing with the water of the Word, God was judging the thoughts of her heart, demolishing lies about her identity and establishing His truths. And when truth prevails, victory is assured.

In both these victories, Angelique did more than *possess* her weapon of the Word. She had *trained* with the Word to proficiency. And yet, there was something even more than proficiency. God had given her specific *rhema* verses for the battles, and she was not running aimlessly. She was not beating the air. As she followed the *Holy Spirit's strategy* precisely as led, pondering each piece of the armor and what it meant for her personally, He anointed His Word and it penetrated her heart.

Do you not know that those who run in a race all run, but only one receives the prize? Run in such a way that you may win ... Therefore I run in such a way, as not without aim; I box in such a way, as not beating the air ...   1 Corinthians 9:24, 26

Angelique partnered with Jesus, and together they demolished those fortresses of suicide and depression and vanquished the dark cloud of demons (Heb 2:14-15, Rev 1:17-18).

Angelique had spent every morning in the deepest of prayer times in the Word. Ultimately, I think how prayer works is a mystery. But we don't need to fully comprehend in order to obey.

Let's explore two additional aspects of prayer to understand in greater measure how prayer can be used to overcome the enemy: praise and thanksgiving, and praying the Word.

Prayer: Praise and Thanksgiving

As we progress through this book, we will see how the alignment of our hearts with God's is *imperative* for victory. Thanksgiving can facilitate that alignment. Think of how the Israelites were to stop their usual work or even their war on the battlefields in order to observe specific feasts and to celebrate and thank the Lord (Ex 12:14, 23:15, 34:22-23, Ps 100:4, 145:1-7). Think about how Jesus *requested* nothing, but simply *gave thanks* over the five loaves and two fishes (Jn 6:1-14).[12]

Jesus instructs us to remember our position as His child, and begin our prayers with praise (Matt 6:9-10) – and no wonder, for praise *silences* the enemy:

From the lips of children and infants
you have ordained praise
because of your enemies,
to silence the foe and the avenger.

Psalm 8:2 NIV, emphasis added

The word silence here is actually Sabbath[13] – our praise forces the enemy *to take a sabbath!* Sabbath means "to rest, cease, sit still ... to desist from exertion ... to put down."[14] So when we praise the Lord, Satan must cease his attack! He must put down his weapons! He must sit down and rest! He must shut up! When we praise and worship the Lord, He shuts the mouths of the lions and silences our enemies (Dan 6:22, Ps 58:6, 2Tim 4:17, Ps 143:12 NIV).

Come with me to meet the daughter of my friend Lauren. This young child learned the power of this weapon of praise.

One night, I heard some noise from my three year-old daughter's bedroom. I listened at the door, and heard singing. I cracked open the door and asked if she was okay. "Yes, Mom," Selah replied. "I'm doing what you taught me to do when the demons come. I just sing worship and they go away."

Lauren Taylor
Dallas, Texas

If a three year old child can shut the mouth of the lion with her song in the night, how much more should we be wielding this weapon with proficiency!

Ponder, Pray, and Journal

Read Second Chronicles 20:1-30, and journal the weapons King Jehoshaphat used. What was the ultimate result?

King Jehoshaphat began with humility, dependence, surrender, and prayer with fasting. When Israel began singing and praising and thanking the Lord, God caused such *confusion* among the enemy armies that those three enemy armies fought against themselves and destroyed each other. When the army of Jehoshaphat arrived on the scene, all that was left to do was to collect the plunder.

It seems God views praise and worship as an invitation to move on our behalf. Hezekiah's battle with the Assyrian King Sennacherib gives us another illustration of how praise moved God to send His angels (2Kg 18:17 – 19:37).

Hezekiah prayed before the LORD and said, "O LORD, the God of Israel, who are enthroned above the cherubim, You are the God, You alone, of all the kingdoms of the earth. You have made heaven and earth. Incline Your ear, O LORD, and hear; open Your eyes, O LORD, and see ... I pray, deliver us from his hand that all the kingdoms of the earth may know that You alone, O LORD, are God." 2 Kings 19:15-16, 19

God's answer included not only protection from the current assault, but King Sennacherib was soon murdered in his homeland as he was worshiping his false god! Additionally, the nation of Assyria never conquered Jerusalem, despite repeated assaults on that city.

When we are tired, weak, weary, hopeless, or depressed, know that praise is a weapon to drive out the spirit of despair (Isa 61:3). I also find praise and worship to be a powerful defensive weapon when Satan is falsely accusing me, churning up false guilt or shame, denouncing my identity in Christ, stirring up doubts, tapping into fears, or tempting me to sin. Sometimes, when I praise, victory is instantaneous. Other times, persistence over hours or even days is necessary, as the Lord uproots lies and replaces them with truth. And when truth prevails in my heart, **the song of the ruthless is silenced** (Isa 25:1,5).

I have to admit that I have tried to orchestrate a victory myself with praise and worship in a manipulative and controlling sort of way. My heart was not right – and you can imagine how completely unsuccessful that was! I have come to understand that the worship that pleases Him emanates from the depth of my heart, with no ulterior motive and no agenda other than to love, please, and glorify Him (Jn 4:24). This kind of true heart worship opens my heart to the work He may want to do in it right then and there. It also invites Him to move, leaving the how and the when up to Him. Additionally, it prepares my heart to *recognize* and *receive* His move, no matter what His answer may look like.

Through Him, then, let us continually offer up a sacrifice of praise to God, that is the fruit of lips that give thanks to His name.   Hebrews 13:15

I have asked my friend Tamar back again to share the outcome of a time when she worshiped in her pain, offering the Lord a sacrifice of praise.

We were going through a very challenging time. Financially we were completely drained, unable to find a home, with time running out on our lease and so many uncertainties ahead. Overwhelmed, I fell to the floor and just wept. "I didn't know this move would cost me everything!" I cried out to the Lord. "You called us here, but this isn't what I thought it would look like!"

After sobbing for what felt like a long time, I heard a soft voice gently say, "Am I worthy?" In that moment, everything changed. I just started saying, "Yes, Lord. I'm so sorry. You are worthy. Worthy of all of it." I just cried and cried and continued to praise Him. I had been looking at what it had cost me to follow Him, not what it had cost Him on the cross.

I suddenly saw the most beautiful vision of incense coming up into His nostrils. The Lord showed me how my worship in my deepest pain was a sweet aroma to Him. Just as when Mary broke open the alabaster jar, and the oil that spilled out produced a sweet fragrance, somehow my being broken, my dying to self but still choosing to praise and worship Him simply because He is worthy, was a pleasing aroma rising up to Him.

Tamar

Tamar had just walked out this verse:

I call upon the LORD who is worthy to be praised, And I am saved from my enemies.   Psalm 13:3

In her heartache, she had praised the only worthy One, and He banished fear. And then, not long after, the Lord took Tamar to this verse, confirming the vision He had given her:

May my prayer be set before you like incense; may the lifting up of my hands be like the evening sacrifice.   Psalm 141:2 NIV

Tamar had felt as if she was being crushed as olives are in the olive press. I have heard it said that the more severely the olives are crushed, the purer the oil that is released. Just as Paul and Silas worshiped in prison (Acts 16:25), just as Tamar worshiped in the depth of her pain, our worship in the crushing is a beautiful offering to our Savior. As Tamar fixed her eyes on Jesus, the Lord brought victory as He freed her from fear.

Praying the Word

When prayer is combined with the Word and anointed by the Spirit, it seems to multiply in power. When we have saturated ourselves with

His Word, memorizing it and speaking it out loud, it will become a part of us. Then, when we pray, the Holy Spirit may just naturally pour Scriptures forth.

We can also be very intentional about praying the Word by turning a verse or a passage into a prayer. Here's what I mean.

Read Ephesians 1:17-19 first, so you can see where this prayer has leapt from. (I used the NLT so my prayer would not come out too stilted.) Then read my prayer for my husband John.

Lord, I pray You will give to John spiritual wisdom and insight so that he might grow in his knowledge of You. I pray that John's heart would be flooded with light so that he can understand the confident hope he has in You as one of Your holy people. And I pray John will understand the incredible greatness of Your power for him. Amen.

We can also use Scripture as a base, and let our prayers grow from it, just as Jesus taught His disciples in Matthew 6:9-13. Here's an example. Read Romans 12:1-2 first, so you can see where this prayer has leapt from. (This time I used the NASB, since that is the version I read from the most.) Then read my prayer for you below, opening your heart to receive it.

Lord God, when we comprehend Your mercy of our forgiveness through the death of Jesus Christ, it seems our only response is surrender to You. I pray that each person reading this book would comprehend Your mercy and would offer to You their bodies, their lives, their gifts and talents, their soul and mind and heart, as a living sacrifice. I pray that each day of their lives they would set themselves apart, holy unto You, to serve You and walk in Your ways, and that the Holy Spirit would sanctify them and make their humble offering acceptable to You.

I pray that they will not allow the world to shape and mold them and control their thinking, but they would daily renew their minds with the truth of Your Word, and through this renewing You would transform them in greater measure into the image of Christ.

And I pray that the result of this transforming will be an ability to comprehend Your perfect will for their lives, and that You will give them the courage to walk it out. Amen.

Ponder, Pray, and Journal

Now it's your turn. Read Colossians 1:9-12, and ask the Holy Spirit for whom He would like you to pray. Then form a prayer directly from His Word. Write it in your journal.

Our Weapons Are Divinely Powerful

... for the weapons of our warfare are not of the flesh, but *divinely powerful* for the destruction of fortresses.

2 Corinthians 10:4, emphasis added

All of our weapons are *completely ineffective* unless they are empowered by the blood of Jesus, the name of Jesus, and the anointing of the Holy Spirit. ***Divinely*** empowered with the wisdom, direction, and fortitude necessary to be fully victorious in Jesus. God has provided divinely powerful spiritual weapons for us, and when we wield them in *surrender, humility, and obedience*, the Holy Spirit can infuse them with His power, making them **mighty through God** (KJV).

Many of the methods you are already using to grow in the Lord are really *weapons* (we may consider them to be tactics) and are *divinely powerful*. As we go through the next few sections, you may discover that some of these methods you haven't yet recognized to be weapons or tactics, even though you may be proficient with them. For others, you may learn some new battle techniques or warfare strategies here. Some we will touch briefly on; others we will go into greater depth.

Remember, I am considering something a "weapon" or "tactic" if the Word demonstrates the power it has to advance the Kingdom and defeat the enemy. Let's explore.

Repent, Surrender, and Obey

**The righteous cry, and the LORD hears
And delivers them out of all their troubles.
The LORD is near to the brokenhearted
And saves those who are crushed in spirit.
Many are the afflictions of the righteous,
But the LORD delivers him out of them all.**   Psalm 34:17-19

The meaning of crushed is "contrite"; a derivative of the same root word is translated "contrite" in Psalm 51:17, David's psalm of repentance after his sin with Bathsheba.[15]

We are very familiar with repentance, as it has been a key part of our journey through the *Triumph* series. I want to pause a moment and emphasize here that God requires us to take the time to repent not only of specific current sins, but also of *specific sins of our past* that we have **formerly practiced** (2Cor 12:21 AMP). It seems He wants all the bases covered.

Clearly repentance, surrender, and obedience position us for deliverance. I believe that some of our battles would come to an immediate and victorious end if we simply repented and obeyed His commands (Ps 119:45). If we surrendered and were convinced that He would guard what we have entrusted to Him (2Tim 1:12, Rom 8:32). This kind of walk of humility is a life lived in utter worship of Him. I have invited my friend Nicolle to illustrate this.

A high-powered MBA and CFO in the hotel industry, Nicolle is bold and persevering as one of my *Triumph* Servant Leaders. In her battle against control, repentance and surrender were key.

Surrendering my parents to God was not easy. I used to call myself a classic A personality because I needed to be in control of everything that was going on around me.

When I started taking care of both of my parents as they began battling terminal illnesses, I struggled with that control. I couldn't make them better. I couldn't make my mother's cancer disappear; I couldn't heal my father's lungs. God had placed me there for the sweetest moments of caring for my mother. But as I watched my mother endure so much pain, and slowly lose her ability to dress and bathe herself, my world changed.

The Lord showed me that I had to surrender her to Him. She was His child first, and my mother second. He was in control, and I was not. I spent weeks of prayer on my knees, repenting of my control and surrendering her, then taking back control, and repenting and surrendering her yet again. As she declined, God showed me again and again that He was the only One in control of this situation.

My mother went into the hospital for the last time on Mother's Day. There was a moment that I knew she was not long for this earth, and would be seated with God soon. My prayers changed from, "Lord, heal her," to "Lord, she is in Your hands. If You choose to take her home, then so be it; give me the peace to know that she is in Your arms." I knew my surrender was complete.

Two weeks later, my mother stepped into heaven. I was not sad; I had surrendered her to God and I knew that as she took her last breath on this earth and her first in heaven the Lord was waiting for her. He granted me the peace I asked for.

After this wrestle to surrender, it was somehow easier to surrender my father to His will. I no longer felt that I must control everything, and I had peace when soon after my mother passed, the Lord took him home also.

I used to call myself an "A personality who had control freakazoidness." My friend reminded me that the power of life and death is in the tongue, and pointed out that I was cursing myself. Once she said that, I made the choice to stop. Taking those labels off myself was another big step in releasing me from the stronghold of control, and it helped me release control not only of my parents, but also in other areas of my life. My job requires some level of control, but I am less hyper-focused on controlling the outcome of everything.

Nicolle Nie
Triumph Servant Leader
Jupiter, Florida

Nicolle may not have known it at first, but she was in a battle with control. This was not an overnight victory; she repented, surrendered, and took back control a number of times before her surrender was complete. And as the Lord demolished control, the Holy Spirit swept in and provided His peace.

Gird Up the Loins of Your Mind

Be transformed by the renewing of your mind (Rom 12:1). **Taking every thought captive to the obedience of Christ** (2Cor 10:5). **Wake up from your spiritual stupor** (1Cor 15:34 AMP). **Prepare your minds for action** (1Pet 1:13), which is literally translated "gird up the loins of your mind." This is a reference to the clothing worn in Biblical times – soldiers would "bind up their long flowing garments by a girdle or belt about their hips" to free themselves up to run or to battle.[16]

Drugs, alcohol, pornography, and other addictions can dull our minds. Additionally, research shows that lack of sleep can impair our minds in a way that is equivalent to intoxication.[17] I think that too much of video games, television, sports, and busyness can blunt our minds too. And it seems to me that overwork, too much serving, no rest in the Lord, and not taking good care of our bodies can deaden our minds also.

Our prayer group prays often for us all to "finish strong." Thinking about some of the kings of Judah who walked so strongly with the Lord yet fell at the very end (for example, Asa (2Chr 16:7-10) and Jehoshaphat (2Chr 20:35-37)), I am reminded of the necessity of constantly keeping our guard up (Gal 6:9, Dan 7:25, Matt 24:13, Rev 3:11).

Therefore, prepare your minds for action, keep sober in spirit, fix your hope completely on the grace to be brought to you at the revelation of Jesus Christ. As obedient children, do not be conformed to the former lusts which were yours in your ignorance, but like the Holy One who called you, be holy yourselves also in all your behavior; because it is written, "YOU SHALL BE HOLY, FOR I AM HOLY." 1 Peter 1:13-16

There is a lot in this passage; let's break it down.

- *Keep sober.* The enemy will kick us when we are down, will mount an all-out frontal attack after an exhausting battle and victory, and will torment us in times of rest. He will shamelessly manipulate and delude. We can gain the victory when we remain alert and rely on God's grace. Walking in our own strength is a place of pride and invites the enemy to trip us up and make us fall (Jas 4:6, Dan 4:37, 1Cor 10:12).

- *Forsake lusts.* Do not covet what is forbidden (1Jn 2:15-17). Lusts are deceitful desires "which seduce to sin and lead to disappointment."[18] Remember from *Triumph of Surrender* how selfishness and idolatry can cause God's voice to be distorted through an idol.[19]

- *Seek holiness.* We are not of this world, we are set apart for His purposes, and we are to live as if we are set apart. We are to align our lives with God's commandments and leave no open doors for the enemy (Jn 15:19, 2Pet 2:9, 2Tim 2:21).

Girding up the loins of our minds also entails renewing our minds and forsaking lies, as we studied extensively in Chapter 2.

Seek Unity

When it comes to spiritual battles, it seems that when we work together, our power increases exponentially.

But you will chase your enemies and they will fall before you by the sword; five of you will chase a hundred, and a hundred of you will chase ten thousand, and your enemies will fall before you by the sword.   Leviticus 26:7-8

Our differences make it easy for Satan to cause strife and division: if he can rip us asunder and isolate us, we are much more vulnerable to enemy takedown. Think how exposed a single sheep is to the hungry lion. Separated from the herd, he is alone and defenseless. But united, the enemy will fall before us by the sword of the Spirit, the Word of God.

Unity is not uniformity. Uniformity is when all are the same, identical, with no variation. If we had uniformity, we would have no need for unity. But unity seems to *require* there to be differences and uniqueness and individuality in order for there to *be* a melding into oneness, a glorious harmony produced when we are united in Him (Eph 4:3, Phil 1:27, 2:1-4).

Seeking unity will require us to battle the *real enemy* (Eph 6:12), and walk in forgiveness, grace, and mercy. It will entail compassion, understanding, and discernment. It will require us not to think of ourselves more highly than we ought (Rom 12:3). Honesty, authenticity, and vulnerability are mandatory. It will be imperative to know deeply in our hearts that those that seem weaker are actually necessary and indispensable (1Cor 12:22). And it won't happen without persevering in prayer and humbling ourselves by relinquishing *our plan* and opening our hearts as we ask the Lord what *His plan* is here.

Compromise, or meeting in the middle, is a *human* method that two dissimilar people can use to work together. Compromise can be useful and healthy, particularly when interacting with unbelievers. But *seeking unity* is an entirely different way, a *spiritual* way that can be only achieved by the work of the Holy Spirit.

Now may the God who gives perseverance and encouragement *grant you* to be of the same mind with one another according to Christ Jesus, so that with one accord you may with one voice glorify the God and Father of our Lord Jesus Christ.   Romans 15:5-6, emphasis added

Seeking unity involves valuing and *capitalizing on* our differences and unique giftings as we rely on the supernatural work of the Holy Spirit to mature us and bring our unity to completion. Only He can grant this kind of spiritual unity – and He then *commands* His blessing when we walk in it! (Ps 33:1-3, 2Cor 13:11).

Now watch how powerful a weapon this kind of unity is:

"... that they may be one, just as We are one; I in them and You in Me, that they may be perfected in unity, *so that the world may know* that You sent Me, and loved them, even as You have loved Me."   John 17:22-23, emphasis added

In a mysterious way that I can hardly comprehend, when we are in unity, people may come to know that Jesus came from God and that God loves them deeply!

Battle Jealousy, Discontentment, and Coveting

Jealousy, discontentment, and coveting are three weapons in Satan's hand, and he will use them mercilessly to divide us and to derail our calling. We can counter Satan's offensive attack with a few defensive weapons. Look up these verses, and journal how you will use these weapons to battle jealousy, discontentment, and coveting:

- Focus on Jesus and not on your own abilities. Become God-fident, not self-confident: Hebrews 12:1-2, 2 Corinthians 3:4-6.
- Trust Him to fully equip you for each assignment He gives you: Hebrews 13:20-21.
- *Choose* gratitude: Colossians 3:15-17.
- *Learn* contentment: Philippians 4:11-13.

Not only can these weapons help us gain victory when jealousy, discontentment, or coveting are attacking, but training with these weapons in advance can prevent us from even falling there in the first place.

Come Into the Light

Denial and deception give the enemy ammunition to ensnare us in fear of exposure and shame. This is a deep topic, and we are going to explore it more in Chapter 17. But for now, I want to get on your radar how coming into the Light invites the Lord's victory:

... but if we walk in the Light as He Himself is in the Light, we have fellowship with one another, and the blood of Jesus His Son cleanses us from all sin ...   1 John 1:7

Keep Your Eyes Fixed on Jesus

The enemy is relentless and tenacious. He is working to wear down the saints (Dan 7:25). Fixing our eyes on the Author and Finisher of our faith protects us from becoming weary and giving up (Heb 12:2-3). We cannot free ourselves; only He can:

My eyes are ever on the LORD,
For only he will release my feet from the snare.
Psalm 25:15 NIV

Fear the Lord

If you address as Father the One who impartially judges according to each one's work, *conduct yourselves in fear during the time of your stay on earth*; knowing that you were ... redeemed ... with precious blood, as of a lamb unblemished and spotless, the blood of Christ.   1 Peter 1:27-29,emphasis added

Fear of the Lord is more than a deep reverential awareness of His majesty. It is a holy fear that He is God and we are not (Ps 86:10, 100:3). It is a humbling fear that knows the cost of our redemption, and does not want to trample on that blood (Heb 10:29). It is a trembling fear that we will stand before Him for an accounting (2Cor 5:9-10, Matt 12:36, Heb 4:13).

The fear of the Lord invites His deliverance and unveils His protection (Ps 34:7, Prov 14:27).

"But the LORD your God you shall fear; and He will deliver you from the hand of all your enemies."   2 Kings 17:39

Additionally, God's eye and His lovingkindness are on those who fear Him (Ps 33:18). And the fear of the Lord brings forth His wisdom and His blessing and keeps us away from evil (Ps 103:17, 111:10, 128:1, Prov 16:6). How do we receive fear of the Lord? By obedience to His Word (Deut 17:18-20).

In amazement I see that the fear of the Lord invites Him to share confidences with us:

**The LORD confides in those who fear him;
he makes his covenant known to them.**   Psalm 25:14 NIV

Love

Love is the hallmark of a Christian (Jn 13:35), and it is through love that the spirit of fear (2Tim 1:7) is cast out:

There is no fear in love; but perfect love casts out fear, because fear involves torment. But he who fears has not been made perfect in love.   1 John 4:18 NKJV

And unconditional nonjudgmental love may be the hardest thing God asks us to do.

Owe nothing to anyone except to love one another ... if there is any other commandment, it is summed up in this saying, "YOU SHALL LOVE YOUR NEIGHBOR AS YOURSELF." Love does no wrong to a neighbor; therefore love is the fulfillment of the law.
Do this, knowing the time, that it is already the hour for you to awaken from sleep; for now salvation is nearer to us than when we believed. The night is almost gone, and the day is near. Therefore let us lay aside the deeds of darkness and put on the armor of light.   Romans 13:8, 9-12

Awaken from sleep, forsake darkness, put on the armor of light, and love one another deeply, for love covers a multitude of sins (1Pet 4:8). **Don't just pretend to love others. Really love them** (Rom 12:9 NLT).

Before we leave this chapter, we will visit one more stockpile of weapons that you may not even recognize are weapons. Fasten your seatbelt; the enemy does not want you to know this.

An Arsenal of Weapons

You may not realize that you have an additional *arsenal* of weapons at your disposal. This storehouse is composed of the *unique and personal gifts* that the Lord has given you.[20] There are three areas of this arsenal that I would like to highlight: our talents, our spiritual gifts, and our testimonies.

Our Talents, Skills, and Abilities

Recall Bezalel in Exodus who was filled with **the Spirit of God, giving him great wisdom, ability, and expertise in all kinds of crafts** (Ex 31:3 NLT) in order to make everything necessary for the tent of meeting. **"In the hearts of all who are skillful I have put skill"** (Ex 31:6).

The combination of talents, skills, and abilities that God has given you are *unique* within you. Whether these gifts are artistic skills, engineering abilities, musical talent, scientific knowledge, compassion and understanding, financial expertise, speaking ability, people skills, athletic prowess, or any other gifting, God has designed you this way *in order to fulfill His purposes*. You are *unrepeatable*, and *you alone* can reflect the piece of His heart that God designed you to reveal.[21]

There may be lots of wonderful things we can do with our talents and abilities, and we can certainly use them for worldly purposes, good or evil, but when we are using them *according to His will* (Eph 2:10, Col 1:10, Rom 12:1-2), He will move mountains and vanquish the enemy for us:

> **If you abide in Me, and My words abide in you, ask whatever you wish, and it will be done for you. My Father is glorified by this, that you bear much fruit, and so prove to be My disciples.**
>
> John 15:7-8, emphasis added

Ask whatever you wish and it will be done for you – *if*. A little word that packs a lot of meaning.

Our Spiritual Gifts

The Holy Spirit *distributes* spiritual gifts, according to His will, and for His purposes (1Cor 12:1-31, Rom 12:6-8, Eph 4:7-16, 1Pet 4:10-11).

But to each one is given the manifestation of the Spirit for the common good ... But one and the same Spirit works all these things, distributing to each one individually just as He wills ... Since we have gifts that differ according to the grace given to us, each of us is to exercise them accordingly ...

1 Corinthians 12:7, 11, Romans 12:6

These gifts and anointings are *special* for us, distributed by the Holy Spirit as He wills, and according to His grace. We are commanded to be good stewards of these gifts and to serve the Body of Christ with them (Eph 4:7-16, 1Pt 4:10, Rom 12:6-8). These gifts are to be used to build up the body of Christ (Eph 4:12) – truly a warfare assignment.

These spiritual gifts are *indispensable* weapons of our warfare, and we can see from these passages that if we do not develop or utilize the special gifts the Holy Spirit has given us, we are being *disobedient* to God's commands. If we have the gift of prophecy but don't speak because of fear, if we have a heart of evangelism but do not take the time to grow in that gift, if we have the gift of teaching but are too busy to teach, if we have the gift of tongues but do not use it in prayer or allow the Holy Spirit to pray through us and to develop it – not only are we rebelling against God's commands, but the Body of Christ is missing out on an entire *arsenal* of weapons.

Our Testimonies

"Now the salvation, and the power, and the kingdom of our God and the authority of His Christ have come, for the accuser of our brethren has been thrown down, he who accuses them before our God day and night. And they *overcame him* because of the blood of the Lamb and *because of the word of their testimony*, and they did not love their life even when faced with death." Revelation 12:10-11, emphasis added

In all honesty, it's not *our* testimony; it's *God's* testimony. It is the story of His working in our lives; it belongs to Him and He has given it to us to steward. Exactly what Satan used to try to destroy us, in God's hands becomes a weapon against him.

Stewarding our testimony means we do not hide it under a rock because we are fearful, embarrassed, or prideful. Stewarding it means we use it to give glory to God. Our greatest failures covered by His grace. Our greatest weaknesses overcome by His strength. Our greatest sins forgiven in His blood. When we openly and honestly tell others what God has done for us, we present them an opportunity to glorify Him, as Paul did, announcing that he was the foremost, the chief, sinner (1Tim 1:15).

"He [Paul] who once persecuted us is now preaching the faith which he once tried to destroy." *And they were glorifying God because of me.* Galatians 1:23-24, emphasis added

Our accuser is thrown down when we rid ourselves of our ego and our concerns about our reputation and allow Jesus' name to be magnified through our God-story.

Re-read the passage in Revelation and circle the three things listed that enable us to overcome.

It's more than just our testimony. Of course it's the blood of the Lamb, who gave Himself for our sins. And the third element? We do not love our lives even when faced with death. Physical death, yes. But

I think there are other layers of meaning here:

- When faced with persecution and rejection, we still courageously and vulnerably share our testimonies.

- When we are called to die to ourselves, we willingly surrender all to Him.

- And we give testimony to Jesus by glorifying God in death as well as life (Phil 1:20), allowing Him to choose the way He will call us home.

Before we wrap up this chapter, I'd like to focus on a familiar Old Testament passage in order to emphasize the importance of *contentment* with the unique armor, weapons, and equipping that God has provided for us.

In First Samuel 17, we see David recognized that God had equipped him for the encounter with Goliath through his battles with the lion and the bear (1Sam 17:33-37). Next, when King Saul offered David his armor and his sword, David put them on, but then realized that those were weapons designed for Saul, not for him. David then went forth against Goliath with the weapons God had provided for him, a sling and a stone, and as his armor, the name of the LORD of hosts. Watch what happened next.

Thus David prevailed over the Philistine with a sling and a stone, and he struck the Philistine and killed him; but there was no sword in David's hand. Then David ran and stood over the Philistine and took his sword and drew it out of its sheath and killed him, and cut off his head with it. When the Philistines saw that their champion was dead, they fled.

1 Samuel 17:50-51

As God did with David, when we learn to proficiently use the weapons God has given us (the sling and the stone), He will give us more (the sword). Don't think the sling is not enough and delay entering the battle until you have been given the sword.

Recall also that although the Lord gave David Goliath's sword to use for that moment in battle, He did not give David possession of the sword until much later, when he was trained and ready to handle it (1Sam 21:8-9).

Ponder, Pray, and Journal

It seems that the enemy fights ever so viciously against the development of our talents, spiritual gifts, and testimony. Maybe because he knows it is an *arsenal*. Maybe because he knows the *potential* this arsenal has to inflict serious damage on his kingdom. Spend some time in prayer, asking God to highlight for you the talents, spiritual gifts, and testimony He has given you uniquely, and ask Him how He wants you to develop and use these weapons to advance His Kingdom.

Sometimes, the Holy Spirit stirs a desire for a particular gift or ability. Ask the Lord to check your motives and expose any jealousy or covetousness, and if your motives are pure, ask Him for what is on your heart! He loves to give good gifts to His children (Matt 7:11).

This was a very full chapter! Be sure you are suited up with your armor and skilled in the weapons God has provided for you, because as we enter the next section, we will put Satan under a magnifying glass and scrutinize some of the weapons, tactics, and strategies that *the enemy* uses.

PART II:
ANALYZING
THE ENEMY

For our struggle is not against flesh and blood, but against the rulers, against the powers, against the world forces of this darkness, against the spiritual forces of wickedness in the heavenly places. Ephesians 6:12

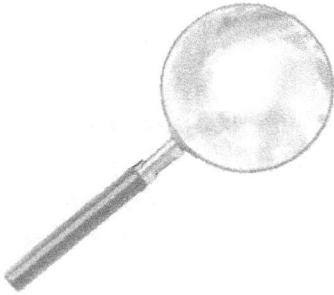

Chapter 6
Know Your Enemy

he Word tells us that the flesh is weak and the world is corrupt (Matt 26:41, 2Pet 2:20). Indeed these would be battles enough. But Satan and his demons capitalize on this weakness and corruption, masterminding temptations to lure us away from God and from the Kingdom work He has planned for us. We are battling three enemies simultaneously: our flesh, the world, and demonic forces (Rom 7:14-25, 1Jn 2:15-16, Eph 2:2-3, 6:12).

Spiritual warfare is the clash of unseen forces in the heavenly places. God's angel armies are battling Satan and his demon armies for the influence of the hearts of men. Each is trying to advance his kingdom rule. Satan, utilizing our weak flesh and the corrupt world, wars for the destruction of the destinies of the saved and the obstruction of salvation of the unsaved. Jesus wars for abundant life for the saved and salvation for the unsaved, for His Kingdom to come.

Satan's attacks are spiritual, but he also uses *physical* weapons, tactics, and strategies to fight *spiritual* battles. His *spiritual* goal is to destroy our relationship with God, to demolish our Kingdom assignments, to totally shatter us. He may do that with an overt demonic attack. But perhaps even more often, he utilizes our weak flesh and the corrupt world to accomplish his spiritual goals. What seems to be a physical struggle against our fleshly desires and worldly temptations may actually be a spiritual battle.

Satan is very adept at making a spiritual battle appear to be merely a physical one. Remember when the army of the Arameans encircled Dothan, and Elisha's servant was terrified.

So he [Elisha] answered, "Do not fear, for those who are with us are more than those who are with them." Then Elisha prayed and said, "O LORD, I pray, open his eyes that he may see." And the LORD opened the servant's eyes and he saw; and behold, the mountain was full of horses and chariots of fire all around Elisha.   2 Kings 6:15-17

This was indeed a physical battle, but the deeper reality was that it was primarily a spiritual battle. In this chapter, we will research how Satan exploits our flesh and the world to serve his diabolical purposes, and learn how we can be victorious as we use the weapons God has given us. In the first half of the chapter, we will concentrate on our flesh and the world, and in the second half of the chapter, we will look at how Satan *teams up* with our flesh and with the world. As we investigate, we will of course keep our eyes on our Victor and Savior, the Lord Jesus Christ.

Suited up and weapons in hand? Let's go.

The Weak Flesh

Since the Fall, we are all born into sin.

Therefore, just as through one man sin entered into the world, and death through sin, and so death spread to all men, because all sinned ... For I know that *nothing good dwells in me*, that is, in my flesh ... *evil is present in me* ...
Romans 5:12, 7:18, 21 emphasis added

Let's pause a moment and clarify. This word **flesh** as used in the Bible can have more than one connotation, and we will need to understand the context of each passage to recognize the meaning. In some passages, our flesh can simply mean our physical body. Our physical body is not our enemy; we are not to attack it or battle against it, but we are to nourish and cherish it (Eph 5:29).

But in many other passages, **flesh** means our inherently sinful nature, as in Romans 7:18 above. There will indeed be a day when our flesh is fully redeemed, when our bodies are glorified and the battle against our flesh has come to its victorious resolution – but that is not yet for today. Today our bodies on this earth are still broken and inherently sinful. Today all creation is groaning, and we long for our bodies to be released from sin and suffering, to be made holy in Him (Rom 8:22-25, 1Cor 15:51-53). Today our inherently sinful nature, our **old self** or **old man** or **natural man**, is constantly at war with our **new self** or **spiritual man** or **inner man** (Eph 4:22, 1Cor 2:14, Rom 7:22).

Ponder, Pray, and Journal

Read Romans 7:14-25, in more than one translation to help with understanding. Meet me back here when you are finished.

I want to do what is right, but I can't. I want to do what is good, but I don't. I don't want to do what is wrong, but I do it anyway.   Romans 7:18-19 NLT

And Jesus sums it up succinctly: **"The spirit is willing, but the flesh is weak"** (Matt 26:41). Our fleshly desires wage war against our very souls (1Pet 2:11). Since our flesh is not yet fully redeemed, while *we are on this earth, we are simply going to want things that God has forbidden.*

Recognize that *temptation is not sin*. We may be drawn to something that God has forbidden – but that temptation is not sin. It is a desire of the flesh, and we are commanded to deny ourselves and to abstain from these sinful desires (Matt 16:24).

Before we came to Christ, we were living solely according to the flesh. Carnal, as the King James says it. But once we surrendered to Jesus, the Holy Spirit has come to live within us; as we cooperate with Him, He begins to conform us to Christ and teach us how to walk according to His Spirit. Daily, we can choose to walk in the flesh, or walk in the Spirit. We can choose to be led by the flesh, the inherently sinful members of our body – or we can choose to be led by the Spirit (Rom 8:5-6,12). We can choose God's bright and righteous way, or Satan's dark and wicked one (Prov 4:18-19).

Ponder, Pray, and Journal

Study the following passages, and in your journal, write down the rotten fruit of walking in the flesh.

- Romans 8:5-8
- Galatians 5:16-21
- 1 Corinthians 3:1-3

Is there anything the Lord is speaking to you about right now?

Satan Seeks To Devour Our Weak Flesh

Sometimes there may be more to our battles with the flesh than meets the eye. In his letter to the Ephesians, Paul spends Chapters 4, 5, and the first half of 6 explaining how to walk worthy of the Lord, how to put off the old self and put on the new self, how to walk as children of the Light – and follows up these commands with the teaching that our struggle to obey is not merely a battle against the flesh, but is a battle with demons:

For our struggle is not against flesh and blood, but against the rulers, against the powers, against the world forces of this darkness, against the spiritual forces of wickedness in the heavenly places. Ephesians 6:12

Similarly, Paul explains in Second Corinthians that **though we walk in the flesh, we do not war according to the flesh** (2Cor 10:3). And James begins Chapter 4 speaking about battles with the flesh and the world, and by verse 7 is teaching how to resist Satan.

Reading through Romans Chapters 5 through 8, I am pondering this verse:

Do you not know that when you present yourselves to someone as slaves for obedience, you are slaves of the one whom you obey, either of sin, resulting in death, or of obedience, resulting in righteousness? Romans 6:16

Ponder, Pray, and Journal

Slavery. Bondage. Captivity.

- Slaves of sin. How can sin actually make us a slave?
- **Slaves of the one whom you obey.** What does it mean to **obey** sin? Is there more going on here? Think about the **spirit of slavery** mentioned in Romans 8:15. And think about how Paul wraps up these chapters:

But in all these things we overwhelmingly conquer through Him who loved us. For I am convinced that neither death, nor life, *nor angels, nor principalities*, nor things present, nor

things to come, *nor powers,* nor height, nor depth, nor any other created thing, will be able to separate us from the love of God which is in Christ Jesus our Lord.

Romans 8:37-39, emphasis added

Journal what the Holy Spirit reveals.

The Word uses the analogy of Satan as a lion:

When evildoers came upon me to devour my flesh ...

Psalm 27:2

David is writing about real physical enemies – but we can see this as a spiritual battle also. Paul writes about being delivered from the lion's mouth and from the wild beasts at Ephesus (2Tim 4:17, 1Cor 15:32, 16:8-9), and Peter gives us a clear spiritual parallel:

Your adversary, the devil, prowls around like a roaring lion, seeking someone to devour.

1 Peter 5:8

As I read through all these passages, it seems apparent to me that, whether people are believers or unbelievers, *being led by the flesh means we are putting ourselves under Satan's influence.* Because the deeds of the flesh align so closely with the hallmarks of Satan, as we discussed in Chapter 2, I think he can easily and constantly utilize our uncrucified flesh in his attack against us. Beware.

Victory Over Our Weak Flesh: Crucify It and Live By Faith

Our flesh wants things that God has forbidden. Escalating the battle, Satan may ruthlessly exploit our own weak flesh by bringing within our reach things which are forbidden. But God's plan for us is our continued sanctification (1Thess 4:3, Heb 10:14). We are to **cleanse ourselves from all defilement of flesh and spirit, perfecting holiness in the fear of God** (1Cor 7:1). This battle against the flesh will require the Holy Spirit for victory (Gal 3:3).

Galatians shows us that the way to victory over our flesh is twofold: crucifying our fleshly desires, and living by faith:

I have been crucified with Christ; and it is no longer I who live, but Christ lives in me; and the life which I now live in the flesh I live by faith in the Son of God, who loved me and gave Himself up for me. Galatians 2:20

Crucifying the flesh means we repent of our sins and die to ourselves, surrendering to the Holy Spirit's control, giving up what *we* desire and wanting only God's will. *Living by faith* means trusting in Him to give us the grace and strength to walk by the Spirit. We actively *choose* to feed our spirit and not our flesh, and we seek to be led by His Holy Spirit.

Now those who belong to Christ Jesus have crucified the flesh with its passions and desires. If we live by the Spirit, let us also walk by the Spirit. Galatians 5:24-25

We join Christ in His death by dying to ourselves, and we join Him in His resurrection by walking in newness of life (Rom 6:4-5).

... knowing this, that our old self was crucified with Him, in order that our body of sin might be done away with, so that we would no longer be slaves to sin; for he who has died is freed from sin ... consider yourselves to be dead to sin, but alive to God in Christ Jesus. Therefore do not let sin reign in your mortal body so that you obey its lusts ... Romans 6:6-7, 11-12

That our body of sin might be done away with. This dying to ourselves is a daily death, a daily laying aside of the old self and putting on the new self (Eph 4:22-24). We **consider** ourselves to be dead to sin. This means we assess, take everything into account, realize we have died with Christ, and choose to die to our sinful desires. We have been granted all the grace we need to walk in victory over the flesh, to daily crucify our flesh and choose to walk by the Spirit (Rom 8:12-13). We cannot accomplish this on our own; we will be victorious only by submitting to the Holy Spirit's control (Gal 3:3).

Ponder, Pray, and Journal

Pause and write in your journal the fruit of the Spirit (Galatians 5:22-23).

- Why do you think these are the *fruit* of the Spirit instead of the *deeds* of the Spirit?
- What needs to be put to death in your life in order for the Spirit to bring forth His fruit?

We crucify our flesh by surrendering our desires, our will, our plans to God's plan, minute by minute, day by day. We will wrestle in this way against the flesh all the way up until we meet Jesus in heaven.

Ponder, Pray, and Journal

In the Agony in the Garden, during Jesus' last night on this earth, He gave His disciples instructions on battling the flesh. Read Matthew 26:36-46, and notice the two commands in verse 41. Write them in your journal.

The word **watch** throughout this passage is a very telling word in the Greek.

It denotes ... a mindfulness of threatening dangers which, with conscious earnestness and an alert mind, keeps it from all drowsiness and all slackening in the energy of faith and conduct ... watching indicates that the Christian is alert or vigilant in order to defend himself against a spiritual foe. He is properly prepared for any surprise or sudden change in his circumstances, and above all, in order that his fellowship with God in prayer may be undistracted and efficacious.[1]

Based on the passage you read in Matthew 26 and this definition, what will you do to do your part in fighting for victory on this battlefield?

Look up the following Scripture verses and record in your journal how God commands us to battle the temptations of the flesh:

- 1 Timothy 6:3-11
- 1 Corinthians 6:15-18
- 1 Corinthians 10:7-14
- 2 Timothy 2:21-23
- 1 Peter 2:11

God promises that there is no temptation beyond what we can bear, and that He will show us a way out when we ask. In order to be victorious, we must walk this out *in the physical*. Scripture commands us to treasure His Word in our hearts so that we may not sin against Him. The Word commands us to flee temptation, and to seek Him when in temptation for mercy and grace. (1Cor 10:13, Ps 119:11, 2Tim 2:22, Heb 4:15-16.) Additionally, we are instructed to

... put on the Lord Jesus Christ, and make no provision for the flesh in regard to its lusts.   Romans 13:14

We are to make **no provision for the flesh** that simply lusts after what is forbidden. Set up Godly boundaries and keep them in place.

The Corrupt World

God created a perfect world, but through Adam sin entered into the world, and death through sin. Satan is the god of this world and the world lies in his power. He will fully exploit it in order to annihilate us. (Rom 5:12, 2Cor 4:4, 1Jn 5:19.) Ephesians explains that those who are unsaved walk according to the course of this world, **according the prince of the power of the air, the spirit that is now working in the sons of disobedience** (Eph 2:2). This battle against the world will require the Holy Spirit for victory.

Let's pause a moment and clarify. Just as the word **flesh** in the Bible can have more than one meaning, this word **world** as used in the Bible can have more than one connotation also, and we will need to understand the context of the passage to recognize the meaning. In some passages, the world can simply mean the physical earth. We are not to hate the physical earth or battle against it, but to appreciate the glorious beauty of God's creation, to see His lovingkindness in the works of His hands (Ps 104, Ps 8, Rom 1:20-21).

In other passages, the **world** means the people of the world (Jn 3:16).

But in other passages, the **world** means the systems, order, and concerns of our life down here in contrast to eternal life. The ideas, morality, belief systems, values, and philosophies of the world. The *culture* of the world. What the world would define as right and wrong.

Pastor Mark Bubeck, founder of International Center for Biblical Counseling, in his book *The Adversary* defines the world in this way:

> As our enemy, the world is the whole organized system, made up of varying and changing social, economic, materialistic, and religious philosophies which have their expression through the

organizations and personalities of human beings. The world system in its function is a composite expression of the depravity of man and the intrigues of Satan's rule, combining in opposition to the sovereign rule of God.[2]

He goes on to say that the reason the world is so corrupt is because "the world system seems to be best understood as an extension of man's two very real enemies – Satan, and man's fleshy interests (or old nature)."[3] The Word tells us that the earth is polluted by its sinful inhabitants and is in slavery to corruption, and we are commanded to keep ourselves unstained by the world (Isa 24:5, Rom 8:21, Jas 1:27).

I have often heard it said that world culture is like a river, in direct opposition to the ways of God, with a strong current pulling us away from the things of God. If we stop fighting that current for a moment, we will be swept away with it. We have a lifelong battle fighting the current of the world.

Now watch how the flesh and the world collude to destroy us in this passage from James. Remember from Romans 7 that your members are your inherently sinful nature, your flesh.

What is the source of quarrels and conflicts among you? Is not the source your pleasures that wage war in your members? You lust and do not have; so you commit murder. You are envious and cannot obtain; so you fight and quarrel. You do not have because you do not ask. You ask and do not receive, because you ask with wrong motives, so that you may spend it on your pleasures. You adulteresses, do you not know that *friendship with the world is hostility toward God*? Therefore whoever wishes to be a friend of the world makes himself an enemy of God. James 4:1-2, emphasis added

Also note that James is speaking to *believers*: note the repeated use of **you**. Go read the entire passage, verses 1-10, with particular attention to verse 5, so you know that this passage is for believers.

James is teaching that if we are united in friendship with the world, we stand *opposed* to God *as His enemy*. This is very grave. Second Peter explains that man's desires have corrupted the world. The Amplified expounds:

... moral decay (rottenness and corruption) that is in the world because of covetousness (lust and greed) ...

2 Peter 1:4 AMPC

The unrestrained desires of our flesh corrupted the world, and now in many ways the world is no longer a safe place, but a place full of even greater temptations intended to ensnare us into deeper and deeper sins of the flesh. I can see Satan's seducing influence upon this vicious cycle – and no surprise, for he is the ruler of the world (Jn 12:3). No wonder we are commanded not to love the world:

Do not love the world nor the things in the world. If anyone loves the world, the love of the Father is not in him. For all that is in the world, the lust of the flesh and the lust of the eyes and the boastful pride of life, is not from the Father, but is from the world. The world is passing away, and also its lusts; but the one who does the will of God lives forever.

1 John 2:15-17

Some of the ways of the world are not necessarily in and of themselves sinful, but with their excesses and extremes they can bring us to wrong priorities. Pride and lack of self control loom large in this passage. Billboards erected on the highway and ads assaulting us on our social media can inundate us with temptations to overindulgence in alcohol, expensive purchases, entertainment. Movies, books, social media, cell phones, computers, and the internet can all work to lure us into similar traps.

And other times, what the world offers is clearly against God's

Word. Corrupt, appealing to our sinful fleshly cravings, those same billboards and social media and internet ads can entice us to sexual sins, addictions, materialism, greed.

The materialism of the world beguiles with its flashy yet empty promises of satisfaction through possessions, relationships, power, position, titles and degrees. The world systems and culture and deceptive philosophies work to derail our good intentions and entice us away from Godly pursuits. Pastor Mark Bubeck lists governments, educational systems, music, and literature as part of the world system that "tries to dictate our values."[4] Make no mistake: God Himself calls the world **this present evil world** and **this present wicked age and world order** (Gal 1:4 KJV, AMPC). We are living in enemy territory.

And Jesus specifically teaches us that just as He is not of this world (Jn 17:14), we are not of this world either:

"If the world hates you, you know that it has hated Me before it hated you. If you were of the world, the world would love its own; but because you are not of the world, but I chose you out of the world, because of this the world hates you."

John 15:18-19

And understand this:

We know that we are of God, and that the whole world lies in the power of the evil one.   1 John 5:19

Since the whole world lies in the power of Satan, being led by the world means we are putting ourselves under Satan's influence. Walking according to the ways of the world is **obeying the devil** (Eph 2:2 NLT). Because he is the **god of this world** (2Cor 4:4), he can easily and constantly utilize the world in his attack against us. Beware.

Victory Over the Corrupt World:
Overcome It

How do we battle with an enemy so vast it seems ubiquitous? Once again, this battle will rage until we are in heaven with Jesus.

"I have given them Your word; and the world has hated them, because they are not of the world, even as I am not of the world. I do not ask You to take them out of the world, but to keep them from the evil one." John 17:14-15, emphasis added

God's Word will be a decisive weapon here. Hiding in our Strong Tower for protection will position us to be kept from the evil one. And remember that Jesus Himself has prayed for us (Jn 17:20).

Let's look at three more weapons and tactics that are necessary for victory over the world: our faith, our transformation, and our firm stand in the truth. As we study these weapons, think about how you will walk this out in the physical world.

Our Faith

"I have told you these things, so that in me you may have peace. In this world you will have trouble. But take heart! I have overcome the world." John 16:33 NIV, emphasis added

For whatever is born of God overcomes the world; and this is the victory that has overcome the world – our faith. Who is the one who overcomes the world, but he who believes that Jesus is the Son of God? 1 John 5:4-5, emphasis added

Overcome, *nikao* in the Greek, means to conquer, to gain the victory, to prevail, to defeat the enemy.[5] Jesus has overcome the world, and He gives us His Spirit to enable *us* to overcome the world through our faith. Faith is such deep certainty in God that we live our lives in trust of

Him, relying on the strength His Spirit provides. We will be less likely to succumb to the world's temptations or be swept downstream by the river of culture when our hearts deeply trust that God knows what's best for us, and that His commands are for our good.

Our Transformation

And do not be conformed to this world, but be transformed by the renewing of your mind ...   Romans 12:2

We refuse to be conformed to the world. As we studied in Chapter 2, we immerse in the truth of the Word and constantly renew our minds to invite Jesus to transform us into His image in greater measure. As we are transformed, we daily learn God's will and His way. And as we seek to be led by the Holy Spirit and we mature in Him, as we seek first His Kingdom and His righteousness, as we find out what pleases the Lord (Matt 6:33, Eph 5:10, Gal 1:10), "the things of the world will grow strangely dim in the light of His glory and grace."[6]

Our Firm Stand in the Truth

See to it that no one carries you off as spoil or makes you yourselves captive by his so-called philosophy and intellectualism and vain deceit (idle fancies and plain nonsense), following human tradition (men's ideas of the material rather than the spiritual world), just crude notions following the rudimentary and elemental teachings of the universe and disregarding [the teachings of] Christ (the Messiah).   Colossians 2:8 AMPC

See to it that you are not captivated by the world's nonsense. Philosophies and intellectualism and human traditions. Idle fancies and materialism. Some of the ways of the world will lead us astray because they are just plain nonsense.

But other teachings will destroy us because they go *against* the teachings of Christ. They contradict the Word of God – overtly, or deceitfully subtly. *Disregarding Christ* indicates that people are seeking knowledge and revelation *apart from* Christ. I can see Satan's fingerprints on this. He can take the world's nonsense and infuse it with his deception, rebellion, and power. See to it that you are not captivated by teachings that go against the Word.

Let's put this verse in context to study God's battle strategy here.

I want them to have full confidence because they have complete understanding of God's secret plan, which is Christ himself. In him lie hidden all the treasures of wisdom and knowledge.

I am telling you this so that no one will be able to deceive you with persuasive arguments ... And now, just as you accepted Christ Jesus as your Lord, you must continue to live in obedience to him. Let your roots grow down into him and draw up nourishment from him, so you will grow in faith, strong and vigorous in the truth you were taught. Let your lives overflow with thanksgiving for all he has done.

Don't let anyone lead you astray with empty philosophy and high-sounding nonsense that come from human thinking and from the evil powers of this world, and not from Christ. For in Christ the fullness of God lives in a human body, and you are complete through your union with Christ. He is the Lord over every ruler and authority in the universe.

Colossians 2:2-4,6-10 NLT

Ponder, Pray, and Journal

Read through that passage in Colossians again, underlining all the aspects of God's battle strategy. Write them in your journal, and anything the Holy Spirit is speaking to you about.

Have you been captivated by empty philosophies and high-sounding nonsense? What drew you to these ideas? Do they seem more interesting than the teachings of the Bible?

Knowing Jesus, living in obedience to Him, growing deep roots of faith, and overflowing with thanksgiving, will give us full confidence in Christ. Our confidence in Him protects us from being led astray **with empty philosophy and high-sounding nonsense that come from human thinking and from the evil powers of this world.**

See to it. This is our responsibility.

Satan Is Our Ultimate Enemy

Satan escalates the temptations of our flesh and the world as he capitalizes on their corruption. But seeking to understand how demons operate and choosing to engage in warfare against them can feel very intimidating. It can seem much easier to remain blissfully unaware. But I will emphasize *seem*. If we remain in denial, when the enemy's sword slashes through our families and our lives, we will have absolutely no idea what hit us, and we will be ill equipped to fight back. I have invited my husband John to share his journey of awareness of the spiritual world.

When the topic of spiritual warfare comes up, many people tiptoe out of the room. If someone defies the majority by believing in something that is not tangible, they are immediately outcasts, thought to be weird or mentally disturbed.

I was once one of those who tiptoed out of the room. It was always uncomfortable to hear people talking about demons and spiritual oppression and all that "crazy stuff." I was very content with my happy little picture of a Garden of Eden paradise heaven with angels and cherubs floating around. I did not want to believe in dark places with demons. That was the stuff of bad movies and grotesque fantasies.

But on the other hand, these spiritual things <u>are</u> mentioned in the Bible. So why did I resist believing? <u>By design of the enemy</u>. The enemy does not want us to know he exists, and if we do already know, then he wants us to believe he is harmless. How does he accomplish this blindness?

Intangibility: He convinces us that if we cannot see, touch, taste, smell or hear it ... then it must not exist. We don't rely on other evidence of his existence, such as cause and effect, eyewitness accounts, and the Word of God.

Trivialization: He persuades us he is harmless. He wants us to think of him the way we think of Santa Claus and Easter Bunny: a cute little red costumed pixie carrying a pitchfork and sporting horns, sitting on our shoulder tempting us to eat sweets.

Persecution: Those who believe in demons and warfare are labeled deranged.

Distraction: He keeps us too busy to even think about it.

Blinding our leaders: He knows we tend to believe the same things that people whom we look up to believe.

Influencing the media: Most movies portray demons in such a hyperbolic way that we compartmentalize them in our minds as the frightening or entertaining stuff of movies; we simply cannot believe that they exist.

Pride: Once we have mocked those who speak of spiritual warfare, pride keeps us from admitting we were wrong.

How did I start the process of assimilating the concepts of the spirit world and warfare into my God journey? I began with the Word of God. If the Bible is inerrant, then there must be something to this and therefore I must investigate. I humbled myself and acknowledged that I didn't know everything. I realized I was like a kindergartner trying to learn algebra, that I needed to grow into understanding, and that there will certainly be some things I will never fully understand until eternity. I don't understand the Trinity. I don't understand infinity. I think of my understanding as illuminated with headlights. My headlights only go out so far.

Just as a child might not understand nor want to believe that there are people out there who want to rob, kill, and destroy, we, too, may want to close off our minds to the possibility that Satan and demons exist. But just as parents educate their children to be street smart and aware of potential dangers, God wants us to be street smart and aware of the existence of demons. And just as parents do not want to create fearful and paranoid children, neither does God want us to become frightened and paranoid about demons.

Just as children must mature before they are able to discuss with parents topics such as politics, astrophysics, or sex, we must mature in the Lord to be able to handle the topic of spiritual warfare.

John Li, M.D.
Jupiter, Florida

Satan has a mission with a singular agenda: to annihilate the Kingdom of God. Do not forget that the forces of darkness hate us with violent hatred (Ps 25:19). Satan's ultimate goal is to prevent people from coming to know Christ. He tempts mankind to trade eternal life with Christ for the corrupted glitter of the world.

Then Jesus said to His disciples, "If anyone wishes to come after Me, he must deny himself, and take up his cross and follow Me. For whoever wishes to save his life will lose it; but whoever loses his life for My sake will find it. For what will it profit a man *if he gains the whole world and forfeits his soul?*

Or what will a man give in exchange for his soul? For the Son of Man is going to come in the glory of His Father with His angels, and WILL THEN REPAY EVERY MAN ACCORDING TO HIS DEEDS." Matthew 16:24-27, emphasis added

If Satan fails to prevent someone from coming to Christ, he next maneuvers to thwart them from growing in their faith. And if that fails, he battles to frustrate their fruit-bearing and hinder them from fulfilling their God-ordained destiny. He is the god of this world (2Cor 4:4), so it is simple for him to manipulate and control the world.

There is yet another tactic Satan uses to exploit us, which I call *teaming up* with our flesh and with the world.

Demons Team Up With Our Flesh and the World

Remember what we discussed earlier in the chapter: *while we are on this earth, we are simply going to want things that God has forbidden.* It is the way our fallen flesh is wired. Additionally, the systems of this fallen world are working to carry us downstream into the corruption of sin. If we do not desire to live a life of obedience, if we do not discipline ourselves to set our minds on the Spirit, if we do not flee temptation, if we do not set up Godly boundaries, if we do not rely on the Spirit to show us the way out and to give us the strength to take that way of escape, we are apt to fall into sin and remain mired in it. This gives the devil a foothold (Eph 4:27), inviting demons to exploit our flesh.

It seems that when our battles are against the flesh or the world, temptations can be quite hard to resist. But when the battle has demonic overlay, the pressure to sin becomes maximally harder to resist, and our resolve to walk in the Spirit may be somehow weakened. Let's explore.

We know that we can fall into regular old everyday sins of the flesh when we do not discipline ourselves to walk in obedience to God's Word and follow His commands. We can fall into sins of the flesh when we don't say "No" to the lusts of the flesh, those desires of our flesh that God has simply forbidden (1Jn 2:16, Rom 6:12). We are susceptible to fall into sins of the flesh when we don't gird up the loins of our minds and instead try to battle in loose-fitting robes (1Pet 1:13, as we discussed in the last chapter). We may fall into sins such as worry, lies, unforgiveness, unrestrained anger, a stumble into impurity, or any number of other sins.

Now when we move from an isolated sin to a repeated sin, when sin becomes accepted and entrenched, when sin becomes a lifestyle, when sin becomes part of our everyday lives with no true genuine repentance, we invite demons to *team up* with our flesh. Any sin is an invitation to demons, but it seems that *repeated sin* really opens the door for a *spirit related to that sin* to oppress us. We are going to examine these concepts further in the chapters on Open Doors, but let's get an overview now.

Pastor Todd Mullins helped me to understand this concept when he taught on the verse, **God has not given us a spirit of fear** ... (1Tim 1:7 NKJV). He explained, "Fear is a spirit. A spirit of fear does not come from God, so we know where *that* spirit comes from."[7]

Pastor Todd is not talking about healthy appropriate fear that galvanizes us to jump out of the way of an oncoming car. Nor is he referring to brief lapses of worry. What he is talking about is deep-seated fear that won't go away. Incessant thoughts that won't be silenced. Thoughts that keep you up at night – or wake you up in the middle of the night. Thoughts that stymie your decision-making abilities by tying up your mind, causing it to churn around and around without rest. Irrational fears, panic attacks, or worry as a lifestyle. First Timothy states that God has not given this spirit of fear to us; it does not come from God; since it is a *spirit*, the only other place it can come from is Satan. Jesus would call this an **unclean spirit**, or a **demon** (Mk 5:8, Lk 11:18-19).

So for example, if someone is worrying about a problem, and he does not obey Jesus' commands to discipline himself to stop worrying, to take his thoughts captive, to surrender the situation to God and to set his mind on the things of the Spirit (Matt 6:25-34, 2Cor 10:5, Rom 8:5-8, Phil 4:8), he is opening a door for demonic influence. Worry is fear; worry is distrust of God. Sinning in his fear invites the **spirit of fear** to influence or oppress him. When the spirit of fear is influencing, it may cause irrational fears or uncontrolled worry or constant unrelenting anxiety or stress. The spirit of fear may cause overwhelming uneasiness and an inability to shut down his racing mind. The spirit of fear can cause anxiety or panic attacks or fears that are out of proportion to the situation. As this spirit of fear teams up with his sinful flesh, he may then find it *much more challenging* to stop worrying. The temptation to stay mired in worry can simply become *much harder to resist.* First Peter describes the weapons needed for victory:

Therefore humble yourselves under the mighty hand of God, that He may exalt you at the proper time, casting all your anxiety on Him, because He cares for you. Be of sober spirit, be on the alert. Your adversary, the devil, prowls around like a roaring lion, seeking someone to devour. But resist him, firm in your faith, knowing that the same experiences of suffering are being accomplished by your brethren who are in the world. After you have suffered for a little while, the God of all grace, who called you to His eternal glory in Christ, will Himself perfect, confirm, strengthen, and establish you. To Him be dominion forever and ever. Amen.   1 Peter 5:6-11

Ponder, Pray, and Journal

Circle the weapons listed in the First Peter passage. If you are struggling with worry or fear, what will you do to conquer?

From this passage, should we always expect *immediate* victory when we battle with these weapons?

First Timothy 1:7 which teaches about a spirit of fear is a pretty well-known verse. In the last chapter we discussed Angelique's victory over the **spirit of heaviness** or **spirit of despair** (Isa 61:3 NKJV, NIV). But did you know there is also a **deceiving spirit** (1Kg 22:22) and a **spirit of a destroyer** (Jer 51:1)? Have you noticed the verse in Hosea that speaks of a **spirit of harlotry** (Hos 5:4)? Are you aware there exists a **perverse spirit** (Isa 19:14 NKJV), also called a **spirit of distortion** (NASB) or **spirit of confusion** (ESV)? Romans describes a **spirit of bondage** or **spirit of slavery** (Rom 8:15 NASB, NKJV). It seems there may be many unclean spirits seeking to amplify temptations by teaming up with our flesh.

Additionally, First Corinthians states that there is a **spirit of the world** (1Cor 2:12). So not only are the world systems our enemy because Satan is the god of this world, it seems the **spirit of the world** can team up with the systems of the world and amp up pressures and temptations.

Satan's Mission and Strategy

Satan is unscrupulous, secretive, and coy. A duplicitous double-dealing archenemy, Satan roams the earth, where he has a throne, a synagogue, and a domain (Job 2:2, Rev 2:9,13, Acts 26:18). Do not underestimate him.

His *mission* from age to age remains unchanged. But his *strategy* is uniquely tailored for each different arena, for each new era, for each distinct season. And his *tactics* are adapted and personalized for our individual weaknesses. Ephesians 6:12 teaches us we are wrestling, *pale*, in up-close, individual, hand-to-hand combat full of trickery and cunning, and requiring deftness and speed.[8] Yet don't allow those truths to drive you to a place of fear. Keep in mind:

- **Greater is He who is in you than he who is in the world** (1Jn 4:4).

- **The battle is the LORD's** (1Sam 17:47).

- **The Son of God appeared for this purpose, to destroy the works of the devil** (1Jn 3:8).

There will be times to battle with our spiritual weapons, and there will be times **the LORD will fight for you; you need only to be still** (Ex 14:14 NIV).

Satan is working to demolish the plan of God, to crush the Kingdom of God, and to shatter the children of God – and he will use everything in his power to do that. He will exploit people who are in his grasp in order to drive them to attack, torment, and reject God's people. He will utilize the lures of the world to try to derail our commitment to obey God. He will tempt our flesh with the most tantalizing offers. His ultimate goal is to kill – literally. He is instigating violence and murder and is speaking suicide and abortion to many people in many generations. Jesus calls him a murderer from the beginning and his intent is to kill us if only God would remove His hedge of protection. (Jn 10:10, 2Tim 2:26, Jn 8:44, Job 1:10, 2:6.)

His goal is to steal our destiny and drive us away from our closeness with Jesus. It is no secret that he is out to kill us spiritually, emotionally, mentally, and physically. Satan and his horde of demons intend to dupe and discourage us, frighten and frustrate us. When we have scored a victory in Jesus, they backlash with a counterattack, hoping to catch us off-guard. They connive to distract us from our Kingdom assignment by luring us into worthless and exhausting activities or by seducing us to drift away from our faith. They work to discourage and wear us down by their incessant attacks. They are weaving intricate webs of lies to ensnare us. (Ezra 4:1-4, Mk 4:19, Heb 2:1, Dan 7:25, Jn 8:44.)

They endeavor to drive us to question God's character and His goodness, and cause us to distrust the magnitude of His forgiveness and deep love for us. They work to confuse us so that we will doubt who we are in Christ and question even our salvation. (Gen 3:1, 2Pet 1:9.)

They attempt to rip apart marriages, families, friendships, and churches by sowing disunity, division, strife, and jealousy. They work tirelessly to deceive, beguile, entice, and seduce us to sin – then drive us to shame over our sin. They seek to blind our minds to the truth and bring confusion to our paths. They attempt to convince us that what is good is evil and what is evil is good, and to persuade us to substitute darkness for light and light for darkness. (Gal 5:19, 2Cor 11:3, Ps 69:18-19, 2Cor 4:4, Isa 3:12, 5:20.)

They lure us to believe that we can be like God, or even believe that we ourselves are divine. They create cults and counterfeit religions, and noble-sounding yet empty philosophies, reasonings, doctrines, and ideologies. They aim to delude us with persuasive arguments and take us captive through hollow philosophy and empty deception. They mastermind worldviews that run counter to the truth of the Word. (Gen 3:4, 1Tim 4:1-2, 2Cor 11:13-15, Col 2:4-8.)

They are so shrewd that they can even succeed in convincing us that *they don't even exist*. They dupe us into believing that these philosophies and ideologies are simply from the world and not from Satan – yet the Word says that the whole world lies in the power of the evil one. Satan's strategies are subtle, crafty, and cunning, and he knows nothing about fighting fair. We are as prey to his roaring lion, and he works to ensnare people in order to hold them captive to do his will. (Eph 4:14, 2Tim 2:22-23, 1Jn 5:19, 1Pet 5:8, 2Tim 2:26.)

Ponder, Pray, and Journal

Go over those last six paragraphs slowly and carefully. Ask the Holy Spirit to reveal any ways the enemy has been attacking you. As the Lord leads, go to the Scriptures referenced.

Search the Scriptures for divinely powerful spiritual weapons to battle each of these attacks.

Studying the Enemy

There is no question that our focus in the war must be on our Lord and Savior Jesus Christ. And yet the importance of knowing about the enemy we are up against cannot be underestimated. I'd like to tap into some military expertise to help us understand why we must analyze our enemy if we want to be victorious.

Tim Miller is a friend of my husband and mine. Tim is truly a man after God's own heart, and we have watched him use the Bible again and again as his war manual for victory on the spiritual battlefront. And we know why he approaches the enemy in this way: this man understands war. As a Lieutenant Colonel in the Marines, he has seen combat. As a law enforcement officer, he has protected the public on the streets. As a secret service Special Agent, he has guarded presidents and vice presidents. And his company, LionHeart International, works today to provide security support and training to churches, businesses, and other venues, as well as the nation of Israel. I have asked Tim to help us understand why our study of the enemy is vital.

The U.S. Military studies their enemy carefully, in order to know the enemy's weak spots, strengths, strategies, and likely responses. They want to know how the enemy thinks and plots and schemes. They read books, study previous battles, and interview others who have fought the enemy. But they learn the most by actively engaging the enemy themselves in battle.

When they have lost a battle, instead of sticking to established patterns of doctrines or practices, they adapt their strategies to seek victory next time. The military understands that remaining flexible and aware is the key to defeating an often changing enemy.

Detailed study of the enemy is imperative for victory, and without it we are likely to face defeat. We want to get the full picture of what we will be up against, to understand as much about the enemy as we possibly can.

We want to know how he fights and what his <u>capabilities</u> are. We want to know how many units he has, and where each unit is located, because we always want to focus our strength against the enemy's weakness.

We want to know the enemy's <u>history</u>, the strategies and tactics that he has used in the past.

And we also need <u>real</u> <u>time</u> <u>intel</u> to ensure his new weapons and tactics are understood and addressed. We never want to fight only with information from the last war, but always want to be focused on current intelligence information. To accomplish this, we will utilize fly-over satellites, drones, communications, and human intelligence methods to find out where he is and what he is doing right now.

Once we have gathered all that information, we next formulate our plan of attack. We believe we will win if we are trained, prepared, and fully committed to the cause we are fighting for. We have learned that much of the victory in battle begins before the battle ever begins. A common saying in the military is this: "The more you sweat in peace, the less you bleed in war." Being trained, committed, and studied allows us to enter the battle with victory on our minds rather than with an unsubstantiated hope that we will win.

Lieutenant Colonel (Ret) Timothy Miller
Founder and CEO, LionHeart International
Juno Beach, Florida

Tim's words are packed with instructions. Let's break it down. Some of his instructions we are already following:

- We have been "sweating in peace" with the training we have been doing in this book and the other books in the *Triumph* series.

- We are fully committed to the cause, fully surrendered to Jesus Christ and His plan for our lives.

- We are going in with victory on our minds. We have spent the first few chapters of this book immersing in our Victor. We know that the war was won at the cross, that there will be a day the guerrillas are silenced, and that right now we are merely *enforcing* the victory.

- When we lose a battle, we learn from our mistakes and adapt our strategies to seek victory next time.

To add to all we have been already doing, in these next chapters we will study the enemy. Tim has outlined for us the way the U.S. Military investigates the enemy, and we will do likewise:

- *Capabilities:* We will learn about Satan's nature and how he fights. We will discover what his capabilities are by examining Scripture verses that call him by name.

- *Enemy's history:* We will study Scriptures that detail some of the tactics and strategies that he and his demons have used in the past.

- *Real-time intelligence:* Because Satan is constantly adapting his strategies to our culture, we will study modern day attacks. Because this master of deception is constantly re-naming and re-packaging to try to catch us unaware, we will educate ourselves so that we are not naïve. Real life testimonies throughout each chapter will allow us to see how he is working right now. We will see how warriors today partner with Jesus to hold crucial positions in battle, and how they co-battle with Him to bring Satan's strongholds down.

We will spend the next few chapters gathering information on the enemy's *character and strategies.* Following that, we will scrutinize exactly *how* he constructs his strongholds, and how he *operates* out of them. Then we will learn how we may inadvertently *open doors* and invite him in to oppress us – *and how to close them.* And in the final chapters of the book, we will learn how to go on the offensive *to tear his strongholds down.*

God is omnipresent and able to be everywhere at once, but Satan is a limited being and can only be in one place at one time. Yet it appears he does preside over an army of demons that do his bidding. Throughout this book, we will use "Satan" or "darkness" to refer to Satan himself, or to his army of demons who are operating under his orders. And in order to accurately comprehend the enemy, we will also call them "demons" or "unclean spirits" just as Jesus did (Matt 12:28, 43, Mk 5:8, 7:29, Lk 11:20, 24).

Please be aware of the words you use. Words such as "warfare," "battles," "captivity," "freedom," and "darkness" indicate we are in some way oppressed or influenced or under attack by Satan and his demons. We will learn more about this in Chapter 8, but for now, recognize that if we are *battling*, we must be battling against someone – and that "someone" is Satan and his demons. And if we have just been granted *freedom*, we must have been spiritually in chains or prisons or dungeons – and it is Satan and his demons that imprison us and hold us in bondage. I am careful not to use spiritual warfare terminology flippantly.

God Created All Things For His Purposes

As we learn more about Satan and his power, don't lose sight of God's undisputed invincible sovereignty. Don't forget Who the Ultimate Authority always was and always will be.

Who can speak and have it happen if the Lord has not decreed it?   Lamentations 3:37 NIV

Yours is the dominion, O LORD, and You exalt Yourself as head over all ... To the only God our Savior, through Jesus Christ our Lord, be glory, majesty, dominion and authority, before all time and now and forever. Amen.

1 Chronicles 29:11, Jude 1:25

Ponder, Pray, and Journal

Do not forget the truth that God retains complete and ultimate control of all of heaven and all of earth. Satan and his demons are *completely* subject to Him. We need only read the first chapter of Job to realize that Satan cannot even *sneeze* without God's approval.

Also recognize that in some mysterious way, God continues to use these fallen angels for *His* purposes. Read Second Chronicles 18:1-22, and journal what the Lord shows you.

We will be relying on the Word to learn what God wants us to know about our enemy. But before we begin, remember that Satan and his demons *were created by God.* They are created – and fallen – beings (Rev 12:3-9, Matt 25:41). And Jesus? He *is* the Creator. *No one* created Him.

For by Him all things were created, both in the heavens and on earth, visible and invisible, whether thrones or dominions or rulers or authorities — *all things have been created through Him and for Him.* He is before all things, and in Him all things hold together.

Colossians 1:16-17, emphasis added

Not only did He create all things, but He created them *for Himself.* His purposes will stand, and He will accomplish all He desires:

"Worthy are You, our Lord and our God, to receive glory and honor and power; for You created all things, and because of Your will they existed, and were created."   Revelation 4:11

Will is the word *thelema* which carries the meaning of both God's will, and His pleasure.[9] What *pleases* Him. For *His* purposes. The King James says **for thy *pleasure* they are and were created.**

"For I am God, and there is no other;
I am God, and there is no one like Me,
Declaring the end from the beginning,
And from ancient times things which have not been done
Saying, 'My purpose will be established
And I will accomplish all My good pleasure.' " Isaiah 46:9-10

He created all things for Himself, for His purposes. *All things.* And what is His purpose for us?

And we know that God causes all things to work together for good to those who love God, to those who are called according to His purpose. For those whom He foreknew, He also predestined to become conformed to the image of His Son ... For this is the will [*thelema*] of God, your sanctification.
Romans 8:28-29, 1 Thessalonians 4:3

Understand that living in a fallen world was not God's cherished plan for mankind. Nor was it God's cherished plan for those angels to fall. He gave them the same precious gift He gave humans: free will. Yet God knew in advance these angels would rebel and reject Him; He knew in advance mankind would rebel and reject Him; His overarching plan took all this rebellion into account. He created them (Satan and his demons), knowing full well they would fall, and without violating their free will or ours, is using *them* to conform *us* to the image of Christ, and thus reveal His glory. Pause a moment and take that in.

Ponder, Pray, and Journal

Meditate on the Scriptures in the previous section.

Why does God continue to tolerate Satan and his demons? Write in your own words the answer to that question. How does this change your perspective on spiritual warfare?

Realize that whether we are warring against the flesh, the world, or demonic powers, all these battles will require the Holy Spirit for victory. Keep your eyes on Jesus, because in the next chapter we will begin to learn about Satan's nature, methods, and strategies as we study his names.

Chapter 7
Satan's Names Reveal His Character

*O*n this chapter we will explore passages where Satan is mentioned by name, and ask the Holy Spirit to teach and reveal. We will see how these names uncover some information about his character, his methods, and his power.[1] We will study these names and do as Lieutenant Colonel Timothy Miller instructed:

- We will investigate his *capabilities* to see his nature, and how he fights.

- We will examine his *history* to learn his tactics and strategies detailed in the Word.

- And we will gather *real-time intelligence* from warriors of today who have engaged the enemy.

Satan is a spirit, **the prince of the power of the air ... the spirit that is now working in the sons of disobedience** (Eph 2:2). He tries to convince us that he *is* God, he tries to deceive us by mimicking the *works* of God, in short, he tries to *be* God (2Thess 2:9, Isa 14:14). But all he can create is a cheap *counterfeit* of the Holy Spirit's work, a forgery, a shoddy and often perverted imitation. The deeper we know the Lord, the less we will be fooled by Satan's glitzy frauds. As we travel through this chapter and learn about his character and his methods, be on the alert for examples of his worthless counterfeits.

We will first take a look at some of Satan's names that are pretty familiar, and then we will ponder some passages that reveal additional names that may be a bit more obscure. As we study these names of Satan, please don't use what you are learning to revile angelic majesties. Trust the Name Above All Other Names for His protection and victory. Hold your heart in humility and follow the archangel Michael's example, standing back and allowing the Lord to be the One to rebuke Satan (Jude 1:8-10).

The Serpent

Now the serpent was more crafty than any beast of the field which the LORD God had made. And he said to the woman, "Indeed, has God said, 'You shall not eat from any tree of the garden'?"
Genesis 3:1

After Eve gave Satan her inaccurate account of what God had commanded,

The serpent said to the woman, "You surely will not die! For God knows that in the day you eat from it your eyes will be opened, and you will be like God, knowing good and evil."
Genesis 3:4-5

This is the first mention of Satan in the Bible. Revelation calls him the **serpent of old** (Rev 12:9). Isaiah calls him the **Leviathan the twisted serpent** (Isa 27:1). Second Corinthians points out that the serpent deceives by his craftiness (2Cor 11:3). A few aspects of his nature are deeply underscored in the Garden temptation:

- He is crafty. Skillful in an underhanded sort of way. He is a master of perversion and twists the truth.

- He sows seeds of doubt and uncertainty.

- He knows how to play into our weaknesses: our pride, our desire to be God-like in power, our craving to know things that God has kept out of our reach.

- He tries to delude us to believe that we know better than God does what is best for us.

My *Word Study* explains that like a serpent, Satan "eyes his objects attentively."[2] He studies us, and seems to know what will most effectively tempt and entrap us. Because he pays such close attention to us, he knows just how to trip us up.

Cunning. Subtly beguiling. Wily, sneaky, and untrustworthy. But also clever and shrewd, full of devious schemes and underhanded strategy. Watch these traits play out in the Garden.

In Eden, it was *Yahweh Elohim* who gave the command not to eat of the tree of knowledge of good and evil (Gen 2:16). But when Satan approached Eve with his devious question, he omitted the deeply personal name *Yahweh* and used only *Elohim* (Gen 3:1). And when Eve gave her answer, she followed Satan's lead, using only the name *Elohim*. Nathan Stone, in his book *Names of God*, speculates that perhaps Satan omitted *Yahweh* with intent to deceive; perhaps Eve suppressed the name because she couldn't speak that very personal and intimate name and sin at the same time.[3]

Now this is very important as we study Satan's tactics. Notice that Satan never explicitly said, "Obey me." He merely spoke a half truth (that is, a lie), offering a deceitful trade to Adam and Eve. In effect he was promising that if they obeyed him they would become like God – but in reality this was an offering so violent its end result was death. Satan played into Eve's doubts and weaknesses, nudging her in the direction he desired, seducing her to make the free will choice to eat. The end result? Both Eve and Adam chose to disobey God, and to obey Satan.

Ponder, Pray, and Journal

With everything in the previous section as background, read God's command in Genesis 2:15-17, then the interaction between Satan and Eve in Genesis 3:1-7.

I want you to see clearly that Eve did not know the Word of God. Think about what we studied in Chapter 5, how Jesus overcame Satan in the wilderness temptations. The importance of knowing the Word of God cannot be overstated.

The Dragon

And the great dragon was thrown down, the serpent of old who is called the devil and Satan ...   Revelation 12:9

An enormous fire-breathing serpent, with wings to extend his reach into places that should be off-limits and armor-plated scales to protect from attack. This word dragon, *drakon* in the Greek, comes from a root word meaning "to behold." The Greeks considered the dragon a species of serpent which had very acute sight.[4] Not only is he eyeing his objects attentively, he is able to see them keenly. This serpent of old is equipped with perspicacity gained through thousands of years of battle experience. His temptations will be precisely placed to play into our weaknesses. He is a formidable foe indeed.

The dragon is able to set people up in places of power, position, and authority (Rev 13:2, Matt 4:8-9). Realize that Satan can bless also – but know that his "blessings" will forever remain forgeries (Mk 8:36-37).

Satan

"The sower sows the word. These are the ones who are beside the road where the word is sown; and when they hear,

**immediately Satan comes and takes away the word which has
been sown in them."**   Mark 4:15

Satan is a transliteration from the Hebrew, as used in Job, First
Chronicles, and Zechariah. This name means "adversary ... oppose,"[5]
or "resistor,"[6] one who comes against. When Peter rebuked Jesus for
speaking about His death, Jesus rebuked Peter, **"Get behind Me,
Satan,"** I think because Peter was resisting and opposing the will of
God (Mk 8:33).

Satan stations himself against God and anything that has to do with
God. He viciously attacks God's Kingdom and His people, and works
to thwart God's plan in any way he can. He stands, poised, alert, and at
the ready, waiting to snatch away truth that the Holy Spirit has sown in
the hearts, depriving people of the freeing power of truth (Lk 8:12, Jn
8:32). Attacking both believers and unbelievers (Matt 16:23, Lk 22:3),
he resists God's will and tempts us to do the same.

For decades Satan had opposed God's plan for my friend Chuck.
Chuck had learned much about the Lord since childhood, but Satan
stole truth from his heart by speaking lies to him through childhood
wounds and Vietnam War traumas. Eventually, the adversary thwarted
his destiny by ensnaring him in alcohol addiction. But God had the
ultimate victory.

*Before I knew Christ, Satan held me in bondage to alcohol, tobacco,
and general disregard for God. I believed the lies and half-truths the
enemy shouted to me, and was trapped in doubt for decades.*

*But God used those many years of rejecting Him as His training
ground. In His sovereignty, He closed the doors of addiction and
taught me surrender and obedience. Then, as I shared my story, He
healed me, freed me, and redirected my path.*

Chuck Dettman
Triumph Servant Leader
Jupiter, Florida

Surrender, obedience, and healing were necessary for victory. Through the grace of God, Chuck has now become an ordained pastor, founded the worldwide marriage ministry *Today's Promise*, and authored seven books on marriage and relationships. Chuck and his wife Mae, as both marriage mentors and Couples *Triumph* Servant Leaders, are leading other couples to the freedom that Chuck and Mae now know. As I look at the fruit of these many ministries that this couple is involved in, it is no surprise that the enemy worked so hard to keep Chuck down for so many decades.

It seems that Chuck's opening of his heart to God in repentance and obedience was God's invitation to enter in, to free and deliver and do as He pleased with Chuck's life. Chuck is truly a living testimony to this verse describing God Most High:

"He does as he pleases
With the powers of heaven
And the peoples of the earth.
No one can hold back his hand
Or say to him: 'What have you done?' "   Daniel 4:35 NIV

The Devil

During supper, the devil having already put into the heart of Judas Iscariot, the son of Simon, to betray Him ... John 13:2

Diabolos in the Greek, devil means "a false accuser ... one who falsely accuses and divides people ... a slanderer."[7] Notice the dual nature of this definition: accuses, and divides. And not simply accuses, but *falsely* accuses. Jesus called Judas *diabolos* because he would falsely accuse and betray Him (Jn 6:70-71).

The devil falsely accused Jesus, and he will falsely accuse us, stirring up people to deceitfully and dishonestly accuse us of failures and shortcomings and to slander our name:

"A disciple is not above his teacher, nor a slave above his master. It is enough for the disciple that he become like his teacher, and the slave like his master. If they have called the head of the house Beelzebul, how much more will they malign the members of his household! ... Remember the word I said to you, 'A slave is not greater than his master.' If they persecuted Me, they will also persecute you."

Matthew 10:24-25, John 15:20

The devil may use people to maliciously persecute us. Slander and gossip are from the devil. And the devil also works to divide marriages, families, friendships, churches, workplaces, neighborhoods, and countries – sometimes with malicious gossip, but other times through simple misunderstandings or miscommunications. Where there is dissension, strife, conflict, schisms – Satan is the mastermind behind it all. The weapon *seeking unity* that we discussed in Chapter 5 will be crucial in battling these kinds of attacks.

Realize that the devil may also attempt to get us to accuse and persecute *ourselves*. Driving foreign thoughts into our minds, trying to convince us that these thoughts are our own, he assigns condemnation where God's truth tells us there is no condemnation possible (Rom 8:1).

The Father of Lies

You belong to your father, the devil, and you want to carry out your father's desire. He was a murderer from the beginning, not holding to the truth, for there is no truth in him. When he lies, he speaks his native language, for he is a liar and the father of lies.   John 8:44 NIV

Satan is the **father of lies**. He is the first liar, and the "author, source, beginner"[8] of all lies. In contrast, God is the **Father of lights**, in whom there is no variation or shifting shadow (Jas 1:17). God is Light, and in Him there is no darkness at all (1Jn 1:5).

All lies *originate* in Satan. I believe deception is possibly Satan's most powerful weapon and the one he wields most frequently.

There is no truth in him. *It is impossible for Satan to speak the truth.* Every word out of his mouth is a lie. His promises are false, his accusations are a lie, his temptations are shrouded in delusion. When he quotes Scripture, he twists it, misapplies it, infuses it with legalism, takes it out of context, omits parts of it, or adds to it (Matt 4:6). His declarations are half-truths, perverted to lure us into sin (Gen 3:4). Lying is his native language. *It is the only language he speaks.*

Sometimes his lies are obvious, but more often they are subtle and insidious. He can *distort* our vision of our Heavenly Father to try to cause us to be unable to *receive* our Father's love. He wounds us to trick us into believing his lies in order to *warp our perception* of our identity. And when it comes to relationships, he can *blind* our minds with lies and delusions that cause rifts and divisions of astronomic proportions.

Satan can be very subtle as he ensnares people into deception, even drawing young children to lie to avoid parental disapproval or punishment. Consciences become more and more insensitive with each lie, hearts become hardened, and strongholds of lying can become entrenched. I have asked my friend Brad to give us a window into how this can happen.

My husband and I have known Brad for many years, but the depth of his struggles were not known to us until recently. Brad had learned deception probably before he even knew what it was. By the time he was an adult, lying was so ingrained in him it was simply the way he operated. He didn't really know any different way to live. I've asked Brad to explain how he became ensnared in Satan's labyrinth of lies from childhood.

The root of deception was implanted when I was very young. When I was five years old, my mother, desperate to get out of a relationship with my father, took my brother and me from our home in the Northeast and brought us down to South Florida. We arrived with nothing. Raising kids as a single parent in poverty was not easy. Additionally, my mother had been traumatized by abuse and brokenness, and had few inner resources. She had to "reinvent" every area of our lives, from where we would live to how we would make money and where we would find community. And "reinvent" she did.

My need for love and approval was not met by my distant father or my overworked mother. Desperately searching for approval, I began seeking to please people. I would say anything to make the pain and emptiness go away. This created a level of co-dependency that would begin to build a lifetime of deception. I became adept at "reinvention" and misrepresentation to simply survive, and skilled at exaggeration and distortion to win approval. I could spin anything in my favor. Omission became my mode of operation.

Over the decades, my relationship with God lost its intimacy and I ended up on a performance track. My life would be defined by a series of "atta-boys" as I climbed a success ladder – a success ladder that never truly existed except for inside of my mind. I found myself creating projects and connecting with people of significance, from working on campaigns with the top marketplace leaders, to becoming a movie producer, to launching national tours. As I climbed this imaginary ladder, my "survival skills" continued to be put to use. Every step of the way required me to stretch the truth in order to make myself look as great as I thought I needed to look. Even if it was just a façade. I held the narrative closely to make sure I could control who heard it and how it was told.

Brad

Brad's deep heart pain from his childhood losses fostered a desperate search for love and approval, and drove him to lie to obtain it. What started as a defense mechanism and a grasping for acceptance developed into a life of illusion. Once passionate for Jesus, Brad eventually succumbed to a superficial and legalistic relationship with the Lord. "Ministry and family had depleted me," he explained. "I was constantly helping people, and eventually I was operating with no reserves. I was reading the Bible every day, but only to help the people I was serving. I was not reading the Word to open my heart to God. Additionally, as a pastor, I had no safe place for accountability, no safe place to be vulnerable, no safe place to fall apart. And, as I realized later, I was only as accountable as I wanted to be. When I left my position as pastor and launched into my own ministry, I still did not *choose* accountability."

God, in His graciousness, eventually called Brad to account. We will read about his painful battle to demolish this stronghold of deception in Chapter 17.

Ponder, Pray, and Journal

God calls lying an **abomination** (Prov 12:22) and will cast **all liars** into the lake of fire (Rev 21:8). It seems lying is a particularly disturbing sin to God, perhaps because it so closely aligns our hearts with Satan's.

The types of sins that fall under the umbrella of lying include manipulation, hypocrisy, and perverting, as well as more subtle deceptions such as embellishment, denial, and half truths. Pause and ask the Holy Spirit to search your heart.

If you are struggling with deception, repent and seek the Lord's help. We will learn more about tearing down strongholds as we work through this book together. But for now, begin to pray for the Holy Spirit to fill you with purity, truth, integrity, fear of the Lord, and a determination and boldness to live a life of "no compromise."

The Enemy

"Behold, I have given you authority to tread on serpents and scorpions, and over all the power of the enemy, and nothing will injure you."   Luke 10:19

Satan is the archenemy of God. His kingdom of darkness is at war with God's Kingdom of Light (Matt 12:25-29, Rev 12:7). Simply because we are citizens of God's Kingdom, Satan counts us his opponents also. From the moment of salvation, he has declared war upon us and our loved ones – whether we have decided to wage war against him or not. The word enemy literally means *hatred*.[9] As we approach the end of time, Satan will fight like a cornered animal, **having great wrath, knowing that he has only a short time** (Rev 12:12).

Our Adversary, the Roaring Lion

Be of sober spirit, be on the alert. Your adversary, the devil, prowls around like a roaring lion, seeking someone to devour.   1 Peter 5:8

The **roaring lion** has fangs that rip out our hearts and claws that rake scars intended to last a lifetime. The name **adversary** literally means "an opponent in a lawsuit."[10] He is legalistic and abounds in justifications and arguments that on our own we cannot defend or argue against. In Chapter 12, we will study his legalistic attacks in more detail, how he contorts the Law to beguile us to sin, then contorts it again to shame us for our sin. Both furtive and vicious, he is a foe who never signs a cease fire.

Satan's roaring lion is a weak counterfeit to the *Lion of Judah*. The Lion of Judah has overcome; He is infinitely more powerful than this prowling lion. With one roar He will once and for all demolish the enemy, for He has overcome as The Lamb That Was Slain, purchasing us with His blood (Rev 5:1-8).

Ponder, Pray, and Journal

Let's pause and apply what we have learned so far. Go over these names of Satan again, and journal what you have learned about his character, plans, and mode of operations through these names.

Has the Holy Spirit opened your eyes to ways you are under attack? Or, is the Holy Spirit revealing that any of your behaviors are lining up with Satan's character?

In the last half of this chapter, we will analyze some less well known names of the enemy, and hear three more testimonies from those in the thick of the battle.

The Commander of the Powers of the Unseen World

Not only is Satan the **god of this world** (2Cor 4:4), but he is also **Beelzebul the ruler of the demons** (Matt 12:24). As we discussed above, Satan is a spirit (Eph 2:2) – and many theologians believe his hordes of demons are fallen angels who rebelled against God and refused to submit to His dominion (Rev 12:3-9, Matt 25:41).

Satan presides over his demons as **the commander of the powers in the unseen world** (Eph 2:2 NLT); some theologians believe his demons are arranged in some sort of hierarchy (Rom 8:38, Col 3:15, Eph 6:12, 1Cor 15:24). Satan and his army are "world dominators;"[11] as **world forces of this darkness** (Eph 6:12) they hold the world in their power (1Jn 5:19).

Our Accuser

... for the accuser of our brethren has been thrown down, he who accuses them before our God day and night.

Revelation 12:10

Satan accuses us of sin, failure, insufficiency, deficiencies, weaknesses, shortcomings, and defeat. To accuse means "to condemn or accuse mainly in a legal sense ... as if he were standing in a court of law."[12] Parallel to the name adversary, the essence of legalism appears again in the name accuser. The accuser sets us up to fail, then floods us with false guilt and shame when we do. Unless we learn how to silence him, these attacks will persist day and night.

The accuser may utilize people to cloud and confuse our minds, and cause us to believe lies and succumb to false guilt and shame, as he did with my husband's friend Bill. I have asked Bill to share this season in his life when the Lord trained him for battle and led him to victory against the accuser of the brethren.

This training didn't happen overnight. Bill had to *learn* to develop a deep intimate relationship with the Lord and *learn* to be led by the Spirit. He had to *learn* how to rely on Jesus for the victory. He had to *learn* how victory occurs when truth prevails. Bill saw victory in warfare only through abiding in Jesus. God did mighty things through His power at work in him and through him – and Bill realized he must be deeply and constantly connected to the Vine for that power to flow (Eph 3:20-21, Jn 15:4-5). And as Bill drew closer to God, the Lord opened his eyes, purified him, and shattered his chains.

When the subject of domestic abuse comes up, people generally think of angry men domineering over meek women. The opposite is harder to believe and rarely discussed. I mean, how can a woman ever abuse a strong manly man? There must be something seriously wrong with the guy. Or ... could it be a bit more veiled and not so easy for the unaware to see?

Many years ago, before the subject of mental health and personality disorders were openly discussed, I found myself in a relationship with an abusive woman. Those who know will tell you the abuse starts in small increments, then over time various forms of manipulation will increase until it consumes a person's life.

Mine took that track, starting with verbal and mental abuse (gaslighting*), until eventually all aspects of abuse, including physical, became a regular part of our relationship (note: I was raised to never strike a woman).

At that time there was little information on this subject and even less for men experiencing it. This lack of support left me isolated and in a continuous battlefield of mental fog and self-doubt.

During those dark times, I remember thinking, "Nobody is ever going to believe me and what I am going through." Voices of shame as well as my own "male" pride were weapons Satan used through this relationship to keep me isolated and in bondage. For years I lived in confusion, feeling trapped and embarrassed as there was no admirable way out.

Bill Unger
Jupiter, Florida

God commands us to stand up against injustice – whether that injustice is towards others or towards ourselves (Isa 1:17, Ps 82:3, Prov 17:15). Bill had fallen into Satan's deception that it was sinful to confront injustice. He mistakenly thought it was Christlike to lie down and take the abuse, to stuff his pain, to allow himself to be manipulated to take the blame for things that were not his responsibility. But in this next season, the Holy Spirit taught him that it was *not* loving to allow someone to mistreat him. God called Bill to stand up for justice while

---

* The American Psychological Association defines gaslighting as "to manipulate another person into doubting his or her perceptions, experiences, or understanding of events." https://dictionary.apa.org/gaslight accessed 9/7/23.

simultaneously walking in forgiveness and humility.[13] Courageously, he refused to tolerate the abuse and refused to succumb to the manipulation. And as he did, the battle exploded. But as Bill steadfastly stood for truth and justice while still maintaining this heart of nonjudgmental love, the Lord orchestrated His victory. I'll let Bill explain what that looked like.

I could have remained this way with my eyes downcast in shame. But thankfully, I made the right decision. I asked God for wisdom, and began going deeper into the teachings of the Bible for understanding. It was during this time that <u>God</u> led me into a men's Bible study and a greater spiritual awareness.

At first, I did not understand that my battle was completely spiritual in nature. But as my wisdom grew I began to see that I was fighting a spiritual enemy with weapons of the flesh, and I was losing. The battle turned in my favor the moment I embraced Ephesians 6:12 as truth:

For our struggle is not against flesh and blood, but against the rulers, against the authorities, against the powers of this dark world and against the spiritual forces of evil in the heavenly realms.   *Ephesians 6:12 NIV*

When I realized what I was battling was not of the flesh, I stopped fighting it that way and began understanding the spiritual war. As I grew in new-found strength, I began to grasp the magnitude of God's love and protection around me. During my battles, I could feel His presence next to me: **the Lord is close to the broken hearted, and saves those who are crushed in spirit** *(Ps 34:18 NIV).*

I was both humbled and strengthened knowing what Jesus did for me on the cross, and that gave me unshakable faith to never fear death nor the dark forces of this world. I embraced the cleansing power of repentance, and through it I began to understand the true enemy in this war.

My spiritual strength for battle grew as I studied the Biblical accounts of how Jesus dealt with demonic forces within people. He faced them without fear, straight on, and in turn they withered in His presence. I embraced this same plan. For the demonic forces understood what God was now teaching me: that He is the ruler over all and no weapon that is formed against me will prosper (Isa 54:17).

Once I began to engage directly with the dark spirit, very intense battles ensued. My commitment to God's truth was being tested and it was then that the Armor of God became very real.

This was a very exhausting time in my life, but in my quiet moments I knew I was on the right path. So, I picked my head up, embraced His gift of salvation with authority, and began walking in my true identity as the son of the King through the battle.

Looking back, I can now see God was there through it all. He never gave up, and never stopped the work He was doing in me. He allowed this pain in order to teach me to rely on Him. I learned that when I truly trust in Him, He always delivers His strength and peace, the peace that surpasses all understanding.

God taught me firsthand about spiritual warfare. I learned that the battle forces are not equal, because God and Satan are not equal. The powers of Satan are weakened when the truth of God is present.

Through this spiritual battle, God gave me the great understanding of spiritual strength over physical environment. I understand who my enemy is and the clever ways he presents himself to entrap me. But more importantly, I know as a son of the King that the enemy has no power over me unless I give him a foothold. When I fully grasped this understanding, true freedom followed.

But whenever anyone turns to the Lord, the veil is taken away. Now the Lord is the Spirit, and where the Spirit of the Lord is, there is freedom.   *2 Corinthians 3:16-17*

I live now without fear of Satan or death, or the dark forces that are all around this world, for I know that God will take care of me and my loved ones. That is not to say that future hardships, heartbreaks, and the deaths of loved ones will not come my way. For all of that will come (Jn 16:33). But my response is to understand that what passes through His hands for me is meant for my refinement. I used to look at my life's challenges as burdens, but now I see them as a spiritual call to conquer higher ground.

I am no longer restrained in any way, for I am healed. I am scarred but better for it. I have reenlisted into the war and returned to the battlefield. Right back to the front lines to share my story, helping others who are in the midst of warfare to learn how to battle with spiritual weapons, how to seek God and allow Him to refine us through the trial.

Bill Unger
Jupiter, Florida

This testimony is packed with battles, weapons, and victories. Let's take it apart.

The accuser of the brethren had an agenda: to take Bill out. Bill immersed in the Word of God, and learned that victory lies in a walk of humility, and would require abiding, repenting, surrendering, embracing truth, and trusting in God. His dynamic relationship with God filled him with hope and trust, giving him the wisdom and strength to stand against the abuse, thwarting the accuser's attempts to discourage and dupe him and drive him away from the Lord. His strong foundation of his identity in Christ now makes it impossible for the enemy's accusations to stick.

Notice how Bill used basic weapons of prayer and connection with his church family in a deep Bible study. He sought God for wisdom and healing. He recognized that Satan's powers are limited *unless he gives him a foothold* (we will discuss what this means in more detail in the next chapter). And Bill then used the weapon of repentance to obliterate any footholds.

This weapon of repentance is critical. Satan – rightly or wrongly – accuses us of sin. If he is wrongly condemning us, we renounce his lies. But if what he is saying is truth, or if he is *accurately* calling out our sins, the only path to victory is to agree with him, take it to God in repentance, and declare the *whole* truth, that we are forgiven in Jesus.

I think this could be what Jesus means here:

"Agree with your adversary quickly, while you are on the way with him, lest your adversary deliver you to the judge, the judge hand you over to the officer, and you be thrown into prison. Assuredly, I say to you, you will by no means get out of there till you have paid the last penny." Matthew 5:25-26 NKJV

We agree with truth and repent to avoid enemy torment and bondage.

As Bill utilized all these weapons, look how God moved! He demolished lies and spoke truth into Bill's heart, teaching him to confront injustice, telling him that he is forgiven and loved. God freed him from pride, shame, and fear and gave Bill peace and trust. He taught Bill in deeper measure who He is, and He restored his identity as the son of the King. He sanctified him as he repented. The victory was in Bill's own heart, and he began to realize that Satan's accusations were groundless. Additionally, the enemy was eventually silenced, because Bill no longer tolerated the abuse and manipulation.

Bill deeply understands that spiritual warfare is for his refinement – and he is on mission for the Kingdom, helping others to learn to battle to victory. He is walking out this verse:

... in no way alarmed by your opponents – which is a sign of destruction for them, but of salvation for you, and that too, from God. Philippians 1:28

The Destroyer

They have a king over them, the angel of the abyss; his name in Hebrew is Abaddon, and in the Greek he has the name Apollyon. Revelation 9:11

Abaddon is Hebrew, "the prince of the infernal regions," literally meaning "wound, destruction"[14] and "perishing."[15] Its Greek translation is **Apollyon,** "to destroy, corrupt."[16] Some scholars think this is Satan; others think this is a high ranking demon. Either way, this name reveals much about the forces of darkness.

Jesus calls Satan a **murderer from the beginning** (Jn 8:44). From Satan's first encounter with mankind in the Garden, his plan has always been to kill. He tempted Eve to eat of the forbidden tree, knowing what God had said, **"in the day that you eat from it you will surely die"** (Gen 2:17). From the beginning, the intent of this murderer has been to **steal and kill and destroy** (Jn 10:10), and his mission remains unchanged today. He cannot steal our inheritance in heaven, so he attempts to steal our peace on earth. He cannot kill our relationship with God, so he works to kill the closeness of our fellowship. He cannot destroy our position as God's child, so he tries to destroy our trust in our Heavenly Father. He works to kill us – not only spiritually, emotionally, and mentally, but also physically.

Satan specializes in wounding, and the younger we are when he wounds us, the deeper the gash will be. As we go through life, wounds on top of wounds work to prevent healing, for his aim is to distort and destroy our identity, our peace, our joy, our purpose in Christ.

Pause, Pray, and Journal

Do you have unhealed wounds from the attacks Satan has orchestrated against you? I am praying healing will come to you as your work through this study. We will learn more about the Lord's healing in Chapter 24, but for now, if you see you are in need of healing, begin to ask the Lord to bring His healing to you, and ask Him how He wants you to partner with Him in your healing.

The Tempter

And the tempter came and said to Him, "If You are the Son of God, command that these stones become bread."

Matthew 4:3

The tempter knows just what will intrigue us, beguile us, ensnare us. He knows our weaknesses and exploits them mercilessly with his temptations. Often, seemingly innocently, he'll dangle in front of us exactly what he knows will tantalize us, for the dragon with the sharp eyes has learned just how to seduce us to cross the line into sin.

We discussed in Chapter 5 the nature of his attack on our Lord: trying to cause Jesus to question His own identity. **"*If* You are the Son of God ..."** (Matt 4:3, emphasis added). Satan was trying to sow seeds of doubt, just as he did in the Garden. **"Did God *really* say ..."** (Gen 3:1 NIV, emphasis added).

The Deceiver, Disguised as an Angel of Light

Satan, the deceiver of the whole world (Rev 12:9 ESV). As deceiver he leads astray, causing people to form wrong judgments and seducing them into rebellion.[17] *Seduces.* Ponder that word.

This word deceive also includes to "err" and to "wander."[18] Notice the subtlety. Causing us to merely "wander." Yet how seriously does God take "wandering"?

You rebuke the arrogant, the cursed,
Who *wander* from Your commandments.

Psalm 119:21, emphasis added

Very seriously.

As part of his deception, **Satan disguises himself as an angel of light** (2Cor 11:14) – a striking example of Satan's perverted forgery.

The NIV translates it **masquerades**. Without discernment, we can be duped into believing that his darkness *is* light. And there is more. Listen to the whole passage:

For such men are false apostles, deceitful workers, disguising themselves as apostles of Christ. No wonder, for even Satan disguises himself as an angel of light. Therefore it is not surprising if his servants also disguise themselves as servants of righteousness, whose end will be according to their deeds. 2 Corinthians 11:13-15

Not only does Satan masquerade as an angel of light, *his servants do also.* Jesus teaches that many will come in His name and mislead many (Matt 24:5). John instructs us to test the spirits because many false prophets have gone out into the world (1Jn 4:1-3). If we are not maturing in the Lord, attuned to the Holy Spirit and abiding in Him, we are vulnerable to being deceived by Satan or his servants. Grasping the depth of this passage is critical in the war. Keep it in mind, for we will refer to it often in this book.

You met my friend Lynn in Chapter 1, the woman now glowing in the Lord who was driven to deep surrender to Him through the traumas of her life. In her younger years, Lynn was deceived by men disguising themselves as servants of righteousness. She was seeking a Christian husband, but lacked the discernment to see when someone was merely masquerading as a Christian. I'll let her explain.

I was attending church but not living as a Christian. I met a man on a Christian online chatroom who would pray for hours on the phone with me. I was certain he was a Christian. Many times I prayed and God told me to run, but I was so engrossed in my own fantasy that I ignored Him. I married this man and ended up caught up in a nightmare of lies and scams that cost me so much money.

After my divorce, I was attending church again and growing closer to God. I so wanted to be married and have a baby. I met a man who acted as though God was an important part of his life. He wanted to marry me and it felt good to be wanted. We were married five months later, but on our honeymoon he stopped attending church, stopped praying with me, and became very verbally abusive. Soon we were divorced. All I could do was cling to God.

Lynn
Florida

When Lynn met her first husband, although she knew the Lord, she was not living in obedience to Him. She was walking in the flesh, wanting her own way, and that left her prey to Satan's traps. She lacked discernment and was snared by this man masquerading as an angel of light.

When she met her second husband, she was growing in Christ but was not yet mature in the Lord, so she was still quite open to being deceived. Additionally, she was so focused on marriage and children that these had become her idols, and these idols thwarted her from hearing clearly from God. She married another ungodly man who had disguised himself as a servant of righteousness. "One thing I learned," she explained, "was that I needed to know the Bible because my second husband always changed the Scriptures when he quoted them." As Satan perverts Scripture, his servants will also. It is imperative that we know the Word, and understand it.

As Lynn has grown in the Lord, she is now more Biblically grounded, more discerning, and stronger in Him. Note how Scripture instructs us to *develop* discernment:

But solid food is for the mature, who *because of practice* have their senses trained to discern good and evil.

Hebrews 5:14, emphasis added

Belial

Do not be bound together with unbelievers; for what partnership have righteousness and lawlessness, or what fellowship has light with darkness? Or what harmony has Christ with Belial, or what has a believer in common with an unbeliever?   2 Corinthians 6:14-15

My *Word Study* books describe **Belial** as "wicked, vile, corrupt, lewd, profligate, licentious,"[19] "worthless, and destructive."[20] I looked up lewd and its synonyms and found "unrestrained or excessive indulgence of sexual desire."[21] I explored profligate and licentious and found descriptions like "utterly and shamelessly immoral," "having no moral restraints."[22] Malevolent indeed. But as I read through the passages referring to Satan as **Belial** in the Bible, even these definitions really don't fully explain the depth of twisted evil this name represents. Let's go to two of these passages to hear about the ways Satan maliciously perverts.

First Samuel 2 introduces us to Eli and his sons, who were priests serving at the tabernacle of the Lord in Shiloh. When the Israelites would come to offer a sacrifice to the Lord, Eli's sons would demand from them the meat intended for sacrifice, and then eat it themselves. If necessary, they would even **take it by force**. Eli's sons also **lay with the women who served at the doorway of the tent of meeting.** They **despised** God and had utter disregard for the things of God and the people of God (1Sam 2:16-30). Scripture calls them **sons of Belial** (1Sam 2:12 KJV).

In another passage that uses the term Belial, Judges 19, an old man offered a traveling man shelter in his home for the night. A group of men from the city demanded to have sexual relations with the traveler. The old man refused, but because the men of the city were so angry, the traveler gave them his concubine. The men of the city raped her to death. The men of the city who did this are called **sons of Belial** (Judg 19:22 KJV).

Yes, these horrific passages have Satan's fingerprints all over them.

Ponder, Pray, and Journal

Lucifer. A well-know name of Satan in the secular world – but I don't find it in my Bible. Where does this name come from?

We will finish up this chapter studying one more challenging passage. Isaiah 14 is a prophecy of Israel's release from Babylonian captivity, and the destruction of the king of Babylon. Realizing that Biblical prophecy can have dual meanings, ask the Holy Spirit to reveal to you, then read Isaiah 14:1-21 a few times. As you read, take note of anything that could indicate that this passage is describing a spiritual power and not merely an earthly king. Meet me back here when you are finished.

Lucifer

Theologians debate whether or not Isaiah 14 describes Satan. As you ponder this question yourself, consider this passage:

The seventy returned with joy, saying, "Lord, even the demons are subject to us in Your name." And He said to them, "I was watching Satan fall from heaven like lightning."

Luke 10:17-18

"I was watching Satan fall from heaven like lightning." Could it be that Jesus is seeing the downfall of Satan and his demons and is referring to this verse:

**"How you have fallen from heaven,
O star of the morning, son of dawn!"**   Isaiah 14:12

This also brings to mind the great dragon being thrown down at the end of time (Rev 12:9).

As I study Isaiah 14:1-21, it appears to me that this is not merely a historical description of an earthly king coming to a humiliating end. The king in this passage attempted to raise his throne **in the recesses of the north** where God is enthroned (Ps 48:2) and to make himself like God Most High:

> **"But you said in your heart,**
> **'I will ascend to heaven;**
> **I will raise my throne above the stars of God,**
> **And I will sit on the mount of the assembly**
> **In the recesses of the north.**
> **I will ascend above the heights of the clouds;**
> **I will make myself like God Most High."**   Isaiah 14:13-14

This king was thrust down to Sheol. He has fallen *from heaven.*

This king is called **star of the morning.** The King James translates it **Lucifer**, from the Latin: *lux* meaning light, and *ferre* meaning to bear or carry – thus "light-bearing."[23] The morning star is commonly used as a name for Venus, the brightest object in the sky (after the sun and moon). Venus appears in the eastern sky before dawn – and soon disappears in the brightness of the sun.[24] Satan may be a **star of the morning**, but *Jesus* is **the *bright* morning star** (Rev 22:16, emphasis added), infinitely more brilliant, radiant in His resplendence, life-giving in His Light:

> **"I am the Light of the world; he who follows Me will not walk in the darkness, but will have the Light of life."**   John 8:12

If we believe this passage describes Satan, we see him as the perverted counterfeit, for his "light" leads to death (Matt 6:22-23, 7:13-14, Prov 14:12). Perhaps Isaiah referring to Satan as **star of the morning** demonstrates Satan disguising himself as an angel of light, mimicking Jesus or impersonating His angels in order to dupe us. Or perhaps Satan was once a beautiful **star of the morning** but now he is fallen. I think the most striking thing about the Hebrew word translated **star of the morning** is that its root means "to shine; hence, to make a show, to boast."[25]

Ponder, Pray, and Journal

To make a show. To boast. Go back to the passage in Isaiah and note the five "I wills" that Satan said in his heart. Journal what you learn about Satan from the "I wills."

Now sit still before the Lord, and allow the Holy Spirit to show you any areas of your life that Satan has tempted you to fall into pride or self-idolatry. As the Holy Spirit reveals, take the time to repent and choose to walk in humility. Ask the Lord what to do next.

One final assignment. I found this very impacting when I worked through Kay Arthur's book, *Lord Is It Warfare? Teach Me To Stand*, and I invite you to try it: Write out five "I wills" that you desire to live out in your own life. Let them be a counterattack against the enemy's "I wills."[26]

Think about how this passage may be describing Satan's end, and ponder these verses:

And it will be in the day when the LORD gives you rest from your pain and turmoil and harsh service in which you have been enslaved ... the whole earth is at rest and is quiet ...
Isaiah 14:3,7

I am thinking of the time when the devil will be thrown into the lake of fire, the time of the new heaven and the new earth, when God will wipe every tear from our eyes and there will no longer be any death, or mourning, or crying, or pain (Rev 20:10, 21:1,4), for He indeed has compassion on us.

Ponder, Pray, and Journal

Go back over this last set of names and journal what you have learned about Satan's character, plans, and tactics.

Are you beginning to comprehend with greater gravity the seriousness of the war? Satan is not playing games. He is out to steal, kill, and destroy. Spiritually, mentally, emotionally, physically.

But Are My Personal Troubles *Really* Caused by Satan?

We have spent the past two chapters studying our enemy, and you may be wondering, When it comes to my own struggles and trials on this earth, are they *really* spiritual warfare? Let's slow down and ponder this a bit.

Jesus declared that we would have trouble on earth – God's once perfect world now shattered by sin. We know deep in our hearts that God is sovereign, and overall we know that our misfortunes, calamities, suffering, pain, illnesses, and wounds are because we live in a fallen world that lies in the power of the evil one (Jn 16:33, Gen 1-3, Rom 8:20-22, 1Jn 5:19). Yet there is more to it than that.

Sometimes, our suffering and pain is a consequence of our own sins. Sometimes, our pain is due to the impact of the sins of others. Sometimes, we are led astray because we have not disciplined ourselves to immerse in and obey His Word. Sometimes, our illnesses are the result of germs and infections that are part of this fallen world. Sometimes, our physical pain is because this is not our real home, and outwardly we are wasting away. Sometimes, our pain is so that the works of God may be displayed in us. And other times, forces of darkness could be directly or indirectly involved in our troubles. (Ps 119:67, Heb 12:15, Jn 14:23, Mk 16:17-18, Heb 11:13, Phil 3:20, 2Cor 4:16, Jn 9:3, Lk 13:11, Mk 9:17-27.)

For me, it seems to take much practice to have my senses trained in discernment to know when demonic forces are involved. Sometimes I think it's a spiritual battle when it's really not, and other times I don't realize it's a spiritual battle when it really is. Sometimes, I miss the reality that I was just in a spiritual battle until I have fought the spiritual forces of evil in the heavenly realms with weapons of the flesh, and lost. Other times, I discover after a battle that I was simply dealing with this fallen world, and had been shadow boxing with a suspected enemy who proved to be nowhere around.

As we studied in earlier chapters, many of our spiritual battles against the flesh and the world can be won by fleeing, obeying, repenting, surrendering, being filled with the Spirit and walking in Him. By disciplining ourselves to read the Word *and do it*. By worshiping and praying and connecting in church and in Christian community. By crucifying our fleshly desires and learning how to be led by the Spirit and not by the flesh.

But if we are caught in addictions or strongholds or bondage or besetting sins, or if we cannot shut down ungodly thoughts, or if we are walking closely with the Lord and there is still an area of our lives where victory seems elusive, where we repeatedly fail to walk righteously – we may be up against forces of darkness. Demons may have conspired with the world and with our flesh in order to manipulate our thought processes, influence our wills, and seduce our hearts.

My friend Myriam is a woman with a heart brimming with compassion, eyes full of sparkles, and a smile as bright as the sun. But it wasn't always that way for her. Her eyes used to hold a sadness so profound it seemed she was drowning in it. You will hear more of her testimony in an upcoming chapter, but for now, I want you to see her real life example of why, despite her relationship with Christ, victory eluded her.

I had angry outbursts with everyone I loved. I hated them. I was convinced <u>they</u> were the problem. I belittled them. I tormented them

Then I would apologize, receive their forgiveness – and then do it all over again. And again and again and again for over fifteen years. I was hateful and vengeful and absolutely out of my mind. I ran to God. I pleaded. I studied. I prayed. I begged Him to take this anger from me.

*As I grew in the Lord, my spirit knew it was wrong to be this way, and I did not want to do these things, but my flesh continued to do the same sins over and over again. There were demons oppressing me, and my flesh would not, could not, change. **"The spirit is willing, but the flesh is weak"** (Matt 26:41). I needed help, I just didn't know it yet.*

Myriam DeSantis
Jupiter, Florida

Myriam had a relationship with Jesus. She was studying the Word and going to church and praying. She was begging God to take this anger away. At first, she did not know that demons had teamed up with her flesh and trapped her in these vicious cycles of anger and hatred. There is a breathtaking victory to this story, and I'll invite her back to share later in this book. But for now, I just want you to see what it may look like when demons capitalize on our fleshly sins.

In the next chapter, we will explore *to what extent* demonic forces can attack or influence us. Let us pray for discernment, and seek the Lord for His victory, knowing, believing, trusting, that Jesus has come to set the captives free. Let's end this chapter in prayer.

Lord God, You alone are a Defense for the helpless, a Defense for the needy in time of distress. We are powerless ourselves – but Satan is no match for You. Your power is infinite, Your presence is indomitable, Your wisdom is inscrutable. We run to You, our Refuge from the enemy's oncoming storm, our Shade from the enemy's blistering heat.

The enemy breathes out violence against us like a hurricane against a wall. But we hide not behind any ordinary wall, but in the Fortress of the Creator of the Universe. The breath of the ruthless is like heat pressing down in the desert; but Your oasis of Living Water subdues their uproar. You dissipate the relentless heat of the enemy like a cloud bringing shade, and as Your presence arrives, the song of the ruthless is silenced. Hallelujah! Amen.[27]

Chapter 8
Levels of Demonic Activity

*A*s I read the Word, I see that demonic forces can attack and influence people to varying extent. I have found it helpful to envision demonic activity as arranged into what I think of as different *levels* of depth. Although there may be some overlap, making some distinctions into different levels helps me personally by giving me a framework to grasp the extent of their influence. The words we will be using to conceptualize these levels come from the Scriptures.

In this chapter, I have stratified demonic activity into three levels, using words and passages directly from Scripture. Here are the three levels we will discuss, starting with the more superficial levels of attack, and moving into more penetrating levels of access:

- *Level 1: Flaming arrows.* These are attacks from a distance. We see in the Word descriptions such as temptation, seduction, opposition, hindrance, and harassment.

- *Level 2: Access.* In this level, we have opened the door for the enemy to begin influencing or impacting. We have fallen into sin, and a line has been crossed. We see in the Word descriptions such as outwitting us, taking advantage of us, sifting us, and holding us captive. We also see oppression, bondage, and torment to describe this level.

- *Level 3: Domination.* This is complete control by Satan or his demons. Some would refer to this as "demon possession."

I'd like to pause a moment and address "demon-possession." I agree with many theologians who believe that a born-again Christian *cannot* be "demon-possessed." Let's talk about two reasons why.

Possession Implies Ownership

Since born-again Christians belong to the Lord Jesus Christ, we cannot be *owned* by Satan. Born-again Christians have become *God's own possession:*

For He rescued from the domain of darkness, and transferred to the kingdom of His beloved Son, in whom we have redemption, the forgiveness of sins. Colossians 1:13-14

But you are a chosen people, a royal priesthood, a holy nation, *God's special possession*, that you may declare the praises of him who called you out of darkness into his wonderful light. 1 Peter 2:9 NIV, emphasis added

But if anyone does not have the Spirit of Christ, he does not belong to Him. Romans 8:9

The Word describes how Satan and his demons can possess a *non-Christian* (for example, the man with the legion of demons in Mark 5:1-20), but since a born-again Christian is God's possession, *Satan cannot possess us.* Satan can tempt and seduce, attack and sift like wheat, torment and oppress and even exert a *level of influence* on a born-again Christian, but Satan and his demons cannot *possess* a born-again Christian.

Possession Implies <u>Complete</u> Control

Another way to understand "possession" is *complete control.* This may be called total mental, emotional, physical, and spiritual *domination.* The man in Mark 5 whom a legion of demons had entered is a Biblical example of possession, or domination (Matt 8:28-34, Mk 5:1-20, Lk 8:26-39).

But a born-again Christian is a temple of the Holy Spirit. Christ dwells in our hearts through faith, and the love of God is poured out within our hearts through the Holy Spirit who was given to us. The Holy Spirit as rivers of living water flows from our innermost being. The sons of God are led by the Spirit of God. (1Cor 6:19, Eph 3:16-17, Rom 5:5, Jn 7:38-39, Rom 8:14.)

Satan and his demons can dominate a non-Christian, but since the Holy Spirit lives inside a born-again Christian, Satan cannot dominate us. Again, Satan can tempt, seduce, attack, sift like wheat, torment, oppress, and even exert a *level of influence* on a born-again Christian, but Satan and his demons cannot *dominate, possess,* or *completely control* a born-again Christian.

With that understanding clarified, let's consider each level. Got your armor on? Let's go.

Level 1: Flaming Arrows

... in addition to all, taking up the shield of faith with which you will be able to extinguish all the *flaming arrows* of the evil one ...   Ephesians 6:16, emphasis added

In my understanding, flaming arrows are an attack from afar. The enemy may have noticed that we are intensifying our spiritual disciplines or stepping out in Kingdom work. He may try to resist the Kingdom's advancement with a flaming missile aimed to cause fear or to disrupt God's plan. We may be attacked with a single flaming arrow, or harassed by many and repeated arrows in an attempt to distract us and to derail God's Kingdom work. These arrows, although they come from afar, can be searing and painful as they pierce our lives and our hearts.

These flaming arrows may come from situations outside of our control, perhaps a sharp criticism by a friend, a loss of job when our company folds, a medical diagnosis, a wayward child, a spouse's betrayal. These are tactics Satan may use to try to wound us and drive us to places of unforgiveness, worry, fear, confusion, or perhaps anger at God.

These flaming arrows can also come in the form of *temptations*. The enemy has studied mankind for millennia, and us individually for decades, and with his keen eye he is an expert at selecting the most enticing traps. The Biblical word *seduce* underscores the deviousness, subtleness, cunning, and craftiness of the enemy as he tries to lure and entrap.

Now the Spirit speaketh expressly, that in the latter times some shall depart from the faith, giving heed to seducing spirits, and doctrines of devils. 1 Timothy 4:1 KJV

Seduce, *planao* in the Greek, means "go astray, deceive, err, seduce, wander ... to cause to roam from safety, truth, or virtue."[1] This word is translated *lead astray* or *deceive* in the NASB, but I think the KJV translation as *seduce* underscores the way demons deceive with sneaky underhanded schemes. It emphasizes how closely they study us in order to allure and beguile. Remember what we studied in the last chapter about Eve. The serpent does not *force* us, but *entices* us to go astray (Gen 3:13, 2Cor 11:3 KJV). And note also from this passage in First Timothy that there is a *spirit* of seduction or a *spirit* of deception.

Additional flaming arrows may be opposition, hindrance, and harassment, which may come as an isolated flaming arrow or a volley of arrows. As we are pressing in to advance the Kingdom, Satan pushes back. This could take the form of continued distractions such as physical illness, dissensions at work, financial crises, or relationship strife. This move of the enemy is *resistance* to the work of the Lord and an attack upon our commitment to Him. Satan may attempt to thwart us, distract us, harass us, wear us down physically or emotionally, exhaust us mentally, throw up stumbling blocks, confuse us, destroy our identity, flood us with doubts, or burn us out so that we simply give up. And he often uses the world and the people in it to accomplish his task.

Acts 13 describes a time of enemy opposition to Barnabas and Saul (Paul) as they brought the gospel to Salamis. Elymas the **magician, a Jewish false prophet,** was hindering them.

This man [the proconsul] **summoned Barnabas and Saul and sought to hear the word of God. But Elymas the magician (for so his name is translated) was** *opposing* **them, seeking to turn the proconsul away from the faith.**

Acts 13:7-8, emphasis added

This passage goes on to describe how Paul, filled with the Holy Spirit, declared that the hand of the Lord would blind Elymas, this "son of the devil." As Elymas was blinded, Satan's opposition lifted, and the proconsul came to believe in Jesus (Acts 13:9-12).

In another passage, Paul described a time when he felt strongly that he was to return to Thessalonica to encourage these believers who were under great persecution, yet Satan opposed him.

For we wanted to come to you – I, more than once – and yet Satan *hindered* **us.** 1 Thessalonians 2:18, emphasis added

This word **hindered** in the Greek literally means "to cut down, to strike."[2] This is strong enemy opposition, impeding the advancement of the Kingdom. Whether it is advancement of the Kingdom in our own hearts, or others' hearts, don't be surprised when you encounter hindrance. And when we are advancing the Kingdom by operating in our unique talents, our spiritual gifts, or the sharing of our testimony, expect wicked resistance.

To help us understand how enemy resistance may feel to us, I have asked my friend Kolleen to share a few details about some battles she has faced. Kolleen is a high-powered attorney who is also a mighty prayer warrior with a passionate relationship with Jesus. As part of her daily routine, she prays as she walks her dogs, then fills herself with Jesus as she runs to praise music, and then spends time listening for His still small voice as she immerses in the Word and journals.

A few years ago, Kolleen was about to dive deeply into a heavy Bible study, and she was poised for much freedom and deliverance. It seems the enemy knew that more than she did. Come listen to this story of enemy opposition.

As I entered the first night of Triumph Over Suffering Class, my emotions churned within me, my heart was racing, I was drenched with sweat, and my head was about to explode. I almost didn't make it to class. As I opened up and shared my pain with the class, somehow, chains were broken like I'd never experienced before, and peace came over me physically. Nothing about my situation had changed, but my heart and perspective had. At that moment, a great weight was lifted off my shoulders, and I no longer felt overwhelmed by my circumstances. I had walked into class consumed with grief, anger, and devastation over my divorce. However, in one instant God took all those feelings from me. I no longer railed against God; I acknowledged that He was sovereign and that He had handpicked my trials, preparing me for greater things and to advance His Kingdom. What a breakthrough! For the first time I was experiencing true freedom in Christ's love for me.

Kolleen Bannon
Triumph Prayer Team
Jupiter, Florida

Honestly sharing her pain with the class invited the Lord to break the bonds of grief, anger, and devastation. Her transparency brought dark things into the Light, and the demons who were resisting her physically, emotionally, and mentally were forced to flee. Yet the battle wasn't finished yet.

The next few weeks were filled with a lot of deep heart work and time spent with God. I had committed to rid my life of as many distractions as possible in order to focus on the class, to grow my relationship with God, and to work towards healing my battered heart. And it was working! I had never before experienced such peace and love in my heart – but one night that peace was shattered. The enemy surely did not want me joining class that night, for I was under attack again.

I walked into the meeting feeling a very strong and irrational sense of anger. I felt resistant to everything I'd come to love about our meeting time: the praise music, the time of sharing. My body felt under attack: my palms were burning up and sweating, my head felt like it was in a vice grip, my neck hurt severely. My body was fidgety and I felt such a sense of unease that I couldn't sit still.

I was angry, furious! Angry that I was still fighting against the same things I'd been fighting against for years – and I wasn't seeing any change. I was sad that I'd lost so much time with my kids because of the timesharing arrangement with their father. Every time I had to say goodbye to them was brutal and painful. My heart gets ripped out of my body every single time.

When it was my turn to share, I wasn't sure I could speak, and I felt like I had no control over what I was going to say. But I opened my mouth and the words came out, words of anger and disappointment. The leader listened compassionately, and suggested that I tell God how I was feeling. She reminded me that He already knew my thoughts, so it wasn't very helpful to attempt to hide those feelings from Him.

I carried these troubled and angry thoughts through the night and into the next morning. Still, I continued my routine of praying during my morning walk with the dogs, and I played praise music during my morning run. It helped, but I was still distracted, still angry. So finally,

I did what the leader had recommended: I sat down at my computer and wrote a letter to God. I let Him know everything that I was feeling, I let the anger pour out of my mind and onto the computer screen, all to God. As I was writing my feelings to Him, the tears started to come. I had spent much of the past three years crying – and I do not like crying! It usually leaves me feeling exhausted and drained – but this time it was different. I hadn't shed a tear since beginning the class, but now the tears ran down my face, and I could feel God's comforting presence. I heard Him tell me in my heart that He knew what I was feeling and that He was holding me in His arms. What a feeling of comfort! Writing that letter with complete transparency before God had somehow opened me up to His comfort and released whatever hold had been gripping me over the past few days. I left my time of tears not feeling exhausted or drained, but energized and ready to face the challenges ahead of me, with God by my side!

From my perspective today, I think both these times the enemy somehow knew that I was on the cusp of finding true freedom. He had attacked me physically, emotionally, and mentally, doing his best to keep that from happening.

Our God is so good and He promises that no weapon formed against us will prosper. After staying faithful and fully surrendering to His will time and again, month after month, God answered my prayers! The fight has turned to peace and my sadness to joy. As only God can, He has healed the areas of my heart that I once believed were beyond healing.

Kolleen Bannon
Triumph Prayer Team
Jupiter, Florida

Observe Kolleen's obedience that led to victory. She didn't know deliverance was imminent, but despite the vicious resistance, she still came to class. She opened her heart to the women during the first class, she brought her pain and struggles and sin into the Light, and she was freed. Weeks later, she opened her heart to the Lord and poured out her soul to Him – and He responded by breaking the chains that were entrapping her, speaking comfort deeply to her troubled heart, and encircling her with His tenderness and love. And as she has persevered in her journey of surrender, the Lord has touched her with the deepest of healing.

> **"I know that You can do all things,**
> **And that no purpose of Yours can be thwarted."**   Job 42:2

Do you wonder how the demons knew more than Kolleen did that the Lord was moving and a battle was imminent? I wonder too. I have heard it said that the demons don't really know, but they leap into action when they see God's angels lining up for battle!

Ponder, Pray, and Journal

Does reading Kolleen's testimony bring to mind any times you have encountered enemy resistance? Ask the Holy Spirit to give you new spiritual revelation of these battles.

We're going to take this up a notch and seek to comprehend the difference between enemy *resistance*, and Holy Spirit *restraint*.

The Holy Spirit's Restraint

This discussion is going to require *discernment*. We will compare the passage from First Thessalonians where we saw Satan thwarting Paul from his ministry work, to a somewhat comparable event in Acts.

Watch closely, though. Although the *resistance* in both these passages appears very similar, the cause and the outcome are vastly different.

In Acts 16, Paul is on his second missionary journey. He and his companions had preached in the cities of Derbe and Lystra in the region of Galatia. Hear what happens next.

They passed through the Phrygian and Galatian region, having been forbidden by the Holy Spirit to speak the word in Asia; and after they came to Mysia, they were trying to go into Bithynia, and the Spirit of Jesus did not permit them.

Acts 16:6-7

Forbidden in the Greek means "to cut off, weaken, and hence generally hinder, prevent, restrain."[3] This word is a synonym for the Greek word for **hindered** in First Thessalonians that we discussed earlier in the chapter. **Did not permit** in this passage above is another parallel word.[4]

Hmmm ... The roadblocks set up by the Holy Spirit and the hindrances established by Satan may feel pretty similar. How will we know when it is the Holy Spirit restraining us, and when it is Satan opposing us? This will indeed require much discernment, prayer, and listening. Sometimes, we may not know that it is the Holy Spirit until much later. Sometimes, it really is Satan resisting, but God is using Satan's hindrances for *His* own purposes. Let's continue the passage in Acts 16 to see how this played out.

A vision appeared to Paul in the night: a man of Macedonia was standing and appealing to him, and saying, "Come over to Macedonia and help us." When he had seen the vision, immediately we sought to go into Macedonia, concluding that God had called us to preach the gospel to them.   Acts 16:9-10

As Paul and his companions entered Europe, the gospel exploded in Philippi, Thessalonica, Corinth.

Let's see a modern day parallel. There was a time over fifteen years ago that my husband and I thought we were battling enemy resistance

– but it was actually the Holy Spirit's restraint. I invite you to hear this humbling story.

I had felt that God had given me a heart for Africa for many years. But my husband John did not feel led to go, and God just didn't seem to be opening the door. I waited and prayed and cried and prayed some more, asking, constantly asking, for Him to open that door.

After five years of asking, it seemed that God unlocked the door and threw it open wide. My husband, an Ear, Nose, and Throat surgeon, was invited to be the keynote speaker at a Conference in Nigeria, Africa, and he invited me to come with him. I was sure it was a message from God. It was time.

Over the next six months, I prayed and fasted and worked with my church to network. I also worked to connect with some missionary organizations in Nigeria. I managed to make some tentative connections. As the time drew near to leave, I felt a bit uneasy about having no particular plan. Since I really like to have things planned out, I thought perhaps God was growing my trust in Him. At one point, in a desperate prayer time, God reassured me, "My powerful hand is upon you."

John and I arrived at the airport check-in, and our trip ended before it even began. Why were we not allowed to board the plane? The simple answer was that our visas were not in order. But at that moment, the only thing I was sure of was that it was <u>God</u>.

John spent the next two hours calling Nigeria, the ambassadors, the WHO, but no visas could be produced. God's powerful hand was upon me, all right, holding us in Florida. Deep in my heart I knew there was no way we were getting past God.

I accepted immediately that He had put a stop to our trip. But what I did not initially accept was the <u>way</u> He stopped us. I was angry. If He wasn't going to let us go, couldn't He have stopped us a month ago? A week ago? Even the day before? It took a full day for me to realize my sinfulness, and surrender not only to His plan, but to also surrender to <u>how</u> He chose to accomplish His plan.

At the moment God stopped us from boarding that plane, my entire relationship with Him was turned upside down. I had <u>thought</u> I knew how to hear His voice. I <u>thought</u> I knew what He wanted and what my purpose was in His Kingdom plan. But now, I knew nothing. <u>Every time</u> that I thought I had heard His voice over the past five years since I had come to know Him, now needed to be re-evaluated. <u>Everything</u> I ever thought I knew about God was thrown into question. My life hung in the balance. Somehow, I had no idea how, I had built my house on the sand, and when the rain fell, and the floods came, and the winds blew and slammed against that house, it fell—and great was its fall (Mt 7:27).

I had already had the time off from work, so I used this time to really press in to God. Surprisingly, He took me to Balaam's story in Numbers. To recap, the Moabites asked Balaam to curse the Israelites. Balaam asked God, and God said no, so Balaam declined. The Moabites returned soon with the same question. Balaam told them he'd check with God again. This time, God told him to **"rise up and go with them."** *But two verses later, we see that* **God was angry with him for going, because his way was contrary to God's.** *So an angel of the Lord blocked his path – first in a field, then in a narrow path in a vineyard, and finally* **in a narrow place where there was no way to turn to the right hand or the left** *(Num 22:20, 22, 32, 26).*

As I was reading and re-reading this passage, God spoke in the quietest of whispers into my heart: "You are Balaam. I stopped you at the ticket counter, that narrow place where there was no way to turn to the right hand or to the left, because your way was contrary to Me."

Contrary to Me? Hadn't God set my heart on fire for Africa, locked the door for years, and then opened it? Hadn't He sent me? I wasn't sure I wanted to hear what was coming next, but I so desperately wanted Him to tell me how I had heard wrong. He spoke ever so quietly, graciously enlightening me.

Like Balaam, God had told me no. Like Balaam, I went back and asked again. Again and again. I had pestered God repeatedly to let me go to Africa, and although my way was contrary to His, God finally said to me, "You want to go? Then go." It is only because of His mercy that He stopped me in the narrow way where I could not turn to the right hand or to the left. **"Your way is contrary to Me."** *It is only because of His mercy that He did not kill me (Num 22:33).*

Celeste Li
Jupiter, Florida

Discerning if a roadblock is Satan's resistance or Holy Spirit's restraint may require a deep seeking of the Lord. I do not think that I would have received so much revelation if I did not utilize my already scheduled time off to seek God with all my heart.

Before we move into the next level, I'd like to take us to a passage about Paul's *harassment.*

So to keep me from becoming conceited because of the surpassing greatness of the revelations, a thorn was given me in the flesh, a messenger of Satan, to harass me, to keep me from becoming conceited. 2 Corinthians 12:7 ESV

I have chosen the ESV translation so we can see the word **harass.** This word in the Greek is *kolaphizo,* which means "to strike with the fist, to buffet."[5] The NKJV translates it **buffet** – that give us a great word picture. (Although the NIV and NASB use **torment,** *kolaphizo* is different than the word we will see translated **tormentors** or **torturers** later on in this chapter when we discuss bondage.)

In this passage, Paul goes on to explain that he asked the Lord to remove this harassment, but the Lord's answer was, **"My grace is sufficient for you, for my power is made perfect in weakness"** (2Cor 12:9 ESV). Paul concluded that surrendering, yielding himself, invited Christ's power to rest upon him. Because of his humility, it would be Christ's power at work, not his own strength:

Therefore I will boast all the more gladly of my weaknesses, so that the power of Christ may rest upon me. For the sake of Christ, then, I am content with weaknesses, insults, hardships, persecutions, and calamities. For when I am weak, then I am strong. 2 Corinthians 12:9-10 ESV

It seems the harassment involved a buffeting of weaknesses, insults, hardships, persecutions, and calamities. Notice there is something going on here that is more than simply resistance to Kingdom advancement. God used this messenger of Satan *to keep Paul from becoming conceited.* Not *because* he was conceited, but to *prevent* his fall into pride. As we discussed in Chapter 1, Satan will always be God's servant, unwittingly serving Him and furthering His plan (Gen 50:20, Col 1:16).

Warfare that we have been discussing so far, flaming arrows, temptations, opposition, hindrance, and harassment are all attacks from a distance. *Satan and his demons are on assignment:* to steal, kill and destroy (Jn 10:10). So even if we want nothing to do with taking enemy territory, even if we are running away from any offensive battle, even if we desire to be civilians instead of soldiers in active duty, we will not escape this kind of enemy attack.

Indeed, all who desire to live godly in Christ Jesus *will be* persecuted.   2 Timothy 3:12, emphasis added

As always, remember that God is in full control, and nothing can enter our lives without His permission, for His good purposes.

Recognize also that *temptation does not mean sin.* As we studied in Chapter 5, our sinless holy Savior was **tempted** in the wilderness (Matt 4:1-11). It is when we *fall* to the temptation, when we *give in* to the seduction, that we have sinned. A line is then crossed, and that fall can open a door for the enemy to begin *influencing* and *accessing.*

Before we move into this next level, I want to re-iterate that I do not believe a born-again Christian can be possessed, dominated, or completely controlled by Satan or his demons. Because we belong to the Lord Jesus Christ and the Holy Spirit resides in us, we cannot be *owned, possessed, dominated,* or *completely controlled* by Satan or his demons.

However, although they cannot completely control us, Satan and his demons *can* attack and tempt and seduce and sift and torment and even exert a *level of influence* on a born-again Christian. In this next section we will study how *deeply* they can affect us, how much *influence* they can have. Biblically speaking, enemy access can occur when we *give the devil a place*. Let's explore what that means.

Ponder, Pray, and Journal

Read Ephesians 4:17-32 in NKJV. Note this is written to born-again Christians. Meet me back here when you are finished.

Giving Place to the Devil

… nor give *place* to the devil.

Ephesians 4:27 NKJV, emphasis added

The word **place**, or **foothold** in the NIV, **opportunity** in the NASB, is the Greek word *topos*; our word "topography" comes from this word. Let's scrutinize some of the definitions in my *Greek Word Study*.[6]

- "A place … as occupied or filled by any person or thing, a spot, space, room."
- "To give place to someone means to make room."
- "Figuratively, place, opportunity, occasion."
- "A place in which one dwells, sojourns, or belongs; a dwelling place, abode, home."
- "In a geographical or topographical sense, a place or part of a country."
- "An inhabited place, a city, village, quarter."
- "A tract of country as a district, region, desert place."

Theologians debate precisely where this **place** is and exactly what this word means, but the important lesson for us is that it seems the devil and his demons can create some type of spiritual influence; they can establish a means of impacting, of spiritually accessing – and they are able to do this when we, by our sins, **give** them that foothold.

Now don't miss this. The Greek translation for that word **give** in this verse means "to give of one's own accord and with good will."[7] This is very grave. We **give** Satan a foothold *voluntarily* and *with good will*. I think giving with good will means that we are aligning ourselves with Satan. It is our sin that demonstrates that we have aligned ourselves with him, that we are *in agreement* with him. And that opens us up to access and influence as we give him a place.

Satan and his demons are fighting fiercely for a place of access or influence in our hearts. But God has another plan. When we are seeking the direction *of the Holy Spirit* and desire to be led by Him, when we obey our Lord Jesus Christ and walk in His ways, *we give place to the Spirit.*

Jesus answered and said to him, "If anyone loves Me, he will keep My word; and My Father will love him, and We will come to him and *make Our abode* with him."

John 14:23, emphasis added

Abode, *mone* in the Greek, translated **home** in the NIV and **dwelling place** in the AMP, is defined in my Greek *Word Study* as "a mansion, habitation, abode."[8] It seems to me that God's word choices here, *topos* and *mone*, are quite intentional. *Topos* seems like Satan's cheap counterfeit to the Lord's *mone*. Let's go to Ephesians and Galatians to see just where God establishes His home in us.

... that He would grant you, according to the riches of His glory, to be strengthened with power through His Spirit in the inner man, *so that Christ may dwell in your hearts* through faith; and that you, being rooted and grounded in love, may be able to comprehend with all the saints what is the breadth and length and height and depth, and to know

the love of Christ which surpasses knowledge, *that you may be filled up to all the fullness of God.*

Ephesians 3:16-17, emphasis added

The Greek word translated **dwell** in this passage means "a certain, fixed and durable dwelling."[9] Christ *dwells* in our hearts.

Because you are sons, God has sent forth the Spirit of His Son *into our hearts*, crying, "Abba! Father!"

Galatians 4:6, emphasis added

When we are born again, Jesus Christ by His Holy Spirit makes His **abode** *in our hearts*. Jesus, His Holy Spirit, takes up residence and establishes a fixed and durable dwelling place there, making Himself at home. Then, each time we come to a greater surrender to Him, we invite Him to exert greater influence. We decrease, and He increases (Jn 3:30). We entreat Him to expand His home in our hearts, as we discussed in Chapter 2, that we **may be filled up to all the fullness of God.**

Remember our analogy in *Triumph of Surrender* how the Holy Spirit desires to flow through us unimpeded, and when we remove the rocks hindering Him, we give Him access and freedom to flow.[10] When we are led by the Spirit, we allow Him to guide our thoughts, plans, and actions. The more we surrender our hearts and lives to His control, the more He will influence all those outflows of our heart. The more we rely on the Holy Spirit to enable us to align our beliefs with the truth of His Word, the more we feed our spirit, the greater His degree of influence upon our lives will be, and the more we will become like Him, conformed to His image.

Satan could not influence Jesus. He had no access – because Jesus was completely sinless (Heb 4:15). There was no darkness in Him, no foothold for the enemy. *Satan could not even penetrate.* God's goal for us is Christlikeness (Rom 8:28): no darkness, only Light in our hearts (Lk 11:36).

Ponder, Pray, and Journal

This concept of spiritual *place* is important for engaging the enemy. Go back and re-read the last section, and journal about this spiritual place in your own words.

Ask the Holy Spirit to show you if you have given the enemy any footholds. Then meet me back here, because I've got an important question for us to address right now.

Can a Born-Again Christian "Have" a Demon?

Certainly a non-Christian can "have" a demon. But can a born-again Christian "have" a demon?

We can easily see how even a born-again Christian can fall into temptations or suffer hindrances. And we already discussed that a born-again Christian cannot be owned, possessed, dominated, or completely controlled by Satan or his demons. But can a born-again Christian be *influenced*? What kind of *access* to a born-again Christian can a demon have?

Discipleship trainer and apologist Dr. Karl Payne, in his book *Spiritual Warfare: Christians, Demonization, and Deliverance,* provides a helpful analogy.[11] He talks about swimming with leeches, which can attach themselves to the outside of our bodies and suck out our life blood. They attach to the *outside* and affect the *inside*. In a parallel way, Dr. Payne explains, if we give demons a place, an opportunity, they may, from the outside, affect the inside. They can suck out our ability to serve Jesus effectively, they can suck out our peace and joy, they can suck out our determination to obey the Lord – until we repent of our sins that gave them access and exercise our authority to remove them.

Can a born-again Christian be *both* Holy Spirit-filled *and* demon-influenced *simultaneously?* Dr. Payne gives another helpful analogy.[12] He describes a house whose owner has given authority to his landlord to maintain the house. If the landlord decides to rent out rooms to renters who are evil and who destroy the rooms they have rented, this does not change *ownership* of the house. The landlord has the authority and responsibility to remove a bad renter, but if he fails to take responsibility and exercise his authority, the bad renter may begin to take over other rooms of the house.

When Jesus becomes our Savior, He is our rightful owner because He paid the debts held against our house. He desires full submission, complete control of every room in our house – but He has given us the free will privilege and responsibility as landlord to choose to give Him control of each room, or not. As landlords, stewards, we have the authority and ability to rent out rooms, to allow other forces to influence or access those rooms – and the only rooms for rent are those not submitted to Christ's control. Rooms we have rented to demons, where we have allowed demons to exert influence, do not jeopardize our salvation because they do not determine who *owns* the house, but they do limit our connection to Christ and the effectiveness of our ministry.

Once we have given demons permission to rent one room by refusing to submit it to Christ, they may attempt to access other rooms, and even invite other demons to move in with them. Jesus, however, remains the owner of the house, and fills the rooms we have submitted to Him. As landlords, we have been given authority in Christ to evict bad renters. If we do not, the owner of the house may decrease our responsibilities and give us fewer opportunities for Kingdom work.

Don't get hung up on this **place**, trying to figure out if it is a physical place as well as a spiritual **place**. Theologians worldwide debate this. It is enough to know that there exists a spiritual place, and by our sins, by our alignment with the ways of Satan, we invite demonic forces to influence or access from that **foothold**. Let's now move into the next level and discuss what may occur when we have given demons that foothold.

Level 2: Access

If we fall to Satan's seduction, by our sin we **give** the devil a **foothold**, a **place**, an **opportunity** (Eph 4:27), which allows him a measure of leverage and connection. If we continue with our analogy from Chapter 2 and consider the ultimate battlefield to be in our hearts, we can imagine him gaining a spiritual foothold, a place of *influence*, in the territory of our hearts. As we discussed in Chapter 2, that foothold allows the enemy a measure of influence upon the *outflow* of our hearts – our words and behaviors, our mind and our thoughts, our beliefs and moral compass and conscience, our desires and emotions, our intentions and plans, our obedience and will. Although our intent may be to walk in righteousness, the enemy can now use that foothold of influence to derail our good intentions.

Yes, we have the Spirit of God within us. As born-again believers, we can choose to walk in the flesh, or in the Spirit (Gal 5:16). As we yield to Holy Spirit's control, we will be led by Him. But if we yield to our sinful nature, if we do not obey God's laws, we are *not* being led by the Spirit. We are in rebellion against God; we are aligning our beliefs with Satan and giving him a place. As we discussed in Chapter 6, once Satan and his demons have entered the door we have opened to them, they can team up with our flesh. Our struggle with the flesh can then become a struggle with demonic forces (Eph 6:12, 2Cor 10:3, Jas 4:7). It seems that Satan deftly and shamelessly utilizes our uncrucified sinful flesh as his beachhead to gain greater access and influence. Our continual, habitual, unrepented sins give more spiritual territory to Satan, and he can then expand his territory beyond a mere foothold. As Jesus said, **".... Everyone who practices sin habitually is a slave of sin"** (Jn 8:34 AMP).

Ponder, Pray, and Journal

In a born-again believer, how extensive can that influence be? Read Matthew 18:21-35. Note carefully whom Jesus is addressing. Meet me back here when you are finished.

Let's discuss the deeper enemy influence of torment, oppression, and bondage.

Torment

Note that Jesus teaches *Peter*:

"And his lord, moved with anger, handed him over to the torturers until he should repay all that was owed him. *My heavenly Father will also do the same to you,* **if each of you does not forgive his brother from your heart."**

Matthew 18:34-35, emphasis added

Clearly, Christians can be not merely *influenced* by demons, but even *held in prison and tortured*. **Torturers**, or **tormentors**, in the King James. This word in the Greek simply means "one who applies torture."[13] This parable teaches us that, Christian or not, unforgiveness will hold us in bondage, will lock us in a dungeon, will open us to torturers. Unforgiveness invites demons to terrorize, torture, and torment. Romans shows us specifically that there is a spirit of slavery, or spirit of bondage (Rom 8:15 NASB, NKJV).

In another passage, we see that *Christians* are warned not to allow themselves to be taken captive:

Therefore as you have received Christ Jesus the Lord, so walk in Him ... See to it that no one *takes you captive* through philosophy and empty deception, according to the tradition of men, according to the elementary principles of the world, rather than according to Christ.   Colossians 2:6,8, emphasis added

Oppression

Another word we read in Scripture that I think is similar to this type of enemy torment is **oppression.** Jesus came to **proclaim release to the captives** and to **set free those who are oppressed** (Lk 4:18):

"You know of Jesus of Nazareth, how God anointed Him with the Holy Spirit and with power, and how He went about doing good and healing all who were *oppressed by the devil,* for God was with Him."   Acts 10:38, emphasis added

Oppression is cruel, unjust, or excessive exercise of power. It also includes a sense of being weighed down in body or mind.[14]

Francis Frangipane, pastor and international teacher of church leaders, expounds on demonic oppression:

> ... Christians can be *oppressed* by demons, which can occupy unregenerated thought systems [strongholds of lies we believe] ... The thought, "I cannot have a demon because I am a Christian," is simply untrue. A demon cannot have you in an eternal, possessive sense, but *you can have a demon* if you refuse to repent of your sympathetic thoughts toward evil. Your rebellion toward God provides a place for the devil in your life.[15]

Bondage

My friend Carol is a woman of tenderness and compassion. With a Masters in Biblical Studies, this *Triumph* leader does not shy away from speaking truth when the Holy Spirit leads. However, Carol admits that years ago she was trapped in a prison of unforgiveness. The Bible uses such words as **captives, slavery, enslaved,** and **yoke of slavery** to indicate this bondage (Lk 4:18, Rom 8:15, Gal 4:9, 5:1). I've invited Carol to explain what this bondage was like, and how the Lord freed her.

Growing up, my relationship with my parents was very good. Though we were never particularly demonstrative about love, I always felt secure and happy.

All that changed, however, when I went away to college, and Mom left Dad. What Mom said was "for a season" turned into a two-year separation. She eventually handed Dad divorce papers, but he did not touch them for months.

Dad finally signed the divorce papers because he wanted to re-marry. When Mom discovered that the woman he wanted to marry was his first love, a woman in whose shadow she had stood for so long, she became bitter and angry.

Mom's wrath fell on me. My close relationship with my dad and growing love for my new stepmother, as well as the physical distance of my siblings, set me up as a target. I felt I was being put into the middle of a situation I didn't deserve to be in. My dad was completely supportive and protective of me, while my mom was basically asking me to take her side against him. It was an extremely difficult time for me.

Soon, even ordinary conversations with my mom turned into bitter arguments, and I found myself becoming angry most times we were together. This caused me to develop a deep-seated bitterness and resentment towards my mom, which was such a torment that I dreaded being in her company. Summers home from college were almost unbearable. When I graduated and moved away, I succeeded in avoiding her. I managed to keep her at a distance, and the anger and resentment went undercover.

After I married and had children, my mother moved nearby in order to be near the grandkids. She was constantly at my home, and the resentment resurfaced. The anger and bitterness that had been smoldering for so many years exploded into a fire of torment that burned a hole in my heart and soul. I felt this anger was not who I was, but I was forced to live in it every time I was with her – which was very often! I dreaded every moment I would be with her, for I knew I could not escape the torture.

A few years later, the Lord found me. As a new Christian, I immersed myself in my church and Bible study. But my resentment continued. I felt my mom deserved my anger because of what she had done to me. I felt it was "righteous" anger, so I did not feel the need to forgive. When my father passed a few years later, the anger really peaked, and I continued to live in this torment of anger and bitterness. But it was another ten years before the Holy Spirit really convicted me of the necessity of forgiveness.

The Lord began to make it clear that He was <u>commanding</u> me to forgive. My anger was holding me back, but I could not evade His conviction. I remember wrestling with the Lord so well – pacing on my back patio, so, so mad, anguishing over my angry heart. I cried out to Him to take this anger from me, but He did not. Finally, in an act of obedience, I deliberately laid all the years of pain at the foot of the cross. I gave them up, putting them one by one into His hands. And at that moment, He answered my prayer and lifted off me all my anger, unforgiveness, bitterness, and resentment. As He delivered me, I felt a great weight taken off me. I felt such a lightness, and an indescribable peace!

After this deliverance, the hard work of walking it out began. My mother did not change. But my <u>response</u> to her did. I learned to feel more compassion for her challenges in life. When trying circumstances inevitably surfaced and my anger returned, I would have to lean harder on God to seek a deeper level of forgiveness. I had forgiven the traumas of the past, but the wounding was still ongoing, and each *new offense required another release of anger and a choice to forgive. God graciously gave me the strength to forgive each time, layer upon layer, and brought healing to my heart.*

God is so faithful! Even though my mom didn't change, when she passed away a few years ago, our relationship was peaceful and loving. I was even privileged to pray with and for her in her last days.

Carol Virelles
Triumph Servant Leader
Wellington, Florida

Anger is indeed a red flag. It may indicate that someone has wounded us, abused us, violated our trust, crossed our boundaries, betrayed us, disrespected us, or devalued us. This person has done something to us that is going to *require* forgiveness. But instead of forgiving, Carol felt that she had a "right" to be angry. She felt her anger was "righteous" so that she didn't need to forgive.

Anger is certainly a normal human response to what Carol had endured. However, whether we think our anger is "righteous" or not does not excuse us from forgiving. Additionally, as Joni Earekson Tada teaches, "righteous anger" moves us *towards* God.[16] Righteous anger galvanizes us to action in Holy Spirit-led ways. Carol's anger was certainly *not* moving her towards God, and could hardly be called righteous.

... the anger of man does not achieve the righteousness of God.   James 1:20

Carol's anger and unforgiveness led to resentment and eventually to bitterness. Her continued unrepented sin was an open door, inviting demons to team up with her flesh and make it even harder to forgive. She was trapped in a prison of torment, dreading her mother's company because of the *fire of torment that burned a hole in her heart and soul.* She remained captive to this spirit of bondage *until* she forgave her mother *from her heart*. We are only able to forgive **from the heart** because of Jesus' forgiveness given to us and the Holy Spirit's power flowing through us. Carol's utter surrender, her release of her anger to God and her *choice* to forgive her mother, obliterated Satan's foothold and invited Jesus' deliverance. Her surrender opened her to the Holy Spirit's power which enabled her to forgive, and this forgiveness closed off access as Jesus freed her from the power of the demonic torturers.

As we have learned in the *Triumph* series, forgiveness does not equal *reconciliation*. Before restoration of the relationship can even begin, heart work is necessary *for both parties*. If we do our part, but the other person does not do their part, we may be able to have some level of connection as the Holy Spirit leads and if the relationship is safe, but we will not be able to have true deep connection or restoration. Carol did everything God called her to do, and God freed her as she forgave and released. The Holy Spirit enabled her to have a peaceful, although not restored, relationship with her mother, and He graciously provided some level of connection.

Additionally, forgiveness does not equal *healing*. Forgiveness is a *choice* to release, and is not dependent upon anything the other person says or does. We are commanded to forgive, to release our offenders to God's hands, to give up our desire for revenge, to rip up the I.O.U. and let it between them and God. Forgiveness means we no longer hold their sin against them or demand restitution. But *healing* is an encounter with Jesus, a supernatural touch from the Lord that lifts the pain from our hearts as He fills us with Himself. We *position* ourselves to receive His healing by forgiving, but God's *timing* to release His healing is His decision. We can see from Carol's testimony that as she chose to forgive, the Lord stepped in and brought her healing, granting her indescribable peace.

Notice also how the ongoing injuries required Carol's ongoing forgiveness and the Lord's ongoing healing. Yet Carol was in a different place after her deliverance. The demonic torturers had been banished, the Holy Spirit had filled her with forgiveness and healing, and it was much easier for her to forgive and release each subsequent time.

Ponder, Pray, and Journal

We live in a fallen world, so we all will have need to forgive. Spend some time in prayer, asking the Holy Spirit to search your heart for any residual unforgiveness.

Unforgiveness gives the enemy an engraved invitation to come and wreak havoc in our lives and souls. If you are struggling to forgive, go back and work through the forgiveness chapters in *Triumph Over Suffering* and *Triumph of Surrender*.

Greater enmeshment in Satan's lies, more feeding of our flesh, more entanglement in the ways of the world, deeper disobedience to the Word, all invite Satan's influence in greater measure. Aligning our thoughts, words, and behaviors with evil creates a foothold. Satan can build on footholds to construct strongholds (2Cor 10:4). The extent of the reach of his oppression, bondage, and torment depends on the number and size of his strongholds. We will explore strongholds in Chapter 10, but for now, understand that from these strongholds the enemy can wield powerful influence over our thought life, our belief systems, our emotions and will and behavior. The more spiritual territory we have given to Satan, the greater his access and his ability to influence, take advantage of, and manipulate us, even reaching levels of oppression, bondage, and torment.

Before we move in to the final level, I'd like to discuss two more ways Satan uses to access: traps, and sifting.

Enemy Traps

The Scriptures are replete with passages about the enemy's traps, snares, pits, and nets, and full of commands to remain on the alert (Ps 37:7-8, 31:4, 1Tim 3:6-7, 6:9, 1Pet 5:8, Eph 6:18, 1Cor 16:13). When we fall into his traps, he is able to *take advantage of us*:

But one whom you forgive anything, I forgive also; for indeed what I have forgiven, if I have forgiven anything, I did it for your sakes in the presence of Christ, *so that no advantage would be taken of us by Satan*, for we are not ignorant of his schemes.   2 Corinthians 2:10-11, emphasis added

Paul is teaching how unforgiveness gives Satan a foothold from which he can take advantage of us, **outwit us** in the NIV. What I want to highlight here is how Satan schemes to gain the upper hand. Manipulative and coy, he utilizes his footholds to steer us into his traps. I will share an example of my own life to illustrate how my sins gave Satan a foothold and drew me into his trap.

My son and his wife were arranging for their newborn son to be dedicated, and they invited us to Canada to be part of the occasion. I leapt at the opportunity to see my grandson again. I also wanted to go help out the new parents, and I so wanted to hold him! "I don't even need to pray about that!" I declared. "I'll be there!"

So I consulted with my family on the time frame, and bought tickets. Deep inside I felt a bit uncomfortable, but I pushed it aside. I generally pray about everything and consult with the Lord for His will on every decision, big and small. But not this time. My determination to accomplish my agenda trumped the Holy Spirit's voice.

I was scheduled to fly out in a week. Over the course of that week, I felt a void and a lack of peace as the Holy Spirit tried to get my attention. Next, I injured my back – how would I be able to even carry my grandson? Then an eye infection. I didn't want to bring that to them! Finally, during a sleepless night, I went to the Lord in prayer. After a great wrestling, I repented of being on my own agenda. I asked Him what His will was, and if He even wanted me to go at all. I admitted I hadn't asked Him because I was afraid He might say no. As I prayed and repented and listened, the Holy Spirit then opened my eyes to see my idolatry of my grandson. I surrendered and laid it all down at His feet. I would go or not go, whatever He willed. I sensed a tremendous release as I surrendered.

It was Friday, and my tickets were for Sunday, just two days away. In the stillness that followed after I had surrendered, to my surprise, I felt He said to delay the trip until Wednesday. In obedience, I turned on my computer to change my flight. Right there in my inbox was an email from the airlines offering flight change without penalty!

When I was in mid process of making the flight change, work called to inform me of a very critical emergency meeting on Monday. They were concerned because they knew I would be away and would not be available. But now I wouldn't be away. I realized that God wanted me present for the crucial events that unfolded on Monday and Tuesday, and if I had not sought Him, I would have missed this Kingdom assignment.

I flew out on Wednesday, now in the center of His will – and with both my back and my eye healed.

Celeste Li
Jupiter, Florida

My idolatry of my grandson and determination to accomplish my own agenda were the open doors that gave Satan a foothold. He now had access and influence. He knew the grave issues and dissension brewing at work, probably because he had caused them. Now I am not saying I am so important that my presence was necessary on those days, but somehow the Lord wanted me there, and Satan was (almost) able to remove me by drawing me right into his trap. Thoughts of how lovely it would be to hold my grandson and how helpful I was going to be taking care of him so his parents could get some rest paraded through my mind. Without forcing or coercing, without violating my free will, Satan preyed on my idolatry and lured me to make decisions apart from God. He almost outwitted me with his *manipulation*.

Was this really a spiritual battle, or was it just a battle with the flesh? Oh, you ask the best questions. And I can't say I always have the answers to these kinds of questions. But the intensity of the wrestling, the release upon surrender, and the realization of the Kingdom assignment Satan was working to thwart, all make me sense that this was more of an Ephesians 6:12 battle, a struggle not against flesh and blood.

Idolatry, wrong priorities, and fear are some things that seem to make us susceptible to Satan's ability to take advantage of us. And thinking about what we studied about Eve in the last chapter, how Satan manipulated Eve to make the free will choice to eat, I see also how Satan plays into doubts and weaknesses and fleshly desires,

Satan weaves his nets to entrap us. But God's agenda may be *sifting*. I am so, so grateful that the Holy Spirit persisted in His convicting work within me before I flew to Canada. I have a sense that if I had flown out on Sunday as I had planned, not only would I have missed that Kingdom assignment, those days in Canada would not have gone well for me. God was gracious to sanctify me in time so that I did not completely fail. Though I stumbled, I was not hurled headlong, for He held my hand (Ps 37:24).

Sometimes, though, we do plummet into Satan's pit during the sifting. Let's read.

Sifting

And there arose also a dispute among them as to which one of them was regarded to be greatest …

"Simon, Simon, behold, Satan has demanded permission to sift you like wheat; but I have prayed for you, that your faith may not fail; and you, when once you have turned again, strengthen your brothers."

But he said to Him, "Lord, with You I am ready to go both to prison and to death!"

And He said, "I say to you, Peter, the rooster will not crow today until you have denied three times that you know Me."
Luke 22:24, 31-34

Mark's version adds that Jesus said all would fall away, but Peter said to Him, **"Even though all may fall away, yet I will not."** And he kept saying **insistently, "Even if I have to die with You, I will not deny You!"** (Mk 14:27-31).

During the agony in the garden, Jesus instructed Peter, **"Keep watching and praying that you may not come into temptation; the spirit is willing, but the flesh is weak"** (Mk 14:38). But Peter fell asleep.

This sifting was a trap of a most horrid kind. Satan took advantage of Peter's pride. His arrogance, coupled with prayerlessness, made him an easy prey for Satan's sifting. All Satan needed to do was nudge a few slaves and bystanders to ask some innocent questions, and Peter succumbed to the temptation to deny he even knew Jesus.

Now don't miss this. Wheat is sifted to separate the chaff from the grain. The worthless, unwanted chaff is removed, leaving the pure and precious harvest of grains of wheat. It seems Peter's sifting humbled him and brought him to repentance, and he wept bitterly (Lk 22:62). Notice that the telling of Peter's denials is in all four gospels – and the most detail in Mark, which is believed by many theologians to be Peter's gospel account. It seems Peter's pride was exposed and removed and replaced with humility – a humility so deep it led to full transparency about his fall. I think this was part of the equipping that was needed to prepare Peter to lead the church; once again, Satan was God's servant.

We will wrap up this chapter on demonic activity discussing the deepest level: domination. Remember, although Satan and his demons can dominate a non-Christian, since the Holy Spirit lives inside a born-again Christian, Satan cannot dominate us.

Level 3: Domination

Someone with dominion is ruling over a territory. They are in a place of command and control. *Merriam-Webster* gives this definition of dominion: "absolute or exclusive use, control, ownership, or possession of property."[17]

Of course God has utter sovereign **dominion** over everything:

His dominion is an everlasting dominion
Which will not pass away;
And His kingdom is one
Which will not be destroyed.   Daniel 7:14

Domination is the exercise of rule or control over the place of dominion. Domination can carry a negative connotation, indicating loss of free will because of control of the dominator. Although God possesses undefeatable sovereign dominion, He never *dominates* people, but gives them free will and draws their free will choice to obey by His love.

Satan also has a dominion (Acts 26:18, Col 1:13), and we will study in the next chapter how he usurped territory to capture this domain. In contrast to how God rules His domain, Satan uses his power and manipulates by fear in order to *dominate* people.

Recall the passage in Luke 8:26-39 which describes a very violent man, who broke through shackles and chains, gashing himself with stones and screaming among the tombs.

When Jesus had stepped out on land, there met him a man from the city who had demons. For a long time he had worn no clothes, and he had not lived in a house but among the tombs ... Jesus then asked him, "What is your name?" And he said, "Legion," for many demons had entered him.

Luke 8:27, 30 ESV

It seems this man was under utter domination by these demons. They had *full access* and *full control* of his speech, actions, thoughts, beliefs, will, intentions. When Jesus delivered him, he sat at His feet, in his right mind and fully clothed, and then went forth to proclaim throughout the whole city what great things Jesus had done for him.

What would open the door for domination? The Word is not explicit, but I think rebellion can play a big part here. Let's go to an Old Testament passage, the Genesis account of Cain and Abel, to read about the consequences of Cain's rebellion. First John tells us that Cain **was of the evil one** (1Jn 3:12).

Recall that the Lord looked with favor on Abel's offering from the firstborn of his flock, but He did not look with favor on Cain's offering of some fruit offered in the course of time (Gen 4:2-5).

So Cain was very angry, and his face was downcast.
Then the LORD said to Cain, "Why are you angry? Why is your face downcast? If you do what is right, will you not be accepted? But *if you do not do what is right, sin is crouching at your door; it desires to have you, but you must master it."*
Now Cain said to his brother Abel, "Let's go out to the field." And while they were in the field, Cain attacked his brother Abel and killed him.   Genesis 4:5-8 NIV, emphasis added

Sin is crouching at your door. Very graphic. Can you see it with spiritual eyes?

Although Scripture doesn't give the details, Hebrews indicates that Abel's offering came from faith, and Cain's did not (Heb 11:4). Abel's offering was righteous; Cain's was evil (1Jn 3:12). God expected Cain to **"do what is right."** Cain, in disobedience, did not. Jude describes Cain as a rebellious one who rejected authority (Jude 1:8,11). I think his rebellion coupled with his anger at God's rejection of his sacrifice opened a door to the enemy, and Satan demanded permission to enter. Satan was poised at this open door, ready to be permitted to pounce. The NLT translates it this way: **"Sin is waiting to attack and destroy you, and you must subdue it."**

In His graciousness, the Lord gave Cain a chance to repent, to master those sins, to do what was right and thus receive the Lord's forgiveness and acceptance. It seems Cain's repentance would have closed the door, causing the enemy to slink away in defeat. But Cain declined God's grace. He left the door open, and the enemy leapt through, perhaps even bringing domination. The forces of darkness led him down a dark pathway that probably included resentment, bitterness, jealousy (1Jn 3:12), and hatred, and that culminated in murder.

Let's also take a look at what the Word tells us about Judas. Watch the progression.

We learn first that Judas was **a thief, and as he had the money box, he used to pilfer what was put into it** (Jn 12:6). We next see that by the time of the Last Supper Satan had *already* **put into the heart of Judas Iscariot, the son of Simon, to betray Him** (Jn 13:2, emphasis added).

During the Last Supper, Jesus announced that one of them would betray Him, and indicated to John that the one to whom He gave the morsel was the one. Sharing food in Jesus' time was a gesture of peace and friendship. It almost feels as if Jesus gave Judas one last chance to turn back from the path of betrayal he was on. But *after the morsel,* **Satan then entered into him** (Jn 13:27, emphasis added).

Ponder, Pray, and Journal

Before we wrap up this chapter, we will visit two passages that describe Satan's workings. Spoiler alert: theologians debate much about these passages, and we are going to ask questions that may remain unanswered. We will pray and ponder and listen to what the Holy Spirit would say to us at this time.

Read 2 Timothy 2:14-26, and meet me back here when you are finished.

I am pondering this: **... the snare of the devil, having been held captive by him to do his will** (2:26).

Are those in this passage who have **gone astray from the truth** (2:18) born-again believers who were once walking in truth but now have fallen away from it? What does it mean to be **in opposition** (2:25)? Are they fallen away believers, or are they unsaved? Or, is it possible to abandon your salvation, and these are born-again believers who had abandoned their salvation? *Can a born-again Christian be held captive by Satan to do his will – oppressed by Satan but not dominated?*

I have similar questions about Ananias and Sapphira. Read Acts 4:32 – 5:11. Meet me back here when you are finished.

I am pondering this: **... why has Satan filled your heart to lie to the Holy Spirit?** (5:3).

Were Ananias and Sapphira, who were part of the congregation of believers, born-again believers themselves? Or were they unsaved? Or, is it possible to abandon your salvation, and Ananias and Sapphira were born-again believers who had abandoned their salvation? *Can Satan fill the heart of a born-again Christian – and can the Holy Spirit still reside there also?*

As you ask the Holy Spirit to open your mind to understand the Scriptures, recall this verse we discussed in Chapter 2, addressed to *the brethren:*

Take care, brethren, that there not be in any one of you an evil, unbelieving heart that falls away from the living God.

Hebrews 3:12

Journal what the Holy Spirit reveals to you.

We have covered a lot of ground so far in this book, from understanding that "Command Central" is our heart, to watching how the enemy plots and strategizes, to comprehending the different levels demons can exert their influence upon us and others. Let's synthesize what we have learned so far and visualize an enemy attack.

Enemy Attack

Any area of our heart that is submitted to the Lord Jesus Christ is in the Light and under His control and protection. When we first surrender our hearts to Jesus, we give to Him all that we can spiritually comprehend at that moment. The Holy Spirit desires us to embark on a lifetime of surrendering more and more to Him, releasing more and more to His control. These surrendered areas become territories of Light, areas in our hearts, minds, bodies, emotions, wills, and lives where:

- Our submission to Him is absolute, our surrender is complete.

- Jesus is reigning and controlling, and we are walking in obedience to His commands.

- Our thoughts and belief systems are aligned with the Truth of God's Word.

- We desire God's will and not our own.

- Our minds are set on the Spirit and we are led by the Spirit of God.

These territories of Light are *where God is.* We have given Him *rule* here. Satan can *tempt* in these areas, he can hurl *flaming arrows,* he can *seduce* and *resist* and *hinder* and *oppose* us – but if we stand firm, he will have no access; he will be unable to *influence, outwit, manipulate, oppress, hold us in bondage,* or *torment* in these submitted areas.

So what does that mean regarding the parts of our hearts that are *not* submitted to Jesus? The unsurrendered parts? The rebellious, disobedient, or unbelieving parts? The parts that we, knowingly or unknowingly, have not yet placed under His control? Also, what happens when the enemy shoots flaming arrows at a sinless area, and we fall and remain unrepentant? Such good questions.

Of course our goal is Christlikeness, full surrender to our Lord's rule, so that we will be filled up to all the fullness of God (Eph 3:19). Our lifelong journey of sanctification is a journey of deeper and more complete surrenders. Areas of our lives and hearts that we have not yielded to the Spirit are areas where Light cannot penetrate. In these unsurrendered areas, in these areas of habitual sin, we have given place to the devil. We have given him an opportunity to influence, take advantage of, oppress, sift, torment, or hold in bondage. These territories of darkness are areas in our hearts, minds, bodies, emotions, wills, and lives where

- We have not surrendered to the rule and control of Jesus, or where our submission is incomplete.

- We are habitually sinning or walking in unrepented disobedience.

- Our belief system is mired in Satan's lies and not aligned with the Truth of God's Word.

- We desire *our* will be done.

- We are being led by our flesh or the world or demons, instead of being led by the Holy Spirit.

These areas of unrepented sin can give Satan a *foothold* from which he may begin to *influence* us. The deeper access of strongholds invites him to manipulate, oppress, hold us in bondage, or torment us.

It seems that when demons have found a foothold and are exerting some level of influence, their impact is *limited* to that area of the foothold. Healing and deliverance ministers John and Mark Sandford in their book *Deliverance and Inner Healing* explain that all examples of demonic influence in Scripture, with the exception of Legion, describe people "beset in some way by demons ... but not completely taken over and controlled." They give examples of the spirit of infirmity who crippled a woman for eighteen years, deaf and dumb spirits, demons that specialize in deception, and the demon that terrorized Saul emotionally (Lk 13:11, Mk 9:25, 2Tim 2:17,18,26, 1Sam 16:14). The Sandfords point out that each one of these people, "apart from the demons' area of specialization, was otherwise in control of his or her faculties ... Each still had a sense of his or her own identity and thought processes."[18]

The way I envision these spiritual battles, the forces of darkness and the forces of Light clash in our hearts. The battles are raging for *influence* of this spiritual territory. Although the topic is very complex, the basic concept is quite simple: Darkness and Light cannot co-exist in the same place. We witness this every daybreak: from the darkest of nights, the sun emerges over the horizon; as its light pierces through, darkness is vanquished.

Wherever Jesus is reigning, darkness is overpowered. When Light comes in, then darkness, the weaker of the two, is forced to flee.

The light shines in the darkness, and the darkness has not overcome it.　　　　　　　　　　John 1:5 NIV

God's Light is so infinitely overwhelmingly powerful, banishing all darkness, that darkness and light are the same to Him!

Even the darkness is not dark to You,
And the night is as bright as the day.
Darkness and light are alike to You.　　　　　　Psalm 139:12

Defensive spiritual warfare involves battles of standing firm and defending the Strongholds of Light that Jesus has built, fortresses such as righteousness, humility, trust, and truth. *Offensive spiritual warfare* involves conquering Satan's strongholds of sin and deception. *Deliverance* occurs when Jesus frees a person from being affected by demons. The Bible uses this word deliverance whether those demons are attacking from the outside (flaming arrows, temptations, opposition, hindrance, harassment, or resistance) or whether those demons have secured a place and are able to more deeply impact (influencing, taking advantage of, manipulating, oppressing, tormenting, holding in bondage, or, as in the case of a non-Christian, dominating). Simply put, *deliverance means demonic forces were involved and forced to flee.*

Satan works to build strongholds of darkness. Jesus Christ works to build Strongholds of Light. They battle to prevent the other from building more strongholds, and they battle to tear down the strongholds that the opposition has already built. The battle is on. Who will win? *We choose the victor.* It's all Him and only Him, but we have a part to play: when we surrender to our Lord Jesus Christ, we *choose* Him as our Victor.

In the midst of this cosmic battle, we have an assignment as a soldier in active duty. Are you asleep in the Light? God has given us free will, and we *choose* whether we will surrender to Him, or not.

God has a plan for your life. Satan has a plan for your life. *You cast the deciding vote.*[19]

I think I can hear your questions already. We can perhaps comprehend attacks and opposition, but exactly *how* can Satan and his demons exert any *influence* upon us? How do they *gain access?* How do they *secure a place?* It's time to face these tough questions head-on. Take a deep breath. We're diving down under.

Chapter 9
Authority, Access, and Power

*O*n this chapter, we are going to study together from Scriptures how Satan may be able to influence us, oppress us, torment us, or hold us in bondage.

Although Satan is a powerful being, and his demons also possess great powers, their power is *limited*. God restricts them – and their power – to a specific place: areas of darkness. Let's hear how the Word explains it.

And angels who did not keep their own domain, but abandoned their proper abode, *He has kept in eternal bonds under darkness* for the judgment of the great day.

Jude 1:6, emphasis added

Angels who did not keep their own domain, who did not stay within the limits of authority God gave them (NLT), seem to be angels who rebelled against God and refused to submit to His dominion (Mt 25:41, Rev 12:4). Francis Frangipane, pastor and international teacher of church leaders, illuminates Jude 1:6 for us, explaining that Satan and his fallen angels, "have been relegated to live in darkness."[1] *They cannot touch areas of Light.*

Peter's writing seems similar to Jude's.

For if God did not spare angels when they sinned, but

cast them into hell and *committed them to pits of darkness,* reserved for judgment ...					Peter 2:4, emphasis added

When Judas betrayed Jesus and the chief priests and officers were arresting Him, Jesus declared, **"... but this hour and the power of darkness are yours"** (Lk 22:53).

My understanding is limited here; these are certainly spiritual mysteries. It seems from these verses, however, that God has consigned fallen angels to territories of darkness, and their power is active in darkness. Their presence and their reach is limited to places where *God's Light* is absent. These verses seem to indicate that Satan and his demons have been relegated to areas of spiritual darkness – both *allowed* there, and *assigned* there.

Demons "Traffic" in Dark Places

Because God keeps Satan and his demons **in eternal bonds under darkness** (Jude 1:6), they have a *right* to be there – indeed, they have been *banished* there; darkness is the only place their presence, their influence, or their power is permitted. They are not permitted to access any areas of Light. God has assigned them the dark territories, and they *influence* those areas of darkness and *operate out of* those areas of darkness. I think we can see how they operate out of the darkness in the world and the darkness that exists in unbelievers' hearts. But what does that mean for born-again Christians?

We are God's own possession, and the Holy Spirit lives in our hearts. As we have discussed, we are all in mid-process of sanctification, and we have areas in our hearts that are surrendered to the Lord, and areas that are as yet unsurrendered. The surrendered territories of our hearts are full of Light and are off-limits to Satan and his demons. They cannot manipulate, influence, oppress, torment, or hold in bondage these areas of Light. However, they can *attack* these areas. They can *shoot flaming arrows* at these areas. They can *resist, oppose,* and *harass* from the outside. And they can indeed repeatedly *tempt us to sin,* trying to wear us down and seduce us to participate in unfruitful deeds of darkness in an effort to drive us to open the door and invite their influence in.

God's gift to us at salvation was to rescue us from the domain of darkness (Col 1:13). Our hearts have become the home of Jesus by His Spirit, and Satan no longer has any *right* to influence our hearts. He has no *legitimate* authority. We belong to God and not to Satan. When we follow Jesus, we do not walk in darkness; we have the Light of life (Jn 8:12). But areas of our hearts where we are not following Jesus, that we have not yet fully surrendered to God, remain an open door for Satan to *usurp* access and exert his power to influence. He is accessing illegally; he is *trespassing,* but he is still in a position to impact. He has no *legitimate* authority in these areas because we have been rescued from his domain. He is a usurper and has seized access by force – *at our invitation.*

Francis Frangipane explains that territories of darkness in people's hearts are territories open to Satan's influence, territories in which the demons have been relegated to "traffic" (Isa 47:15):

> ... we have been delivered out of the domain or "authority" of darkness (Col 1:13) ... But if we *tolerate* darkness through tolerance of sin, we leave ourselves vulnerable for satanic assault. For wherever there is willful disobedience to the Word of God, there is spiritual darkness and the potential for demonic activity ... *The devil can traffic in any area of darkness, even in the darkness that still exists in a Christian's heart.*[2]

We learned that one of Satan's names is Adversary, an opponent in a lawsuit, and we can see from this name that Satan operates in legalism. He has been studying God's Law for thousands of years, legalistically he is more of an expert in it than we could ever be, and he manipulates it to his advantage. If he can convince us that he legitimately has the right to access our hearts, he's won half the battle already. But the Word says he has *no right*:

The sting of death is sin, and the power of sin is the law; but thanks be to God, who gives us the victory through our Lord Jesus Christ.   1 Corinthians 15:56-57

But now we have been released from the Law, having died to that by which we were bound, so that we serve in newness of the Spirit and not in oldness of the letter.   Romans 7:6

Jesus nailed the certificate of debt to the cross (Col 2:14). He fulfilled the Law *for us* so that it might be fulfilled *in us* (Matt 5:17-18, Rom 8:4). And in so doing, He *disarmed* the forces of darkness:

When He had disarmed the rulers and authorities, He made a public display of them, having triumphed over them through Him.   Colossians 2:15

Disarmed. They have lost their weapons and their access to those who belong to Jesus - unless we give them weapons and access by opening doors to darkness and inviting their influence in.

Satan has no right to our hearts, minds, or bodies. He can only influence when we willingly give place to him. He has no legitimate authority over us. And yet his power is persistent and real. He forces his way into unprotected areas and violently seizes access, usurping what is not rightfully his. He is fighting guerilla warfare. And it is our surrender, our death to our own will and desire, that invites Jesus to step in and block his power.

This concept of Satan trafficking in darkness will become increasingly important as we study warfare. For any area that we have not submitted to the Lord is an area that is fair game from Satan's perspective. He must ask permission, of course, for our Lord God is supremely and ultimately sovereign, but realize that Satan has been *relegated* to areas of darkness, and he will attempt to use those areas of darkness as his beachhead to launch further attacks.

Understanding the interplay of authority, access, and power is critical, so let's spend some time grappling with these concepts.

All Authority Belongs to God

God created the world, and He remains the rightful owner.

**The earth is the Lord's, and all it contains,
The world, and those who dwell in it.**   Psalm 24:1

All authority ultimately belongs to God, for He is Sovereign Lord. In His hand is power and might; His is the dominion, and He rules over all (1Chr 29:10-13).

For there is no authority except from God, and those which exist are established by God.   Romans 13:1

Jesus answered [Pilate], **"You would have no authority over Me, unless it had been given you from above."**   John 19:11

God Delegated Authority to Man

When God created the world, God *delegated* authority[3] to mankind.

**The heavens are the heavens of the Lord,
But the earth He has given to the sons of men.**   Psalm 115:16

Hebrews, quoting from Psalm 8, echoes these words:

"You have crowned him [man] **with glory and honor,
And set him over the works of Your hands.
You have put all things in subjection under His feet."**

For in that He put all in subjection under him, He left nothing that is not put under him. But now we do not yet see all things put under him.

Hebrews 2:7-8 NKJV

God chose to place mankind as *ruler* over the earth and all that is in it. Hear how Genesis explains this:

Then God said, "Let Us make man in Our image, according to Our likeness; and let them *rule* over the fish of the sea and over the birds of the sky and over the cattle and over all the earth, and over every creeping thing that creeps on the earth." God created man in His own image, in the image of God He created him; male and female He created them. God blessed them; and God said to them, "Be fruitful and multiply, and fill the earth, and subdue it; and *rule* over the fish of the sea and over the birds of the sky and over every living thing that moves on the earth."   Genesis 1:26-28, emphasis added

Let them rule over all the earth. Fill the earth and subdue it and rule over it. Mankind is the legitimate ruler over all the earth, ruling by God's delegated authority.

The territory that a ruler controls is his *domain*. When one in authority entrusts, or delegates, command to a ruler, the ruler has obtained this domain legitimately. This is how man was given authority and rule by God.

God *delegated authority* to mankind and gave him *rule* over the earth and all that is in it, and commanded mankind to steward the earth for Him. Satan had no authority, rule, or dominion on earth. And because Adam and Eve were in communion with God and submitted to God's authority, because they were walking in His Light, Satan had no authority, rule, or dominion over the hearts of man either. God of course retained – and continues to retain – utter dominion, for He is forever the Ultimate Owner and Sovereign Lord with supreme undeniable irrevocable authority – but He had delegated rule and authority of the world, and rule and authority of their own hearts, to Adam and Eve *as His stewards*.

Satan Usurped Rule and Authority

In Genesis 3, we see God ordained a test for Adam and Eve, permitting Satan to attack and tempt. Satan had no *authority* and no *rule* over Adam and Eve – but he did have *power*. His power was limited and restricted by God. Adam and Eve fell to this seduction. They rebelled against submission to God, and forfeited their communion with God. By their free will action, they gave their *right to rule,* their *authority,* of their hearts and lives over to Satan. Adam and Eve willingly, but probably unknowingly, entered into Satan's domain. They handed over to Satan the authority that God had delegated to them. Satan admits that the authority he has was not originally his (**"It has been delivered to me"** Lk 4:6). Satan now had *illegitimate* authority. He had *usurped* authority by using his power to seduce, wresting authority from them by luring them into sin. Their fall had far-reaching consequences, since through Adam sin entered the world, and death through sin (Rom 5:12). Adam and Eve had, again probably unknowingly, handed over to Satan *rule over the earth* (Heb 2:8c). Jesus called Satan **"the ruler of this world"** (Jn 12:31, 16:11). So earth had become Satan's territory, and all men are now born into Satan's domain (Col 1:13).

Now don't lose sight of the truth that God retains *ultimate* authority. He remains *sovereign*. He possesses unlimited power, unparalleled supremacy, and utter control. He limits Satan's *rule*; Satan still must ask *permission* to wreak his evil (Job 1:9-12, Lk 22:31). Satan's plans will never trump God's overarching purposes.

Jesus Won Back Rule and Authority at the Cross

God had given Adam and Eve authority as His stewards. They disobeyed God, and that choice enslaved them to Satan. They handed over their *right to rule* to Satan, giving up their delegated authority to him, clearing the way for him to usurp rule. But the Father's plan to divest Satan of his rule was the cross. Hear Jesus' words near the end of His life:

"Now judgment is upon this world; now the ruler of this world will be cast out. And I, if I am lifted up from the earth, will draw all men to Myself." But He was saying this to indicate the kind of death by which He was to die.

John 12:31-33

At the Last Supper, Jesus explained that He was going to the Father, and **"the prince of this world now stands condemned"** (Jn 16:11 NIV). By His death and resurrection, He won back all *authority* over the enemy, and was given *authority* over all flesh (Jn 17:2). He explained to His disciples just before His ascension:

And Jesus came up and spoke to them, saying, "All authority has been given to Me in heaven and on earth."

Matthew 28:18

Ephesians elaborates on what "all authority" means:

... He raised Him from the dead and seated Him at His right hand in the heavenly places, far above all rule and authority and power and dominion, and every name that is named, not only in this age but also in the one to come. And He put all things in subjection under His feet ...

Ephesians 1:20-22

God through Jesus has triumphed over Satan at the cross, stripping him of his rule and authority and crushing his power, making a public spectacle of him. But as we studied in Chapter 1, we are still in the midst of guerilla warfare. Jesus will not *abolish* all rule, authority, and power until the end of the world (1Cor 15:24-26).

We looked at Colossians 2:15 a few pages back; let's put it into context here to better understand.

When you were dead in your transgressions and the uncircumcision of your flesh, He made you alive together

with Him, having forgiven us all our transgressions, having canceled out the certificate of debt consisting of decrees against us, which was hostile to us; and He has taken it out of the way, having nailed it to the cross. *When He had disarmed the rulers and authorities, He made a public display of them, having triumphed over them through Him.*

Colossians 2:13-15, emphasis added

The **certificate of debt** is the payment due for our own sins – a payment that we could never afford to pay. A debt that could only be paid by the holy blood of sinless Jesus.

I have heard it said that in Old Testament times, if a man had a debt that he could not pay, he would be in danger of losing his land, and he and his family in danger of being sold as slaves. He would nail the paper that detailed his debt to the doorpost of his home. But sometimes his kinsman may come by and mercifully pay that debt for him, stamping on the certificate of debt, "It is finished." The kinsman would then gain possession of the land. (Lev 25:25, Ruth 3:9, Lev 25:8-34.)[4]

Jesus took on flesh and blood, becoming our kinsman:

Therefore, since the children share in flesh and blood, He Himself likewise also partook of the same, that through death He might render powerless him who had the power of death, that is, the devil, and might free those who through fear of death were subject to slavery all their lives.

Hebrews 2:14-15

Jesus mercifully paid our debt. He took the certificate of debt out of the way and nailed it to the cross. His last words on the cross:

"It is finished!" And He bowed His head and gave up His spirit. John 19:30

At the cross, He **disarmed** Satan and his demons. My *Greek Word Study* books say disarmed literally means "stripped"[5] ... "divest ... despoil."[6] I was unfamiliar with these words and had to look them up.

Divest means "to strip of rights."[7] Despoil is "to strip of possessions, things of value, etc.; rob, plunder, pillage."[8]

Jesus has canceled our certificate of debt and stripped Satan and his demons of their greatest weapon: the rule and authority that Adam and Eve had handed over to them. Satan and his demons now have *no right to rule*. They have *no authority*. They lost it at the cross.

What occurred at the cross was a powerful spiritual exchange, as Jesus paid mankind's debt and offered freedom for every person. He offers each one of us His free gift, and we receive that gift when we come to Him. When we surrender our lives to Jesus, the exchange for us individually is completed; our debt is paid and we are freed from Satan's dominion, extricated from his authority, released from his rule.

He rescued us from the domain of darkness, and transferred us to the kingdom of His beloved Son.

Colossians 1:13

We are transferred to God's Kingdom and have placed our hearts under His authority. Jesus has become the Possessor of the territory in our hearts. Hear it once again in Jesus' own words,

> **"The Spirit of the Lord is on me,**
> **because he has anointed me**
> **to preach good news to the poor.**
> **He has sent me to proclaim freedom for the prisoners**
> **and recovery of sight for the blind,**
> **to release the oppressed,**
> **to proclaim the year of the Lord's favor."**   Luke 4:18-19 NIV

To free the prisoners. We are set free from the domain, the authority, the rule of Satan.

I have heard that the year of the Lord's favor is a reference to the Jubilee Year, which was to be celebrated in Old Testament times every fifty years. Leviticus 25 tells us that in the Jubilee year, debts were to be canceled, slaves were to be set free, and property was to be returned to its original owner. Yes, Jesus came to set us free from Satan's captivity, to release us from an oppressing debt that we could never pay, and to restore property to its original owner. To free our hearts from slavery to Satan, and to restore our hearts to *His* authority.

We Share Jesus' Authority

Now this is astounding to me. Read this passage carefully:

But God, being rich in mercy, because of His great love with which He loved us, even when we were dead in our transgressions, made us alive together with Christ (by grace you have been saved), and raised us up with Him, *and seated us with Him in the heavenly places in Christ Jesus.*

Ephesians 2:4-6, emphasis added

We are seated *with Jesus* in His place of authority, in the heavenly places, far above all rule and authority and power and dominion and every name that is named! Spiritually, Jesus has *delegated* authority to us. We are positioned with Jesus' authority.

When He rescued us from the domain of Satan, He restored the rule of our hearts back to us as God's stewards. We steward our hearts well when we daily surrender to Him, moment by moment placing our hearts under His control (Rom 6:22).

All Creation Still Groans

Although Jesus triumphed at the cross, the entire earth still reels under the curse set in motion by Adam and Eve's sin. The whole world is still in bondage to decay. All creation groans under the yoke of slavery. Although we belong to God and are protected by God, the whole world still lies in the power of the evil one (1Jn 5:18-19). We do not yet see the world back under the God-delegated authority of man (Heb 2:6-8).

For the creation was subjected to futility, not willingly, but because of Him who subjected it, in hope that the creation itself will be set free from its slavery to corruption into the freedom of the glory of the children of God. For we know that the whole creation groans and suffers the pains of childbirth together until now.   Romans 8:20-22

This passage goes on to describe how although we have the first fruits of the Spirit, we await the final redemption of our bodies as the whole earth awaits its redemption. The guerilla warfare persists.

Ponder, Pray, and Journal

The progression we have just studied is very important in understanding warfare. Go back through these sections listed below, and summarize what you have learned in your own words:

- *All Authority Belongs to God*
- *God Delegated Authority to Man*
- *Satan Usurped Rule and Authority*
- *Jesus Won Back Rule and Authority at the Cross*
- *We Share Jesus' Authority*
- *All Creation Still Groans*

Satan Retains Power

Because we are seated in the heavenly places with Jesus, we share His authority. Satan and his demons now have *no right to rule* a born-again Christian. They have *no authority* over a believer. They lost it at the cross. They can only access and exert their power *where we invite them in*. Satan is an unscrupulous usurper with no legitimate authority to reign over born-again Christians, and whose power is active in darkness (Lk 22:53). Relegated to darkness, Satan and his fallen angels may reach into territories that we leave in the dark, where our sin or our refusal to surrender invites their influence in. They are trespassing; they are accessing illegally. We have given them this illegitimate access by continuing to walk in darkness, and they sustain their illegitimate access by means of their power. Satan is a defeated foe, yet he is still battling – for he is fighting *guerilla warfare*.

Additionally, although we were set free from Satan's authority and rule at the moment of our salvation, there may be areas where we are still in bondage and have not yet escaped from his torment. The chains are broken, but we must still run free (Ps 124:7). We are free, but we may not yet be *free indeed* (Jn 8:36).

And in the areas where we *have* broken free, Satan can still attack from afar. He can shoot flaming arrows, he can oppose and resist and tempt and harass and attack in all sorts of ways, but he cannot permanently destroy us. He can hurt us, but he cannot *touch* us, meaning he cannot reshape us eternally for his purposes:

We know that everyone who has been born of God does not keep on sinning, but he who was born of God protects him, and the evil one does not touch him.   1 John 5:18 ESV

Touch, *haptomai* in the Greek, means "to exert a modifying influence ... touching for the purpose of manipulating."[9] He can try to manipulate us and customize us for his plans – but if we are abiding in Christ, he will not be able to integrate us into his designs.

Because Satan has lost his authority at the cross, he has *no legitimate right* to influence, oppress, hold us in bondage, or manipulate us with his power. However, if we *give him a place, an opportunity, by continuing to sin,* if we refuse to *close* the doors to darkness – or if we *open* doors to darkness and invite the influence of the guerilla warriors in – we give Satan dark places to traffic in. For with his formidable power, he will indeed attempt to usurp access in places where he legitimately has no authority, and he will claim he legitimately has the right to access because we have invited him in to influence. If we succumb to his temptations, falling into repetitive sins and remaining unrepentant, this may culminate in bondage to him, for although he has no legitimate authority, we have voluntarily and with good will given him a place.

The Holy Spirit Infuses Us With His Power

We are also given power to resist Satan's attacks, power to walk uprightly, power to crush the enemy, power to take territory in our hearts for the Lord – a power that is not our own, but is the Holy Spirit's power.

"... but you will receive power when the Holy Spirit has come upon you; and you shall be My witnesses both in Jerusalem, and in all Judea and Samaria, and even to the remotest part of the earth."   Acts 1:8

... to be strengthened with power through His Spirit in the inner man ... Now to Him who is able to do far more abundantly beyond all that we ask or think, *according to the power that works within us*, to Him be the glory in the church and in Christ Jesus to all generations forever and ever. Amen.

Ephesians 3:16, 20-21, emphasis added

This Holy Spirit power within us is the *same power* that raised Jesus in victory from the dead and seated Him in the heavenly realms:

... and what is the surpassing greatness of His power toward us who believe. These are in accordance with the working of the strength of His might which He brought about in Christ, when He raised Him from the dead and seated Him at His right hand in the heavenly places ...

Ephesians 1:19-20

This Holy Spirit power to us and for us and within us and through us is *infinitely* greater than Satan's power (1Jn 4:4).

Ponder, Pray, and Journal

In your own words, explain the difference between authority and power, and how that relates to our battles with Satan.

Ponder Ephesians 1:18-22 and 2 Corinthians 4:7. Journal your thoughts.

Ponder, Pray, and Journal

Now if ...

- Jesus has disarmed the rulers and authorities, and
- Satan no longer has authority over us, and
- The Holy Spirit power in us is greater than Satan's power

... then why can't we just go around casting demons out of every one and every place? (I admit I tried it; it didn't work for me.)

Have you ever commanded a mountain to move – and it didn't? What could be the reason? No peeking at the next section!

Power Activated

Jesus has given us His authority, yet *power* is necessary for action to happen. The way I see it, the Holy Spirit's power within us must be *activated*. It seems to me that there are three important conditions to position ourselves for *activation* of Holy Spirit's power:

- We are fully submitted to God and are resisting the enemy.
- We humbly recognize it is *not* our power, but the Holy Spirit's power.
- We are in the Father's will.

Let's dive into the details here.

Positioned for Activation of Holy Spirit Power: Fully Submitted to God and Resisting the Enemy

James 4 talks about battles with the flesh and the world. It speaks of humility and repentance. And it teaches about battles with Satan:

Submit therefore to God. Resist the devil and he will flee from you. Draw near to God and He will draw near to you.

James 4:7-8

Notice the order here. Our opening move is **submit**. Second, **resist**. Third, **the devil flees**. *Then* we can draw near to God and He will draw near to us. Let's break it down.

Submit

Full and complete surrender to God's will and His plan comes first. God does not want us going into battle unprepared. He is setting us up for victory, not for defeat. One of the ways He may **equip** us is by **working in us that which is pleasing in His sight** (Heb 13:20-21). He sanctifies us in order to close doors to the enemy to ensure the victory.

We may think of "accessing the Holy Spirit's power," but I think that thought process is flawed. Each deeper surrender to the Holy Spirit allows *Him* to access *us* in greater measure. Realize that the Lion of Judah overcame by becoming the sacrificial Lamb (Rev 5:5-10). We overcome when we fully surrender and obey the Father's will.

This positions us to be vessels for His power to flow through us, as Colossians describes, **striving according to His power, which mightily works within me** (Col 1:29). Read this verse from Ephesians once again:

Now to Him who is able to do far more abundantly beyond all that we ask or think, *according to the power that works within us* ...   Ephesians 3:20, emphasis added

Resist

My friend and *Triumph* leader Sandy helped me to see that this word **resist** may not mean attacking and pushing and forcing your way in, criticizing or condemning Satan, or throwing your entire weight against him in hand-to-hand combat. Those techniques put all the focus on Satan. But think of the Archangel Michael's strategy:

But Michael the archangel, when he disputed with the devil and argued about the body of Moses, did not dare pronounce against him a railing judgment, but said, "The Lord rebuke you!"   Jude 1:9

Let's check out **resist** in the Greek: *anthistemi*. You can see *histemi* in this word – to stand firm. *Anthistemi* simply means to stand firm against.[10]

We can try to resist Satan's attacks on our minds as he condemns us and shames us by arguing with him that he is a liar, trying to prove ourselves, or defending ourselves against him – or we can **resist**, *anthistemi*, by refusing to even discuss it, standing firm on who God's Word says we are, and focusing on God in thanksgiving. By walking as a child of the Light, in goodness and righteousness and truth (Eph 5:9), and letting *God* deal with Satan.

We can try to beat Satan's temptations by going head-to-head with him, commanding him to leave, and hopelessly trying to demonstrate that our flesh is stronger than his temptations – or, we can **resist** by standing firm against him, admitting our weaknesses, and relying on the Holy Spirit's strength as we refuse to cave in to the temptations. By walking in holiness and uprightness, and, as the Archangel Michael did, asking *God* to take care of Satan.

I am thinking of an exercise my parenting teacher did with us many years ago in parenting class. She had my husband role-play the "child," while I role-played the "parent." We stood as instructed, facing each other, hands raised, palms pressed against each other. When she said "Go," we were to push against each others' palms as hard as we could. My husband's "child" face was sheer glee with the joy of opposing.

Then our parenting teacher pulled me aside and gave me new instructions, which my husband did not hear. I was instructed, when she said "Go," to disengage and drop my hands. My husband entered the battleground beaming with excitement to get to do this again. When she said "Go," and I disengaged, his face fell in utter disappointment. The battle immediately ended, because my "child" had no one to battle with.

The Devil Flees

Imagine if we handled a demonic attack in this way: resisting by facing him, refusing to cower or flee, and standing firm on truth and in obedience. Imagine if we refused to engage him in battle, but relied on God to force him to flee. Notice James 4:7 doesn't say "resist the devil and command him to flee from you." It says **resist the devil and he *will* flee from you**. Very subtle difference. There may be times when the Holy Spirit will lead us to command the enemy to leave (we will discuss this in Chapter 26), but it seems from this passage that resisting is a key strategy.

Let's move into the second condition necessary to prepare ourselves for the Holy Spirit to activate His power.

Positioned for Activation of Holy Spirit Power: Humility to Know it is Not Our Power

We have no authority apart from Jesus – and we have no power apart from Jesus either:

"Abide in Me, and I in you. As the branch cannot bear fruit of itself unless it abides in the vine, so neither can you unless you abide in Me. I am the vine, you are the branches; he who abides in Me and I in him, he bears much fruit, for *apart from Me you can do nothing.*" John 15:4-5, emphasis added

I have head knowledge that the power within me is only the Holy Spirit. I know the Scriptures on this. And I *think* my heart knows it also. But sometimes, my heart can get proud. Sometimes, I can start to think I'm all that wonderful myself. Sometimes, I am not abiding. And in that heart state, I am thwarting the Holy Spirit's power from flowing to me and through me and from me.

I want my heart to be as certain as Peter and John, as Jesus used them to heal the lame man at the gate called Beautiful:

When Peter saw this, he said to them: "Men of Israel, why does this surprise you? *Why do you stare at us as if by our own power or godliness we had made this man walk?* The God of Abraham, Isaac and Jacob, the God of our fathers, has glorified his servant Jesus ... By faith in the name of Jesus, this man whom you see and know was made strong. It is

Jesus' name and the faith that comes through him that has completely healed him, as you can all see."

Acts 3:12-13, 16 NIV, emphasis added

I want that kind of deep heart humility! A heart that unequivocally knows,

"Not by might nor by power, but by My Spirit," says the LORD of hosts.   Zechariah 4 6

The name **the LORD of hosts** indicates that we are talking about *warfare*.[11] This title of God indicates His position as Commander-in-Chief of His host of heavenly angels. He is Captain of the Angel Armies. When we read this Name in the Word, let it remind us that we must hold our hearts in a place of deep humility, most especially in times of battle, recognizing that it is not *our* power, but *His* power, flowing through us as we abide in Him and are fulfilling His will. If we are seeking to glorify ourselves, we impede His power, for He declares in Isaiah, **"I will not give My glory to another"** (Isa 42:8).

First Thessalonians emphasizes this. Paul prays that the Lord will fill their faith-filled works with power, *so that* Jesus will be glorified:

To this end also we pray for you always, that our God will count you worthy of your calling, and fulfill every desire for goodness and the work of faith with power, *so that the name of our Lord Jesus will be glorified in you,* and you in Him, according to the grace of our God and the Lord Jesus Christ.

2 Thessalonians 1:11-12, emphasis added

And now for the final condition needed to prepare ourselves for the Holy Spirit to activate His power, the condition that trumps everything else.

Positioned for Activation of Holy Spirit Power: In the Father's Will

"Not My will, but Yours be done."   Luke 22:42

We so desire the anointing of the Holy Spirit's power to continuously flow through us. When the Holy Spirit has given us a special assignment to accomplish the will of the Father, it seems He desires to anoint us with His power to complete His work. But I don't think that flow of His power is constant. Even for Jesus, we see limitations in the presence of the Holy Spirit's power:

One day He was teaching ... and the *power of the Lord was present* for Him to perform healing. Luke 5:17, emphasis added

On that particular day, the Holy Spirit's healing power was present. I think that verse may imply that on other days, the Holy Spirit's healing power was not. Hear this passage:

And He could do no miracle there [in His hometown of Nazareth] **except that He laid His hands on a few sick people and healed them. And He wondered at their unbelief.** Mark 6:5

At the pool of Bethesda, there was a **multitude** of sick and infirm people, but Jesus healed only one (Jn 5:1-17). Yet there were other times when He healed **all who were ill**, when He healed **every kind of disease and every kind of sickness** (Matt 8:16, 9:35).

Once, when He was walking with a large crowd jostling and pressing up against Him, only the woman who touched the fringe of His cloak was healed (Lk 8:42-44). And another time, **as many as touched it** [the fringe of His cloak] **were cured** (Matt 14:36).

Why such extremes? Recall that Jesus had emptied Himself (Phil 2:7). Perhaps one of the things He emptied Himself of was His power. It seems that Jesus limited Himself to do only those miracles that were according to His Father's will, as the Father revealed His will to Him, and granted Him power.

"Truly, truly, I say to you, the Son can do nothing of Himself, unless it is something He sees the Father doing; for whatever the Father does, these things the Son also does in like manner ... I can do nothing on My own initiative ... I do not seek My own will, but the will of Him who sent Me ... For I have come down from heaven, not do to My own will, but the will of Him who sent Me." John 5:19, 30; 6:38

Jesus did nothing unless He saw the Father doing it. He was completely subject to the will of the Father.

The same seems to be true for His disciples: at times the Holy Spirit's power is present; at times it is not. In Luke 9, Jesus sent out the twelve, **and gave them power and authority over *all* the demons and to heal diseases** (Lk 9:1, emphasis added). Yet later in Chapter 9, the disciples were unable to cast out a demon from a boy with seizures (Lk 9:40).

I believe it is the same with us. There may be times when we are anointed with the Holy Spirit's power for use of our spiritual gifts, for preaching and teaching and evangelizing and prophecy, for healing and miracles and deliverance – and other times when we are not. If we are not aligned with God's perfect will, we will enter the battle alone, without His protection and power, and we will lose. (See Numbers Chapters 13 and 14, especially verses 14:40-45 for an Old Testament parallel.)

We have no power outside of His will. We exist for His pleasure, and we work for His pleasure (Rev 4:11, Phil 2:13).

This is the confidence which we have before Him, that, if we ask anything *according to His will*, He hears us. And if we know that He hears us in whatever we ask, we know that we have the requests which we have asked from Him.
1 John 5:14-15, emphasis added

Our work in the Lord is completely dependent upon our submission to our Heavenly Father. It is not our own authority we walk in, it is the authority of Jesus. It is not our own plans and will; it is *God's* will revealed to us. And it is not our own power, it is the *Holy Spirit's* power granted to us as we are obeying the will of the Father.

Ponder, Pray, and Journal

Now that we have explored this concept of activated power, let's revisit the questions I posed a few pages ago: Have you ever commanded a mountain to move – and it didn't? What could be the reason?

I have another burning question. When our hearts in all humility recognize it is Holy Spirit power, when we are in accordance with His will, resisting the enemy, and fully submitted to Him, will we then be *overflowing* with power activated within us? Well, not so fast. Recall the account of the disciples' inability to drive out a demon that we discussed above. In Matthew's version, Jesus explains it was because of the *littleness of their faith*, and that **this kind does not go out except by prayer and fasting** (Matt 17:19-21).

Additionally, God may prepare us through skirmishes with the enemy in order to train us and strengthen us for greater battles. Realize that after His baptism, Jesus **was full of the Spirit** (Luke 4:1). But after He was tempted by the devil for forty days, He came out of the wilderness **in the power of the Spirit** (Lk 4:14).

In order to partner with Jesus as He destroys the works of the devil, I think we must *develop in power*. As you work through this next section, remember that all the training and expertise in the world is useless in warfare if we are not in the center of His will. The will of God trumps *everything*.

Ponder, Pray, and Journal

What do I mean when I talk about developing in power? I imagine it to be similar to Josiah's story. Read 2 Chronicles 34:1 – 35:19. Meet me back here when you are finished.

Growing in Power

At eight years of age, Josiah was crowned king and given the *authority* to be king. He had the authority to quash a rebellion and put the rebellious ones in prison. It was his right. That is not disputed.

But he had no *power*. He could make all the laws he wanted, but without the backing of the military might, he would be unable to *enforce* those laws. It was not until he was twenty-six years old that we see him exercising his authority. Now, at age 26, reigning with power, we watch as he took control of Israel, leading the country in the burning of idols, the destruction of the high places of idol worship, and the purging of the temple and the land. He was now able to exert his rightful authority and take control by *wielding* his power.

We may own the sword, but we must grow in strength to heft it and we must develop the skill to wield it. We have Jesus' authority over all the power of the enemy, yet we must grow in power to be able to effectively *exert* that authority. And that, I believe, is a lifetime of training and equipping.

Like Josiah, when we are newborn babes in Christ, just recently rescued from the dominion of Satan and transferred to the Kingdom of Light, we have Christ's *authority*, but we probably don't know how to rely on Holy Spirit's *power*. We may not even know about our weapons, and certainly have not trained in using them. And it is not enough to merely be adept at using these weapons during practice in the safety of our homes and churches. We must also learn to wield these weapons on the battlefield *and with strategy*. Not aimlessly or fruitlessly, but with intention and purpose in order to advance His Kingdom (1Cor 9:24-26). We must learn how to abide in the Vine and, with Holy Spirit power, overcome the world, crucify our flesh, and stand firm against Satan, as we battle to take over territory of our hearts and submit it to Jesus for His rule.

Ponder, Pray, and Journal

Read 1 Samuel 17:50-54, and 21:8-9.

David was first given Goliath's sword at the moment of that victory, but the Lord did not place it in his hands for further use until many years later. Ponder all that transpired between these two passages. Journal your thoughts.

I'd like to share with you a physical parallel from my life to help us visualize these concepts.

The phone jangled in the early hours of the morning. My mother told me she was taking my father to the hospital for abdominal pain.

I walked into turmoil when I met them in the Emergency Room. Emergent decisions had to be made, but my mother was distraught and my father was in extreme pain and unable to make decisions.

I reached into my purse and handed the staff some papers. Suddenly, chaos was replaced by order. Decisions were made, tests were completed, surgeons were called in, and my father was quickly taken to the operating room for emergency surgery.

How did confusion change to order so immediately? Because the papers in my hands were legal documents declaring me to be my father's healthcare surrogate. But more than that, I knew the authority they gave me, and I was adept at using them strategically.

Just the week before, my father had a lawyer draw up the healthcare surrogate documents, and my father had signed them, "just in case." We had met with the lawyer, and he taught me exactly what those papers gave me the authority to do, and what those papers didn't cover. Additionally, my years of training and experience as a physician prepared me to quickly evaluate the situation, understand the options, and make wise decisions on my father's behalf. I didn't know what I would encounter when the phone rang that morning, but I walked into the Emergency Room equipped and ready. In the time of battle, I pulled out my "weapon" and wielded it with both authority and expertise.

Celeste Li
Jupiter, Florida

In a similar way, we need to know our *spiritual* weapons and be proficient in their use. We need to know the authority behind them. Most especially, we must be strong in our knowledge and understanding of the Word of God. And we will need to know God's *will*, His *strategy*, and His *timing*, and receive the Holy Spirit's assignment and anointing before engaging the enemy. We must know that the goal is the glory of God and the advancement of His Kingdom, and understand that in humility and surrender to Him lies the victory.

It seems to me that our growing in the Lord includes training for warfare and *maturing into the power* that He desires to work in us and through us. I believe that as we grow spiritually, as we implant the Word in our hearts and the Holy Spirit grants us understanding, as we learn to so closely abide in Him, as our ears are attuned to hear His voice, as we humble ourselves and surrender more completely and obey more instantaneously, we invite the power of the Holy Spirit to flow through us, unimpeded. As we learned in *Triumph of Surrender*, removing the rocks of our sins is removing the obstructions to the flow of the Holy Spirit.[12]

Maturity is indeed critical (Eph 4:13-15, 2 Cor 2:6, 3:1-3). And yet, let's go back to a passage from the last chapter to see what is *truly* imperative for growing in power:

But he said to me, "My grace is sufficient for you, *for my power is made perfect in weakness*." Therefore I will boast all the more gladly of my weaknesses, so that the power of Christ may rest upon me. For the sake of Christ, then, I am content with weaknesses, insults, hardships, persecutions, and calamities. For when I am weak, then I am strong.

2 Corinthians 12:9-10 ESV, emphasis added

Made perfect is *teleo*, accomplished, fulfilled, completed, brought to perfection or to its destined goal.[13] Even more important to grasp, **weakness** is *astheneia*; one of its meanings is "impotence."[14] When we grow in humility and truly recognize that our human abilities are *powerless*, when we are fully *dependent* upon Christ's power, then His power in us grows and develops to reach its destined goal.

As Paul walked in humility, yielding himself and surrendering to God's plan, he no longer operated in human strength, but the power of Christ worked through him. Christ's power increased in him as he walked in greater surrender and humility. **"My strength and power ... show themselves most effective in [your] weakness"** (2Cor 12:9 AMPC).

Ponder, Pray, and Journal

Read the following passages:

- 2 Corinthians 12:7-10
- 1 Corinthians 2:1-5

What does it mean to you to develop in power?

So ... once we develop in power, will we always retain that power? Oh, you ask the best questions. Let's go to the Word.

"Power Had Gone Out of Me"

And a woman who had a hemorrhage for twelve years, and could not be healed by anyone, came up behind Him and touched the fringe of His cloak, and immediately her hemorrhage stopped. And Jesus said, "Who is the one who touched Me?" And while they were all denying it, Peter said, "Master, the people are crowding and pressing in on You." But Jesus said, "Someone did touch Me, *for I was aware that power had gone out of Me."*   Luke 8:43-46, emphasis added

When this woman was healed, power was released from Jesus. Would He need to seek the Holy Spirit for refilling of that power, or did He have an infinite source of power within Him? When He went off to secluded places to unite with His Heavenly Father in prayer, did the Holy Spirit replenish His power? Scripture does not clarify things here, but we do know that Jesus was fully God and fully man (Phil 2:6-7, Col 2:9). As fully God, 100% divine, the Holy Spirit had full access to Him, and He always had full access to the Holy Spirit and always had full power of the Holy Spirit. The Father had given Him **the Spirit without measure** (NIV **without limit**, Jn 3:34). And as fully man, 100% man, Jesus always prayed and did nothing apart from God.

Ponder, Pray, and Journal

Read the following passages and journal when Jesus prayed. Was it before, during, or after the battle? Why do you think He prayed at those times?

- Mark 1:29-39
- Matthew 14:13-23

Jesus prayed before, after, during – He was constantly connecting to His Heavenly Father. Perhaps Jesus needed to be refilled. Read about the Holy Spirit descending upon Jesus in Mark 1:9-11, and about angels ministering to Him in Matthew 4:9-11 and strengthening Him in Luke 22:39-44.

How will you seek filling and replenishing?

In this chapter, we have learned the difference between authority and power. We learned where our authority comes from, how we can invite Satan's influence even though he has no legitimate authority. We learned how to position ourselves for the Holy Spirit to activate His power within us, and how to develop in power. In upcoming chapters, we are going to discuss how, when we are in the center of His will and abiding in Him, we can stand in our God-given authority and rely on the Holy Spirit to work powerfully through us for destruction of strongholds. But before we can learn how to *tear down* strongholds, we will first learn how they are *formed*.

PART III:

SATAN OPERATES OUT OF STRONGHOLDS

For though we walk in the flesh, we do not war according to the flesh, for the weapons of our warfare are not of the flesh, but divinely powerful for the destruction of fortresses [NIV strongholds]. We are destroying speculations and every lofty thing raised up against the knowledge of God, and we are taking every thought captive to the obedience of Christ, and we are ready to punish all disobedience, whenever your obedience is complete.   2 Corinthians 10:3-6

Chapter 10
Formation of a Stronghold, Part I

*W*hy, if I am a Romans 8 girl, do I sometimes feel like I am living in Romans 7? If the law of the spirit of life in Christ has set me free from the law of sin and death, why then am I not practicing what I want to do, but I am doing the very thing I hate? Is this simply a battle with my flesh, or have the demonic teamed up with my flesh so now I'm battling a stronghold? Does a stronghold necessarily imply something demonic? Can a Christian really have a demonic stronghold???

Let's go to the Word right away. We are going to be referring back to these next two passages frequently as we travel through this chapter, so take some time to read and ponder them slowly and prayerfully.

For our struggle is not against flesh and blood, but against the rulers, against the powers, against the world forces of this darkness, against the spiritual forces of wickedness in the heavenly places. Ephesians 6:12

For though we walk in the flesh, we do not war according to the flesh, for the weapons of our warfare are not of the flesh, but divinely powerful for the destruction of fortresses [NIV strongholds]. We are destroying speculations and every lofty thing raised up against the knowledge of God, and we are taking every thought captive to the obedience of Christ,

and we are ready to punish all disobedience, whenever your obedience is complete. 2 Corinthians 10:3-6

War and **strongholds** are words that indicate battles with demonic forces. Note Paul's use of the words **our** and **we**. He is clearly including *himself* in this warfare against strongholds.

Healing and deliverance ministers Chester and Betsy Kylstra, and John and Mark Sandford, write about strongholds *in themselves* that they have battled to bring down. And Francis Frangipane, pastor and international teacher of church leaders, writes unhesitantly,

> It is foolish to assume that our salvation experience has eliminated all the wrong ideas and attitudes – the strongholds – which are still influencing our perceptions and behavior. Yes, old things passed away, and truly new things have come, but until we are walking in the fullness of Christ, we should not assume that the process of change is over ... being a Christian has not made us perfect. There are still many strongholds within us. Therefore, let us identify some of these spiritual fortresses. Rare is the Christian who is not limited by at least one of the following strongholds: unbelief, cold love, fear, pride, unforgiveness, lust, greed, or any combination of these as well as the possibility of many others.[1]

As we have been discussing, we cannot blame all our hardships, sins, trials, and failures on demons. Yes, the world is corrupt and Satan can manipulate it to tempt us mercilessly. Yes, nothing good dwells in our flesh, and Satan can exploit our weaknesses to draw us into pride and jealousy and rebellion and lust and control and idolatry and many other sins. Yet it is our responsibility to feed our spirits, to implant His Word in our hearts, to flee temptation, to renew our minds, to abide in the Vine, to see to it that we are not deceived. (Jude 1:20, 2Pet 1:4, 1Jn 2:15-17, Rom 7:18, Jas 1:14-15, Rom 8:5-8, Jas 1:21, Ps 119:11, 2Tim 2:22, 1Tim 6:11, 1Cor 6:18, Rom 12:1-2, Jn 15:4, Col 2:8.)

Sometimes, however, when we are walking closely with the Lord, immersed in the Word and the disciplines of Christ, obedient and surrendered, renewing our mind and fleeing temptations and feeding our spirits, victory over sin may *still* elude us. That is the time to consider that we may be in a battle with demonic forces.

If we are dealing with ...

- A sin we cannot defeat,
- An addiction or stronghold that we cannot break free from,
- Negative or ungodly or blasphemous thoughts that we cannot shut down – or that persistently recur when we do squash them,
- A lie we cannot uproot from the deepest part of our heart,
- A besetting sin,
- An inability to accept something written in His Word,
- A spiritual or emotional or mental wound that will not heal, or perhaps even a physical illness that defies medical explanation or evades all treatments,
- A particular sin that seems to run in our family,
- An area where we can get free, but can't *stay* free, or
- Any area where victory seems to slip through our fingers

        ... it is possible we may be up against a demonic stronghold.

Ponder, Pray, and Journal

Let's pause a moment and pray for the Lord to bring us out of denial, and to reveal any strongholds in our hearts that He wants to deal with during this season.

Lord God, You are the only One who knows our heart. You search the heart, You test the mind, You weigh the heart and know its thoughts and intentions. Search me, O God, and know my heart. I am conscious of nothing in myself that is not aligned with You, but I do not acquit myself – only You examine me. Don't allow me to remain mired in denial and deception. I know that You confide in those who fear You; please, dear Lord, reveal to me anything in my heart that is not pleasing to You. Amen.[2]

Be still before Him and allow Him to speak. Ask Him if He has brought you to this book to deal with any strongholds.

Write on this line any strongholds He is unveiling:

_____

If He has revealed something to you, rejoice! The Holy Spirit does not reveal in order to discourage, but because He is intending to work. I believe He has brought you to this study because He is inviting you to partner with Him in the destruction of this stronghold – so persevere through this course! Jesus wants you to be *free indeed* (Jn 8:36).

Before we can fully comprehend Satan's strongholds of darkness, I think we must understand God's Strongholds of Light. Let's explore.

Defining Strongholds of Light

Strongholds of Light are territories in our hearts where Jesus is reigning. Where we have surrendered to Him and asked Him to take control. Where we have become obedient from the heart to Jesus' teaching. Where we are continuing in His Word, walking in the Light as He is in the Light. In these Strongholds of Light, Jesus is the foundation. And remember the concept of spoils of war: whatever area Jesus rules in our heart translates to His rule in all the outflow – our minds, bodies, actions, thoughts, words, intentions, consciences, and beliefs in that same area.

In contrast, strongholds of darkness are territories in our hearts where Satan has access. Where we have refused to surrender to Jesus, or are walking in continual unrepented sin. Where we have aligned our thought processes or behaviors with Satan, and thus invited his influence. In these demonic strongholds, Satan has laid the foundation. And I use the concept of spoils of war to mean that whatever area Satan influences in our heart translates to his impact in all the outflow: our minds, bodies, actions, thoughts, words, intentions, consciences, and beliefs in that same area.

In the battle over territory of our hearts, Jesus' plan is to build and fortify His Strongholds of Light. The larger, stronger, and more towering a particular fortress of Light is, the more impregnable it will be from enemy take-over. Although he may shoot flaming arrows and tempt and harass, Satan will not even be able to find a foothold.

Scripture teaches us that God *Himself* is our Stronghold of Light, for He has **made Himself known as a stronghold** (Ps 48:3).

The LORD is my rock and my *fortress* and my deliverer,
My God, my rock, in whom I take refuge;
My shield and the horn of my salvation, my *stronghold*.
I call upon the LORD, who is worthy to be praised,
And I am saved from my enemies.   Psalm 18:2-3, emphasis added

The LORD of hosts is with us;
The God of Jacob *is our stronghold*.   Psalm 46:7, emphasis added

How are these Strongholds of Light created? Only by Jesus, since the Strongholds *are* Jesus, but it seems He desires us to co-labor with Him in the process (2Cor 6:1, 1Thess 3:2). I am going to use some poetic license and talk about *co-battling* with Jesus. Of course we know that He doesn't *need* us; the battle is the Lord's, and the Lord God fights for us, just as He promised (2Chr 20:15, Josh 23:10). But because He gave us free will, in order to be victorious with Him, it seems He generally requires us to *cooperate* with Him in the battle.

I believe that we invite Him to lay the foundation of His Stronghold by our repentance and surrender to Him. When we cast down lies and choose by faith to believe the truth of His Word, whether it *feels* true or not. When we trust Him so fully that we walk out in obedience, even if we do not understand completely.

It seems we invite Him to build up His Stronghold, block by block, when we immerse in Scripture study, when we are devoted to prayer, when we choose to walk in contentment, joy, and thanksgiving. We invite Him to fortify the walls of His Stronghold as we are connected to our church family in fellowship and prayer and accountability and community worship. And repentance and confession as a way of life reinforces the walls, while praise and worship sustains them.

Cooperation demands that we humble ourselves and trust in Him. When we fully surrender to His sovereignty, when we invite Him in to control and rule, when we choose His way and not ours, *then* His victory is complete in that territory in our hearts.

Ponder, Pray, and Journal

Go back to the last three paragraphs and underline the ways we co-battle with Jesus as He builds His strongholds in our hearts. Journal anything the Lord is bringing to the forefront of your mind right now.

The Word reveals that *trust in His Name* is necessary for development of His Strongholds:

The Lord also will be a stronghold for the oppressed,
A stronghold in times of trouble;
And those who know Your name
Will put their trust in You,
For You, O Lord, have not forsaken those who seek You.

Psalm 9:9-10

And Strongholds of Light will not be built *without obedience to His will* for our lives:

The *way of the LORD* is a stronghold to the upright.

Proverbs 10:29, emphasis added

Some of the Strongholds of Light that I pray for the Lord to build in me are humility, surrender, obedience, submission, purity, truth, integrity, love, trust, dependence, contentment, gratitude, and fear of the Lord.

Ponder, Pray, and Journal

Take some time to pray about what Strongholds of Light you would like to ask Jesus to build in your heart, and ask Him to do just that. Write your requests in your journal – and buckle your seatbelt.

We are now going to turn our attention to strongholds of darkness. Let's explore the Word on this topic.

A Stronghold of Darkness Means Demonic Activity

Go back to the passages at the beginning of this chapter, Ephesians 6:12 and Second Corinthians 10:3-6. Read these passages again and circle the words or phrases that indicate that Paul is writing about spiritual warfare and battles with demons. Meet me back here when you are finished.

A stronghold of darkness *equals* demonic activity. I am careful not to use the terms "spiritual warfare," "freedom," "deliverance," "oppression," "bondage," "stronghold," or "fortress" flippantly, because, as we discussed in Chapter 6, *these words mean that demons are present*.

Francis Frangipane echoes these thoughts. He explains that strongholds of Biblical times were

> ... physical structures, usually caves high on a mountainside, and were very difficult to assault. It was with this imagery in mind that the inspired writers of the Bible adapted the word "stronghold" to define powerful, vigorously protected spiritual realities ... When we speak of strongholds we are not talking about random thoughts or occasional sins. Rather strongholds ... are so hidden in our thinking patterns that we do not recognize them nor identify them as evil ... Wherever a stronghold exists, it is a demonically induced pattern of thinking. Specifically, it is a "house made of thoughts" which has become a dwelling place for satanic activity ... spiritual fortresses wherein Satan and his legions hide and are protected.[3]

Wherever a stronghold exists, it is a demonically induced pattern of thinking. Where Satan and his legions hide and are protected. A dwelling place for satanic activity. Frangipane has declared without hesitation that a stronghold involves demonic forces. He *includes* demonic infiltration as part of his definition of a stronghold. Many other freedom and healing ministers agree.[4] I believe this is why destruction of strongholds is so hard: we are not fighting flesh and blood; *we are battling demons* (Eph 6:12).

Warfare is a spiritual reality that is impossible for our limited minds to fully comprehend. As we discussed in Chapter 8, don't get hung up on whether demons are "inside" or "outside" and where the "place" is. What we are looking at is the *level* of demonic activity. Flaming arrows, attacks, temptations, opposition, hindrance, resistance, and harassment do *not* indicate a stronghold. These are attacks from the outside. But when a stronghold exists, demons are involved on a deeper level. Given access, they are able to influence, manipulate, or oppress. If the stronghold is more entrenched, demons may be able to torment or hold people in bondage. The size and strength of the strongholds determine how impacting the demonic reach will be. In the unsaved, if demons have erected many strongholds, it may even lead to domination.

Comprehending Strongholds

My comprehension of a stronghold took on new depths when our family traveled to Israel a number of years ago. We visited Masada, an ancient fortress built around 30 BC. Even in its ruined state, we could envision Masada as an invincible fortress, a heavily armed castle constructed on a high mountain plateau that would be very difficult to assault. Clearly it was not merely the structure itself, but the geographic location of the fortress that provided for its impenetrability. As we traveled 1000 feet up to the ruins by cable car, I imagined what would be necessary for an invading army to conquer those sheer cliff walls.

The word **stronghold**, *ochuroma* (okh-oo'-ro-mah) in the Greek, is derived from a word that means "to hold fast."⁵ Bible teacher, author, and prayer warrior Pastor Dutch Sheets explains that a stronghold means "in essence, Satan has a place of strength *within* believers from which he can hold on to them strongly."⁶ This is very grave. When we have a *stronghold*, Satan *holds onto us strongly*. Pause a moment and take that in.

How Does Satan Construct a Stronghold?

How exactly *does* Satan create a stronghold? Good question. I'd like an answer to that too.

I have immersed in the Word, I have experienced warfare personally, and I have prayed for others as they have battled. I have studied theologians on this topic; some of their books are listed in the *Resource Section* at the back of this book. As we discussed in the *Introduction*, remember that these Bible scholars do not always agree on everything, but I think their writings mostly seem Biblically sound and carefully balanced, and appear to be a good foundation for understanding this topic. Some of my writing in this chapter and the next has leapt from the writings of these authors. **Examine everything carefully; hold fast to that which is good** (1Thess 5:21), and do not follow any teaching contrary to the Word of God (Gal 1:8).

One thing seems fairly certain to me: Satan's work is not random or haphazard. His schemes and strategies appear to be well-thought out and carefully calculated. As we mentioned in Chapter 7, some theologians even believe that his demons are arranged into some sort of hierarchy (Col 1:16, Eph 6:12, 1Cor 15:24).

The way I envision it through the study of Scriptures, as Satan maneuvers to gain the advantage, there are six ploys he aims to use in order to construct his stronghold. I will list them here as an overview, and then we will go into depth regarding each component.

1. Priming the ground with iniquities of our ancestors.
2. Laying the foundation with unhealed wounds.
3. Finding footholds of anger, unforgiveness, and more.
4. Entangling us in a network of lies, the cement holding the stronghold together.
5. Building towers with blocks of pride and idolatry.
6. Persuading us to open doors by our sin, particularly rebellion and habitual, repetitive, continual, unrepented sin.

When Satan has these components securely in place, our hearts become a place of rest for demons (Mt 12:43). And once demons enter, the *structure* becomes a *stronghold*. All these components may not be necessary for a stronghold to be formed, but it does seem to me that the more of these components Satan has in place, the greater the likelihood that he will be able to erect a stronghold.

In this chapter, we will focus on the ploys of wounds, footholds, and lies. In the next chapter, we will focus on iniquities of our ancestors, pride and idolatry, and habitual unrepented sins – and then we will see what it means to have created a resting place for demons.

In these next sections I will be leaping from Chester and Betsy Kylstra's visual depiction of a stronghold in their book, *Restoring the Foundations.*[7] I am pretty visual, so I am going to describe pictorially the way I visualize Satan and his demons creating a stronghold. We will start with the way I envision him laying the foundation.

The Foundation of a Stronghold: Unhealed Wounds

I agree with many freedom and healing ministers that Satan and his demons often begin by inflicting deep heart wounds. It seems that if they can effectively manipulate this fallen world and its imperfect people to cause us deep wounding, especially when we are young children, they have successfully laid their foundation.

Some deep heart wounds may be called trauma. Traumas are deeply painful experiences, including physical and emotional injury. Trauma also encompasses abuse of all categories – physical, emotional, mental, spiritual, and sexual, as well as abandonment and neglect. Traumatic experiences also include violence, witnessed or experienced, as well as natural disasters and losses, such as losing a loved one through death, divorce, abandonment, betrayal, or other ways. Illnesses and medical diagnoses – your own or that of a loved one – can fall into the category of trauma. Loss of dreams, health, finances, career, security, or even loss of life *as we know it* can also be traumas.

And yet, wounding does not need to fall into what the world would acknowledge as "traumatic" in order to be a deeply painful heart wound. Anything that overwhelms our ability to cope can be considered trauma. This fallen world is so rife with pain, violence, sin, hatred, indifference, selfishness, ignorance, that it doesn't take much for Satan to orchestrate wounding. An overly harsh parent. Thoughtless laughter of friends when we stumble. Careless remarks by a teacher. Biting criticism of a schoolyard friend. A physically or emotionally absent parent. A long term illness of a caregiver. A controlling older sibling. A failure to earn a spot on the football team. A report card with a D in math. A betrayal of a friend. As a child, we are so vulnerable and naïve, up against a powerful, cruel, and wily enemy who has had thousands of years of experience. And often we don't know where to go with our pain. Our wounds remain unhealed.

Often, it seems Satan carefully builds on these wounded areas. Wound upon wound. Pain upon pain. Abusive parent followed by abusive boyfriend followed by abusive boss followed by abusive spouse. A failing grade in school followed by failure to make friends followed by failure in the workforce. Betrayal of a childhood friend followed by betrayal of an adulthood friend followed by betrayal of a spouse. For Satan knows that a wound on top of a bleeding laceration will be much more painful than a wound on top of a strong healthy part of our body. He comes to steal, kill, and destroy; he wars ruthlessly and he has no concept of fighting fair.

Once the foundation is laid, Satan seeks a foothold. Even a toehold will do, for he is skillful and adept. When we are wounded, and we remain in anger or unforgiveness, we have provided just such a foothold he is searching for.

The Footholds of a Stronghold: Anger, Unforgiveness, and More

"In your anger do not sin": Do not let the sun go down while you are still angry, and *do not give the devil a foothold.*
Ephesians 4:26-27 NIV, emphasis added

We have studied anger in *Triumph Over Suffering* and *Triumph of Surrender*, and you know it is a normal human response to pain or heartache.

When our anger is due to injustice inflicted upon others, know that we are sharing God's anger, because He hates injustice also and calls it an abomination (Prov 17:15, 6:16-19). We can process our anger with God and allow Him to use our anger to *propel us* to fight for those who have been unjustly wronged (Micah 6:8, Jas 1:28, Rom 13:4).

When our anger is due to our own pain, the processing will be different. As we discussed in Chapter 8, anger may help us to recognize that someone has wounded us, violated our trust, crossed our boundaries, disrespected or devalued us. Realize that God is furious because of the pain inflicted upon us (2Sam 22:5-9). We can go to God to process our anger, *choose forgiveness*, and ask Him to heal us and direct us how to stand up against the injustice (Micah 6:8, Prov 31:8-9, Rom 12:19-21).

When our anger is due to circumstances beyond our control, the pain of loss or the heartache that life is not turning out as we had planned, we can turn to God to process our anger and *surrender* to His plan.

We can choose to trust that He is working for our good (Rom 8:28-29), even if it does not appear to be that way right now. If we remain mired in anger, it could be because we are believing that we know how to run the universe better than God does. We may be unable to trust Him, His hand, His timing. This kind of anger is a rejection of the sovereignty of God.

God's plan for our anger is to use it to draw us to Him. But if we turn away from Him in our anger, it becomes not only a barricade to our relationship with Him, but also, as Ephesians explains, an invitation for the enemy to gain a foothold.

Here are some ways we may avoid taking our anger to God:

- Stuffing our anger. Realizing that we are angry, but quashing it down instead of processing through it with God. Thinking that we are spiritually or emotionally mature enough to handle this on our own. Excusing the person who has hurt us, justifying his behavior, instead of acknowledging the pain and, in love as led by the Holy Spirit, confronting the offender.

- Pretending we are not angry. Deliberately creating a "forgiving" façade that in reality hasn't forgiven at all. We can only forgive as deeply as we have acknowledged the wound.[8]

- Denying that we are angry. This is a place of self-deception. We may at first not even realize that we are deluding ourselves. This denial may be fueled by the lie that "good Christians" shouldn't have any anger. Not being "allowed" to have anger in childhood also fuels this denial.

- *Pridefully* refusing to open the wounds of our hearts to God to heal. Determined we can heal on our own, blocking Him out of our pain, seeking the things of the world for healing.

- *Fearfully* refusing to open the wounds of our hearts to God to heal. Not trusting Him to be greater than our pain, refusing to talk to Him about our pain, locking Him out of rooms of our heart.

- *Shamefully* refusing to open the wounds of our hearts to God to heal. And if our shame is from our own sins, we may refuse to let go of the lies that our sin is too great to forgive, that we need to earn our forgiveness, or that we will always be second-class citizens in God's family. Shame causes us to hide our true selves from Him, as Adam and Eve did, and to reject His healing.

My friend Tina has a passion for the Lord and a contagious excitement to serve Him. But it wasn't always that way for her. When she was diagnosed with breast cancer a number of years ago, she became paralyzed with stuffed anger. I have asked her to share how turning away from God in her anger gave the enemy a foothold and invited him in to influence.

I was angry because of my divorce, hysterectomy, breast cancer, double mastectomy, survivor's guilt, and countless other things completely out of my control. I thought I was entitled to be angry with everyone around me – but I didn't think I was allowed to be angry with God.

The one thing I was most angry about was my hair. How dare God take away from me the one thing that I used as my security blanket since I was a child! How dare God take away something a woman prides herself on! How dare God take my identity away! How dare God take away my mini therapy sessions with my wonderful hair stylist!

I dreaded taking a shower, knowing I would be in tears over the large clumps of hair that fell into my hands as I washed. I pleaded with God, please leave the hair on my head! Why, why me God, why!?! But two weeks into my chemotherapy, I was completely bald.

I was raised in a strict Italian household. I was told that showing emotions was a sign of weakness, and I was trained from a very young age not to show emotions to God or to anyone. So even though I was very, very angry, I kept it locked deep down inside of me. My anger put a barrier between God and me. It began to affect my walk with the Lord as I drew further and further away from Him.

Reading <u>Triumph Over Suffering</u>, I learned that anger was a normal human response to my suffering, and that I was allowed to be angry with God! He already knew about my anger; He was just waiting for me to admit it to Him and process it with Him. If I came to Him, He would use my anger to draw me towards Him, and He promised to carry my suffering as I surrendered my anger to Him. Reluctant at first, I decided to test it out.

I really let God have it!!! After my anger / crying session, as I put my anger into His hands, I felt this intense peace come over me like a tidal wave, surging through every inch of my soul. The weight was lifted, and peace has been there ever since. Don't get me wrong, I still get angry, but I quickly realize that the source of my anger is the devil trying to get a foothold. I immediately stop in my tracks and begin thanking God for everything I can think of: sunshine, a roof over my head, clothes on my back, slow growing hair on my head.

It was during this season that I learned how to release my anger to God and choose thanksgiving and peace, no matter what comes my way!

Tina Monaghan
Loxahatchee, Florida

Notice the double sins of anger: dumping unchecked anger on people, and denying her anger against God. These dual anger sins of dumping anger and stuffing anger gave an open door to the enemy. Demons were invited in, and they had a field day amping up her anger and putting a "barrier" between her and God.

To demolish this foothold, Tina needed to process her anger *with* God. When she honestly poured her heart out to Him and surrendered everything into His hands, "the weight was lifted" as God granted her ravaged heart freedom. Peace like a tidal wave indicated her deliverance, as she closed the door and the enemy was forced to flee.

Notice the repeated battles as the enemy still tries to get a foothold and gain entrance again through that anger doorway. But as Tina continues to fight with spiritual weapons, thanking God, surrendering, and releasing her anger to Him, she has locked that door, and demons have been unable to gain entrance again. Her relationship with God remains deeply intimate, vibrant, and active.

Little did Tina know that God had been training her hands for a bigger battle. He wanted her to become very skillful in battling anger, because an even more terrifying season was ahead of her.

A few years later, my twenty-one year old daughter Mary was diagnosed with ovarian cancer. I left the oncologist's office fuming mad but silent – until I got in the car. As the door closed, I punched the steering wheel as hard as I could several times, saying, "I'm angry with You, God! How could You let this happen to my little girl! I know what she is about to endure and it's breaking my heart!" Mary was in the car with me and I remember her reaction, "Mom! You are scaring me!"

I told her that I knew that I had to get this out in the open. God knew I was angry, and this time, I would not let the enemy hold it over my head as he had in the past. As I released my anger to God, and taught Mary to do the same, God held us close and walked us ever so gently through this excruciatingly painful season.

Tina Monaghan
Loxahatchee, Florida

The Lord had indeed trained Tina's hands for war (Ps 144:1). Tina leapt to action and used the spiritual weapons she had learned – and taught Mary to use them too. As Tina pressed in to God and once again released her anger, her daughter, and the whole situation to Him, she gained the victory in Jesus and ensured that door remains locked against enemy entrance.

Ponder, Pray, and Journal

- Have you been wounded? Have you suffered loss? Is life not turning out as you planned?

- Have you admitted your anger and pain?

- Have you taken this to God? Have you poured out your soul and your pain to Him – and then in stillness listened for His response?

If you are not sure how to do this, go back to Chapter 2 of *Triumph Over Suffering*, "Experiencing and Expressing Emotions," or Chapter 7 of *Triumph of Surrender*, "The Life of the Heart," for some help as you walk through this with God.

Unhealed wounds lead to anger. Anger festers into unforgiveness. Anger gives a foothold, and unforgiveness creates an open door We discussed this passage in Chapter 8, but let's revisit it.

... if I have forgiven anything, I did it for your sakes in the presence of Christ, *so that no advantage would be taken of us by Satan, for we are not ignorant of his schemes.*

2 Corinthians 2:10-11, emphasis added

The NIV translates it **in order that Satan might not outwit us.** Wily and crafty, if Satan can successfully cause us to be offended, he can outwit us and gain entrance into our lives.

I think I can hear some of your questions already. But what about childhood pain? How could we be expected to forgive these penetrating wounds?

Yes, God knows. He knows your vulnerability. He knows and He sees. He feels your pain. He cries for you and with you (Jn 11:35). He gives us grace. Maybe we were a child at the time. But we are not children now. There comes a time when God calls us to forgive even what the world would call unforgivable. Remember, however, what we discussed in Chapter 8: forgiveness is release of the offender to God, *but forgiveness does not equal reconciliation.* Reconciliation requires heart work on the part of the other person. And for some relationships, even if the person seems to have repented and been transformed, God may command us to maintain distance for our safety and protection.

We make a choice to forgive, and we trust Jesus to heal us. But we are only able to forgive from the heart because of Jesus' forgiveness given to us and the Holy Spirit's power flowing through us. As followers of Jesus, we are *commanded* to forgive:

"For if you forgive others for their transgressions, your heavenly Father will also forgive you. But if you do not forgive others, then your Father will not forgive your transgressions." ... Be kind to one another, tender-hearted, forgiving each other, just as God in Christ has forgiven you ...

Matthew 6:14-15, Ephesians 4:32

If we withhold forgiveness, or if we judge and condemn those who have hurt us, we have been outwitted by Satan. We have allowed Satan to take advantage of us, to get the upper hand. We have fallen prey to his schemes. We have provided him a *foothold.*

Ponder, Pray, and Journal

Anger and unforgiveness are two footholds listed in Ephesians 4. It seems that many other sins may give Satan a foothold also. Read Ephesians 4:17-32 and list some of the other sins that give Satan an opportunity. (Verse 27 uses the word **foothold** (NIV) or **opportunity** (NASB) or **place** (NKJV).)

Visualize a rock climber attempting to surmount a sheer wall, finding it impossible to make any headway without a foothold. In equally real spiritual ways, areas of our hearts are impregnable to Satan – *unless we give him that foothold*. I have invited my friend Endrea to show you how this might play out.

I think what you would notice immediately about Endrea is her compassionate heart for those who are hurting. Undoubtedly it was her journey of suffering, her courage to turn to God in her pain, and God's miraculous healing that created in her this sensitive heart.

Endrea grew up in Brazil with a physically abusive mother who always made it clear that she was an unwanted mistake. When Endrea was ten, her parents sent her completely alone to the Unites States. She didn't know English and she knew no one. She was sent to live with her siblings, ten years older than her, whom she had never met. For the next seven years she stayed with different people every few years, attending eleven different schools in seven years. Eventually, there came a time when God called Endrea to forgive the seemingly unforgivable abandonment – *so that Satan could no longer outwit her*. Come with me and meet her.

I met the Lord when I was a child. But when my mother and father abandoned me, a deep root of rejection and fear of abandonment was cemented into my soul. I would often beg God to remove that stronghold in my heart and allow me to feel His love, to feel and see what I meant to Him. When I was sent alone to America, I knew He was all that I had, but somehow, the stronghold remained unbroken. Frustrated, I would give up and walk away, only to find myself in complete desperation for Him once again. These cycles of walking with God then turning from God continued again and again. Even though I knew all the Scriptures to tell me otherwise, I still believed the lies that I was unlovable, I wasn't good enough, and I didn't matter.

When the Lord brought me to Triumph Over Suffering *Class, I felt like a dead branch lying on the ground, detached from the Vine. I was ready to whole-heartedly seek Him. I learned to soak in His presence, meditating on Him, and He began to shine His light into my hardened heart, gently showing me my unforgiveness, judgments, and sin which had left no room for Him to enter. By His grace, as I repented and forgave and turned from my sins, He slowly broke down the walls of the strongholds, and as I let Him in, He replaced those strongholds with His love. He showed me that He was there for me and would always be there.*

As I accepted His sovereignty, it brought me so much healing and enabled me to truly trust Him as a good Father. And then He showed me His beautiful exchange: He had worn a crown of thorns so I could wear a crown of jewels. He showed me that I was a daughter of the King of kings, and He demonstrated to me how much He loved me. And finally, I could feel His love for me.

Endrea Elizabeth Jahn
Tequesta, Florida

Endrea had been deeply wounded by abandonment and rejection. Her unforgiveness gave Satan a foothold, her judgments and forsaking of God's ways invited Satan to erect a stronghold, while the lies held the stronghold in place. As she came to repentance, and chose to forgive and release and walk in obedience, the lies were banished by truth, and the whole stronghold began to come crashing down. Endrea was then able to *receive* His love – love that He had been pouring out upon her all along.

Later, when a friend was praying for her for continued healing, her friend prayed that God would give her a new name. Endrea heard the Lord say to her, "Elizabeth." Her Google search revealed that it meant "God's daughter"! At that moment, God spoke so deeply to her heart. She may have been unwanted and abandoned by her earthly parents, but she was loved and chosen by her Heavenly Father, who has claimed her for His own! **My father and mother have forsaken me, but the LORD will take me up** (Ps 27:10). It was such a beautiful seal upon His deep healing that she has taken Elizabeth as her own middle name.

As you saw in Endrea's testimony, Satan caused deep unhealed wounds, and drew her into his traps of anger and unforgiveness. This is one of Satan's prevailing tactics, for he knows that judging, resentment, bitterness, isolation, and defensiveness may follow. Next, we may begin to wall off our hearts to God, and soon be unable to trust God, or people. Our relationship with God now disrupted or non-existent, Satan's first strategy has succeeded: he has gained a foothold, and advanced from there. We are then ripe to fall to his next ambush: lies.

The Cement of a Stronghold: Satan's Lies

It seems to me that it is lies that cement the building blocks of the stronghold in place. The Kylstra's, in their visual depiction of a stronghold, call the lies "the mortar between the bricks or stones."[13] That sounds like a good analogy to me.

You may be wondering how Satan can implant lies in our hearts. Once we've been wounded, I don't think he finds this too difficult. For the pain of our life circumstances will work to speak a different reality than God's truth. These unhealed wounds entrap us into believing Satan's lies. If ...

- We don't know the truth of God's Word fully and completely, or
- We have never heard His truth, or
- We have heard the truth but are struggling to believe the truth, or
- We know the truth but refuse to believe it, or
- We are in doubt or confusion, or
- Our faith flounders upon the traumas life has dealt us

... then our hearts are wide open to grab onto untruths. A young child is of course extremely vulnerable.

Believing Satan's lies only requires us to see the reality of our circumstances. Believing God's truth requires us to see a deeper and more obscured spiritual truth, a truth that is greater than our *perceived* reality – which means that we must believe on faith. Faith is not a feeling; it is a *choice*. A choice to *trust* the truth even when the world, the people of the world, and our experience are screaming otherwise.

Faith ... is being certain of what we do not see.

Hebrews 11:1

Of course these lies are most easily implanted when we are children, before we are even able to read or comprehend His Word. But as we grow older, if we are not immersed in His Word, constantly washing ourselves with the water of the Word, repeatedly cleansing ourselves from Satan's lies and replacing them with God's truths, then we will be as susceptible as children are to fall into his lying snares (Eph 5:26, Titus 3:5, 1Cor 3:1-3, Col 2:8). The pressure Satan exerts via the corrupt world and our own sinful flesh is *relentless*.

I'd like to introduce you to my friend Eva. This precious woman has had her share of trials and heartache, yet through it all she literally glows with the grace of Christ. I've asked her to share how her strict childhood upbringing made her vulnerable to Satan's lies, and how Satan constructed his stronghold on that wounded foundation.

For the majority of my life I have struggled with my body image. In high school I started restricting my diet. I would eat a lot of sweets and then feel guilty, or at times not feel bad at all as if I had deserved it. And if I worked out hard, then all foods were guilt free. I tried to have complete control over what I ate or could say no to. And I would feel proud and empowered if I said no. Food wasn't used for the right reasons. Food was either a punishment or a reward, depending on how I felt. And I was the only one who made the rules, to beat myself up or to reward myself.

I was always thinking of what I would allow myself to eat later, so I had to plan carefully what I ate now. It was exhausting to think about eating all day long. My irrational eating always kept me uneasy. And my feelings dictated what I saw in the mirror. When I was feeling in control, I liked what I saw. When I was not feeling in control, I didn't. And what I saw in the mirror changed with each passing of the mirror, within minutes. I did not like myself one minute, and then thought I looked pretty great the next.

Although I was growing in Christ, reading the Word and going to church every week, I was blind to my dysfunctional approach to food. To me, it was "normal." The pastor at my church preached a series on "Freedom" and encouraged us to pray for freedom from our strongholds. It didn't even occur to me to pray about food and my body image.

Recently, the struggle worsened and the mind games became more exhausting and depressing. The oppression and turmoil were overwhelming. I discussed it with my counselor, and she told me that this was anything but "normal." She helped me to see that my strict childhood upbringing resulted in my feeling that I could never hit the mark. This led to my striving to be perfect. And I suddenly realized that these issues with food and body image were also striving for perfectionism. I knew only Jesus is perfect, but somehow, I kept striving to be perfect myself. I left her office unsettled.

Alone in the elevator, I didn't want to catch my reflection in the mirror. I didn't know if I'd be happy or disgusted with what I saw. But the pull to look was too great. I decided I would look, cautiously – and then I became annoyed with myself. A raging battle began in my mind over what was the right answer to what I saw. Do I look good, or fat? In anger I yelled to myself in my mind, "What is wrong with you?" and immediately the response came, "You want to be perfect!"

Wow, instantly, in that very moment, I realized I was believing a lie: that I needed to be perfect to win His love. And as the lie was exposed and I rejected it, I was set free. I realized that I can't be perfect, and that's okay. As I acknowledged the truth that there is no perfect body, I was suddenly okay with who I am. My healing came as I suddenly realized that I am a child of God, chosen and beloved. He sees me, and He knows my name! I was able to love myself the way God made me.

As I walked off the elevator, I suddenly realized how the media and advertisements are so false, because there absolutely is not one perfect body on earth that has no wrinkle or fat dimple or flawless skin. What a relief. A great weight was lifted off me. A standard that is unattainable in all aspects of life was shattered right then and there, and God has given me such freedom. Freedom to enjoy food, to no longer see it as punishment or reward, but to see that it is for nutrition and enjoyment. Freedom in my mind from the torment of relentless mind games. Freedom to look in the mirror, accept what I see, and to believe that I am pretty. I can now accept myself with my imperfections.

And God freed my mind! It is no longer running around in exhaustive circles planning what to eat, or not to eat. It is calm and at peace. My time with God has become richer, and I can hear Him with greater clarity.

That Sunday in service, the pastor reviewed his messages of the previous few weeks. And it was then that I understood what had happened to me: Jesus had delivered me. I had been absorbing the power of God's Word that was spoken over me at church each week, and that same power was present and active in that elevator. All God was working to free me culminated at the moment in the elevator.

I am in awe of how God met me right where I was and changed my life! I AM FREE! Oh how lavish is His love for you and me.

Eva

Did you see how Satan teamed up with the world to bring this young girl down? Satan's lie that she *could* be perfect dovetailed with the world's lies that perfection was *necessary* for happiness. And from there Eva's heart leapt to the lie that she needed to be perfect to win God's love. Eva unknowingly wrestled with this stronghold for decades. And it was her openness to the Lord and her growth path of Bible study and church that positioned her to be free indeed. Those lies were the cement that had been holding the stronghold in place, and when the Holy Spirit exposed them, Eva chose the humble path of rejecting them.

Imagine the lies as the cement holding the stones in place. When lies were torn down, the cement was suddenly removed. The entire stronghold of perfectionism and control could no longer stand without the cement, and it toppled. Jesus broke her chains, and she ran free.

Notice that even though initially Eva didn't fully understand the pastor's messages on freedom, she continued to listen intently in church each week. She didn't realize it, but the Holy Spirit was gradually working truth into her heart. When she experienced personally what the pastor was teaching, the Holy Spirit opened her mind and her heart to understand those previous messages and to comprehend that Jesus had delivered her.

The lies Satan entices us to believe are often very insidious. My husband, thinking in piloting terms, explains this as "one degree off of center." Satan knows that if he presents us with a lie that is many degrees off from what we believe is truth, we will probably reject it as an outright falsehood. But if he can distort our thought process *just a little bit*, we will start to travel one degree off of center. One degree off isn't much at the start. But over many years, one degree will lead us far off course. To avoid getting off course, we will want to become ...

... mature in the Lord, measuring up to the full and complete standard of Christ. Then we will no longer be immature like children. We won't be tossed and blown about by every wind of new teaching. We will not be influenced when people try to trick us *with lies so clever they sound like the truth.* Ephesians 4:13-14 NLT, emphasis added

Lies so clever they sound like the truth. Oh, Satan is very sneaky indeed. Charles Spurgeon explains that it is not enough to simply know the difference between right and wrong. We must know "the difference between right and almost right."[9]

Just How Does Satan Introduce These Lies?

Let's wrestle through some questions. Can Satan and his demons *influence* our minds? *Read* our minds? *Control* our minds? *Plant thoughts* in our minds? Scriptures are not clear here, and theologians disagree. We don't want to ascribe to Satan powers that he does not have. But nor do we want to underestimate his power here. Let's look at what Scripture *does* reveal on this topic. As you read these four passages, circle what kind of impact Satan *can* have on our minds.

But I am afraid that, as the serpent deceived Eve by his craftiness, your minds will be led astray from the simplicity and purity of devotion to Christ.   2 Corinthians 11:3

The AMPC translates it: Satan *corrupts and seduces* our minds.

When anyone hears the word of the kingdom and does not understand it, the evil one comes and snatches away what has been sown in his heart. This is the one in whom seed was sown beside the road.   Matthew 13:19

You will remember this passage from Chapter 2:

And even if our gospel is veiled, it is veiled to those who are perishing, in whose case the god of this world has blinded the minds of the unbelieving so that they might not see the light of the gospel of the glory of Christ, who is the image of God.   2 Corinthians 4:3-4

Then Satan stood up against Israel and moved David to number Israel ... Now David's heart troubled him after he had numbered the people.   1 Chronicles 21:1, 2 Samuel 24:10

These verses say Satan can lead our minds astray with his deception, corrupting our minds and seducing them away from Christ. He can steal away what God is sowing in our hearts. He can blind minds, and even move a Godly king to sin. The word *moved* is translated *incited* in the ESV and *provoked* in the KJV. The Word does not specify *how he does this,* but somehow it seems he can persuade us to disobey, he can lead us astray with lies, he can induce us to disloyalty. These verses do indicate significant influence upon our minds and hearts. I have asked my son's friend Ty to share a time when the enemy worked to implant thoughts into his mind.

I first met Ty when he was in high school and mentoring my son Alec. My family has watched Ty's deep and devoted walk with the Lord over many years as he completed seminary and is now a pastor. Fourteen years ago, Ty was in Haiti on the mission field.

After a devastating earthquake shook Haiti in 2010, my church sent a mission team to deliver resources and encouragement to our mission partners in the nation. The church in the city of Gonaives received us graciously. Despite this warm reception by the people of Haiti, there was one day when we came into spiritual conflict with a group of Voodoo priests. While we prayed outside their temple, we saw overt signs of spiritual warfare unlike anything I had seen before.

While Voodoo priests cursed our group, the weather and animals began acting bizarrely while we prayed. This was a shocking experience to me. But the demonic activity did not end when we had left the temple area. As we headed back to the local church, I began to feel intense pangs of loneliness and could not shake the belief that I did not belong on this trip or with my fellow missionaries.

These particular thoughts were foreign to me. I belonged to an incredible church, and prior to that very moment had only felt excitement and a passion about being on this trip. Despite that, as we arrived at church and filed into the chapel for a brief service, I continued to wrestle with these negative thoughts and began to sink deeper into a state of isolated frustration.

As we began worshiping, I turned my heart and mind toward the truths we were singing. Upon focusing on who God is, I began to experience freedom from those negative thoughts. Within minutes, I realized that the Enemy had been impressing his thoughts upon my mind. With each passing song, the joy and confidence in the Lord that

I had brought with me into the trip returned more and more fully.

This experience taught me that the Enemy uses a variety of tactics to break the focus of believers. The explicit warfare taking place outside the Voodoo Temple was shocking, but the more subtle attacks on my spirit were even more deadly.

I don't believe these types of attacks are unique to the mission field. In fact, I am confident that attacks such as these happen frequently around the world and go undetected. When the wind is howling, animals are braying, and curses fill the air, Christians may recognize demonic activity and know to keep their guard up. But angry, selfish, and self-loathing thoughts are more palatable to us, so we may not realize that these thoughts are coming from the Enemy. We may not know to seek the Lord's protection.

When I realized how subtle the Enemy can be, I understood how much I need the Holy Spirit to guide me into all truth. When I reframed my focus on the character of God, and sang about it in the congregation of believers, I was given the victory needed to overcome in that trial.

Ty McMillan
West Palm Beach, Florida

We may not be able to really comprehend exactly how the enemy impresses his thoughts on our minds. Perhaps he instigates, motivates, prompts, provokes, or causes obsession. However he might accomplish this, the choice to *act upon* his suggestions remains ours.

Nevertheless, I don't think Satan and his demons can actually *read* our minds. It seems to me that only God has that power and access; the Word says *only God* knows what is in every human heart:

... *You alone* know the hearts of all the sons of men ...

1 Kings 8:39, emphasis added

Satan and his demons *can*, however, read our behaviors, and it seems they can have some access to our minds, hearts, souls. Joni Eareckson Tada, in *When God Weeps*, puts it this way:

> Satan ... taps into people's brains all the time. He's a regular soul hacker – like the techno-geeks on their modems at home, breaking security codes and logging onto sensitive government computer systems. Scripture calls him "the spirit who is now at work *in* those who are disobedient." It describes his access to the human soul: "When anyone hears the message about the kingdom and does not understand it, the evil one comes and snatches away what was sown in his heart" (Matthew 13:19).[10]

Francis Frangipane goes deeper:

> The aspect of the human nature which is most similar in substance and disposition to the nature of the evil one is the carnal thought-life ... It is uniquely in our uncrucified thoughts and unsanctified attitudes that unclean spirits, masking themselves as *our* thoughts and hiding themselves in *our* attitudes, find access into our lives.[11]

When it comes to strongholds, I see it this way. Often Satan orchestrates wounding to lead us to entertain a lie. Maybe Satan speaks the lie through another person. Maybe we read it, or hear it on media. Or maybe he whispers the lie to us, something insidious, just one degree off center. Maybe he implants it, maybe he injects it. Maybe he simply suggests it, and, as Frangipane explains, we think it is our own thought. It could be a thought like, "They must think I am stupid." "They don't want to be with me." Or it may even come in the first person: "I'm no good," "I'm worthless," "I'm unlovable," "I'm a failure." Of course the suggestion coming in the first person would cause us even more so to think it is our own thought.

Initially, we may have no recognition that a particular thought has come from darkness. Because of the pain and circumstances of our lives, this lie may *appear* to be truth. It may be the only reality we know, and if we do not know God, if we do not know His Word, we are unable to combat that lie and stand on the Truth.

So we receive the lie. We meditate on it, churn it around, chew on it. And instead of spitting it out as a repulsive lie, we plant it as truth in our heart.

It is the Word that will expose these lies:

For the word of God is living and active and sharper than any two-edged sword, and piercing as far as the division of soul and spirit, of both joints and marrow, and able to judge the thoughts and intentions of the heart.   Hebrews 4:12

If we are not immersed in the Word, the deceitfulness of these lies may not be exposed, and those lies may become entrenched, very deep roots indeed.

Entanglements of Lies: Logismos

As I study the Greek, it seems to me that strongholds are formed generally not on one isolated lie, but on a tangled web of lies that affect many different parts of our belief system. If Satan can water and fertilize that first little lie with additional woundings, the pain of our heart opens us to latch on to more and more lies. Think about the network of lies in Eva's testimony. I think a stronghold involves a network of interconnected lies, each one feeding on and supporting another.

We are destroying speculations and every lofty thing raised up against the knowledge of God ...   2 Corinthians 10:5

Speculations, or *logismos* (log-is-mos') in the Greek, must be a pretty hard word to translate into just one English word. The KJV translates it **imaginations**, the NKJV **arguments**, the AMP **sophisticated arguments**, and the NLT **human reasonings and false arguments**.

Logismos is the reasoning and reflection that brings us to conclusions that dictate our beliefs and conduct.[12] Our word logic comes from this word. *Logismos* does not mean isolated thoughts, but an *entrenched* thought pattern, a deep reasoning process, involving weighing various options and coming to a conclusion after all the evidence is assessed. This word indicates our viewpoint, or our mindset, our worldview which governs what we believe and how we act. Our *logismos* controls our emotions, our thoughts, and our speech. It determines how we perceive our experiences, how we interpret what people say and do, and what we think of the world around us. It dictates our behaviors, how we see God, and how we define ourselves.

Satan uses deceptive *logismos* to attempt to *annihilate our identity*. Satan's *logismos* can cause us to believe that we are superior and to think of ourselves more highly than we ought. Or to believe that we are unwanted, of no value, with nothing to contribute to the Kingdom. Or to believe that God is not really on our side and that He is not concerned with us personally.

Satan can cause such a great distortion of our personality traits and thought processes so as to cause us to *think* that this delusional identity really *is* who we are. Whenever we encounter confusion about our identity – whether it is our physical, spiritual, emotional, mental, or gender identity – expect to find *logismos* at work.

In Chapter 2, I referred to the way I was ensnared in the "I'm-too-sinful-worthless-and-insignificant" lies and how I was trying to *earn* God's love and acceptance. For me, Satan's deception was not an isolated one sentence thought, but a milieu of degrading and condemning feelings of "not enough-ness" and impressions of worthlessness. I *thought* these perceptions and feelings were my own. I certainly didn't recognize them as specific "thoughts" or "beliefs." They were such a part of my character and life for so many decades that I had no idea that they were lies, or that they were foreign. Satan had embedded his *logismos*.

At first I didn't even know they were even *thoughts*. And I certainly didn't know that they were not *originally* my thoughts. I didn't know that they were lies implanted by Satan, probably inserted when I was wounded throughout my childhood. In my ignorance, I had taken on these thoughts and feelings as my own. I had come to believe that they *were* mine, and thus my heart believed that they were true.

Ponder, Pray, and Journal

Logismos is a complex word. Re-read this section, and summarize in your journal what you have learned.

Ponder, Pray, and Journal

Sometimes, maybe often, we pay no attention to our thoughts. Our minds run in whatever ruts have been worn there, without our intervention. Ask the Holy Spirit to examine your thoughts, and begin to take notice of them. Are they peacefully focused on the things of the Spirit, or racing uncontrollably with worry, anger, guilt, fear, revenge, or addictions?

I'd like to introduce you to Dave Bowerman, a friend of my husband and mine who holds a Master of Divinity degree. This man is now a spiritual powerhouse for the Lord – but for over three decades he had been trapped by the enemy. I've invited him to share his downward spiral into a stronghold of impurity through a *logismos* full of faulty mindsets.

I was trapped in impurity but didn't know it. Influenced by the news, TV, movies, and music, I began to believe I could define truth for myself. With no absolute moral authority, I believed the lie that truth was negotiable. I was soon snared in outright denial that I even had a problem. On days I couldn't quite deny it, I believed that it simply wasn't my fault, blaming my upbringing, bad influences, an identity crisis, and depression. While these were factors, they were never the sum total of my problem.

I minimized the harm it was having on my marriage and my family. My focus was completely on the world, and I failed to see life the way God does. At times when I would realize I was in sin, I believed that God's grace would simply cover my sin, so I had no motivation to change. During the times I did desire to change, I believed I could do it on my own strength. After repeated failures, I embraced the lie that my situation was hopeless. I was defined by defeat.

Pride led me to believe that I could find my own escape, and hindered me from surrendering to God and relying on the Holy Spirit's power. I see now that I had lived out Romans 1:18-32: though I knew God, I did not acknowledge Him but rather thought for myself. I exchanged the truth of God for a lie, and worshiped and served created things rather than the Creator. Therefore, God gave me over to shameful lusts and a depraved mind, to do what ought not to be done.

My thought life behind this stronghold was cunningly beyond my ability to recognize. It created the behavior and continued to fuel it. Until my thought life was transformed, nothing would change.

Dave Bowerman
Author, Higher Pursuits
Port St. Lucie, Florida

We will pick up Dave's story in Chapter 21, but for now, we will let it stand to remind us how Satan uses faulty *logismos* to build his strongholds. And realize that although we are talking about our "mindset," all this reasoning, reckoning, considering, calculating, and reflecting is occurring *in our hearts*. Jesus, speaking to the Pharisees, asks them,

"Why are you reasoning in your hearts?"   Luke 5:22

These activities are carried out in our minds, but the source is *our hearts*. It is our "heartset" that dictates our mindset, for as we learned in Chapter 2, our heart is "Command Central."

What sorts of things influence our viewpoint, our "heartset"? My Greek Word Study explains that the word **stronghold** metaphorically means "arguments in which one trusts."[13] *What we trust*. What we trust is what we rely on to make our decisions. What we trust is what dictates our thoughts and behaviors. Clearly we can see how our education, our reading, our absorption of knowledge impacts what ideas we will trust. To develop a Biblically accurate heartset, we must immerse in the truth of His Word. Immersing in the principles of the world or "wisdom" of the flesh or the doctrines of the demonic will result in a faulty heartset, which will develop a flawed mindset. Feeding the flesh instead of feeding the spirit will result in a *logismos* based on lies. We must guard our hearts, the wellspring of our lives. (2Tim 3:16-17, Jas 3:14-17, 1Cor 3:19, Rom 8:5-8, Prov 4:23.)

Our mind is an amazing gift, but we can abuse that gift by using it to justify our sins or to rationalize our rebellion or to try to make sense of a God who is too massive for our puny minds to make sense of. My husband says we cannot fully trust God if we demand that everything about God "makes sense" to our minds. Faith defies reasoning and explaining. Faith is trusting that He is the LORD, and there is no other, and no one can thwart His plans (Isa 45:6, Job 42:2).

Rationalizing and justifying also includes defending our shortcomings and minimizing our sins. Excusing ourselves. Holding ourselves to a different standard than we hold others to. Thinking that we are above the law. Giving ourselves a free pass. Aligning ourselves with the excuses of Satan instead of confessing and agreeing with God about our sins. Believing we can overlook our sins and God's grace will cover them. Scripture calls this insulting the Spirit of grace (Heb 10:26-29, Jude 1:4).

Ponder, Pray, and Journal

Re-read that last paragraph, and think about Dave's testimony. Can you see how the reasoning based on lies invites the darkness in? Ask the Holy Spirit to search your heart for deceptive justifications and rationalizations.

In this chapter, we have observed how Satan lays the foundation of his stronghold by wounding, finds footholds such as anger and unforgiveness, and ensnares us in his web of lies. Are you beginning to visualize a stronghold being formed?

Now that you have a greater understanding of strongholds, prayerfully ponder the question that opened this chapter: Are there any strongholds the Lord is revealing to you? Write them here:

_____

In the next chapter, we will watch Satan build up the stronghold block by block, and in later chapters, we will learn how to attend to all these components in order tear his fortresses down.

Chapter 11
Formation of a Stronghold, Part II

In the last chapter, we learned how unhealed wounds can lay a foundation for a stronghold, opening us up to believe lies and more lies, and how unforgiven offenses give footholds. Before we see the rest of the stronghold built up and the invitation issued for demons to access, we are going to back up a bit and talk about the groundwork *below* the foundation.

The Groundwork Below the Stronghold:
Iniquity of Our Ancestors

I'd like to discuss a method Satan may use to prepare the ground so his lies may be more readily believed, his traps may appear more enticing, and his foundational wounding may be even more likely to take hold. The Bible calls this scheme **the iniquity of the fathers** (Ex 20:5).

How is iniquity different than sin or transgression? Sometimes, it seems these words are used interchangeably. But other times it seems the Lord has selected these words very specifically, using transgression to mean an action of breaking His law, sin to be the consequences of that, and iniquity to indicate something found within our hearts[1] (1Sam 20:8).

I kept myself from my iniquity ...
Do not let iniquity have dominion over me.

Psalm 18:23, 119:133

The iniquity of the fathers seems to refer to unrighteousness deep within the hearts of members of a family line. This iniquity creates an environment that somehow makes it easier for these family members to fall into repeated sin. In Chapter 24, we will learn how Jesus has made a way for freedom from these iniquities of our ancestors – but we have spiritual concepts to learn and work to do here first. Brace yourself; this will be a heavy section.

The Word explains how iniquity in our ancestors affects us, so we will let Scripture speak.

"I am the LORD your God, who brought you out of the land of Egypt, out of the house of slavery. You shall have no other gods before Me. You shall not make for yourself an idol, or any likeness of what is in heaven above or on the earth beneath or in the water under the earth. You shall not worship them or serve them; for I, the LORD your God, am a jealous God, *visiting the iniquity of the fathers on the children*, on the third and the fourth generations of those who hate Me, but showing lovingkindness to thousands, to those who love Me and keep My commandments."   Exodus 20:2-6, emphasis added

I was thinking about skipping this passage. But God repeated these verses verbatim in Deuteronomy 5:6-10, and also in Exodus 34:7, so He must consider this teaching very important. Let's pause and ask the Holy Spirit to enlighten us.

Holy Spirit, You promise to be our Teacher. Please grant us wisdom and revelation to understand Your Word, and to comprehend the Father's heart with deeper discernment. Help us to humbly accept Your ways, Your purposes, Your mighty hand. Help us to bow our hearts to Your plan, because You are Almighty Sovereign King – and also because You love us deeply, You know what is best for us, Your plan arises from Your heart, and You alone can be fully trusted. Amen.[2]

I'll grab my *Hebrew Word Study* and start with **iniquity**. Iniquity in this passage, *avon* (aw-vone') in the Hebrew, can also be translated **perversion**. Think about perversion deep within one's heart. *Avon* comes from a root word meaning crooked, indicating "twisting or perverting deliberately." This iniquity, this *avon*, results in rebellion against God *and includes the consequences* that result from the rebellion.[3] Understanding the incorporation of *consequences* in this word will help us to understand **visiting**.

Words that are translated "iniquity" in the Greek include in their definitions "obstinate adherence to worldliness or idolatry"[4] and "lawlessness ... contempt of Divine law."[5] Our English word addiction comes from one of the Greek words translated as iniquity, *adikia*.[6]

There is a Greek word translated "sin" that is *hamartia* (ham-ar-tee'-ah), which means "missing the mark ... missing the true end and scope of our lives, which is God."[7] *Hamartia* is indeed very grave, yet iniquity is a vastly different word; iniquity within our hearts results in a much more *deliberate* rebellion, a *definite* twisting, a *calculated* perversion of the ways of God.

Visiting

Visiting has many layers of meanings; let's look at a few that I think are relevant here. Visiting "refers to someone (usually God) paying attention to persons, either to do them good, or to bring punishment or harm ... to cause something to be attended to."[8]

To cause something to be attended to. Our rebellion against God is visited upon our children to cause *us* to attend to our rebellion. This is very heavy. If we are sinning with intentional malice, if we are deliberately twisting and perverting truth, if we are living in habitual unrepented sin, if we are mired in addictions, if we are hardening our hearts to God's correction, if we are in contempt of God's law, if we

are stubbornly holding onto worldliness and idols, if we are refusing
to humble ourselves and grow up in the Lord – and *if we don't attend
to those iniquities when the consequences damage us* – then we may
wake up, come out of denial, and attend to our iniquities *when the
consequences damage our children*. That is God's merciful grace.

Realize that God's ultimate purpose is not to simply inflict
punishment upon us, but to cause us to *attend* to these sins when we see
these sins affecting our children. He has established this consequence
to bring us back to Him, because He loves us – and our children – so
much, and because He knows that only when our relationship with Him
is restored will we receive peace, fulfillment, contentment. He created
us, and He knows exactly what will bring us – and our children – the
greatest joy. (Ps 119:67, Heb 12:5-11, Ps 85:10, Rom 5:1, Gal 5:22-23.)

Another definition of **visiting** is "to search out."[9] God is in the
purification business: it is His will that we be sanctified (1Thess 4:3).
God orchestrates the timing of His sanctification (Gal 6:7-8). He may
graciously protect us from the consequences of our sins for a period of
time, protecting our children from the visitation, as He gives us time to
respond to His gentle correction. But if we remain stubbornly blind to
our iniquities, God may orchestrate the events of our lives so that we
are no longer shielded from the fallout. If our hearts of rebellion remain
hard, our iniquities may be visited upon our children, and our sins will
be searched out and exposed. As Moses told the Israelites, **"Your sin
will find you out"** (Num 32:23).

How many times have we seen this play out? When parents are
addicted to drugs, children suffer. These children may be hungry,
neglected, abandoned, homeless, abused, even introduced to drugs
at very young ages. The iniquity of the fathers visited on the children.
But please don't miss God's heart in all of this! Yes indeed, He set the
universe into motion and with it the consequences for our sins. But there
is deep love and unspeakable grace in the aftermath. Sometimes we see
the parents come to their senses and repent and find God and seek help
conquering their addictions – but not until they saw the devastating

effects that their addictions were having on their children! This is an example of the parents' iniquities being visited on their children *to cause the parents to attend to them*. In our free will, we may choose iniquity, but God is using even that to draw us home to Him. (Ps 33:11, Eph 2:8-9, Gen 50:20.)

Let's explore one more aspect of what it means for iniquity to visit our children. This is the aspect that relates to our study of strongholds: the priming of the ground before the foundational wounding. I am referring to the passing down of iniquities from generation to generation.

Iniquity Visited on Our Children

The American Academy of Child and Adolescent Psychiatry states that "children of alcoholics are four times more likely than other children to become alcoholics themselves."[10] The World Health Organization states that "a child who is abused is more likely to abuse others as an adult so that violence is passed down from one generation to the next."[11] The American Psychological Association states that children of gamblers "are more likely to engage in gambling."[12] Research reveals that anger, anxiety, insomnia, workaholism, depression, and many more run in families.[13] As a family practice physician, I have seen the generational aspect of iniquities repeatedly in my practice, including issues like generational control, anger, bitterness, and unforgiveness. Additionally, it seems that the sins escalate from generation to generation. I have heard it said that what one generation tolerates, the next normalizes, and the next celebrates.

Healing and deliverance ministers Chester and Betsy Kylstra describe iniquity as a *propensity* to sin that results from recurrent sin in the family line. The trap that ensnared our ancestors does not "force" us to sin, but puts a "pressure" on us to sin. "This doesn't automatically mean that we have to sin. But that we are likely to."[14] When someone has the pressure of an ancestral iniquity, I think the temptation simply seems more enticing, and the will to say no seems weak or nonexistent.

We can see this illustrated throughout the Bible, as we read in Kings and Chronicles about the sinful lives of generations of kings. We can see the entire nation of Israel also, repeatedly falling into idolatry and rebellion. Additionally, each generation seemed more evil than the previous one (Jer 7:26).

It seems the passage below from Deuteronomy 28 could be related to the visiting of iniquities. In Deuteronomy 28, the Lord is enumerating the blessings for obedience, and the consequences (curses) for disobedience.

"But it shall come about, if you do not obey the LORD your God, to observe to do all His commandments and His statutes with which I charge you today, that all these curses will come upon you and overtake you:
... You shall have sons and daughters but they will not be yours, for they will go into captivity."   Deuteronomy 28:15, 41

We know how Israel went into captivity in Babylon because of their iniquities of rebellion and idolatry. As we studied in Chapter 8, rebellion against God can open us up to a spirit of bondage, or spirit of slavery.

Could *our own* iniquities and disobedience to God's commandments be contributing to the bondage of our sons and daughters? My heart is pierced through for the many who are in bondage to addictions and iniquities and strongholds; perhaps their parents' opposition and blindness to the truth contributed to that captivity.

And Deuteronomy 30 goes on to explain the pathway out of captivity:

"So it shall be when ... you *return to the LORD your God and obey Him* with all your heart and soul according to all that I command you today, you and your sons, then the LORD your God will restore you from captivity ..."
                    Deuteronomy 30:1-2, emphasis added

Do not forget that **the LORD has caused the iniquity of us all to fall on Him** (Isa 53:6). In Jesus, freedom is available. Repentance and returning to the Lord entreat the Lord to deliver us. Note that if our children are in rebellion, Deuteronomy states that they also need to return to the Lord *themselves* to receive His freedom.

Now one more passage for clarification. Iniquity visited upon the children does not mean they are *responsible* for their parents' sins. This visitation is merely the spill-over effect of their parents' sins. Ezekiel makes that clear:

"The son will not bear the punishment for the father's iniquity, nor will the father bear the punishment for the son's iniquity; the righteousness of the righteous will be upon himself, and the wickedness of the wicked will be upon himself."   Ezekiel 18:20

What does that mean for us? The ancestral iniquity pressures us to sin. We have inherited a heart weakness, a predisposition for a particular sin. But it seems that most often, in order for a stronghold to be formed, more than temptation is needed: we must *enter into* the sin ourselves. (Recall how Jesus warned Peter to keep watching and praying so he would not **enter into** temptation (Matt 26:41)). We inherit the heart weakness, the pressure bears down, and we may fall into the snare of sin. As this sin becomes repeated and unrepented, it can soon become a besetting sin, a continual, habitual sin, a practice of sin – thus becoming harder and harder to break free. Iniquity is then formed in our hearts, full grown, ready to be passed on to the next generation (Ps 66:18, Jas 1:14-15).

Yes, these children who are born into generational sins will have a bigger battle against these sins, but God reassures us that His grace is sufficient for each one of us, and that in Him there is victory (2Cor 12:9-10, 2:14).

Ponder, Pray, and Journal

Spend some time alone with the Lord, and ask the Holy Spirit to reveal any generational iniquities in your family line.

Write on this line any generational iniquities He is unveiling:

_____

If He has revealed, this is a time to rejoice, because revelation is the first step towards freedom. Don't fall into discouragement or shame or false guilt, for the Holy Spirit reveals in His timing, when He is ready to move. Ask Him to begin to show you His intended pathway to freedom; we will learn more about freedom from these curses in Chapter 24.

Our Spiritual Inheritance

Although there are many aspects of these iniquities of our ancestors that I do not fully understand, it does seem to me that they do prepare the ground for the settling in of the stronghold. As Satan orchestrates his wounds and lies are embraced, these generational iniquities seem to predispose us to react with the *same sins* of our ancestors. These habitual unrepented sins contribute to the formation of the stronghold by opening the doors to demons.

The Holy Spirit may be unblinding your eyes as never before, and you may be beginning to discern what is going on in your family. Satan may be working to dishearten and intimidate you. Don't stand for it. Allow me to share ...

I was discouraged. It seemed the battles against these strongholds were interminable. And the walking it out so painful. God was calling me to humble myself and admit I was wrong. Way wrong. Made a big mess of everything in my wrongness. Yet again.

And even worse, Holy Spirit was now showing me with great clarity how my iniquity was visited upon my children, as He unveiled the damage it caused them growing up under the shadow of my strongholds. It was more than I could bear.

Broken and repentant once again over these sins, I poured out my soul to Him, and then sat in stillness. Not that I really expected Him to say anything, but I sort of had run out of things to say. I was counting on His presence, though, to comfort to meet me and somehow strengthen me to go on. So I waited.

He spoke into my heart. "It is your spiritual inheritance." Spiritual inheritance? What does that mean? I didn't remember reading those words paired together in my Bible.

And then in a flood of impressions on my heart He explained how, each time I partner with Him and He demolishes a stronghold, that this <u>freedom</u> is passed down to my children. Not that they would instantaneously be freed. But the <u>spiritual inheritance</u> of my own freedom that I now pass to them makes it <u>easier</u> for them to get free if they become trapped in these strongholds. The pressure is lifted. Somehow, their battle for the territory in their hearts will not be as intense, because Jesus has broken the chains for me, and I have walked out in that freedom.

The joy and encouragement those words infused into my heart and soul gave me the strength I needed to pick up my spiritual weapons and press on in the battle.

Celeste Li
Jupiter, Florida

The Holy Spirit reminded me of what we discussed in Chapter 2: our sanctified hearts are part of our inheritance (1Pet 1:1-9). And then He began to show me Scripturally what He meant by this "spiritual inheritance" being passed down to our children. Come with me to the sweetness of these verses He showed me.

Lovingkindness to Thousands

... but showing lovingkindness to thousands, to those who love Me and keep My commandments.   Exodus 20:5

... But showing mercy and steadfast love to a thousand generations of those who love Me and keep My commandments.
Exodus 20:6 AMPC

... But I lavish my love on those who love me and obey my commands, even for a thousand generations.   Exodus 20:6 NLT

Yes, our iniquities will be visited on our children to the third and fourth generation. *But our obedience causes Him to visit His lovingkindness on our children to the thousandth generation!!* We will pass down a propensity for Godliness to a thousand generations! This will make it easier for our offspring to partner with Jesus as He builds Strongholds of Light, such as humility, contentment, purity, trust in the Lord, obedience, and fear of the Lord. Hear how the Lord explains it further in Psalms:

But the lovingkindness of the LORD
is from everlasting to everlasting on those who fear Him,
And His righteousness to *children's children*,
To those who keep His covenant
And remember His precepts to do them.
Psalm 103:17-18, emphasis added

Who is the man who fears the LORD?
He will instruct him in the way he should choose.
His soul will abide in prosperity,
And his descendants will inherit the land.
Psalm 25:12-13, emphasis added

Yet a little while and the wicked man will be no more;
And you will look carefully for his place
and he will not be there.
But the humble will inherit the land
And will delight themselves in abundant prosperity.
Psalm 37:10-11, emphasis added

Ponder, Pray, and Journal

Every family in heaven and on earth is ordained by God, created by God, named by God (Eph 3:14). Although it is His will that *none* should perish (2 Pet 3:9), it is no secret that *entire families* are on His heart. We see this both in both the Old and New Testaments. Look up these passages and allow the Lord to imprint on your heart His loving desires for your family.

- Joshua 24:15
- John 4:46-53
- Acts 16:14-15
- Acts 16:22-34
- Acts 18:5-8

When we partner with Jesus to demolish strongholds and Jesus sets us free, we give a *spiritual inheritance* to our children. It is the "land" they inherit, areas in their hearts that will be particularly receptive to Jesus and His Spirit. And God grants this blessing not only to us and to our children, but to a thousand generations! Hold this close to your heart as we move into the next parts of a stronghold and watch how Satan lays his blocks and erects his towers.

Building Blocks and Towers of a Stronghold: Every Lofty Thing

The ground has been primed, the foundation laid. Footholds are ready and the network of lies is in place. Our wounds have been ripped wide open, ripe for enemy attack.

Our yearning wounded hearts seek for love, acceptance, affirmation, approval, attention – and Satan is at the ready with the next components of his stronghold. Only God could ever fill our bottomless empty hearts, and without depth of relationship with Him, we naturally turn to *idols* and things of the world to fill us. Additionally, our own *pride* causes us to think that we can heal ourselves, by filling ourselves with ourselves and with anything and everything other than God. Pride and idolatry fortify the structure as **every loft thing** is erected, block upon block.

We are destroying speculations and every lofty thing raised up against the knowledge of God ...		2 Corinthians 10:5

We are going to study the three parts of this component:

- Every lofty thing, *hupsoma* (hoop'-so-mah) in the Greek.
- Raised up.
- Against the knowledge of God.

Every Loft Thing

Hupsoma means "a high place ... figuratively of a proud adversary, a lofty tower or fortress built up proudly by the enemy."[15] Pride echoes strongly in this word. *Hupsoma* includes prideful lofty thoughts, arrogant words, and deeds – even good deeds with prideful motivation. In Dave's testimony in the previous chapter, you can see the *hupsoma* right alongside the *logismos* (faulty mindset).

Raised Up

Raised up encompasses "to lift up or exalt oneself" but also includes the idea of worship.[16] *Hupsoma* is anything that entices us to exalt *ourselves* above God. *Hupsoma* includes idols, anything or anyone that we worship, that we serve above God, that we put above God in importance, that we put our trust in, or that we fear losing.

For example, if we lose someone we love, through divorce or death or abandonment, or course we will indeed grieve and feel heartbroken. But if we are consumed with the pain of the loss, if we cannot lean on the Lord to help us move past the pain, we may have an idol. Or, if someone we care about is going through painful circumstances, and we cannot release her to God, if we cannot accept His sovereign plan, if we cannot trust Him enough to surrender her to Him, we may have an idol. Or, if we have been deeply wounded and we cannot trust Him enough to allow Him into the broken area of our heart to heal and restore, we may have an idol. Additionally, if we turn to something or someone other than God for comfort, we may have an idol.

Idols can be very insidious. Satan, a mastermind at deception, can delude us so that we believe *we have no idols*. It is a work of the Holy Spirit to uncover these idols.

My friend Rebecca always had an infectious laugh and an easy joy about her, her walk with the Lord strong and sure. But one season, her eyes held a heaviness that her laughter couldn't cover. I have asked her to share how the Lord uncovered *hupsoma* in her heart.

My relationship with my children and grandchildren was wonderful. According to the Word, children and grandchildren are truly a gift from God, and I was thoroughly enjoying that gift. Weekly we attended church together, often sitting in the same row. One looking on could say our family was picture-perfect. However, in this fallen world, perfect is really not a possibility.

When circumstances beyond my control collided into my picture-perfect family, my life began to unravel. My daughter and her family began to withdraw, which was very painful. My son and daughter-in-law also became somewhat distant. My whole life seemed to turn upside-down – or at least that's what I believed.

The pain felt like torture and seven years felt like forever. I was invited into <u>Triumph Over Suffering</u> *Class, and God began to reveal that I had set my family up as an idol. At first I questioned God, saying, "But You gave them to me to enjoy and feel fulfilled." But God showed me I had made His gift an idol. Although my idolatry was very subtle and unintentional, God would <u>not</u> accept second place.*

God continued to humble my heart through this class. In order for me to accept that my family was an idol, He had to completely remove my daughter and her family. Then my son and his family also began to further withdraw. But during this time, God did not fail to surround me with Christians who unconditionally loved me and encouraged me to grow in Christ.

This journey of humbling took a number of months, but as I repented of this idolatry, I realized that He had a greater purpose for me, a purpose to know Him, to <u>really</u> know Him. Many times through this journey I became discouraged, thinking I could not make it through another day. But God assured me by his Word, in Phil. 4:13, **"I can do all things through Christ who strengthens me,"** *even though at times this strengthening is moment by moment.*

As the idol toppled, I learned that my identity was not found in my family, but in <u>who He says I am</u>. God wanted total surrender so that I can flourish. I am so thankful for God's patience, comforting me in my pain. He had bigger plans for my life. Proverbs 3:5-6, that I adapted for me, says:

*"Trust in the LORD (not my family) with ALL my heart
and lean not on my own understanding (desires),
but in all my ways (life) acknowledge Him
and He will make my path (life) straight (full/complete)."*

Thank you Jesus, for Your ways are not my ways. Thank you for removing the family idol, for your honor and glory. Living life fully surrendered is my desire. The tap root has been dug out! Praise You Jesus!

Rebecca
Hobe Sound, Florida

God turned Rebecca's life upside-down so He could establish *His* priorities in her heart. The idol of her family had been cemented in place by the lie that her family was her identity. As she repented and renounced that lie, the *hupsoma* toppled.

Over the next few months, I watched as Rebecca partnered with Jesus to tear down the stronghold. She surrendered her family on deeper and deeper levels. She chose the path of obedience for each test He ordained. And, as she grew in intimacy with Him, she embraced her true identity in Christ as His daughter and loved one. This stronghold is now smoldering in the dust. And Rebecca's eyes have a new depth of joy, because it is no longer her family providing her joy, it is her *relationship with her Savior.*

Rebecca's children have not yet returned. But her joy and peace are unshakable. The beautiful fruit of this journey of freedom is her deep heart knowing that her identity is not in her family, but in who God says she is.

Ponder, Pray, and Journal

Go back to the first two paragraphs of this section entitled *Raised Up* and read again what an idol encompasses. Be still before the Lord, and ask the Holy Spirit to expose any idols in your heart. Refer back to Chapter 5 in *Triumph of Surrender* if needed – there is a pretty extensive heart check list in this chapter.

Against the Knowledge of God

Note that *hupsoma* is specifically raised up **against the knowledge of God.** *Hupsoma* stands in opposition not only to God Himself, but to *knowing* God, to *intimacy* with Him. These lofty things, our pride and our idols and our self-idolatry, prevent us from understanding His character, His ways, His heart. They distort our comprehension of *who He really is.* For if we refuse to believe that God is who He says He is in His Word, we are open for enemy infiltration. If we march out in rebellion believing the lie that He is not a God of love, or if we believe the lies that He is not a Righteous Judge and that He is unconcerned about sin, then we are susceptible to enemy influence. If we stubbornly believe that He is vengefully punishing us for our imperfections or that He is not personally interested in our lives, or if we remain entrenched in the lies that we have no value to Him or that we need to earn His love and acceptance, then Satan can easily erect a lofty tower in our hearts.

Hupsoma also includes thoughts such as "I'm worthless" and "I need to earn His love and approval." I know, I know, that sounds the complete opposite of pride. But follow along with me here as we look at one more surprising part of *hupsoma.*

Realize that *unworthiness* is different than *worthlessness.* None of us are worthy of the Lord's love and forgiveness and grace, and it requires great humility to accept these free, unearned, undeserved gifts. But feelings of worthlessness, that we have no value, that we are not enough, that we are not important or not useful to God, are Satan's lies that generally have developed out of deep heart wounds. We are made in the image of God, and this great dignity gives us great worth, value, and importance. And even deeper, as children of God and members of His household, He has chosen us and given us freedom and healing and calling and purpose – we are the apple of His eye and are of infinite value to Him. He expects us to grow up in our identity in Christ and to reject the lies of worthlessness and not-enoughness – no matter what other people, the world, or our experiences are impressing upon us.

Sometimes, we can wear *unworthiness* like a badge, constantly trying to earn what we could never earn and what He has already given us. Other times, we can wallow in *worthlessness* and not-enoughness. Recall my testimony in Chapter 4 about how I was rejecting my identity in Christ and believing lies that I was worthless. Although looking superficially, these thought processes *seem* to be humble, in reality they are prideful and selfish, because they are drawing all the attention to ourselves. My daughter Jenna pointed out to me that this behavior deflects the focus from our true faults and failures by over-exaggerating our defects to an unbelievable level. Additionally, these thought processes assume that we *can* earn His love, we *can* prove our worth – again indicating pride. Lofty thoughts raised up against a God whose love and acceptance we could never earn – *yet who gives it to us anyway. Jesus* makes us worthy, only in Him. He gives us value and tells us we are enough in Him. Self-deprecating behavior is *hupsoma* because it actually is a *false* humility.

True humility is having an accurate estimation of ourselves (Rom 12:3): seeing our faults and shortcomings, and at the same time seeing our God-given gifts and abilities. Rick Warren writes that humility is not thinking *less* of yourself, it is thinking *about* yourself less.[17] And C.S. Lewis takes it up another notch, saying that the humble person is not thinking about being humble; he is actually not thinking about himself at all.[18]

The culmination of *hupsoma* is a destruction of our *relationship* with God. Foundational in our relationship with Him is knowing the truth of who He really is, and knowing the truth of what He thinks of us – as found in His Word. I believe that pride, idolatry, and false humility are three of the biggest barricades to relationship with Him.

We have now seen the groundwork even below the foundation, the ancestral iniquities that make us more susceptible to Satan's attacks. We have watched how the foundation has been laid with woundings, and we have come to understand how the unhealed wounds have led us to believe an entanglement of lies. Our wounded hearts, clouded with deception, have sought love and filling from idols, addictions, and things of this world. Anger, unforgiveness, or other sins have given Satan a foothold, and prideful idolatrous towers have been erected. The Light of God is absent within the structure; it is dark, almost ready for the demonic to access. The only thing needed for demons to gain entrance is an open door.

Open Doors of a Stronghold: Rebellion and Habitual Sin

Everyone who practices sin also practices lawlessness; and sin is lawlessness.　　　1 John 3:4

Sin is disobedience; the *practice of sin* is truly lawlessness, rebellion against God. Sin gives the devil a foothold, inviting demons to *team up* with our flesh. When we have given the devil that foothold, temptations may escalate, the pressure to fall into sin may increase, and our resolve to walk in the Spirit may weaken. Although any sin may open us up to demonic influence, continual, repetitive, habitual, entrenched, unrepented sin is a wide open door.

Jesus answered them, "Truly, truly, I say to you, everyone who commits sin *is the slave of sin.*"   John 8:34, emphasis added

The Amplified elucidates the tense of that word **commits,** demonstrating that it means a *continual practice* of sin:

Jesus answered, "I assure you and most solemnly say to you, everyone who *practices sin habitually* is the slave of sin."   John 8:34 AMP, emphasis added

Although in this passage Jesus is speaking to unbelievers, He states that *everyone* who practices sin habitually is the slave of sin. *Everyone.* The King James says **whosoever.** Whether sin is practiced by believers or unbelievers, disobedience is rebellion against God's commands, against His will, against His plans, against His timing, against His sovereignty, against God Himself. The practice of sin is the hallmark of Satan. Lawlessness and opposition against God are the hallmarks of the antichrist. Disobedience to God means we have aligned ourselves with the ways of Satan. (1Jn 3:8, 2Thess 2:3-4, 1Jn 2:22, 4:3.)

I think that *strongholds* are not generally formed by occasional sins or failures of integrity. Repeated deep-rooted heart sins and continued sinful behaviors without repentance are the ones which seem to open doors to stronghold formation. Such repetitive sins may include sins such as pride, fear, control, idolatry, lying and deception, rebellion, disobedience to the Word, contempt of God, sexual sins and impurity, perversion, addictions, occult involvement, distrust of God, and self-hatred. Unforgiveness, judgment, bitterness, resentment, jealousy, and unforgiveness of self can become habitual entrenched sins also. There are indeed many more.

Let's pause to review once more.

When Satan schemes to erect a stronghold, it seems he uses iniquities of our ancestors to prime the land. He then rakes his claws over our heart, leaving a raw wound. This foundational wound is a set-up to persuade us to believe his lies. Our anger and unforgiveness then provide him the first footholds he needs, and he begins to build his structure with *logismos*, his complex networks of lies that will cement the blocks in place. The structure grows block by block as he deftly draws us into *hupsoma*, towers of pride and idolatry, using his network of lies to cause confusion about who God is and uncertainty of our own identity. The Light of God is absent from this structure, creating a welcoming place for demons seeking rest. Then, if we fall to Satan's temptations and rebel against God's commands, our sins, especially our continual repetitive unrepented sins, can become the open door that invites the access of dark forces. Once demonic activity is present, the *structure* has become a *stronghold*.

Creating a Place of Rest for Demons

Jesus, teaching on demons, explains,

Now when the unclean spirit goes out of a man, it passes through waterless places seeking rest ...   Matthew 12:43

We are going to discuss this passage a bit further in Chapter 16, but for now, let's focus on that word **rest**. Demons seek *rest*. Rest in the Greek means "inward tranquility while one performs necessary labor."[9] Reading that definition causes my heart to leap into my throat. Demons find a comfortable place of *tranquility*, a place where their darkness is undisturbed, *so that* they are able to accomplish their devastating work in our hearts and its outflows, stealing, killing, destroying. We give them rest, and in that rest they are able to work.

Demons find rest when the area they occupy is *comfortable* for them. We give them a restful place when our viewpoint, our words, our thought life, our heartset, or our behavior resonates with their dark ways. We can make it downright cozy for them when our thoughts and plans are in harmony with darkness and sin. Remember they are *relegated* to darkness, and the darker the area, the more comfortable it will be for them. Any Light filtering in will disturb their rest.

When demons find cooperation with their ways, they settle in. When they are able to move from *a position of attack* into a *place of influence*, then a *stronghold* has been formed. When they are able to move from simply *attacking* (shooting flaming arrows, hindering, resisting, or harassing), to *influencing* (manipulating, oppressing, tormenting, holding in bondage, or, in the unsaved, dominating), they have crossed the line and formed a stronghold.

Ponder, Pray, and Journal

What kind of environment would create a comfortable, restful place for demons? They will find us peaceful and inviting to them when our thoughts, words, intentions, or activities are in accord with their purposes and desires. I have listed some things that create a comfortable place for demons. Grab your pen and circle anything that the Holy Spirit is revealing to you about the state of your heart right now.

- Lying, deceiving, cheating, stealing
- Impurity, sexual sins
- Violence, hatred
- Unforgiveness, bitterness, resentment
- Anger, impatience
- Unwholesome talk, foul language, coarse jesting
- Gossip, criticism, slander
- Addictions
- Fear, worry, anxiety, doubt, unbelief, or distrust
- Rebellion
- Independence
- Selfishness
- Arrogance and pride

- Low self worth, self deprecation, false humility
- Jealousy, envy, and discontentment
- Hardness of heart
- Self-pity and mentality of a victim
- Self-righteousness, judgment, contempt
- Prejudice
- Unconfessed sin
- Lovelessness, cold love
- Legalism
- Idolatry

Spend some time alone with the Lord and allow Him to deal with anything you have circled.

In the next few chapters, we will see how Satan conquers territory in our hearts in order to construct and expand his strongholds. We will consider how he cleverly weaves his traps, and how we can, with the Holy Spirit's strength, avoid them – or climb out if we have fallen in. Additionally, we will see how he operates out of his strongholds in order to influence and manipulate. Let's move into the next chapter and inspect his devious and wicked ways.

Chapter 12
Satan Operates in Legalism

*O*n Chapter 9, we learned that we have been rescued from Satan's domain, from his *authority*, so he now has *no right* to our hearts or lives (Col 1:13, 2:13-15, Eph 1:20-21, 2:5-6, Lk 4:18-19, 1Cor 15:56-57, Rom 7:6). But remember, although he is a defeated foe, he is fighting guerilla warfare, and seeking every opportunity for a foothold. If we choose to align ourselves with the ways of darkness, we give him that foothold and invite him to access. Go back and review Chapter 9 if you are not clear on these concepts.

When we give Satan a foothold, he can use it for his beachhead and start to build up strongholds. The larger and more numerous his strongholds, the greater can be his access and the greater can be the extent of his *influence* on the outflows of our hearts: our minds, beliefs, thoughts, consciences, bodies, emotions, wills. The more robust his fortresses, the more powerful his *oppression* and *manipulation* of our decisions and our thought processes can be, even leading to torment and bondage.

It seems Satan seizes every opportunity to wound us, to set us up to believe lies, to lure us to fall into fear, deception, unforgiveness, pride, idolatry, and more. Our sins, particularly repetitive unrepented sins, open the doors into a structure where demons feel welcomed.

It seems often that Satan attacks when he believes we are weak.

Recall how he tempted Jesus after a 40-day fast. Jesus was physically weak – but He was spiritually strong. As Satan slunk away in defeat, watch his final ploy:

When the devil had finished every temptation, he left Him *until an opportune time*.   Luke 4:13, emphasis added

Satan seeks an opportune time. He counterattacks in the high after victory. And in times of discouragement, he fights dirty, kicks us when we're low, and inflicts wound on top of wound. He attacks when our guard is down, when we're sick or exhausted or overwhelmed or too busy to have time alone with the Lord. He works to pierce us with his first wounding when we are young children, for he knows our vulnerability and intends to build on that pain. He shamelessly takes advantage of open doors. He demands to sift us like wheat when we are walking in sin. He is on the lookout for chinks in our armor in order to thrust in his sword (1Pet 5:8, Eph 6:18, 1Cor 7:5).

When we are in trials, his attack may be very intense. Hear Paul's concern that the Thessalonians, new Christians under severe persecution, would fall away from their faith:

That is why, when I could bear it no longer, I sent Timothy to find out whether your faith was still strong. I was afraid that the Tempter had gotten the best of you and that all our work had been useless.   1 Thessalonians 3:5 NLT

But the Tempter did not win that battle; the Thessalonians remained strong in faith and love (1Thess 3:6).

In this chapter and the next, we will see two legalistic tactics Satan utilizes to create an opportunity to expand his reach and usurp access:

- Satan works to ensnare us into breaking God's laws, anticipating that we will reap the *consequences* of our law-breaking.

- Satan tempts us to succumb to a *law-keeping position* under God, instead of developing an intimate relationship with God. When we live in intimacy with God, we obey out of love, we rely on the Holy Spirit's power for the strength to obey, and we depend on God's grace when we fail.

Ponder, Pray, and Journal

The Pharisees of Jesus' day were trapped in legalism. Jesus describes them as self-righteous and focused on keeping the law to the letter, instead of seeking relationship with God. They honored God with lip service, but their hearts were far from Him. They were *spiritually blind* (Matt 15:7-9, 14).

Jesus was quoting from Isaiah 29:9-14, a passage that describes how spiritual blindness was poured out upon Israel because of their hard hearts, because they honored God with their lips but their hearts were not committed to Him. Isaiah explains there is a **spirit of deep sleep** (Isa 29:10) – so we see that spiritual blinding is indeed demonic.

Only the Holy Spirit can unblind. Spend some time with the Lord, asking Him to reveal any spiritual blindness, or any legalism.

Comprehending Satan's legalistic strategies will equip us to defend against them, so that will be our focus in these next two chapters. But first, we will seek to understand *God's laws* that govern our universe, so that we can then see how Satan exploits them.

God Ordained Physical and Spiritual Laws

God is not a God of confusion, but a God of peace and order (1Cor 14:33). When He spoke the world into existence, He established both physical and spiritual laws that create order in the world. These physical and spiritual laws and the *consequences* of breaking them are woven into the fabric of the universe. God ordained these laws and their consequences *for our good*. He created us, and He knows what is best for us, what will draw us deeper into Him, and what will bring us joy and peace.

I think that Satan with his legalistic mindset is delighted with the ordained consequences of law-breaking, and he capitalizes on them. But before we study just what that means, let's first look at some overarching principles of the physical and spiritual laws that direct the universe.

The *physical laws* dictate how the world operates on the physical level. You've probably learned about some of them through your science education in school. For others, simply living on this planet teaches us the consequences of challenging them.

The *spiritual laws* dictate how the world operates on a spiritual level. Scripture teaches us about these spiritual laws and God's declared consequences of obeying them or rebelling against them.

Both the physical world and the spiritual world are ruled by God's laws; these laws govern animate and inanimate, humans and animals, mankind and spirit beings alike. God's laws are always in action, although we may not readily see those laws unless we – purposefully or inadvertently – challenge them. We can understand that the law of gravity is always at work, although we may not perceive it unless we test it by stepping off a rooftop.

Just because we are in *ignorance* or *denial* of a particular physical or spiritual law doesn't mean that the consequences of breaking that law will be avoided. And our *refusal to believe* His physical or spiritual laws will not protect us from the consequences of challenging those laws either. Refusal to believe in the law of gravity will not prevent the consequences of stepping off that rooftop.

Realize also that at any moment God can violate His own laws, physical or spiritual. He can suspend them, bend them, even break them if it suits His purposes.[1] He can part the sea, cause a human to walk on water, continually fill a flour bowl and an oil jar until the famine is over. He can calm a raging sea with one word, muzzle the jaws of the lions, and raise the dead to life. And as His mercy triumphs over judgment, the Forgiver of our sins and Destroyer of curses can even dispense with the *consequences* of breaking His laws if He so chooses, bringing His good purposes out of the gravest of sins, allowing adulterers and prostitutes and incest survivors to be in the Messiah's family line, raising up a violent persecutor of Christians as His powerful evangelist, ordaining a man who deceived to be the father of the twelve tribes of Israel. (Ex 14:21-22, Matt 14:28-29, 1Kgs 17:14-16, Mk 4:39, Dan 6:22, Jn 20:14, Jas 2:13, Ps 103:12, Gal 3:13, Matt 1:6, 2Sam 11:2-5, Matt 1:5, Josh 2:1, Matt 1:3, 2Sam 13:12-14, Acts 7:58-59, 8:1, 9:1, 22:4, Gen 27:1-29).

Physical Laws

The physical, natural laws are working *whether we understand them or not.* They are in action *even if we don't know they exist.* They are in effect *even when we don't believe in them.* Whether we recognize them, understand them, or believe in them is simply irrelevant. We are governed by those laws and will experience the Creator's ordained consequences.

The earth will revolve around the sun even if we think the sun revolves around the earth. The cycle of rain and evaporation will continue even if we are completely unaware.

Sometimes a challenge to one of God's laws results in immediate consequences. If we touch a hot stove, the law of conduction of heat will move into action, and the inevitable consequence will occur.

A challenge to other natural laws may give delayed consequences. For example, if we don't provide a plant with sunlight and water, it will eventually die.

And yet there are other natural laws which, when challenged, result in almost immediate consequences for some people, delayed consequences for others, and escaped consequences for still others. For example, if we quit brushing our teeth for a month, we may develop gum disease or a cavity immediately, later, or not at all. Perhaps this seeming unpredictability exists because of a complex interplay between other unseen physical realities (such as strength of an individual's teeth), God's sovereignty, our free will, His Kingdom plans, and the purposes of His heart for each individual (Prov 21:30, Ps 33:10-11, Prov 16:9).

Spiritual Laws

The spiritual laws operate similarly. They are working whether we understand them or not. They are in action even if we don't know they exist. And they are in effect even when we don't *believe* in them. Whether we recognize these spiritual laws, understand them, or believe in them is simply irrelevant; they are still in effect. We are governed by those laws and will experience God's ordained consequences for obedience or disobedience to those laws (Heb 2:2).

God did not keep these consequences a mystery. He lays out His spiritual laws in His Word, and the resulting blessings for obedience and consequences for disobedience. He explains that when we walk in His commands, it will go well with us (Deut 4:40, Jer 7:23, Eph 6:3). He tells us that we will reap what we sow (Gal 6:7-8). He declares we will be blessed if we are a doer of the His Word and not merely a hearer (Jas 1:25, Rom 2:13). He describes how our sins will affect our children to the third and fourth generation (Ex 20:5). Jesus tells us that we are blessed if we follow His example (Jn 13:14-17), and blessed when we obey the word of God (Lk 11:28). Not that there is a one-to-one correspondence, but a set of general principles.

In the next chapter, we are going to take a deep dive into some of the spiritual laws, including both the blessings of obedience and the consequences pronounced for rebellion, because understanding how these blessings and consequences operate will be critical in our comprehension of stronghold formation. Satan, operating in legalism, brazenly uses both the blessings and the consequences to ensnare us. If he can lure us into rebellion against any of God's laws, the consequences ordained by God are then set into motion. And, if he can dupe us into trying to *earn* God's blessings with our obedience instead of relying upon God's grace and Holy Spirit's power, he can ensnare us into sins of pride, striving, and works-based mentality. But first, some more groundwork before we go into specifics.

Adversary Means Legalist

We learned in Chapter 7 that the name Satan means Adversary: he is an opponent in a lawsuit, accusing us as if we are standing in a court of law. When it suits his purposes, he will trip us up to ensnare us into sin, and then heap shame upon us by berating us for not following God's laws to the letter.

If we disobey God's law, consequences kick in. It seems Satan claims that he has the right to ensure those consequences are enforced. He comes before God and charges us with breaking God's law, and demands we reap the consequences of our law-breaking (Zech 3:1, Lk 22:31):

For as many as are of the works of the Law are under a curse; for it is written, "CURSED IS EVERYONE WHO DOES NOT

ABIDE BY ALL THE THINGS WRITTEN IN THE BOOK OF THE LAW, TO PERFORM THEM." Galatians 3:10

The Law is the Law of Moses: the Ten Commandments and all the commandments throughout the Old Testament. As we discussed in Chapter 9, **the power of sin is the law** (1Cor 15:56). The Law establishes the consequences (curses) and gives sin its power. And under the Law, in order to be without guilt, we must keep the *whole* Law:

For whoever keeps the whole law and yet stumbles in one point, he has become guilty of all. James 2:10

Satan knows this and attempts to exploit it mercilessly. He contorts the Law to seduce us to sin, then contorts it again to shame us for our sin. He heaps false guilt on top of Holy Spirit's conviction. He often legalistically knows God's laws – and the consequences of breaking them – better than we do. As our legal opponent, he accuses us as if in a court of law.

But do not forget what we learned in Chapter 3: our Advocate in this court of law is the Holy Spirit, the *Paraclete*, our legal advisor and who comes forward on our behalf and advocates for us. I imagine the *Paraclete* to be defending us against Satan's slander and false accusations, pleading our cause before our holy and righteous Judge. But I have also heard that *when we have sinned*, the *Paraclete* is pleading *God's cause* with us.[2] We discussed this verse in Chapter 7 but let's look at another angle here. Remember to read it on a spiritual level, knowing Satan is called our Accuser:

Come to terms quickly with your accuser while you are going with him to court, lest your accuser hand you over to the Judge, and the judge to the guard, and you be put in prison. Truly I say to you, you will never get out until you have paid the last penny. Matthew 5:25-26 ESV

If Satan is rightly accusing us when we have sinned, we are to acknowledge our sins (come to terms quickly with our accuser), repent, and seek God's forgiveness. In these times, the *Paraclete* may be advocating *the Father's cause*, encouraging us to take responsibility for our sins and repent. If we do not, we may end up in bondage.

Similarly, if Satan is speaking a half-truth (which of course is a lie), we can agree with what is true, and then declare the *whole* truth to gain freedom. My friend Endrea provided an example of this verse lived out. I had asked her to pray about *Triumph* leadership. The enemy planted this thought: "You need to pray a lot because you are not ready." Sensing that she was in danger of spiraling down into not-enoughness and fear, she agreed with the part that was true, that she is not yet ready, and then put her trust in Jesus to fully prepare and equip her to be ready. Immediately the thoughts in her head were silenced and replaced with peace and trust in Him.

But Are We Doomed to Reap These Consequences?

Such a good question. I'm glad you asked.

The consequences of breaking God's law still stand because He is a God of justice – *but Jesus!*

"Do not think that I came to abolish the Law or the Prophets; *I did not come to abolish but to fulfill*. For truly I say to you, until heaven and earth pass away, not the smallest letter or stroke shall pass from the Law until all is accomplished."

Matthew 5:17-18, emphasis added

How did Jesus fulfill the Law? By living a perfect sinless life, and dying in our place as the perfect sacrifice. And in so doing, He fulfilled the requirements of the Law *for us!*

Therefore there is now no condemnation for those who are in Christ Jesus. For the law of the Spirit of life in Christ Jesus has set you free from the law of sin and death. For what

the Law could not do, weak as it was through the flesh, God did: sending His own Son in the likeness of sinful flesh and as an offering for sin, He condemned sin in the flesh, *so that the requirement of the Law might be fulfilled in us,* who do not walk according to the flesh but according to the Spirit.

Romans 8:1-4, emphasis added

God delivered us from the curse of breaking the Law through His Son, Jesus Christ. By *becoming* a curse, Jesus *redeemed* us from the curse:

Christ redeemed us from the curse of the Law, having become a curse for us – for it is written, "CURSED IS EVERYONE WHO HANGS ON A TREE" – in order that in Christ Jesus the blessing of Abraham might come to the Gentiles, so that we would receive the promise of the Spirit through faith.

Galatians 3:13-14

Jesus, by His death and resurrection, freed us (redeemed us) from the curse. By paying the ransom price for us, Jesus *became* a curse, and also *destroyed* the curse. This paved the way for us to receive the promise of the Spirit. When we surrendered our lives to Jesus as our Savior and our Lord, He broke the curse *individually* for us, and blessed us with the gift of salvation. We were rescued from the domain of Satan, sealed with the Holy Spirit, and set free.

But now we have been released from the law, for we died to it and are no longer captive to its power. Now we can serve God, not in the old way of obeying the letter of the law, but in the new way of living in the Spirit. Romans 7:6 NLT

Jesus destroyed the power of the Law by His death on the cross; by His death He canceled out everything the Law says we owe (Col 2:14). Sin, Satan, the Law have all lost their power over those who belong to Jesus. We are not under law but under grace (Rom 6:14).

But the law was given through Moses; grace and truth were realized through Jesus Christ. John 1:17

Then Why Do I Still Experience Consequences For My Sins?

You are full of good questions.

Through the blood of Jesus shed for our sins, in Jesus we are guaranteed freedom from the ultimate penalty of breaking God's Law: separation from God in eternity. Additionally, we are offered freedom from curses here on earth – but this is often a freedom we must fight for and walk in, by the power of His Holy Spirit. By walking not according to the flesh, but according to the Spirit (Gal 5:16).

Remember here on earth, Satan is still actively fighting guerilla warfare. He is still world dominator, holding the world in his power (Eph 6:12, 1Jn 5:19), and at work to enforce the consequences of our law-breaking.

Living under grace means we have *access* to God's grace. Jesus' death set us free from the Law – but we must run free from the prison of the Law to be **free indeed** (Jn 8:36). We run free by repenting, by no longer continuing in sin, and by surrendering to the Holy Spirit's leading. **But if you are led by the Spirit, you are not under the Law** (Gal 5:18), and Satan's influence is thwarted. The more we are led by the Holy Spirit, the less we operate as if we are still under the Law of Moses. If we submit ourselves to the Law of Moses again (Gal 4:9-11), we are aligning ourselves with Satan's legalism in that area; we have fallen from grace (Gal 5:4).

Yet God is merciful and gracious and at times shields us from the consequences of our sins here on earth. Sometimes, He delays the consequences because He is graciously giving us more time to repent (2Pet 3:9). Other times, His protection may remain a mystery as He works to accomplish His Kingdom purposes (1Cor 13:12).

And other times, for reasons we may not fully comprehend, although we have escaped the final eternal penalty of our sins, we may not escape the earthly consequences. When we are experiencing His ordained consequences, we do not want to not lose sight of His purpose: God **disciplines us for our good, so that we may share in His holiness** (Heb 12:10). He is using the consequences *that He has ordained* to draw us deeper into Him.

The Law of Christ

Though we are no longer under the Law of Moses, we are now under the Law of Christ, also called the Law of Liberty, the Law of Freedom, or the Perfect Law (Rom 6:14, 1Cor 9:21, Gal 6:2, Jas 2:12, 1:25). What is the Law of Christ?

The Law of Christ is grace. It is forgiveness of all our sins through the cross. God does not ask us to be perfect, but to be repentant and humble, accepting His shed blood for our forgiveness. He desires us to admit our weaknesses, to acknowledge that we cannot be perfectly obedient, to rely on the Holy Spirit's power to obey, and to trust His grace to cover our sins and failures. We do guard our heart, but we do not fall into legalistic traps.

Obeying the Law of Christ is *not* following a set of rules. It is entering into a sacred covenant relationship with our Heavenly Father, where God set us free from sin and death by the death of His own Son, and in our great gratitude we *choose* to please Him and do His will. By His abundant grace, He gives us the will to obey, and the ability to obey (Phil 2:13). He writes His law in our hearts, and promises He is our God, and are His people (Jer 31:33, Heb 8:10). And in this sweet covenant relationship, His commandments are not burdensome (1Jn 5:3).

The commandments under the Law of Christ take the Law of Moses to a new level. The Law of Christ involves loving our enemies and doing good to those who hate us (Lk 6:27). It involves not only avoiding adultery, but refusing to even look at a woman with lust (Matt 5:27-28). Obeying the will of God means that if the Holy Spirit is prompting us to take dinner to the single mom who has just gotten out of the hospital, we do it (Jas 4:17). Our obedience is led by the Spirit and is motivated by love in this covenant relationship.

And finally, the Law of Christ means that He provides everything we need to do His will *by the power of the Holy Spirit* (2Pet 1:3-4, Eze 36:27, Col 1:29, Eph 3:20-21). This is not a work of our own accomplishments, but a work of the Holy Spirit within our surrendered hearts (Gal 3:1-3). It is only the sanctifying work of the Holy Spirit that enables us to obey (1Pet 1:2), and as we grow in Him, we are able to increasingly rely on the Holy Spirit to give us the strength to be obedient.

God is all about *relationship*, not laws. As we grow in intimacy with Him, we will so desire to keep His commands and walk in His ways because we do not want anything hindering our relationship with Him. We will desire to surrender to His will and be led by His Spirit.

God is all about relationship. *But Satan is all about laws.* Yes, God decreed the laws of the universe, but Satan has perverted these laws and seems to have made it his personal business to accuse us when we have broken them. He operates in legalism and he demands we reap the consequences. The path to victory on this battlefront is repentance and dying to ourselves daily. **"He must increase, but I must decrease"** (Jn 3:30).

Dying to Self Is Our Protection From Satan

Now **the law has jurisdiction [authority NIV] over a person as long as he lives** (Rom 7:1). We escape the authority of the Law by crucifying our flesh and dying to ourselves (Gal 2:20, Rom 6:6), **for he**

who has died is freed from sin (Rom 6:7). And we are able to die to ourselves only by the power of the Holy Spirit.

We have died and we are hidden in Christ with God (Col 3:3). We are protected from the power of the law *because* we have died with Christ, and we *walk* in that protection by grace through faith when we daily die to sin. Jesus won our freedom from the penalty of the law at our moment of salvation: He broke open the prison doors. And we *experience* that freedom from the penalty of the law each time we rely on the Holy Spirit for the strength to walk out of the prison cell by crucifying our own desires and surrendering to God's will. We battle daily to walk in the freedom that Jesus has provided for us, to be **free indeed** (Jn 8:36).

Remember Jesus has destroyed the curses through His death and resurrection, and Revelation reassures us that at the end of time, when Satan is thrown into the lake of fire, there will no longer be any curse (Rev 22:3). But here on earth, we are still in the thick of the battle, as guerilla warrior Satan fights to enforce the curses. We battle against his deceptive tactics and seek to walk out the freedom Jesus purchased for us at the cross (Gal 3:13-14, 5:18).

Ponder, Pray, and Journal

The sections we have just studied will become very important as we study Satan's legalistic approach to warfare. Go back through these sections listed below, and summarize what you have learned in your own words:

- *Adversary Means Legalist*
- *But Are We Doomed to Reap These Consequences?*
- *Why Do I Still Experience Consequences for my Sins?*
- *The Law of Christ*
- *Dying to Self Is Our Protection From Satan*

Before we examine further Satan's legalistic strategies against us, we must truly understand God's grace, so we have just spent a considerable amount of time here. Additionally, there are two more concepts we must thoroughly understand before we grapple with Satan's legalism:

- God takes rebellion very seriously.

- God by His Spirit has given us everything necessary to walk in a manner pleasing to Him.

We will cover both of these truths in the next two sections.

Rebellion Grieves God's Heart

Since we are not under the Law but under grace, does that give us an exuse for sin? Absolutely not! (Gal 5:13, Rom 6:15-16). **Do not use your freedom as a covering for evil** (1Pet 2:16).

Rebellion against God and His laws is a scornful affront to His face, a deep wounding of His heart. The *pride* that drives us to refuse to obey His laws and to defiantly walk our own way was originally Satan's sin. And the Word indicates that *idolatry* is particularly grievous to His heart – so much so that He calls it spiritual harlotry. God expects us to trust Jesus, and to rely on the Holy Spirit to give us the strength to obey. When we sin, He will use the consequences *that He has ordained* to draw our attention to the state of our heart and to the chasm separating us from connection with Him. He desires *intimacy*. (Gen 6:6, Ps 78:40, Isa 63:10, Eph 4:30, Ex 34:15-16, Gal 5:16, Ps 119:67, Heb 12:4-11, Ex 3:14-15.)

The Word is very clear that we are not to *presume* that He will give us grace. We are not to take our sins lightly, cavalierly counting on His forgiveness to be available. **Are we to continue in sin so that grace can increase? May it never be!** (Rom 6:1-2). We die to sin so we don't continue to walk in it. We do not use our freedom as a covering for evil; we use it to serve God (1Pet 2:16, Jude 1:4). Hear this very convicting passage from Hebrews:

If we deliberately keep on sinning after we have received the knowledge of the truth, no sacrifice for sins is left, but only a fearful expectation of judgment and of raging fire that will consume the enemies of God. Anyone who rejected the law of Moses died without mercy on the testimony of two or three witnesses. How much more severely do you think someone deserves to be punished *who has trampled the Son of God underfoot, who has treated as an unholy thing the blood of the covenant that sanctified them, and who has insulted the Spirit of grace?* For we know him who said, "It is mine to avenge; I will repay," and again, "The Lord will judge his people." It is a dreadful thing to fall into the hands of the living God. Hebrews 10:26-31 NIV, emphasis added

If we know the truth and continue to deliberately sin, there is no other sacrifice available to cover our sins. We are scorning God's provision of forgiveness: Jesus' blood shed on the cross.

God has created His laws *for our good,* to show us what is best for us. He wants us living an abundant life, a life overflowing with blessings and joy and peace. And since He created us, He knows what will lead to abundant life for us. Although nothing can separate us from His love, if we flagrantly disregard His ways, we are walking away from His offer of abundant life, unable to receive His love and deliberately hindering our fellowship with Him (Rom 8:35-39, Jn 10:10, Isa 59:1-2). Additionally, we are trampling underfoot the Son of God, treating His blood as unholy, and insulting the Spirit of grace. Other translations describe this as profaning His blood, spitting on His blood, and disdaining and outraging the Spirit of grace.

Ponder, Pray, and Journal

What does it mean to "presume" that God will give us grace?

Take some time to study and meditate on Hebrews 10:26-31 above. Is there any area in your life or your heart where you are trampling underfoot the Son of God, profaning the blood, or insulting the Spirit of grace?

God Gives Everything Necessary for Godliness

We cannot walk in obedience on our own strength. Hear Paul's warning in Galatians:

You foolish Galatians, who has bewitched you, before whose eyes Jesus Christ was publicly portrayed as crucified? This is the only thing I want to find out from you: did you receive the Spirit by the works of the Law, or by hearing with faith? Are you so foolish? *Having begun by the Spirit, are you now being perfected by the flesh?*

Galatians 3:1-3, emphasis added

Salvation is by the Holy Spirit. Sanctification and obedience is by the Holy Spirit also. If we are striving to perfectly obey God's laws on our own human strength, Satan has ensnared us into sins of striving, earning, legalism, and works-based mentality. Pride, independence, and self-idolatry are at play also. What God desires is a humble and repentant heart, a heart that relies on *the Holy Spirit's power* for strength and *God's grace* when we fall short.

"I will give you a new heart and put a new spirit within you; and I will remove the heart of stone from your flesh and give you a heart of flesh. *I will put My Spirit within you and cause you to walk in My statutes,* and you will be careful to observe My ordinances." Ezekiel 36:26-27, emphasis added

We humbly rely on the Holy Spirit for strength to crucify the desires of the flesh and to walk in obedience (Rom 7:6).

But I say, *walk by the Spirit, and you will not carry out the desire of the flesh.*   Galatians 5:16, emphasis added

... for if you are living according to the flesh, you must die; but if *by the Spirit* you are putting to death the deeds of the body, you will live. For all who are being led by the Spirit of God, these are sons of God.   Romans 8:13-14, emphasis added

As we surrender more deeply to Him, our wills become more aligned with His will. We are then more powerfully led by the Holy Spirit, and He enables us to obey His commands in the newness of the Spirit. Learning to be led is a lifetime of maturing in Him.

The more our hearts are aligned with Him, the more our thoughts, words, and behaviors will be also. When our hearts are truly surrendered to *His* will, the Holy Spirit will give us even the *desire* to obey.

... work out your salvation with fear and trembling, for it is God who is at work in you, both *to will* and to work for His good pleasure.   Philippians 2:12-13, emphasis added

And, as we admit our weakness and rely on His Holy Spirit power at work within us, the Holy Spirit will also give us the *strength* to obey (Eph 3:20-21).

By his divine power, *God has given us everything we need for living a godly life.* We have received all of this by coming to know him, the one who called us to himself by means of his marvelous glory and excellence. And because of his glory and excellence, he has given us great and precious promises. These are the promises that enable you to share his divine nature and escape the world's corruption caused by human desires.   2 Peter 1:3-4 NLT, emphasis added

God has granted us everything we need to walk in holiness through Scriptures (His **precious promises**) and the power of His Holy

Spirit within us (His **divine power**). We grow in Christ and come to know Him deeper through His Word, and His Spirit fills us more and strengthens us to hear and obey. And, as we discussed in Chapter 8, the more we obey, the closer we draw to God, and the deeper He fills us:

"If you love Me, you will keep My commandments ... If anyone loves Me, he will keep My word; and My Father will love him, and We will come to him and make Our abode with him." John 14:15, 23

Additionally, the more obedient we are, the more we are positioned to be used by Him:

But God's firm foundation stands, bearing this seal: "The Lord knows those who are his," and, "Let everyone who names the name of the Lord depart from iniquity."
Now in a great house there are not only vessels of gold and silver but also of wood and clay, some for honorable use, some for dishonorable. Therefore, if anyone cleanses himself from what is dishonorable, he will be a vessel for honorable use, set apart as holy, useful to the master of the house, ready for every good work. 2 Timothy 2:20-21 ESV

Ponder, Pray, and Journal

We truly want to be a vessel of honor, sanctified and useful to the Master. Spend some time of transparency with the Lord. Is there a sin you repeatedly fall into? Could you be relying on your own strength instead of surrendering and relying on the power of the Holy Spirit to walk uprightly?

Indeed, God does command obedience. Yet right here is where obedience can morph into legalism.

Satan's Traps of Legalism

Satan may try to beguile us into working to *earn God's favor and blessings* with our obedience. He also may try to dupe us into believing we can keep God's commandments and obey His will *on our own strength*. Since this is working to obey a set of laws, I think of these sins as sins of legalism. These sins of legalism spring out of pride, thinking that we somehow *can* be wonderful enough to earn God's favor and acceptance and *are* strong enough to be obedient.

Here are some ways Satan may legalistically twist and pervert God's Word, and the corresponding truths:

- Satan insists we need perfect behavior to be in right standing with God,
  ... but God weighs our hearts (Pr 21:2, Jer 17:10, 1Sam 16:17).

- Satan would like nothing better than to have us believe that we can *earn* our right standing with God by obeying a set of laws,
  ... but we are given Jesus' righteousness by grace through faith (Eph 2:8-9, Gal 3:1-3, 2Cor 5:21).

- Satan will berate us every time we fail in our obedience,
  ... but what God wants is our surrendered hearts (Hos 6:6, Isa 29:13, Mt 9:12-13, 15:8-9).

- Satan works to shame us when we sin,
  ... but **there is no condemnation for those who are in Christ Jesus** (Rom 8:1), and **those who look to Him are radiant; their faces are never covered with shame** (Ps 34:5 NIV).

- Satan claims if we are obedient *in our outward behavior* that is sufficient,
  ... but it is only when we are **obedient *from the heart*** that we are freed from sin (Rom 6:17-18, emphasis added).

- Satan claims he has the right to sift us like wheat when we sin, ... but God must first give him permission. And through the sifting we can become slaves to righteousness, resulting in sanctification (Rom 6:19).

God *does* command obedience – but He also grants us *the ability to obey by His Spirit*. The Bible calls the *consequences* of obedience "blessings" and the consequences of disobedience "curses."

"But it shall come about, if you do not obey the LORD your God, to observe to do all His commandments and His statutes with which I charge you today, that all these curses will come upon you and overtake you." Deuteronomy 28:15

Deuteronomy Chapters 27 and 28 detail these curses that will result from rebellion against God's commands, and the blessings that result from obedience. Keep in mind that Jesus redeemed us from these curses, but it is a redemption we must walk in. Remember we are not under the Law *if* we are led by the Spirit:

But if you are led by the Spirit, you are not under the Law.
Galatians 5:18

Greek and Hebrew scholar and international Bible teacher Derek Prince points out that the basic requirements for covenant relationship for the Israelites under the Old Covenant are the same basic requirements for covenant relationship with God under the New Covenant: listen to His voice and obey Him (Jn 10:27).[3]

In the next chapter, we will look at some specific spiritual consequences that are the result of rebelling against God's laws. But before we wrap up this chapter, let's look at how we can position ourselves for spiritual blessings, and how Satan exploits God's laws to bring spiritual curses.

Positioned for Spiritual Blessings

Some of God's blessings are for all of mankind. His love is for the entire world. He causes His sun to rise on the evil and the good, and sends rain on the righteous and the unrighteous. (Jn 3:16, Matt 5:45.)

Some of His blessings are reserved for believers. Because of Jesus' blood spilled out for us and our acceptance of Him as Savior, our sins are forgiven and we are adopted as His children, given every spiritual blessing in the heavenly places, filled with His Spirit, made a new creation, and given a place with Him in heaven. (Eph 1:5-7, Rom 8:15, Eph 1:3, 2Cor 5:17, Jn 14:2-3.)

And many of His blessings for us as believers are *conditional*. As we explore His conditional blessings, be alert for sentences that fall into an "If ... then ..." pattern.

Ponder, Pray, and Journal

Look up the following precious verses and transcribe them in your journal in an "If ... then ..." fashion.

- 1 John 1:9
- Luke 6:38
- 1 John 5:14-15
- Jeremiah 17:7-8
- Psalm 5:12

Now be still before the Lord, and allow the Holy Spirit to speak His love to you through those passages.

Positioned for Spiritual Curses

We learned in Chapter 9 that God has relegated Satan and his demons to darkness (Jude 1:6, 2Pet 2:4), and that they have a legitimate right to oppress us when we have areas of darkness in our hearts and lives. And we also learned how, if God gives them permission, they will "traffic" in those areas of sin in our hearts and in our lives, because they are assigned there, and their mission is to steal, kill, and destroy. Let's look more closely at what it means for Satan to "traffic."

We have learned that whoever influences a portion of our hearts influences the outflow of that portion – thoughts, beliefs, behaviors, conscience, will, desires, plans. For example, if we are stuck in anger, we have given Satan a foothold in our hearts (Eph 4:27), we have given him *access* to our hearts, and he has the right to torment areas of our lives from that foothold. If we are living in selfishness, the spiritual laws of this world give Satan permission to oppress us from that beachhead that he accesses in our hearts. If we are walking in pride or deception or independence or hatred or bitterness or unforgiveness or control, Satan has the power we have given him to utilize these areas to wreak havoc in our lives, even to hold us in bondage. This is what I mean by "trafficking." The Bible also calls the spiritual consequences of our rebellion "curses."

If we could just see with God's eyes, how our sins and the sins of our ancestors have given Satan an engraved invitation to brutally tromp all over our lives ... And, even more importantly, if we could just see God's hand of protection holding him back, as God allows Satan to go only so far (Job 1:12). We discussed this passage in Chapter 8, but let's revisit it here.

"Simon, Simon, behold, Satan has demanded permission to sift you like wheat; but I have prayed for you, that your faith may not fail; and you, when once you have turned again, strengthen your brothers."   Luke 22:31-32

Demanded permission in the Greek means "to claim back, to require something to be delivered up."[4] I think that Satan alleged that there was darkness in Peter's heart. I think that Satan claimed that because he was relegated to darkness, he therefore had the *right* to access Peter's heart, and he **demanded** God deliver him up. Possibly the darkness he saw there was pride, as we notice that the disciples were discussing who was greatest in verses 24-30.[5] Satan **demanded** permission to attack. He insisted Peter be delivered up to his power to manipulate and oppress.

We know the rest of the story. God granted Satan permission – not because God had to, not because God wanted Peter to fail, *but because of God's own plans,* possibly to purify Peter (Gen 50:20, 1Thess 4:3), possibly in order to prepare him for his role as apostle and leader of the church (Lk 22:32).

> **There is no wisdom, no insight, no plan**
> **that can succeed against the LORD ...**
> **He does as he pleases with the powers of heaven**
> **and the peoples of the earth.**
> **No one can hold back his hand**
> **or say to him: "What have you done?"**
>
> Proverbs 21:30, Daniel 4:35 NIV

Notice that Satan had to *ask permission*. Satan wants to run rampant in our lives – and indeed we have invited him in. But God in His sovereignty prevails. He chooses. With great love and care, with complete omniscience, *God hand-picks our sufferings.* He sets up the hedge, and He takes it down, always limiting Satan, always decreeing what is only for our good and His glory (Job 1:9-12, Rom 8:28-29). And don't miss what else Jesus told Peter:

> **... but I have prayed for you ...**   Luke 22:32

Jesus prayed for Peter when He was being sifted like wheat, and He also lives to intercede *for us:*

Therefore He is able also to save forever those who draw near to God through Him, since He always lives to make intercession for them. Hebrews 7:25

In the next chapter, we will examine some specific spiritual laws found in Scripture that Satan seems to love to exploit. We will study these laws so that we can see how Satan can claim that he has a *legitimate right* to influence our hearts when we disobey. We will want to learn how we have opened the door and welcomed him in, so we can learn *how to close off his access.*

Chapter 13
The Consequences of Obeying –
Or Disobeying –
God's Laws

criptures are clear that there are consequences for our sins:

For he who does wrong will receive the consequences of the wrong which he has done, and that without partiality.
Colossians 3:25

Another word Scripture uses for consequences is *curses*. Satan in his impertinence demands these consequences be enforced. He knows God's commandments and the consequences God has ordained for disobeying them, and it seems he has legalistically made it his job to demand permission to *enforce* those consequences.

Does God need to pay heed to Satan? Of course not. But as we learned in Chapter 1, God uses Satan and his demons for His own good purposes: to draw us to Himself, to conform us to the image of Christ, to advance His Kingdom, to reveal His glory. We must also acknowledge that there are things going on in the heavenlies that we cannot possibly begin to fathom (Job 1:6-12, Dan 10:12-13, 1Pet 1:12).

In this chapter, we will take a look at three spiritual laws that we find in the Word, and the consequences of obeying or disobeying these laws:

- The Law of Sowing and Reaping
- The Law of Honoring and Dishonoring
- The Law of Condemning Judgment

Recognizing the consequences that God has woven into the fabric of the universe, Satan works to seduce us to rebel against God's laws, and then demands those consequences be applied. Satan already knows these spiritual laws and their consequences, and exploits our ignorance mercilessly – so let's catch up in our own knowledge so we can know what we are up against.

We'll start with a law that holds in both the physical and the spiritual realms, the Law of Sowing and Reaping, and examine a few different aspects of this law. I think one of the reasons that God uses this principle to teach us about the spiritual world is that it is so easy for us to see it at work in the natural world.

The Law of Sowing and Reaping

Do not be deceived, God is not mocked; for whatever a man sows, this he will also reap. For the one who sows to his own flesh will from the flesh reap corruption, but the one who sows to the Spirit will from the Spirit reap eternal life. Let us not lose heart in doing good, for in due time we will reap if we do not grow weary ... Now this I say, he who sows sparingly will also reap sparingly, and he who sows bountifully will also reap bountifully. Galatians 6:7-9, 2 Corinthians 9:6

Spiritually, when we sow to the Spirit, we reap eternal life and store up treasures in heaven. When we sow to the flesh, we reap corruption, developing sins such as arrogance, immorality, idolatry, impurity, rebellion, and so much more.

Ponder, Pray, and Journal

Look up the following verses and write down in your journal what living in the flesh leads to:

- Romans 8:7-8
- Galatians 5:19-21
- 2 Peter 2:9-10 (look this one up in AMPC)

Of course we are not in the flesh but in the Spirit (Rom 8:9) – but apparently we can still fall into fleshly sins. Be still before the Lord, journaling anything the Holy Spirit is speaking to you right now. Allow Him to convict you and bring you to repentance.

Galatians 6:7 in the Amplified says **He will not allow Himself to be ridiculed, nor treated with contempt, nor allow His precepts to be scornfully set aside.** Ponder how rebellion against God's ways destroys relationship with Him because of *contempt*. Ponder what it means to *ridicule* God, to *scornfully* set Him aside. Pray for fear of the Lord, and journal your heart.

Reaping in Kind

Genesis teaches us that plants and trees bear fruit **after their kind** (Gen 1:12). Plant barley seeds, and we will reap barley. We certainly would not expect to reap corn when we have planted barley.

Similarly, spiritual consequences will come in like kind when we reap what we sow. Let's imagine what this may look like. Applying Galatians 6:7-9 to violence, we see that when we sow violence, we will reap violence. For example, if we are filling our minds with violent movies, games, books, music, online videos and video games, we may begin thinking violent thoughts, and meditating on violence in our hearts. Because out of the abundance of our hearts, the mouth speaks (Lk 6:43-45) we may then begin speaking violence: anger, unforgiveness, sarcasm, criticism, gossip, foul language, slander (Matt 5:21-22). Violent actions may follow. Sow bountifully, reap bountifully. I think my personal example will illustrate it best.

Since my late teens I allowed myself to enjoy mainstream media that fed me a diet of what I now recognize as occult and violent books and movies. It seemed normal at the time. Eventually, the thoughts that paraded through my head were full of darkness and violence.

These thoughts became a torment. No longer were they present only when I chose them – they were present <u>always</u>. Terrorizing me, disturbing me, invading what should have been peaceful and joyful moments. I went to sleep thinking those thoughts. I woke up thinking those thoughts. I was awakened in the middle of the night with those thoughts. I was helpless to control them.

When I came to Christ at age 40, one of the first things God began to speak to me about was my thought life. I had believed that my thought life was, well, private. I believed that no one would ever know – but God was telling me that not only did He <u>know</u> my every thought, He wasn't pleased with my thoughts. And although immediately I tried to be obedient, I had no idea how difficult it was going to be to shut those thoughts down.

I repented and repented and repented and removed them and removed them and removed them hundreds of times a day, but they kept popping back into my mind. Even when I was reading my Bible, worshiping, or listening to the pastor's sermon. I finally admitted that there was nothing I could do to escape those sinful thoughts. I felt I had failed in my Christian walk, and I was ashamed. I continued to seek the Lord passionately, to spend time with Him and study the Word and grow in Him, but this seemed that this unholy thought life was one sin that I was simply never going to conquer.

Celeste Li
Jupiter, Florida

You will hear the Lord's victorious end to this story in Chapter 25, after we have laid more groundwork so that you will fully understand it. For now, I'll let it stand as is, as an example of reaping bountifully what I had bountifully sowed.

Ponder, Pray, and Journal

God speaks of this principle of sowing and reaping a number of times in His Word, perhaps because He finds this principle so critical He really wants to impress it upon us. Read the following Scriptures and summarize in your journal what you learn:

- Luke 6:43-45
- Hosea 10:12
- Job 4:8
- Proverbs 22:8
- Romans 6:21-22 (read NIV to find "reap")
- James 3:18
- Isaiah 17:10-11

Sowing to the Spirit

Realize, joyously, that this principle of sowing and reaping applies to good and not just to evil: **the one who sows to the Spirit will from the Spirit reap eternal life** (Gal 6:8). If we sow to the Spirit, we will reap holiness. The mind set on the Spirit will reap life and peace. Bible study, worship, prayer, solitude, connection in church are seeds that will bring forth a harvest in due time, and will reap a rich relationship of abiding in Him (Rom 6:22, 8:6, Gal 6:9). As the farmer waits for the early and late rains to bring forth the precious produce of the soil, we must be patient (Jas 5:7). Watch this play out in this testimony about my son.

My son Alec has faithfully immersed in his Bible every morning since he was ten years old. When he was in middle school, he determined he wanted to learn how to pray out loud in a group, even though that was very uncomfortable for him. He made a decision to offer to pray out loud every time someone asked for a volunteer to pray, and has faithfully carried out that heart commitment even to today.

When Alec was nineteen, he went on a mission trip to Belle Glade, a rural farming community here in Florida. Much to his surprise, God anointed him during that week as a man of prayer. All week long kids came up to him asking him for prayer. "Mom," he said, "I don't even know where these prayers came from. They just sort of welled up inside of me, and I was praying Scripture verses that I didn't even know that I knew."

How did this happen? At the appointed time, Alec reaped what he had sown. Day after day, he had hidden God's Word in his heart. Week after week, he prayed out loud with his Bible study group, even if it didn't feel comfortable. He had been sowing to the Spirit for nine years, and in due time he reaped beautiful Kingdom fruit.

Celeste Li
Jupiter, Florida

Ponder, Pray, and Journal

Pause and ask the Holy Spirit to show you a time when you have reaped glorious fruit from the good seeds you have sown. Was the reaping delayed?

Multiplying the Harvest

I'd like to expand on the Law of Sowing and Reaping by touching on multiplication. In the physical, it's easy to visualize. From one apple seed grows a tree that bears numerous apples. In the spiritual realm, we can see just one lie resulting in a painful harvest of repercussions.

Jesus describes it in the spiritual this way:

"Give, and it will be given to you. They will pour into your lap a good measure—pressed down, shaken together, and running over. For by your standard of measure it will be measured to you in return." Luke 6:38

For with the measure you use, it will be measured to you (NIV). The amount you give will determine the amount you get back (NLT). When we give generously – whether that be something such as money, time, love, compassion, forgiveness, service, or gifts from the depth of our heart – or whether it is something such as unforgiveness, judgment, or resentment – we will receive back an overflowing amount of the same.

In Due Time

So when we plant seeds, whether sowing to the flesh or sowing to the Spirit, will we harvest the blessing or the curse immediately? Sometimes, the reaping seems to happen quickly. I think if we are sowing to the flesh, and quickly reap the consequences, it is God's grace to us, to open our eyes to our unrepented sin and bring us to repentance.

But other times, the reaping is delayed, sometimes for years: **for *in due time* we will reap** (Gal 6:9, emphasis added). We see this delay in the harvest in the physical world. When we sow apple seeds, it may be many years before they bear fruit. When we sow spiritual seeds, it also may be many years before they bear fruit – for in due time we will reap. *Due time.* God's appointed time. As mere humans, we generally have no knowledge when the time of harvest will be. However, I have read many times – and personally witnessed – that for many, reaping often occurs in three significant seasons: the first year of marriage, the year after the birth of the first child, and the time our children become teens and cannot be controlled.[1]

Let's continue with the analogy God has given us. Repenting and receiving Jesus' gift of freedom from curses will require us to stop planting sinful seeds. But remember that there may already be seeds planted from long ago; some are already at maturity, some are just reaching maturity, and some are just starting to sprout. All these consequences may not disappear overnight when we repent and return to Him. God, in His kindness, may destroy some or even all of this harvest of curses immediately. But I think more often He, for His own good purposes, purposes that we may not fully comprehend, works in a more gradual fashion, allowing some of those seeds to continue to produce their harvest. Additionally, we may not successfully stop sowing to the flesh overnight. Sometimes, yes, God gives us the grace to leave a sin behind and never repeat it. But other times, it is a long road of both victories and defeats before we cease sowing to the flesh in this area. And in the times of our lapses, more seeds of the flesh will have been planted.

As we are transformed and conformed to His image, we will begin to sow to the Spirit. **In due time we will reap if we do not grow weary.** Remember, we are *sowing.* It may require quite a bit of repentance, quite a few seeds sown. It may be a period of time before we witness that harvest of blessing. Sometimes, though, God in His graciousness will miraculously cause some of the seeds we plant to bear fruit overnight, and we will reap blessings. I think He gives us little glimpses of the upcoming harvest to encourage us, for He doesn't want us to become discouraged and weary.

Ponder, Pray, and Journal

Stop and be still before the Lord. Allow Him to show you if you are right now reaping from bad seeds you have sown, or good seeds you have sown – or both. Repent or rejoice. Then allow Him to fill you up with Himself as you take some time alone with Him.

The next law we will learn about in this chapter applies to all of us, since we all have parents. We know the commandment well: **honor your father and mother** (Ex 20:12). But we may not understand the *consequences* of honoring – or dishonoring. Additionally, I think this could be a law Satan exploits to the utmost. It seems his strategy is to wound us when we are young in order to drive us to unforgiveness and dishonoring of our parents so that he can gain his first foothold. Let's look at how he capitalizes on this law for maximal impact.

The Law of Honoring Your Parents

"Honor you father and your mother, that your days may be prolonged in the land which the Lord your God gives you."
Exodus 20:12

This law is written into the Ten Commandments. Deuteronomy amplifies it a bit.

"Honor your father and your mother, as the Lord your God has commanded you, that your days may be prolonged and that it may go well with you on the land which the Lord your God gives you."
Deuteronomy 5:16

Let's explore.

Honoring

I think that honoring our parents means that whether they are still alive on this earth or not, we forgive them as the Lord commands us, no matter the greatness of the wounding. I think it means that we give them unconditional love from a nonjudgmental heart. We appreciate their love, time, efforts, and sacrifices involved in raising us. We do what we can on our part to restore the relationship if it is broken. We ask for forgiveness when we have failed, and offer forgiveness and grace when our parents are not perfect. We understand that they may have been wounded themselves. They may not have been equipped with the skills necessary to parent us well or the inner resources necessary to meet all of our needs. We respect them in their position as parents, for they have been assigned and anointed by God. We realize that God has *chosen* them to be our parents.

We can pray for our parents to grow strong in the Lord, and ask God to give them wisdom and wise counsel that come from deep relationship with Him. We can pray that they will be full of sap and very green:

> **Planted in the house of the LORD,**
> **They will flourish in the courts of our God.**
> **They will still yield fruit in old age;**
> **They shall be full of sap and very green ...**   Psalm 92:13-14

Dishonoring

We dishonor our parents when we withhold forgiveness. We dishonor them when we slander them or gossip about them. We dishonor them when we view them with condemning judgment, or when we pridefully or contemptuously think that we are (or will be) better parents than they were. We dishonor them if God has given them wise counsel for us, and we don't seek that counsel because of pride. We dishonor them when we refuse to humble ourselves and ask forgiveness for our sins, when we close our heart off towards them, when we refuse to be grateful for the good they have provided for us, or when we refuse to do our part in restoring the relationship. We dishonor them when we ignore them or refuse to give them help, saying all our time and money and energy is reserved for God (Mk 7:10-12, Matt 15:4-6).

Forgiving

I think some confusion may arise if we begin to think that honoring our parents by forgiving them means excusing them, or denying the pain of past or current hurts. That is not true. Forgiving means *acknowledging* the depth of our pain – and then *choosing to release* our parents to God. It means recognizing that they owe us a debt they can never repay – and then *tearing up the I.O.U.* Letting it be between them and God. If you are struggling with or confused about forgiveness, go back and work through Chapter 6 in *Triumph of Surrender*, or Chapter 8 in this book.

Obeying

Confusion may also ensue if we think honoring our parents means *obeying* them. Although we are to *honor* our parents our entire lives, only dependent children are commanded to *obey* their parents (Eph 6:1-3, Col 3:20).

Although a young child will not be able to discern good from evil, an older child may recognize when a parent is not walking according to God's laws. In these cases, they are not to obey parents who are commanding them to do evil, to disobey the laws of God, act immorally, or violate their conscience. At these times, they are to obey God and not men (Acts 5:29, Dan 3:16-17). God is the authority we listen to above all else.

Pleasing

I also think some confusion may emerge if we think that honoring our parents means *pleasing* them. We are not to strive to please any people, not even our parents. We are to please *God* alone.

For am I now seeking the favor of men, or of God? Or am I striving to please men? If I were still trying to please men, I would not be a bond-servant of Christ.   Galatians 1:10

Obeying God may at times please our parents, but it may at times *displease* them too. God commands us to seek to please *Him*, and to obey what *He* commands us, and to leave the results up to Him. Indeed, He commands us to **find out** what pleases Him (Eph 5:10 NIV).

Setting Godly Boundaries

Although we are to honor our parents, and often that means helping them and spending time with them, we must always be led by the Spirit. Some parents may demand of their adult children large commitments of time that the Lord is not directing these adult children to give. We must seek the Lord's will to hear His balanced plan for our lives; at times, this may require setting Godly boundaries. His plan will indeed be different for each person and each circumstance.

Finally, honoring can be very confusing if our families are marked by abuse, wounding, or violation of boundaries. It is not loving to continue to allow our parents, or any people, to hurt us.[2] Often, God commands us to confront injustice by lovingly speaking truth – but from a heart of forgiveness (Eph 4:15, 25, 32, Gal 6:1). We may find this extremely challenging! See the *Resource* section for some help in this journey if needed.

So It May Go Well With You

What does Deuteronomy 5:16 mean when it says **so it may go well with you**? Is the corollary true, that if we *dishonor* our parents it will *not go well* with us? I'd like you to see this law and its consequences played out in real life, so I have asked Frank, a friend of my husband and mine, to share. Frank is a man of persistent prayer and deep Bible immersion who holds a doctorate in Biblical studies. He has agreed to share about a time when he walked a path of dishonoring his father.

My mother passed away over a decade ago. There is not a week that goes by when we do not mention her or quote some of her famous phrases. She left a fantastic legacy of wisdom and love for our family. Her name was Bernadette, and she was the most amazing mother in the world. Bernadette has three sons and six grandkids, and was the Godly matriarch of our family. She was loved beyond belief by her family and friends alike. She had a decade long marathon fight with cancer, and eventually passed away, to everyone's sadness.

Four days after my mother's funeral, my father said to me, "I have something I need to tell you." We were in the hospital parking lot, visiting a family member who had become ill during the funeral weekend. After all my father had been through, I was very sympathetic and attentive to his needs. He said he had someone he wanted me to meet. He said it was a woman in the neighborhood whom he had met on his morning walks. He then went on to tell me he wanted me to meet her and that he would like to marry her as soon as possible.

I was stunned, confused, hurt, devastated, betrayed, and upset beyond belief. The events following this announcement and his wedding three months later started a season of pain and relationship discord that would last for years. I became angry and freely vented my unchecked emotions to my family and friends. I refused to go to his wedding; I would not be a witness, a best man, or anything. I did not acknowledge or accept his marriage or his new wife.

After the wedding, I decided I would have nothing to do with my father or his new wife. As a result of my rejection, my lack of participation in the wedding, and my refusal to recognize his marriage, my father became angry with me and talked poorly of me behind my back to our family. The hurt and pain from my mother's death and my father's remarriage caused me to dishonor my father by resentment, disrespect, hardening of my heart, unforgiveness, and withholding of esteem and appreciation toward my father for years.

I avoided my father and his new wife Pat at all costs. For years I went out of town for Christmas, Thanksgiving, birthdays, and any special occasion or holiday. I cut off my father from our family. I simply neglected and rejected him, and I certainly ignored him consciously and intentionally. My attitude dishonored my father.

A few years later, I was still not speaking to my father much, and our family was avoiding him at all costs. But when I was in Key Largo on a family vacation, the Lord softened my heart.

Each morning, I would walk our dog along the same road in the community. Regularly, an oxygen truck delivered oxygen to a homebound older man. But this particular morning, I noticed it. There was no car in the driveway. There were never any visitors at the house. The only person who would visit this older man was the oxygen truck employee.

At that precise moment, I thought of my father. I thought about how he could be that lonely man one day. It was as if the Lord spoke to me with His still small voice as clear as a bell. I have never sensed the Lord nudge me and talk to me as He did at this moment. He spoke to my heart, impressing upon me to "honor my father" and to forgive him. I sensed from the Lord to invite him into my home, and to welcome him into my life again fully and completely.

I stood there in the street. My dog looked up at me, wondering what was going on as I stood there in shock. I knew what I had to do. So I called my father that very day and invited him to our house, to the family birthday parties, every holiday, every graduation, every game, and every big and small event. I even invited my new step-mom Pat too!

My father never apologized for what he did when he married a new woman immediately after my mother's death. He never asked for forgiveness. He never said he did anything wrong. He never said he was sorry for what he did. He never said he was insensitive. He never apologized for how it affected our family and his grandkids. He said nothing. He never mentioned it for the rest of his life. But something happened in <u>my</u> life. I was healed. I was free. Our family was healed, and our family was freed.

A few years after that summer day in Key Largo, my father slowly became sick with Alzheimer's disease. After a year, he faded physically, and quickly passed away. By God's grace, I was able to perform the funeral, honor my father, and accept step-mom Pat into our family.

This change of heart in my life was a miracle from the Lord. As a result of honoring my father and forgiving him, I was healed, and our family was changed forever. Today, there is no big event, birthday, or anniversary that goes by when I don't thank God that I forgave and honored my father before he went to be with the Lord.

Frank B.
Palm Beach Gardens, Florida

What strikes me most about Frank's journey is how one-sided all the heart work was in this father-son relationship. Even after Frank did all he could do to rebuild the relationship, his father never took part in the rebuilding. His father never apologized, never asked for forgiveness, and never acknowledged how his actions had hurt Frank and his family.

And yet God *still* healed Frank and freed him! He honored his father, and now it goes well with him. "It was as if a weight was lifted off me," Frank explained, "and I didn't realize until it was gone just how heavy it was." God called Frank to forgive – and to *walk out* that forgiveness. Notice his forgiveness was not just lip service. He had to find out what pleases the Lord, and then he had work to do. And as Frank followed the Holy Spirit's leading and invited his father – and stepmother – back into his life, the Lord freed him from anger and resentment. Frank had just obeyed this verse:

If it is possible, *as far as it depends on you,* live at peace with everyone.   Romans 12:18 NIV, emphasis added

We learned in *Triumph of Surrender* that forgiveness does not equal reconciliation.[4] As we discussed in Chapter 8, God commands us to forgive, but reconciliation requires *the other person* to repent and seek the Lord for transformation also. Additionally, forgiveness does not equal healing. Forgiveness is our choice; healing is a supernatural work of God in our hearts. In a way we probably cannot fully comprehend, forgiveness invites God to enter and do His healing work in our hearts.

We make a choice to forgive, but we are only able to forgive from the heart because of Jesus' forgiveness given to us and the Holy Spirit's power flowing through us. As we forgive, God will lead us in His plan for rebuilding and restoration. For some situations, particularly situations that are physically or emotionally unsafe, the Holy Spirit may command us to remain far off, and simply be ready to work to restore the relationship when the other party has changed also, and if God shows us it is safe and it is His plan. Sometimes He will ordain no contact for our safety and protection. We are to seek transformation *of our own hearts* as we are waiting. We repent as necessary, apologize as the Lord leads, forgive as needed, pray for them, and set Godly boundaries. **As far as it depends on you.** As much as you can do.

But other times, the Holy Spirit may define **as far as it depends on you** differently than just doing our own heart work and waiting. He may call us to work to rebuild a relationship – *even if the other person has not changed or asked for forgiveness*. God called Frank to do just that, and I believe it is the depth of his relationship with the Lord that gave him the strength to do all God called him to do. And as Frank obeyed

Romans 12:18 by fully submitting to the Lord's commands, through God's grace there was a beautiful level of supernatural rebuilding. True restoration could not happen without his father doing his part. But even though the relationship was devoid of the depth it could have had if his father had owned his mistakes and apologized also, Frank – and his family – still received a full measure of the Lord's healing. I recall Frank speaking at his father's memorial service. Every word was full of love and tenderness that only Jesus could have provided. Frank's heart was clear before the Lord, for he had indeed forgiven his father as the Lord had forgiven him (Col 3:13).

It continues to go well for Frank today, for he has no regrets. "Today, there is no big event, birthday, or anniversary that goes by when I don't thank God that I forgave and honored my father before he went to be with the Lord."

Honor your father and mother so that it may go well with you. In corollary, I think when we don't honor our parents, it won't go well. When Frank allowed bitterness to take root in him, it affected his whole family.

Pursue peace with all men, and the sanctification without which no one will see the Lord. See to it that no one comes short of the grace of God; that no root of bitterness springing up causes trouble, and by it *many be defiled* **...**

Hebrews 12:14-15, emphasis added

When Frank was dishonoring his father, a root of bitterness sprang up, and many were defiled. He – and his family – were trapped in unforgiveness, bitterness, resentment, anger. Their family was marked by division, discord, and strife.

But something miraculous happened when Frank forgave and pursued peace as the Lord commanded him: the Lord *healed* him, and *freed* him.

Frank points out another way it had not been going well with him: the door was opened for his father to slander him. "My father became angry with me and talked poorly of me behind my back to our family."

And one more way it had not been going well with Frank was in his relationship with the Lord. Frank confides in his testimony that what his father had done had "caused me to dishonor my father by ... hardening my heart." As I ponder some passages, I see that hardness of heart causes us to be clouded in our understanding. We will have eyes that cannot see, ears that cannot hear, hearts that cannot comprehend. Hardening of our hearts disrupts our relationship with the Lord, and we may even enter places of striving and earning and be unable to rest in Him (Mk 8:17-18, Rom 11:7, Eph 4:18, Heb 3:3-11). And Isaiah explains that a hardened heart blocks healing. In this passage, the Israelites had continually rebelled and hardened their hearts, and God instructed Isaiah to assess and see that their hearts were insensitive to God:

> **He said, "Go, and tell this people:**
> **'Keep on listening, but do not perceive;**
> **Keep on looking, but do not understand.'**
> **"Render the hearts of this people insensitive,**
> **Their ears dull,**
> **And their eyes dim,**
> **Otherwise they might see with their eyes,**
> **Hear with their ears,**
> **Understand with their hearts,**
> **And return and be healed."**   Isaiah 6:9-10

Now I happen to know that Frank's dog-walking times are prayer walks in disguise. Frank was *pursuing sanctification.* My guess is that as he was in prayer that morning in Key Largo, the Lord graciously opened his eyes and softened his heart. Frank ran to obey, *pursuing peace,* calling his father that very day. His stony heart pulverized, Frank received the Lord's healing – even without a single word of apology from his father.

One more critical point before we move on. I'd like to take us back to a passage from the Ten Commandments that we studied in Chapter 11:

"... visiting the iniquity of the fathers on the children, on the third and the fourth generations of those who hate Me, but showing lovingkindness to thousands, to those who love Me and keep My commandments." Exodus 20:5-6

Do not miss how this played out in Frank's testimony: his family was impacted. When Frank was walking a path of dishonoring his father, *the whole family followed suit.* He led his wife, his children, and their spouses on that same pathway of unforgiveness and division. And when Frank submitted to the Lord's command, *the whole family followed suit.* They all followed Frank on the pathway of forgiveness – and all received the Lord's freedom and healing. "As a result of honoring my father and forgiving him, I was healed, and our family was changed forever." Indeed. Lovingkindness to thousands poured out upon this family, because of one man's obedience.

Ponder, Pray, and Journal

This has been a very heavy section, and the Holy Spirit may be convicting you of dishonoring your parents already. First, take the time to acknowledge the depth of your pain. Pour out your soul to the Lord, and journal in His presence. Then be still before Him, for an equal time that you spent pouring out your heart. Finally, I encourage you to repent and make the choice to forgive and release, and ask the Lord to heal your heart. Meet me back here when you are finished.

This next assignment is for when you are ready. If this is the first time you have worked through forgiveness of your parents, or if wounds run very deep or if you are still being continually wounded today, it may take some time of processing with the Lord and receiving His healing before you are ready. When you are ready, write a letter of encouragement and affirmation to your parents. I don't mean a letter saying, "I forgive you for hurting me ..." All that discussion of pain is in your journal, between you and God. What I mean is a letter that gives unconditional love from a heart that has forgiven, thanking and appreciating them for who they are. Write these letters whether they are alive or not. Ask the Lord if He wants you to send them.

Sometimes, forgiveness comes in layers, and if you are not ready to write a letter of encouragement and affirmation, seek the Lord for deeper layers of forgiveness until you are ready. Remember that forgiveness of deep heart wounds is often not completed in one time of repentance and prayer. There may be layers and layers to process through with the Lord, and we will be in need of His healing. Sometimes, God has us start with the first overarching choice to forgive, and then the Holy Spirit will lead us to forgive specific incidents and situations over weeks or months or longer. Don't be discouraged, just follow His leading. And realize that if the wounding is ongoing, God calls us to set Godly boundaries and to give ongoing forgiveness for each fresh wounding, and He may call us to speak the truth in love.

My friend Maxine wrote a powerful poem that illustrates her journey through layers of forgiveness. When I first met Maxine, she had already been walking deeply with the Lord for many years, led by the Holy Spirit and growing in Him. But this excruciating pain she had buried for decades as she shut the Lord out of these tormented areas of her heart. I have had the great privilege of watching her open her heart to Him and invite Him in. This invitation took much courage, but the result has been healing that words could hardly describe.

They hurt me.
They lied.
They stole.
    You weren't there.

They took my innocence.
    You allowed it.

They abused me.
> *I cried out to you*
> *You did not answer.*

WHERE WERE YOU?
> *I could not see you*
> *I could not find you*

It is so hard to carry
> *This pain*
> *This heartache*
> *The resentment*

How do I know who I am supposed to be?

I hurt myself
I lied
I stole
I allowed myself to be used and abused

I did not look for you
I was ignoring you

I still don't know what to do with
> *This pain*
> *This heartache*
> *The resentment*

I and I still don't know who I am supposed to be

Then one day I see your peace on someone else's face.
You turned toward me, I looked at you

I see you!
I called out to you
You answered me
You lifted my head
Your face shined on me
You answered me!

You tell me how to go
    Hand held tight
    Head held high
    Together – step by step

    Pain is fading
    Heartache lessens
    Resentment lightens

Walls come down
Scales fall off
Face is seen
Heart is open
Arms embrace

I forgive them – me – you
    I forgive the hurt
    I forgive the lies
    I forgive the theft
    I forgive the abuse

You are here
With me
I hear me
I see you
You know me
And I know you

I am becoming who you made me to be

Maxine Taylor
Triumph Servant Leader
North Palm Beach, Florida

Transformed and healed, Maxine now dances with Jesus in sweet relationship with Him.

The Law of Condemning Judgment

Before exploring this law and how Satan capitalizes on it, let's discuss this word "judge." The Bible uses this word at times to mean *condemning* judgment, and at times to mean *discerning* judgment. We must study the context to determine the meaning.

The Bible teaches us that God wants us to use *discerning* judgment – to recognize the difference between good and evil, right and wrong, pure and sinful. But discernment crosses the line into *condemning* judgment when we begin to think we are superior to someone because we don't sin in such a way. When we look down upon someone, think we are better than they, or think of ourselves more highly than we ought. When we think we could do a better job, or would not do it the way they did it. When we are looking at a person from a position of arrogance or self-righteousness. When we view someone with disdain, contempt, or disrespect, or when we despise them in our hearts. (Matt 7:1-5, Rom 12:3, 2Sam 6:16.)

Ponder, Pray, and Journal

Prayerfully read Matthew 7:1-5.

According to verse 1, what will happen to us if we condemningly judge? What specifically would that mean if we are reaping in kind?

According to verse 2, what will happen to us if we are ...

- Holding someone to an impossibly high standard?
- Not giving someone grace?
- Expecting perfection of someone?
- Nit-picking and critical?

According to verse 5, how are we to handle situations where we think someone's walk is not Christlike?

It's about to get heavier as we go to Luke's account of the Beatitudes. We read Luke 6:38 earlier in the chapter when we discussed multiplying the harvest. Read it in a bit more context, Luke 6:37-38.

We see in Luke that Jesus is telling us that when we judge, *we will be judged in return in escalating fashion.* I have asked my friend Cathy to give us a real life example to illustrate the nuances here.

Cathy is an incredible woman of the Lord who has been a mentor to me for many years. She hears from the Lord as if she is sitting right at His feet – probably because she is. She has walked a life of heart-wrenching pain, and as she has pressed into Him in her pain, she has developed an endearing intimacy with Him. I have asked her to share about the first time she realized that these laws of condemning judgment were true and very active in our lives today.

When I was a child, my father constantly criticized me: how I looked, what I wore, the way I walked, the way I talked. This criticism continued into my adulthood and showed no signs of abating. When I became a Christian, I forgave him, and continued to forgive him again and again, but the attacks persisted.

About fifteen years ago, I traveled to see my father. This was in the days before GPS, and as I was leaving, I asked him to draw me a map to help me get back on the highway. He did, and as I asked him to explain it, he began yelling and calling me stupid.

A few years later, I learned about the laws of condemning judgment. I pondered this passage:

Therefore you have no excuse, everyone of you who passes judgment, for in that which you judge another, you condemn yourself; for you who judge practice the same things. And we know that the judgment of God rightly falls upon those who practice such things. But do you suppose this, O man, when you pass judgment on those who practice such things and do the same yourself, that you will escape the judgment of God? Or do you think lightly of the riches of His kindness and tolerance and patience, not knowing that the kindness of God leads you to repentance?   Romans 2:1-4

The Holy Spirit revealed that not only was I <u>judging</u> my father, but that I always expected to be criticized. These <u>expectations</u> grew out of my judgment of him. As the Holy Spirit led, I repented of my judgments and wrong expectations, and prayed blessings over my father.

Not long afterwards, I visited my father again. I actually got lost, and arrived at the house late. I believed that since I had dealt with my own judgments and expectations, I could admit that I had gotten lost and he would not judge and criticize me. And the most amazing thing happened! Not only did he not criticize me, he actually <u>complimented</u> me all weekend – yet continued to criticize my step-mother and others.

Many many visits later, my father continues to compliment me. Over the years, the Holy Spirit revealed judgments in other relationships, and as I repented, He has healed those fractured relationships also.

Cathy Moesel
Inner Healing & Deliverance Ministry
Covenant Centre International
Palm Beach Gardens, Florida

As Cathy condemningly judged her father, her father condemningly judged her. Her judgments led to her expectations that she would be criticized. Her father's judgments of her led to his expectations that she would fail, and brought out his criticisms. Something happened in the spiritual world when she repented of her unforgiveness, judgments, and expectations. She was no longer judging, and no longer judged. The cycle was broken. Her father no longer condemningly judged her, and no longer had judgmental expectations upon her.

Note also that Cathy prayed blessings over her father, as Jesus commands, **"... love your enemies, do good to those who hate you, bless those who curse you, pray for those who mistreat you"** (Lk 6:27-28). And First Peter teaches us another spiritual law: when we bless those who insult us, we inherit a blessing:

Do not repay evil with evil or insult with insult. On the contrary, repay evil with blessing, because to this you were called so that you may inherit a blessing.   1 Peter 3:9 NIV

One more highlight. Do recognize that these laws of condemning judgment have no bearing on *discernment*, the ability to recognize the difference between good and evil, right and wrong, pure and sinful. If the Holy Spirit has granted you the gift of discernment, you may recognize such things as sins, strongholds, or deceptions in other people. But the Holy Spirit has not granted you this gift to judge or to indiscriminately speak out what He has revealed to you.

If you *discern* someone else's sin, a good first step is to take the log out of your own eye (Matt 7:1-8). Ask the Lord to perform a heart check, to show you first if you are judging condemningly, and second, if you are walking in the same sin. If the Holy Spirit reveals that your heart is void of condemnation and sin, and is simply full of discernment and compassion that someone has fallen into Satan's trap, ask the Lord why He has revealed this to you, and what He wants you to do with the revelation. He may be directing you to speak to that person (Matt 18:15-18, Gal 6:1), or perhaps He wants you to pray for *Him* to speak to that person. Perhaps He is calling you to stand in the gap in prayer and repent for them, praying for the Holy Spirit to bring them revelation, to bring them to their own repentance, and to free them (1Jn 5:16). Discerning His plan here will require a very close walk with the Lord indeed.

Ponder, Pray, and Journal

Your turn now. Ask the Lord to search your heart. Do you feel you are being judged?

- Are you judging?
- Are you practicing the same thing?
- Are you *expecting* to be judged and criticized?

Let the Lord lead you on a journey of sanctification. You know what to do.

When the Laws Combine

Sometimes, the consequences of law-breaking may collide for maximum impact. There was a very painful time in my life when the law of condemning judgment was amplified by the law of dishonoring parents and the law of sowing and reaping. A bit of clarification before I share.

Healing and deliverance ministers John and Paula Sandford emphasize that reaping will be *of like kind*, as we discussed above. In their book *Restoring the Christian Family*, the Sandford's reference Deuteronomy 5:16 (that we read earlier in this chapter) and expound on it this way:

> When God commanded that we honor our parents "that it may go well with you," that was a description of the operation of a specific law of the universe. If a child judges his father for lying, by that law of Deuteronomy 5:16 ... he dooms himself to become a liar. When a daughter hates her father for not sharing

himself, being too quiet, and withdrawing from her, that dooms her by law (unless the cross intervenes) to reap the same from her husband and/or her children. If a child rebels against a father's judgmental, hateful ways, he will struggle against his own predilection to judge others until he repents of his judgment of his father.[5]

Unless the cross intervenes. Unless we repent of our judgments and receive Jesus' work on the cross.

Healing and deliverance ministers Chester and Betsy Kylstra describe this law also:

> If a son says, "My dad was a terrible father who beat me all the time. He is no good," that child has judged his father and set the stage to enter into the same sins and to receive that same kind of judgment when he becomes a father himself.
>
> In families of alcoholics, the children are likely to say, "I will never be like my dad (or mom)." In reality, they usually become alcoholics themselves as a result of planting "judging seeds" and then reaping the consequences.[6]

Even though the child's intention was positive (not to become an alcoholic), his vow grew out of a judgment. He will likely become what he judges (an alcoholic, Rom 2:1), or perhaps marry what he judges (an alcoholic). A vow is making a promise with swearing or with an oath, and is taking judgment to a whole new level.

"Again, you have heard that the ancients were told, 'YOU SHALL NOT MAKE FALSE VOWS, BUT SHALL FULFILL YOUR VOWS TO THE LORD.' But I say to you, make no oath at all, either by heaven, for it is the throne of God, or by the earth, for it is the footstool of His feet, or by Jerusalem, for it is the CITY OF THE GREAT KING. Nor shall you make an oath by your head, for you cannot make one hair white or black. But let your statement by 'Yes, yes', or 'No, no'; anything beyond these is of evil."

Matthew 5:33-37

James expounds on Jesus' teaching:

Do not complain, brethren, against one another, so that you yourselves may not be judged; behold, the Judge is standing right at the door ... But above all, my brethren, do not swear, either by heaven or by earth or with any other oath; but your yes is to be yes, and your no, no, so that you may not fall under judgment.   James 5:9,12

If we find ourselves using the words "I will always" or "I will never" – beware, because we may be declaring a vow that is arising from a judgmental heart. If we judge, we will be judged (Matt 7:1). *Unless, of course, the cross intervenes.* Jesus has broken these curses for us – but we must receive that gift of freedom by repentance and walking it out. Now watch this play out in my own life.

When I was young in my walk with Christ, I was completely blind to my judgmentalism. There was a veil over my heart, and I did not recognize this sin. But when my daughter was a teen, I reaped. God orchestrated events in my life to expose this dark area of my heart, and I began to struggle in my relationship with my daughter.

Now I had taken parenting classes since my daughter was two years old. I had even taught parenting classes! And now, I had a rift in my relationship with my own teenage daughter.

This strained relationship with one I loved so deeply drove me to God for answers. And His answers didn't look pretty. He began to speak to me regarding judgment, ever so gently at first, because He knew my deep root of shame made it excruciatingly painful to admit. Shamed and horrified, I tried and tried yet found it impossible to control my judgmental thoughts and words. And soon after He had given me a peek behind the veil over my heart, He pulled that veil back all the way. During a particularly candid conversation, with great accuracy and acute spiritual perception, my daughter declared, "Mom, you're judging me!" My eyes were opened. There was no denying it now. The veil came fully off. My heart was laid embarrassingly bare before her – and before Him.

Nothing in all creation is hidden from God's sight. Everything is uncovered and laid bare before the eyes of him to whom we must give account.					Hebrews 4:13 NIV

But God didn't stop there. He revealed that I was judging my parents – because I felt <u>they</u> had been judging <u>me</u>. With full condemnation I had sworn in my heart, "I will <u>never</u> judge my children in that way." Not only did I make this vow, I asked my brothers to tell me if they ever saw me acting like my parents. But **you who judge practice the same things** *(Rom 2:1). Although I had not said the same judgmental words to my children as my parents did, I had judged them in my heart, and somehow, my daughter could sense that.*

It was decades before I reaped the seeds of judgment that I had sown inside of my heart since childhood. But throw in the law of dishonoring parents and the law of sowing and reaping, and no wonder that when it was due time, when my daughter was a teenager, the harvest was plentiful. I reaped in kind. What I had judged, I became: a judgmental parent. It drove my daughter away from me. And it opened the door for my children to enter into judging me.

Celeste Li
Jupiter, Florida

The Holy Spirit exposed not only my judgmental heart, but also began to expose pride and hypocrisy, and a deep root of perfectionism. Slowly, bit by bit, over time, as I was able to handle His revelations, He opened my eyes to see my holier-than-thou attitude, and my contempt and spiritual superiority that led to the judging.

Eventually, the Holy Spirit also unveiled my judgment of *myself.* He exposed my own fear of failure and expectations of perfectionism that I imposed upon both myself and others, particularly my children. Yet there is only one Lawgiver and one Judge:

There is only one Lawgiver and Judge, the One who is able to save and to destroy; but who are you who judge your neighbor?					James 4:12

If I judge others, or judge myself, I am setting myself up as god! Additionally, if I allow others to judge me, I am establishing them as god in my heart! Only the Lord is to examine my heart (1Cor 4:3-5, Ps 139:23-24).

As I recognized that I had judged my parents, I realized that I also held dual expectations: that they would judge and criticize me, and that they should behave differently. As I repented of my judgments and expectations of both my daughter and my parents, as I repented of my pride and hypocrisy and perfectionism, as I forgave my parents and apologized to my daughter and my parents, the Lord graciously began to rebuild these relationships. I began a long slow uphill journey, as I begged Him to give me a heart of humility, compassion, and grace. I asked Him to expose my heart when I had fallen again. Slowly, slowly, He began to uproot the nasty roots of judgment, pride, and perfectionism and to plant His seeds of humility and unconditional grace. Slowly, slowly, they have begun to grow and bear fruit.

My testimony is also a reminder that we don't always know when the **due time** will be; God holds that mystery in His heart. I believe in His graciousness He may give us time before the harvest of bad fruit appears, perhaps giving us time to recognize our sin and repent before we begin to reap the painful harvest.

Ponder, Pray, and Journal

No parent is perfect, and even people who grew up with loving and tender parents may have accumulated some resentments, judgments, and unmet expectations, and even made some vows. Take some time alone with the Lord, and see what He reveals. You have already worked through unforgiveness of parents and dishonoring parents in the last section. Let's take it another step further and together with the Lord destroy any judgments, expectations, and vows.

We've taken a deep dive into three important spiritual laws, and the results of obeying or disobeying them. Now that our eyes are opened, as we study the Word, we will begin to notice more spiritual laws and their ordained consequences.

In the next chapter, we will see why it is so critical to know God's laws and to obey them in order to be victorious against the enemy. We know that we belong to Jesus, and Satan has no *authority* over us and no legitimate *right to influence* our hearts. But in the next chapter, Scripture will show us how he schemes to *seize access* when we violate God's law and rebel against Him. We will see how, when we walk in disobedience, we have opened the door for Satan to *usurp* access and to wreak havoc as he expands his reach.

Chapter 14
Satan's Strategies to Usurp Access

*R*emember that Satan legitimately has *no authority* over us, because we have been rescued out of his domain. But we have learned that when we align ourselves with his dark ways, we *invite* his power into our hearts and lives. We give him *permission* to usurp *access* over territory where he has no rightful authority. He seizes access by force – *at our invitation*.

Expect Satan to pervert God's laws to entrap us in sin, then pervert them again to shame us for our sin. In the last two chapters we learned that in order to avoid his traps, we must be very familiar with God's laws – *and be obedient to them*. Disobedience and continued sinful behavior – which is rebellion – invites Satan's influence. When we – knowingly or even unknowingly – violate God's laws, we have created an area of darkness. We have invited Satan and his demons to traffic; we have given them a place of rest.

As we discussed in Chapter 6, the wrestling described in Ephesians 6 is *pale*, hand-to-hand combat full of trickery and scheming.[1] We will often find Satan's attacks to be deeply personal, timed at our weakest moments, with blows to our most vulnerable areas and temptations uniquely designed to lure us to sin. His strategies are carefully crafted to pin us to the mat and get us to tap out.

As we ponder some of Satan's strategies in this chapter, keep in mind that in Jesus, ultimately no weapon formed against us will bear fruit. Read this passage with spiritual eyes:

> **"If anyone fiercely assails you it will not be from Me.**
> **Whoever assails you will fall because of you.**
> **Behold, I Myself have created the smith**
> **Who blows the fire of coals**
> **And brings out a weapon for its work;**
> **And I have created the destroyer to ruin.**
> **No weapon that is formed against you will prosper;**
> **And every tongue that accuses you in judgment**
> **You will condemn.**
> **This is the heritage of the servants of the LORD,**
> **And their vindication is from Me," declares the LORD.**

Isaiah 54:15-17

God has created the destroyer who has crafted weapons against us. He created Satan and his demons as holy angels with free will – fully knowing that they would choose evil over Him and fall from holiness. God is the One who created them, and in their wickedness they have forged their weapons. But as we learned in Chapter 1, God is using Satan and his demons to purify us and grow us in Him. Weapons may be formed against us, flaming arrows may assail us, but they will not succeed in their mission. *No weapon formed against us will prosper* – because no matter how hard Satan tries, when we place ourselves in God's hands, God will confound his efforts and the end result will be God's victory: our sanctification, His Kingdom advanced, and His glory revealed. And rest in the knowledge that *God* will be the One to vindicate us. He will clear us, defend us, and avenge us.

In this chapter, we are going to study some passages that give insight into Satan's modes of operation, exploring five different strategies that he may use to entrap us to sin:

- Influencing our minds
- Attacking our bodies
- Masquerading as an angel of light

- Counterattacking after victory
- Condemning us

Satan's goal is to compel us to open a door by our sins, inviting him to usurp access. In Volume II, we will look at how we may open doors to the enemy, and how to close them. But first, let's study some of Satan's strategies.

Enemy Strategy: Influencing Our Minds

In Chapter 10, we studied through the Scriptures how Satan and his demons can influence our minds by corrupting them, leading them astray, seducing them, blinding them, deceiving them.

Additionally, as we studied in Chapter 2, Romans teaches us that those who neglect thanksgiving and worship open the door for Satan to bring mental confusion and darkness to their minds.

For even though they knew God, they did not honor Him as God or give thanks, but they became futile in their speculations, and their foolish heart was darkened.

Romans 1:21

When people do not have hearts of gratitude, when they do not acknowledge God as King and worship and honor Him, they become susceptible to deception regarding who God is, what He is like, His character, His heart, His integrity, His ways. They open the door and invite Satan to begin clouding their minds, causing darkness, depression, hopelessness, and confusion to settle in. Both Romans and Second Timothy explain that for those who oppose the truth, their minds become **depraved** (Rom 1:18, 28, 2Tim 3:8).

Romans 1 and Second Timothy 3:8 are describing those who are unsaved. Yet, as we discussed in Chapter 2, even those who belong to Jesus can struggle with areas of darkness also. And Ephesians teaches that although we were formerly darkness and now are light in the Lord, we still have a choice: we can walk in futility of mind with darkened understanding, or we can walk as children of the Light (Eph 4:17-28, 5:8).

Ponder, Pray, and Journal

If you are struggling with dark thoughts, depression, hopelessness, or confusion, then thanksgiving and worship are crucial weapons in the battle. Take up those weapons and enter the battlefront.

Is This My Thought, God's Thought, or the Enemy's Thought?

How can I know if a thought in my heart or in my mind is from God, from myself, or implanted into my mind from the enemy? Such a good question. I am so glad you asked.

I think we can't always know. But I believe as we grow in the Lord and develop a greater spiritual discernment, we will be able to distinguish the difference with more certainty.

From my own walk with the Lord, I have found that when I am fully surrendered in an area, when the depth of my heart wants the will of the Father no matter what, when I desire to obey with all my heart no matter how hard it will be, then a sinful thought regarding this issue probably doesn't come from me. It has been inserted into my mind by Satan and his demons, and they are hoping I will grab onto it *and make it my own thought* by dwelling on it or expounding on it.

On the other hand, if I am not fully surrendered in a particular area, if the depth of me still wants things my way, if I am disobedient

– or obeying but with reluctance or resentment – then I may have an idol. The thoughts regarding this issue may well be my own thoughts from my own uncrucified flesh. Because I am seeking to have my ears tickled and to hear what I want to hear (2Tim 4:3-4), I may hear the enemy's voice and think it is coming from God. The forces of darkness can surely capitalize on my sinfulness and easily implant their sinful thoughts *in addition* to those of my own uncrucified flesh, resulting in an entanglement of my own ungodly thoughts and the enemy's injected thoughts.

Let's look at three specific attacks on our minds.

Battling Ungodly Thoughts

If we are able to recognize the enemy infiltration and quickly reject an ungodly thought, fixing our minds and hearts on Jesus, our shields of faith have blocked those flaming arrows from going any further. We read Pastor Ty McMillan's testimony about this sort of attack in Chapter 10.

Or, if an isolated sin is the issue, when we do acknowledge our sin or our unsurrendered heart and choose to repent, we are closing the doors that we had opened to darkness. Sometimes the battle in our minds will be immediately over and the ungodly thoughts will vanish.

Sometimes, though, the problem is deeper than that. A persistent thought process that cannot be silenced could well be coming from the enemy.

Relentless Bombardment of Ungodly Thoughts

If, by a *practice of sinning* (Jn 8:34, 1Jn 3:8) we have opened a door to this kind of incessant attack on our minds, we may actually be up against a stronghold. We are going to study demolition of strongholds in upcoming chapters, but for now, realize that in this type of situation, these incessant thoughts will probably only be silenced when we repent, forgive, surrender, and align with God's commands.

Additionally, if trauma and unhealed wounds have given the enemy access to assault our minds, these thoughts will probably require God's healing to be subdued. We will discuss more about receiving God's healing in Chapter 24.

I have asked my husband John to share a time when he could not shut down obsessive thoughts. John had always seemed to have a deep well of peace, but this ordeal truly disturbed his tranquility. Let's hear how he partnered with the Lord for victory.

A few years ago I was ousted off the board of a Christian ministry organization. Having never been fired from anything before, this was very devastating to me. My mind kept swirling over and over again about the same issues. How wrong this was. How I was shut down when I was only trying to be helpful. How this one particular person had made an unilateral decision. How things could've been different. I tried to figure out what I did wrong and what I could do better next time. The constant re-play in my head was counterproductive and was bearing no good fruit.

This was all-consuming. It was hard to think about anything else. All I wanted to do was write letters explaining myself to everyone so that I would not need to be embarrassed. It was hard to concentrate on work. This obsession invaded my peace.

So I did the best I could to bottle things up inside. I left the organization gracefully, without a fuss or making a scene. I stuffed the emotions deep down into a hole. And then I stewed. And then I stewed some more.

I would think about it on the drive to work ... on the drive back home ... in the shower ... before bed ... over lunch ... any time my mind was not otherwise occupied.

With most of my acquaintances, I pretended to be totally at peace. I stayed mum. But when people who cared about me would ask about the situation, I would give them a very detailed, blow by blow recounting of the entire epic saga. It was clearly very consuming!

I prayed about this daily. Constantly. Lord, please take this cup from me! Help me quit thinking about this! I wish that I could say that the Lord granted me complete instantaneous freedom. But it was not so.

First, He said I had to forgive. "What? I didn't do anything wrong, why do I need to forgive? He doesn't deserve it!" Then He told my wife to tell me to forgive. What? Whose side was she on anyway?

For me, forgiveness was not a light switch that I flipped on or off. It was a process. And this process sure was slow.

I started with "Hey, at least he donates a lot of money to the ministry!" There! I said one good thing.

The next was "Hey, at least he spends a lot of time working on the ministry. We need someone who can spend a lot of time on it."

Over many months, through a slow process of choosing to think positive thoughts about him, I became less and less angry with him. I think I actually forgave him. Hey, I even defended him when one of my friends started bashing him.

And now, I am no longer thinking about it every day! It is no longer an obsession. This deliverance was slow and gradual, but I think I am finally free!

John Li, M.D.
Jupiter, Florida

Notice how Satan used the open door of John's sin of unforgiveness to invade his mind. Anger and judgment gave Satan additional footholds, inviting him to expand his reach in John's mind. Obsessive thoughts pervaded his every waking moment.

Notice how the Lord required John to partner with Him to receive his deliverance: John was to forgive and release. As John obediently walked the path marked out for him, doors to the enemy were closed, Jesus delivered John, and the obsessive thoughts were silenced.

Before we leave this section on attacks on our mind, I'd like to study one more of Satan's strategies of mind access: blinding our minds.

Spiritual Blinding

We studied this spiritual blinding extensively in Chapters 2 and 10, and in Chapter 12 we learned that this blinding is caused by the demonic spirit of deep sleep. Satan blinds our minds by deceiving, lying, beguiling, deluding, and misleading. He can dupe us into believing that light is dark and dark is light, that good is evil and evil is good (Isa 5:20). When we are blinded in an area, we are completely unable to recognize truth in that area, and we are *truly convinced* that the lies we are believing *are* the truth. Even the most eloquent and persuasive speakers will not convince us otherwise. Only Jesus can unblind us by His deliverance, for **the veil … is removed in Christ** (2Cor 3:14).

To illustrate this blinding, I'd like to introduce you to John Cintorino. I call this man the "Johnny Appleseed of *Triumph Over Suffering*" because he has given out countless *Triumph* books, planting seeds in so many hearts! He and his wife Phyllis have invited many people into their home, mentoring them and walking them through this study. *Triumph Over Suffering* had taught John to embrace adversity as an opportunity to learn more about God and himself, but for a season, the trials of his present coupled with the pain of his past had blinded him to his own anger.

A few years ago, my wife was diagnosed with cancer, and I became her caregiver. This season of adversity held an intensity I did not know before; it was filled with a great deal of uncertainty.

I turned away from God. It was all about me, me, me. I was sure someone else was responsible for the problems I was having. I was not able to give my wife the love and understanding she badly needed. After three years of being a caregiver, I ran dry. I had nothing left to give. I began to find fault with my wife. The problems in my marriage increased, the pain in my marriage escalated, and the arguments became severe. I thought that I had put God in the center of all I was doing, but it was obvious that I had not. I tried to discipline myself with self-control, but that only silenced my behavior for a short time. It was a while before the Holy Spirit led me to accept ownership of my actions, and I sought counsel from a trusted pastor.

I shared my writings with him. He noted that all my writings were written to teach and instruct other people. He suggested I spend the next week journaling my emotions instead. I did not want to write about my emotions; I just wanted to continue to embrace the lies and remain frozen in my beliefs. But taking a step of faith, I did as the pastor suggested, and it opened the door to the pain of my childhood that I had buried for many decades.

I met again with the pastor the following week. I shared about my early years and my anger. I felt I was born with anger; it helped me survive. My early experiences had brought hate, anger, and destruction into my life. After we discussed my past, he asked me if I was angry with my wife; I said no. He said normally people become angry if their plans for their lives are changed. There was a moment of silence, then the scales fell off my eyes and my hidden anger towards my wife began to surface.

I realized I was angry because my wife was sick. I was angry because my life had taken a radical turn. I was angry because I could no longer do the things I had wanted to do. I had tried to hide my anger, but it came out in arguments with my wife. I was imprisoned by my anger. It seemed I had nowhere else to release the pain I was feeling but to dump it out on my wife. I had also been blind to the pain of my past that was feeding into my present circumstances. But God used this pastor to open my eyes.

The pastor told me to present my anger to God, to spend time *pouring out my anger to God. He told me, "Do not rush." He said after I do that, to spend an equal amount of time waiting for His answer. "When you have understood what He has told you, then ask Him how to treat your wife," he said. Only God could free me from what was holding me captive. These steps were the beginning of my forgiveness, and my surrender.*

What happened next is hard to explain. As I surrendered and forgave the people of my past and my present, I felt free, my burden was lifted, and I felt such happiness. I found the peace and joy I longed for. I just wanted to take in all the beauty I could see. Somehow, miraculously, God opened my eyes and set me free. He removed my selfish thinking and replaced it with His. I now had clarity and understanding, and I was able to love my wife again.

John Cintorino
Jupiter, Florida

"The scales fell off my eyes and my hidden anger towards my wife began to surface." John Cintorino had been completely blinded to his anger towards his wife. He truly believed he harbored no anger.

If someone is blinded, how will they ever be able to see? Revelation of the blindness is completely a work of the Holy Spirit. When He is ready to unblind, He may invite us in to work, as He invited John Cintorino to journal his emotions. The Holy Spirit worked through John's obedience to bring revelation. And once the Lord reveals, we will have work to do, which will probably entail, as it did for John Cintorino, forgiveness and surrender.

As the eyes of John Cintorino's heart were opened and he forgave and surrendered, Jesus delivered him from the blinding spirit, and once again revealed the hope of his calling: to mentor people living in pain and confusion. Freed from the spirit of deep sleep and the bondage of anger, released from the pain of his past and present, God's love once again flows through John Cintorino and to his wife, and to the people he is mentoring.

Enemy Strategy: Attacking Our Bodies

It's easy to see how being laid low with physical illness could take us out of our Kingdom work, and even drive us into irritability, impatience, and any number of other sins. But what we may not realize is that Satan may – directly or indirectly – be the *cause* of physical diseases. Read the following passages to hear Scripture attribute some physical ailments specifically to demons.

- Job 2:7
- Matthew 12:22
- Luke 13:11-16

We know that germs and diseases are part of the fallenness of this world. Satan can orchestrate attacks on our bodies through infection or injury. Additionally, Bible teacher and healing and deliverance minister Derek Prince believes that illnesses that are "extraordinary" or "severe and lingering" or run in families may indicate that demonic forces are in play.[2] Satan is an expert at disguising a demonic attack to appear to be merely something physical. It will require Holy Spirit discernment to know if demonic forces are in play when we are battling physical illness.

Enemy Strategy: Masquerading as an Angel of Light

An imposter and a fraud, a genius of duplicity, Satan deludes and misleads people so they believe his lies. We studied this verse in Chapter 7, but let's review it here.

For such men are false apostles, deceitful workmen, masquerading as apostles of Christ. And no wonder, for

Satan himself masquerades as an angel of light.   It is not surprising, then, if his servants masquerade as servants of righteousness. Their end will be what their actions deserve.

2 Corinthians 11:13-15 NIV

As the father of all lies, the source of all deception, Satan is behind cults and false religions, false apostles, false prophets, and counterfeit doctrines, which the Word calls doctrines of demons (1Tim 4:1-2).

Ponder, Pray, and Journal

Have you ever encountered evil disguised as good? How did you come to discern that what appeared to be light was really darkness?

Does realizing that Satan has created false religions and cults to ensnare the unwary cause you to look at their members with a heart of compassion?

Let's look at two ways Satan may masquerade as an angel of light: by counterfeit miracles and distortion of Scripture.

Counterfeit Miracles

I know it may be hard to believe Satan can perform miracles. But read these passages carefully:

- Matthew 7:21-23
- 2 Thessalonians 2:9-10
- Matthew 24:24
- Revelation 13:11-14

Second Thessalonians calls these counterfeit miracles **false signs and wonders**. Forgeries. These verses state that false miracles are designed to **mislead** and **deceive**. I call these miracles *counterfeit*, because although something in the supernatural may well be occurring, these miracles are *not* authored by God, and any good that seems to result will not be lasting. Only miracles through Jesus Christ are eternal and everlasting.

Distortion of Scripture

Sometimes Satan tries to cause me to stumble by impressing Scripture upon me in a perverted way. Invariably, my first thought is, "This is God's Word, so it must be God speaking." But I have learned that Satan may be twisting Scripture in order to condemn or shame me, or using it out of context in order to tickle my ears and tell me what I want to hear (2Tim 4:3). If I am not careful and discerning, I can be duped.

We studied this tactic of Scripture perversion in Chapter 5 when we examined the temptations of Jesus. Our protection from this entrapment is not merely to know Scripture verses, but to know them *in context*, to know the *whole counsel of the Bible*, and to know *the heart, the character, and the ways* of God. And of course we will also need the power and revelation of the Holy Spirit.

Enemy Strategy: Counterattacking After Victory

Many times I have witnessed people turn to the Lord in repentance, or step out in obedience, or walk away from sinful lifestyles, or press in to know Him more or step out in Kingdom work – and immediately suffer financial loss, relationship havoc, loss of job, attacks on family members, physical illness, family strife, or any number of attacks. I think of this harassment as enemy backlash. It is a retaliation of the enemy, in fury working to derail the Kingdom advancement, or to discourage us and steal away our new-found freedom by attempting to drive us back into old sinful patterns.

Let's look at an Old Testament parallel. In Second Chronicles Chapters 29-31, King Hezekiah, leading his country in mighty strides of repentance and obedience, had repaired and purged the temple and the land. Then,

After these acts of faithfulness Sennacherib king of Assyria came and invaded Judah and besieged the fortified cities, and thought to break into them for himself.

2 Chronicles 32:1, emphasis added

Notice the emphasis: *after these acts of faithfulness*. Yet even this enemy backlash seems to have been part of the Lord's sovereign plan, for Hezekiah's heart was soon exposed. He did not thank God for the miraculous deliverance from the Assyrians, or for the miraculous healing of a mortal illness **because his heart was proud** (2Chr 32:25).

Come meet my friend Betz, a woman I have always known as a bright light. Bubbling, energetic, and constantly serving in church, Betz is also an extraordinary connector of people. I have asked her to share a time of decisive victory, followed by enemy counterattack.

My husband and I had gone through years of infertility treatment and multiple miscarriages, and had tried to adopt from both inside the Unites States and from Romania, but the doors were closed. I then wanted to pursue adoption from China, but my husband refused. I felt my husband had not allowed me to fulfill my dreams of having a baby.

Years after our divorce, I realized that I was blaming my ex-husband that we did not have any children. When I was in a Bible study, the Holy Spirit showed me that I was holding on to unforgiveness of him. I knew I needed to forgive. It was not easy, but with the help of the Lord, I was finally able to forgive him.

Not long afterwards, my older brother's relationship with his adult daughter got rocky. I tried to speak to him about this, asking him, "What would Jesus do?" He attacked me: "What do you know about having kids? You didn't have kids and the reason you don't have any kids is probably because you would not have been a good mother!"

Miraculously, I was able to remain calm and end the call. I did not defend myself or lash back. As soon as I got off the phone I dropped to my knees in tears and cried out, "Jesus! Jesus! Please come!!" Suddenly, I felt like He came and wrapped His arms around me as I wept. I could not believe my own brother had said such horrible things to me. Yet I became very peaceful and was able to forgive him quickly, and even spoke with him a few weeks later without bringing it up.

Betz Fishbein
Palm Beach Gardens, Florida

"Not long afterwards." Such a clear counterattack. Isaiah explains that **he who turns aside from evil makes himself a prey** (Isa 59:15). Betz had quit blaming her ex–husband that she did not have children. She had turned away from unforgiveness and walked out in obedience. And Satan, the prowling lion, targeted her as prey. He pierced her to the core, attacking the most vulnerable place of her heart: her loss of motherhood. Sometimes, Satan attacks after a victory when he thinks that we have become vulnerable by letting our guard down. The Word cautions,

So, if you think you are standing firm, be careful that you don't fall!   1 Corinthians 10:12 NIV

Satan may have thought Betz had let her guard down. But he was mistaken. Satan had no victory here. Betz knew right where to go for comfort, and, out of a heart that has learned how to forgive, quickly forgave her brother.

I'd like to add a P.S. to her testimony, to demonstrate that no weapon formed against us will prosper. Not long after these victories, God gave Betz the desires of her heart. He brought her an amazing husband, a man who prays with her every morning and every night, goes to church with her every week, and serves alongside her in her church's youth ministry and on the welcome team. And along with this Godly husband, God brought Betz a beautiful family of three grown children and four precious grandchildren! She explained, "I told Bob in the beginning that Jesus would always be my #1. His response was, 'That's OK. Can I be your #1A?' "

Ponder, Pray, and Journal

Think of a time you experienced an attack after victory. Did you stand firm? If the enemy scored with his counterattack, how did that happen? Did you let your guard down, or slip into pride or complacency? What will you do next time?"

Enemy Strategy: Condemning Us

Therefore there is now no condemnation for those who are in Christ Jesus.   Romans 8:1

Although Satan has no *right* to condemn us, that won't stop him from trying. Remember he is waging guerilla warfare, and we can fall prey to his condemnation. We'll look at two types of condemnation: *warranted*, and *unwarranted*.

Warranted Condemnation

If we are sinning, Satan is justified when he condemns us. Let's take a Biblical example.

SATAN'S STRATEGIES TO USURP ACCESS

After the Israelites had returned from captivity, Joshua the High Priest was walking in iniquity. The Lord gave the prophet Zechariah a vision that gave him a glimpse into what was happening in the spiritual world:

Joshua was standing before the angel of the LORD, and Satan standing at his right hand to accuse him ... Now Joshua was clothed with filthy garments and standing before the angel.
                                                         Zechariah 3:1,3

We see in the next verses that Joshua the High Priest was in opposition to God. His opposition left him open to the accuser of the brethren's attack of condemnation. But God was gracious and He rebuked Satan. Joshua's filthy garments were removed and a clean turban put on his head. The angel of the Lord said to him,

"See, I have taken your iniquity away from you and will clothe you with festal robes."
... And the angel of the LORD admonished Joshua, saying, "Thus says the LORD of hosts, 'If you will walk in My ways and if you will perform My service, then you will also govern My house and also have charge of My courts, and I will grant you free access among these who are standing here.' "
                                          Zechariah 3:4, 6-7, emphasis added

Joshua's rebellion against God's ways opened him up to condemnation. To close the door to Satan's oppression, Joshua would need to walk in God's ways and perform the assignments God had given him. The rewards of obedience included reinstatement over the temple, and deep intimacy with God: **free access [to My presence] among these who are standing here** (Zech 3:7 AMP).

If we, like Joshua the High Priest, are not walking uprightly and we remain unrepentant, we are open to enemy accusation.

We can also invite Satan's condemnation by our sinful heart attitudes. For example, if we fear being imperfect, the door is open for Satan to fill our minds with obsessive self-critical thoughts.

Other times, we may have repented and left a sin behind, but we still position ourselves for Satan's condemnation by remaining in the dark. If we hide our sins instead of bringing them into God's Light, Satan can flood us with shame.

In these cases, we can fight to victory by acknowledging our sin (Matt 5:25-26), repenting, and trusting the blood of Jesus to cover all our sins. In the passage in Zechariah, the Lord graciously took away Joshua's iniquity, and required that he walk in His ways to remain free.

Unwarranted Condemnation

There are also times when Satan's accusations are undeserved.

When we sin yet repent, although our sins are immediately forgiven and forgotten, if our hearts don't believe that God has put our sins as far away from us as the east is from the west (Isa 43:25, 1:18, Ps 103:12), we may be open to this kind of attack. Satan can berate us incessantly with condemnation. He can accuse, slander, criticize, and heap on shame and false guilt. Note, however, that it is *our sin of refusing to believe God's Word about His forgiveness* that opens us up to this attack.

Additionally, when we are wounded, we may be the most open to his lying condemnation. Satan can undercut our identity, telling us we are worthless, unwanted, and unloved. We may hear Satan's voice in the first person, causing us to think it is our own thought. "I'm no good." "I am of no value to God." Although we cannot know another's thoughts (1Cor 2:11), we may hear Satan's voice as others' thoughts: "They probably think I'm stupid. "They probably don't want to be with me." Note that often, it is our sin of unforgiveness that opens us up to this attack.

My friend Sylvie possesses an ability to ignore her own feelings and remain steady and calm. These traits have served her well as an

Emergency Room physician, enabling her to think on her feet when everyone else is panicking. But these same traits did not serve her well when it came to dealing with her childhood wounds. I have asked her to share her testimony, how Satan used the pain of her past to undermine her worth with his incessant condemnation, and how she battled to victory.

By the age of ten, I had attended eleven schools in three countries across two continents in two different languages. This would have been disruptive enough, but by the age of ten I had also been raped twice. The trauma destroyed my stability and self worth. I had an emotionally distant family environment in which emotions were not discussed, and in which I was expected to be the "perfect" child. We were not a Christ-centered family. I found myself over and over again in a new country and a new school. The despair and darkness that overwhelmed me was indescribable. This is when Satan began his lies. "You are worthless. You are unlovable. You are rejected. No one wants you. You don't belong. You might even want to end it all." The anger, depression, fear, anxiety, and insecurity were crushing. I had attended my parents' church, but because I had not given my life to Christ, I had no power to fight Satan.

I struggled through to adulthood, and gave my life to Christ in 2020. It was then that I learned that contrary to Satan's lies, I am chosen, I am loved, I am a child of the Father, and before I was born, God had known me (Jer 1:5). Satan's lies began to be revealed for what they were.

Through Freedom Class at my church, I discovered that I was in the thick of warfare, and I learned that I needed to forgive. God spoke very clearly to me: "Why are you asking Me to forgive you when you won't forgive?" I began to grasp that forgiveness is worship, and that worship is the ultimate weapon against Satan. And as I spoke out what had happened to me, and forgave those who caused such deep wounds, Satan's lies and the pain of my past began to lose their power over me. I have put on my armor, and the healing has begun.

As the lies have come down, the anger, depression, fear, and insecurity have been banished. My husband has even noticed that when something gets me angry, I am able to release it quickly. And when Satan attacks again with those anxious or fearful thoughts, I pray and go to the verses I learned in Freedom, and Jesus restores my peace.

Sylvie Rimmer, M.D.
Jupiter, Florida

Notice the wounding that opened Sylvie to believe Satan's lies: the rejection, sexual trauma, and inability to forge deep connected friendships because of the constant moving. Her heart and soul were also wounded by a family environment of secrecy, stuffing, and demands for perfectionism. "My parents just didn't have the tools to help me through these things," Sylvie explained. Can you see the strongholds forming? Foundational wounding, next a network of lies, and then unforgiveness gave Satan a foothold and invited his condemnation. Strongholds of anger, depression, fear, anxiety, and insecurity developed.

Notice also the divinely powerful spiritual weapons that Sylvie wielded with deftness and proficiency. Once she recognized the lies, she rejected them and renewed her mind with the truth of God's Word. And she *forgave*. As she partnered with the Lord, He silenced the enemy and brought the victory.

Sylvie and I have known each other for over two decades, and I am truly a witness to her transformation. Sylvie's eyes used to hold distance and tenseness, but now they are warm and inviting, her face lit with a brilliant light that reflects her deep inner peace.

Indeed, there will be a day when our accuser is forever silenced (Rev 12:10), but at this time, we are still embroiled in the guerilla warfare, and Satan will not be quashed unless we learn, as Sylvie did, how to silence him.

Ponder, Pray, and Journal

If you are struggling with worthlessness, false guilt, shame, self-condemnation, self-hatred, self-deprecation, or low self worth, could it be an attack by the accuser of the brethren? Ask the Lord if there is something that makes you open to this kind of attack.

Enemy Goal: Bondage

Satan's goal of these strategies is to expand his reach more and more until he holds us in bondage, thwarting us from growing in our relationship with God and completing our Kingdom work. Scripture is full of words that describe this bondage: captivity, slavery, chains, imprisonment. Satan works to keep us shackled to our sins, our past, our addictions and failures.

When we are in spiritual chains, we become unable to fulfill the calling Jesus has on our lives. My friend Annette had been walking with the Lord and growing in Christ for decades, but was trapped in bondage of fear. I have invited her to share how she was so constrained by her fears she was unable to even travel with her husband.

Since accepting Christ as my Lord and Savior when I was in high school, I have always considered Jesus a very important part of my life. However I have spent most of my Christian life living in fear. Fear of cancer, fear of heights, fear of closed spaces, fear of losing a loved one – and fear of flying, to name a few. My husband of over thirty years is very adventurous and travels a lot. Because of my fears (specifically the fear of flying), I refused to join him on his business and other trips. It was definitely affecting our marriage. He couldn't understand how I could put God first in my life, yet let such fear paralyze me and keep me from enjoying life with him.

I knew I needed to completely trust God with all aspects of my life, but for decades I did not know how to let go of the fear. Through study of His Word, the Lord began to teach me that fear and anxiety can be idols.

By spending alone time with Him every day, I gradually learned to place all of my fears and worries in His hands. My focus turned to God and away from my fears and anxieties. Deuteronomy 6:13 says, **"You shall fear only the LORD your God."** *As I have learned to walk in fear of the Lord, He and only He has become my sanctuary. By having deeper and deeper fellowship with Him, I was eventually able to fully trust Him with my entire life – and God has demolished the chains of fear! In the four months after this surrender, I went on three separate trips that have involved multiple plane rides – and then I traveled overseas to Italy! That is something I would have never done before this surrender.*

God has totally freed me from the fear of flying. It is something I never plan on taking back. In the past, before a very rare plane trip, I would start worrying and having sleepless nights weeks before the trip. But now, I look forward to my vacations and can't wait to plan more. I am actually on the other side of the country in Park City, Utah right now! I am truly free from the bondage that I was in, and I praise God every day for that freedom.

Annette Schumacher
Juno Beach, Florida

Notice how the Lord required Annette to partner with Him to receive this deliverance. She spent time in His presence, which strengthened her to eventually trust Him enough to place everything in His hands. Her surrender opened her to receive the Lord's freedom from the crippling fear of flying. She sought the Lord, and He answered her, and delivered her from *all of her fears* (Ps 34:4).

Released from bondage, Annette now serves in Student Ministries, reaching young girls who are trapped. As she shares her testimony, God is using her as His instrument, setting others free who are similarly in bondage to fear.

Ponder, Pray, and Journal

As we discussed in Chapter 8, Scriptures make it clear that even Christians can be in bondage (Matt 18:34-35). Have you ever been enslaved? Caught up in idolatry? Trapped in an addiction? Are you in bondage now? Is there a repetitive sin you cannot seem to shake?

We studied some rotten fruit in Chapter 6. Let's look at some more. Read Ephesians 2:1-3 and 4:17-20, and journal the rotten fruit of the sons of disobedience. Sit in stillness before Him, and journal anything that applies to you now.

Commit to walk out in obedience of what He is calling you to do. If this is an addiction or a besetting sin or a heart attitude that you cannot shake, you may be battling a stronghold. As we walk together through Volume II, we will seek the Lord for continued freedom from slavery.

Recap: How Satan Builds His Strongholds

Let's take some time to put together what we have studied in the past few chapters. You have worked hard to learn about the components of strongholds and how these fortresses are constructed. Recognize that by gaining this knowledge, you are also being equipped with powerful weapons to dismantle them. Let's recap.

Satan lays the foundation for his fortresses by inflicting deep heart wounds. These wounds entrap us into believing the lies that those wounds seem to prove. These lies develop into tangled deceptive mindsets and heartsets (*logismos*) that are not aligned with the truth of God's Word, and we are then lured into sin. Satan knows the connection between the lies we believe and the sins we commit.

As Satan is shrewdly laying those traps to lure us into sin, he cunningly selects temptations that feed into iniquities that run in our family lines, for somehow these generational curses add an additional pressure to sin. Satan knows our inherent weaknesses in these areas, and he knows that we will be more likely to fall into repetitive entrenched sin here.

Satan is seeking a **foothold** (Eph 4:27), an open door to enter and launch his attack. One very common foothold is unforgiveness. God commands us to forgive, and even if we were wounded when we were very young, there will be a day when He calls us to accountability. If we remain mired in unforgiveness, it may fester into anger, resentment, bitterness, revenge, and hardness of heart.

Once we have cracked open that door by unforgiveness or any number of other sins, demonic forces can slip in to create a beachhead of increased influence from which they can launch further attacks. Our separation from God can develop into pride and idolatry (*hupsoma*), which further distances us from Him. One sinful lapse leads to another, and sins can become repetitive, or **full-grown:**

... but each one is tempted when, by his own evil desire, he is dragged away and enticed. Then, after desire has conceived, it gives birth to sin; and sin, when it is full-grown, gives birth to death.
James 1:14-15 NIV

Our own evil desires, our deep discontentment, and our wanting what we can't have can drag us into sinful places. Our burning passion to have what is forbidden can seduce us to sin. Every sin separates us from God and disrupts our relationship with Him, but when sin is **full-grown**, when it is deep and repetitive, it *fractures* our relationship with Him. This is spiritual death, as parts of our hearts and lives are severed from God, the only Source of Life. Demons are invited to traffic. Once they enter, a stronghold is formed.

When it seems we are completely unable to do the good we want to do in our behavior, thoughts, or words, and we end up doing the evil we don't want to do, when victory evades us, we may be up against a stronghold.

As we continue to sin, we continue to give more spiritual territory to demons. They are able to move from a position of hovering and harassing, to accessing and influencing. From this deeper position they can establish leverage and connection, moving from flaming arrows, attacks, and opposition to influence, manipulation, oppression, and torment. By our continued sin, we invite them to usurp further access and to exert their power to influence. As they are able to expand their base of operations, the stronghold grows, and the results can be bondage, and in the unsaved, domination.

How Demons Operate Out of Our Strongholds

As demons become entrenched in their strongholds, they can exert pressure upon us to continue in sin. Remember that since our hearts are Command Central, the one who has the greatest influence in our hearts influences all the outflows of our hearts. The greater the demons' access in our hearts, the more they will be able to influence, manipulate, and impact our minds, wills, consciences, emotions, desires, behaviors, and speech. We may have all the right intentions, but the overwhelming pressure from the stronghold can drive us to make sinful choices.

In Francis Frangipane's words, "A demonic stronghold is any type of thinking that exalts itself above the knowledge of God, thereby giving the devil a secure place of influence in an individual's thought life ... Whenever there is a habit of sin in a believer's life, expect to find demonic activity in that area."[3]

Any type of thinking that exalts itself above the knowledge of God. Strongholds involve an entangled web of lies and prideful thoughts. *Logismos* (faulty deceptive mindsets and worldviews) and *hupsoma* (prideful lofty thoughts) lodged in our hearts.

Further woundings, greater delusion and deception resulting from belief in even more lies, and continued repetitive sins determine how extensive the stronghold will be. Furthermore, one demon can pave the way for additional demons (Lk 8:2, Matt 12:45). A stronghold may involve a host of demons cooperating and working together. And from this base of operations, the demonic forces exert their influence and their power.

Ponder, Pray, and Journal

Before we leave this chapter, I would like to read one more passage together from Isaiah. Watch the imagery in this passage as you read about how the rebellion and disobedience of the Israelites caused their fortress to be breached and then defeated. And realize that when we rebel against the Lord, we open the door for demons to breach and then destroy the Strongholds of Light in our own hearts.

My heart breaks as I read this passage; I am sure yours will too. As you read Isaiah 30:9-14, take some time to journal this graphic word picture, and how you can relate it to Satan's working in your own life to destroy your strongholds of righteousness.

As we bring Volume I of this study to a close, I want to pause and celebrate all the Holy Spirit has revealed and taught us, and praise the Lord for all the healing and freedom He has done in our hearts already!

Lord God, You are intimately acquainted with all my ways, and You did not let me remain trapped in the miry clay. Instead, You searched my heart; then by Your kindness You brought me to repentance. I sought You, and You answered me and delivered me from all my fears. You brought me up out of the pit of destruction, setting my feet upon a rock. Because of Your great love with which You love me, You granted me healing and freedom. I give thanks to You, O Lord, with all my heart, and Your praise is continually in my mouth. I thank You and bless Your name and tell the world of Your wonders. For You are magnificent and highly to be praised; Your love and power is unfathomable. O magnify the Lord with me, let us exalt His name together! Amen.[4]

We have completed Volume I, but we have not completed the study – there are more concepts to learn and more battles to fight. If you are doing this study with a group, you may have a break between Volume I and Volume II. Use the break to go back over parts of Volume I as the Holy Spirit leads so you will be ready for the next book.

As we move into Volume II, gear up for intense work – yet I think you will find this work very rewarding as we partner with Jesus and take an active role. We are first going to take a hard look at what we have called "open doors." I have used this phrase throughout this book, and in this next Volume we will really delve into the meaning of this.

As you may be suspecting, this next Volume is not for the faint of heart. And regarding your relationship with Jesus, the question I have for you is this:

Do you want to be...

this
close   or  this
close?

I believe you want to be *this close* or you would have not persevered to finish this book. I believe that you want everything the Lord has for you, and are willing to do whatever it takes to break free from demonic strongholds and to know Jesus in a deeper and richer intimacy. So put on the Lord's armor and come.

Appendix 1
Declarations: Who I Am in Christ

Wear new ruts in your brain by declaring these truths, out loud and with confidence, daily until your heart believes it. Look up the verses and write them down so you can refer to them often.

I am His precious child, chosen, adopted, and sealed by His Holy Spirit (Eph 1:4-5, 13).

My citizenship is in heaven (Phil 3:20).

I bear His name, Christian (Jer 15:16, Acts 9:15, 11:26).

I am established, anointed, and sealed by God (2Cor 1:21-22).

I am His workmanship, a royal diadem in His hand (Eph 2:10, Isa 62:3).

I am His friend (Jn 15:14-15).

I am a member of His body (1Cor 12:27).

He accepted stakes through His hands because He loves me so much (Isa 49:16, Jn 10:18, Heb 9:14).

I am not condemned, for I am the righteousness of God in Christ (Rom 8:1, 2Cor 5:21).

He is always working for my good (Rom 8:28).

He has plans and purposes for me as His co-worker (Jer 29:11, 1Cor 3:9).

He will never stop pursuing me (Ps 139:7-10).

Nothing can separate me from His love (Rom 8:38-39).

Nothing and no one can snatch me from His hand (Jn 10:27-28).

I am His warrior, and He is training my hands for war (2Tim 2:4, Ps 144:1).

He is bringing me to look more like Christ each day (Rom 8:29, Gal 4:19).

I have been bought with a price. I am a temple of God's Holy Spirit – God lives inside of me! (1Cor 6:19-20)

Appendix 2
Victory Verses

Go on the offensive by proclaiming these truths out loud. Since God's Word is like a fire, like a hammer which shatters a rock (Jer 23:29), let's use it to demolish strongholds in our hearts and our lives.

"For nothing is impossible with God." Luke 1 37

The LORD is my light and my salvation;
Whom shall I fear?
The LORD is the defense of my life;
Whom shall I dread? Psalm 27:1

Then David said to the Philistine, "You come to me with a sword, a spear, and a javelin, but I come to you in the name of the LORD of hosts, the God of the armies of Israel, whom you have taunted. This day the LORD will deliver you up into my hands ... that all the earth may know ... that the LORD does not deliver by sword or by spear; for the battle is the LORD's." 1 Samuel 17:45-47

... He who was born of God keeps him, and the evil one does not touch him. 1 John 5:18

"For we are powerless before this great multitude who are coming against us; nor do we know what to do, but our eyes are on You." 2 Chronicles 20:12

The LORD will march forth like a mighty man; he will come out like a warrior, full of fury. He will shout his thundering battle cry, and he will crush all his enemies. Isaiah 42:13 NLT

"Every place on which the sole of your foot treads, I have given it to you." Joshua 1:3

Like heat by the shadow of a cloud, the song of the ruthless is silenced. Isaiah 25:5

I pursued my enemies and overtook them,
And did not turn back until they were consumed ...
And [came] trembling out of their fortresses.   Psalm 18:37, 45

"The Lord is a warrior;
The Lord is His name."   Exodus 15:3

"Should anyone rise up to pursue you and to seek your life, then the life of my Lord shall be bound in the bundle of the living with the Lord your God; but the lives of your enemies He will sling out as from the hollow of a sling."   1 Samuel 25:29

But we have the mind of Christ.   1 Corinthians 2:16

..in no way alarmed by your opponents – which is a sign of destruction for them, but of salvation for you, and that too, from God.
                                                         Philippians 1:28

"Have I not commanded you? Be strong and courageous! Do not tremble or be dismayed, for the Lord your God is with you wherever you go."
                                                         Joshua 1:9

"Not by might nor by power, but by My Spirit," says the Lord of hosts.
                                                         Zechariah 4:6

For I will bend Judah as My bow,
I will fill the bow with Ephraim.
... And His arrow will go forth like lightning   Zechariah 9:13,14

"Be strong and courageous, do not fear or be dismayed because of the king of Assyria nor because of all the horde that is with him; for the one with us is greater than the one with him."   2 Chronicles 32:7

Though a host encamp against me,
My heart will not fear;
Though war arise against me,
In spite of this I shall be confident.   Psalm 27:3

"One of your men puts to flight a thousand, for the Lord your God is He who fights for you, just as He promised you."   Joshua 23:10

The LORD will fight for you; you need only to be still."   Exodus 14:14 NIV

He broke the flaming arrows,
The shield and the sword and the weapons of war.   Psalm 76:3

"And they overcame him because of the blood of the Lamb and because
of the word of their testimony, and they did not love their life even when
faced with death."   Revelation 12:11

If God is for us, who can be against us?   Romans 8:31

"Do not fear, for those who are with us are more than those who are
with them."   2 Kings 6:16

As soon as you hear the sound of marching in the tops of the balsam
trees, move quickly, because that will mean the LORD has gone out in
front of you to strike the Philistine army."   2 Samuel 5:24

"Our God will fight for us."   Nehemiah 4:20

Cry aloud and shout for joy, O inhabitant of Zion,
For great in your midst is the Holy One of Israel.   Isaiah 12:6

You are from God, little children, and have overcome them; because
greater is He who is in you than he who is in the world.   1 John 4:4

The LORD is for me; I will not fear;
What can man do to me?   Psalm 118:6

"But you will chase your enemies and they will fall before you by the
sword; five of you will chase a hundred, and a hundred of you will chase
ten thousand, and your enemies will fall before you by the sword."
          Leviticus 26:7-8

The LORD utters His voice before His army;
Surely His camp is very great,
For strong is he who carries out His word.   Joel 2:11

The LORD is my rock and my fortress and my deliverer,
My God, my rock, in whom I take refuge;
My shield and the horn of my salvation, my stronghold.
I call upon the LORD, who is worthy to be praised,
And I am saved from my enemies.   Psalm 18:2-3

"Behold, I have given you authority to tread on serpents and scorpions, and over all the power of the enemy, and nothing will injure you."
                                                    Luke 10:19

"Do not be afraid of them; remember the LORD who is great and awesome, and fight for your brothers, your sons, your daughters, your wives and your houses."   Nehemiah 4:14

"No weapon that is formed against you will prosper."   Isaiah 54:17

"O LORD, the God of our fathers, are You not God in the heavens? And are You not ruler over all the kingdoms of the nations? Power and might are in Your hand so that no one can stand against You."
                                                2 Chronicles 20:6

"With man this is impossible, but with God all things are possible."
                                              Matthew 19:26 NIV

"When a strong man, fully armed, guards his own house, his possessions are undisturbed. But when someone stronger than he attacks him and overpowers him, he takes away from him all his armor on which he had relied and distributes his plunder."   Luke 11:21-22

"Do not fear or be dismayed because of this great multitude, for the battle is not yours but God's."   2 Chronicles 20:15

"I am the LORD and there is no other;
Besides Me there is no God."   Isaiah 45:5

"Behold, I am the LORD, the God of all flesh; is anything too difficult for Me?"   Jeremiah 32:27

... for the accuser of our brethren has been thrown down, he who accuses them before our God day and night.   Revelation 12:10

Resources

Greek and Hebrew Word Study Tools

Baker, Warren and Carpenter, Eugene. *The Complete Word Study Dictionary Old Testament*. Chattanooga, TN: AMG Publishers, 2003.

Strong, James. *The New Strong's Exhaustive Concordance of the Bible, Concise Dictionary of the Words in the Hebrew Bible, and in the Greek Testament*. Nashville, TN: Thomas Nelson Publishers, 1995.

Zodhiates, Spiros. *The Complete Word Study Dictionary*. Chattanooga, TN: AMG Publishers, 1992.

Vine, W.E., Unger, Merrill F., White, William Jr. *Vine's Complete Expository Dictionary of Old and New Testament Words*. Thomas Nelson Publishers: Nashville, TN, 1996.

Bible Study Tools

Halley's Bible Handbook: with the New International Version. Zondervan: Grand Rapids, MI, 2000.

Kohlenberger III, John R., General Editor. *NIV Nave's Topical Bible*. Zondervan: grand Rapids, MI, 1992.

Vos, Howard F. *Nelson's New Illustrated Bible Manners & Customs: How the People of the Bible Really Lived*. Thomas Nelson Publishers: Nashville, TN, 1999.

Youngblood, Ronald F., General Editor. *Nelson's New Illustrated Bible Dictionary: Completely Revised and Updated Edition*. Thomas Nelson Publishers: Nashville, TN, 1995.

Spiritual Warfare Resources

These theologians do not always agree on everything, but I think their writings mostly seem Biblical, balanced, and helpful to increase our understanding of this complex topic. **Examine everything carefully; hold fast to that which is good** (1Thess 5:21), and do not follow any teaching contrary to the Word of God (Gal 1:8).

Anderson, Neil T. *The Bondage Breaker*. Harvest House Publishers: Eugene, OR, 2000.

Anderson, Neil T. *Victory Over Darkness*. Bethany House Publishers: Bloomington, MN, 2013.

Arthur, Kay. *Lord, Is It Warfare? Teach Me to Stand*. Waterbrook Press: Colorado Springs, CO, 2000.

Bubeck, Mark I. *The Adversary: The Christian Versus Demon Activity*. Moody Publishers: Chicago, Illinois, 2013.

Dean, Robert, Jr. and Ice, Thomas. *What the Bible Teaches About Spiritual Warfare*. Kregel Publications: Grand Rapids, MI, 2000.

Frangipane, Francis. *The Three Battlegrounds*. Arrow Publications: Cedar Rapids, IA, 1989.

Ingram, Chip. *The Invisible War: What Every Believer Needs to Know About Satan, Demons, and Spiritual Warfare*. Baker Books: Grand Rapids, MI, 2007.

Kylstra, Chester and Betsy, *Restoring the Foundations: An Integrated Approach to Healing Ministry*, Henderson, NC, Restoring the Foundations Publications, 2001.

Payne, Dr. Karl I. *Spiritual Warfare: Christians, Demons, and Deliverance*. WND Books: New York NY, 2011.

Prince, Derek. *Blessing or Curse, You Can Choose: Freedom From Pressures You Thought You Had to Live With*. Chosen Books: Grand Rapids, MI, 2006.

Prince, Derek. *Pulling Down Strongholds*. Derek Prince Ministries: Charlotte, NC, 1984.

Sandford, John Loren and Mark. *Deliverance and Inner Healing, Revised Edition*. Baker Book House Company: Grand Rapids, MI, 2008.

Sandford, John Loren and Paula. *Restoring the Christian Family*. Charisma House: Lake Mary, FL, 2009.

Shirer, Priscilla. *The Armor of God*. LifeWay Press: Nashville, TN, 2016.

Spurgeon, Charles, *Spiritual Warfare in a Believer's Life*, Emerald Books, Lynwood, WA, 1993.

Healing and Freedom Resources

Allender, Dr. Dan B. Wounded Heart: *Hope for Adult Victims of Childhood Sexual Abuse*. NavPress: Colorado Springs, CO, 1990.

Bevere, John. *The Bait of Satan: Living Free from the Deadly Trap of Offense*. Charisma House: Lake Mary, FL, 2014.

Bowerman, Dave. *Higher Pursuits: Overcoming the Lies that Keep Us from Freedom, Power, and Purpose*. High Value Press: Port St. Lucie, FL, 2015.

Burg, Courtney J. *Loyal To A Fault: How to Establish New Patters When Loving Others Has Left You Hurting*. W Publishing Group, an imprint of Thomas Nelson: Nashville, TN, 2023.

Cloud, Dr. Henry and Townsend, Dr. John. Boundaries: *When to Say Yes, When to Say No, To Take Control of Your Life*. Grand Rapids, MI: Zondervan, 1992.

Hallam, Walter. *From This Day On: Keys to breaking Yesterday's Stronghold on Today*. Creation House: Lake Mary, FL, 2000.

Kubetin, Cynthia & Mallory, James, M.D. *Shelter From the Storm: Hope for Survivors of Sexual Abuse*. Robert S. McGee Publishing: Titusville, FL, 1995.

McClung, Floyd Jr. *The Father Heart of God: Experiencing the Depth of His Love for You*. Harvest House Publishers: Eugene, OR, 1985.

Names of God Resources

Arthur, Kay. *Lord, I Want to Know You*. Waterbrook Press: Colorado Springs, CO, 2000.

Jukes, Andres. *The Names of God: Discovering God as He Desires To Be Known*. Kregel Publications: Grand Rapids, MI, 1967.

Lockyer, Herbert. *All the Divine Names and Titles in the Bible*. Zondervan: Grand Rapids, MI, 1975.

Spangler, Ann. *Praying the Names of God: A Daily Guide*. Zondervan: Grand Rapids, MI, 2004.

Stone, Nathan. *Names of God*. Moody Publishers: Chicago, IL, 2010.

Occult, Alternative Medicine, and False Religions Resources, Christian Perspective

Explore further only as led by the Holy Spirit, for clarity from the Lord or repentance and cleansing of your involvement in these areas. Be discerning about the resources you use. And don't embark on research out of fascination or idle curiosity, but remain **wise in what is good and innocent in what is evil** (Rom 6:19).

Ankerberg, John and Weldon, John. *The Secret Teachings of the Masonic Lodge: A Christian Perspective*. Moody Publishers: Chicago, IL, 1990.

Bickel, Bruce & Jantz, Stan. *World Religions & Cults 101: A Guide to Spiritual Beliefs*. Hasrvest House Publishers: Eugene, OR, 2002.

O'Mathuna, PhD, Donal, Larimore, MD, Walt. *Alternative Medicine: The Options, the Claims, the Evidence, How to Choose Wisely*. Zondervan: Grand Rapids, MI, 2007.

Reisser, M.D., Paul C., Mabe, D.O., Dale, Velarde, Robert. *Examining Alternative Medicine: An Inside Look at the Benefits and Risks*. InterVarsity Press: Downers Grove, IL, 2001.

Rhodes, Ron. *Find It Quick: Handbook on Cults & New Religions*. Harvest House Publishers: Eugene, OR, 2005.

Ridenour, Fritz. *So What's the Difference? A Look at 20 Worldviews, Faiths and Religions and How They Compare to Christianity*. Regal: Ventura, CA, 2001.

Virtue, Doreen. *Deceived No More: How Jesus Led Me out of the New Age and into His Word*. Thomas Nelson: Nashville, TN, 2020.

Wilder, Lynn K. *Unveiling Grace: The Story of How We Found Our Way Out of the Mormon Church*. Zondervan: Grand Rapids, MI, 2013.

Endnotes, Volume I

Introduction: *Asleep in the Light*

[1] God commands us to be **wise in what is good and innocent in what is evil** (Rom 16:19). Innocent in this verse doesn't mean naive, but *undefiled*. Spiros Zodhiates, *The Complete Word Study Dictionary, New Testament*, Chattanooga, TN, AMG Publishers, 1992, p 111 (no. 185 innocent).

Chapter 1: *The Why Behind the Warfare*

[1] These Scriptures were on my heart as I prayed for you: Hebrews 12:2, 1 Timothy 6:15-16, Philippians 2:9-11, Jude 1:25.

[2] Chip Ingram, *The Invisible War: What Every Believer Needs to Know About Satan, Demons, and Spiritual Warfare*, Grand Rapids, MI, Baker Books, 2007, p 73-74.

[3] David L. Allen, *Hebrews, The New American Commentary: An Exegetical and Theological Exposition of Holy Scripture*, edited by Ray E. Clendenen et al, vol 5, Nashville, TN: B&H Publishing Group, 2010, p 390.

[4] Ingram, p 61.

[5] Francis Frangipane, *The Three Battlegrounds*, Cedar Rapids, IA, Arrow Publications, 1989, p 16.

[6] Celeste Li, M.D., *Triumph Over Suffering Workbook, A Companion to Triumph Over Suffering*, Jupiter, Florida, Plum Tree Ministries, 2015, p 45.

[7] Jade Yu, quoted in *Triumph of Surrender*, p 156.

Chapter 2: *Know Your Battlefield*

[1] Zodhiates, p 533 (no. 1537 *ek*).

[2] Greg Laurie, *New Believer's Bible, New Living Translation: First Steps for New Christians*, Carol Stream, Illinois, Tyndale House Publishers, 2019, p 1074.

[3] Zodhiates, p 1103 (no. 3860 *paradidomi*).

[4] Zodhiates, p 968-969 (no. 3339 *metamorphoo* = transform).

[5] Celeste Li, M.D., *Triumph Over Suffering, A Spiritual Guide to Conquering Adversity*, Jupiter, Florida, Plum Tree Ministries, 2013, p 289.

[6] https://www.youtube.com/watch?v=MFzDaBzBlL0, Smarter Every Day, accessed 3/31/22.

[7] Celeste Li, M.D., *Triumph of Surrender: A Walk of Intimacy With Jesus*, Jupiter, Florida, Plum Tree Ministries, 2016, p 284-286.

[8] Derek Prince, *Blessing or Curse, You Can Choose: Freedom From Pressures You Thought You Had to Live With*, Grand Rapids, MI, Chosen Books, 2006, p 249.
Derek Prince explains that proclamation is "shouting forth, shouting aloud," and it indicates "... strong, confident assertion of faith, which cannot be silenced by any form of opposition or discouragement. It implies a transition from a defensive posture to one of *attack*."

[9] My friend and mentor, Cathy Moesel, taught me this term "glorious opposite." We will use this term throughout the book.

Chapter 3: *Know Your Victor*

[1] Ann Spangler, *Praying the Names of God: A Daily Guide*, Grand Rapids, MI, Zondervan, 2004, p 11.

[2] Spangler, p 12.

[3] Herbert Lockyer, *All the Divine Names and Titles in the Bible*, Grand Rapids, MI, Zondervan, 1975, p 17.

[4] Spangler, p 64.

[5] Lockyer, p 17.

[6] Nathan Stone, *Names of God*, Chicago, IL, Moody Publishers, 1944, 2010, p 11.

[7] Stone, p 11.

[8] Stone, p 34.

[9] Stone, p 34.

[10] Andrew Jukes, *The Names of God: Discovering God as He Desires To Be Known*, Grand Rapids, MI, Kregel Publications, 1967, p 53.

[11] Spangler, p 292.

[12] Stone, p 51-53.

[13] Spangler, p 68.

[14] Spangler, p 64.

[15] Floyd McClung Jr., *The Father Heart of God*, Eugene, Oregon, Harvest House Publishers, 1985, p 66.

[16] James Strong, *The New Strong's Exhaustive Concordance of the Bible, Concise Dictionary of the Words in the Hebrew Bible*, Nashville, TN, Thomas Nelson Publishers, 1995, p 87, no. 4899, and *Concise Dictionary of the Words in the Greek Testament*, p 99, no 5547 (Messiah, Christ).

[17] Warren Baker and Eugene Carpenter, *The Complete Word Study Dictionary Old Testament*, Chattanooga, TN, AMG Publishers, p 899 (no. 6382 wonderful).

[18] I first became aware of the juxtaposition of the Lion of Judah and the Lamb Who Was Slain in Revelation 5 when I heard the song *Lion / Lamb* by Joshua Leventhal, album Lion / Lamb, released 2017.

[19] Saint Augustine, *The Works of Saint Augustine: A Translation for the 21st Century, Part II – Sermons, Volume 10: Sermon 375A*, Hyde Press, NY, New City Press, 1995, p 330-331. *Reproduction by Google books at* https://wesleyscholar.com/wp-content/uploads/2019/04/Augustine-Sermons-341-400.pdf

[20] Zodhiates, p 1107 (no. 3875 *Paracletos*).

Chapter 4: *Know Your Identity*

[1] This thought comes from Joshua 5:13-15, and the commentary I read on https://biblehub.com/commentaries/joshua/5-14.htm#, accessed 3/7/19.

Chapter 5: *Divinely Powerful Weapons*

[1] Spiros Zodhiates, *The Complete Word Study Dictionary*, Chattanooga, TN, AMG Publishers, 1992, p 75 (no. 2476 *histemi*).

[2] Pastor Ryan McDermott, sermon at Christ Fellowship Church on 8/6/23.

[3] Strong, *Greek*, pp 71 and 69 (nos. 4102 and 3982 *pistis*).

[4] Zodhiates, p 924 (no. 3056 *logos*) and p 1262 (no. 4487 *rhema*).

[5] Zodhiates, p 409-410 (no 1209 *dechomai* = take).

[6] Charles Spurgeon, *Spiritual Warfare in a Believer's Life: Compiled and Edited by Robert Hall*, Lynwood, WA, Emerald Books, 1993, p 92.

[7] Zodhiates, p 983 (no. 3379 *mepote*, lest at any time).

[8] Spurgeon,p 82.

[9] Zodhiates, p 259 (no. 739 adequate) and p 601 (no. 1822 equipped).

[10] Spurgeon,p 92.

[11] *Holy Bible: Contemporary English Version*. New York: American Bible Society, 1995.

[12] I heard this pointed out somewhere, in a book or a sermon or both, I do not remember where at this time.

[13] Pastor Todd Mullins spoke about this, sermon at Christ Fellowship Church on 3/6/22.

[14] James Strong, *The New Strong's Exhaustive Concordance of the Bible, Concise Dictionary of the Words in the Hebrew Bible*, Nashville, TN, Thomas Nelson Publishers, 1995, p 137 (no. 7674 sabbath).

[15] Strong, *Hebrew*, p 32 (no. 1793 and 1794, contrite).

[16] Zodhiates, p 148 (no. 328 gird up the loins of your mind).

[17] https://www.ncbi.nlm.nih.gov/pmc/articles/PMC1739867/, accessed 10/5/21

[18] Zodhiates, p 207 (no. 529), p 627 (no. 1939 lusts).

[19] Li, *Triumph of Surrender*, p 178.

[20] My friend shared with me that her friend told her he thought "the arts are an arsenal to impact people." My friend then thought that "the arts are an arsenal against the enemy." My writing here leapt from those thoughts.

[21] Julie Woodley, *Into My Arms*, Setauket, New York, Restoring the Heart Ministries, Inc., 2011, p 115.

Chapter 6: *Know Your Enemy*

[1] Zodhiates, p384-385 (no. 1127 watch).

[2] Mark I. Bubeck, *The Adversary: The Christian Versus Demon Activity*, Chicago, Illinois, Moody Publishers, 2013, p 53. This book helped give me clarity on what the Bible means when it speaks about the world, and was influential in my writing in this section.

[3] Bubeck, p 53.

[4] Bubeck, p 56.

[5] Zodhiates, p1011 (no. 3528 nikao, victory).

6 Turn Your Eyes Upon Jesus - Helen Howorth Lemmel, written in 1918. https://www.songfacts.com/facts/helen-howarth-lemmel/turn-your-eyes-upon-jesus, accessed 3/10/20.

7 Pastor Todd Mullins has taught on this multiple times at Christ Fellowship Church.

8 Zodhiates, p 1091 (no. 3823). (*pale* = wrestle)

9 Zodhiates, p 721 (no. 2307 *thelema*).

Chapter 7: *Satan's Names Reveal His Character*

1 Zodhiates, p 419. This page which discusses *diabolos* (no. 1228) expounds on some of the names of Satan, which brought some additional verses to mind for this chapter.

2 Zodhiates, p 1082 (no. 3789 serpent).

3 Stone, p 40.

4 Zodhiates, p 484 (no. 1404 *drakon*, dragon).

5 Zodhiates, p 1282 (no. 4567, Satan).

6 Derek Prince, *Pulling Down Strongholds*, New Kensignton, PA, Whitaker House, 2013, p 30.

7 Zodhiates, p 418-419 (no. 1228, *diabolos* = devil).

8 Zodhiates, p 1128 (no. 3962 father).

9 Zodhiates, p 692 (no. 2190 enemy).

10 Zodhiates, p 191 (no. 476, adversary).

11 Prince, *Pulling Down Strongholds*, p 17.

12 Zodhiates, p 850 (no. 2723 accuser) and p 419.

13 Timothy Keller, *Loving Your Enemies*, podcast by Gospel in Life, 8/28/23, helped me to understand that it is *not* Christlike when we refuse to confront injustice, and what it means to stand for truth and justice with humility, forgiveness, and love.

14 Zodhiates, p 58 (no.3 Abaddon).

15 Strong's *Hebrew* p 1 (no. 11 Abaddon).

16 Zodhiates, p 321 (no. 623 Apollyon).

17 Zodhiates, p 1165 (no. 4105 deceive).

18 Zodhiates, p 1198 (no. 4190 evil).

19 Zodhiates, p 332 (no. 955 Belial).

20 Strong's *Hebrew*, p 20 (no. 1100 Belial).

21 http://www.dictionary.com/browse/lechery?s=t, and http://www.dictionary.com/browse/dissolute?s=t, accessed 6/20/18.

22 http://www.dictionary.com/browse/profligate?s=t, and http://www.dictionary.com/browse/licentious?s=t, accessed 6/20/18

23 Warren Baker, D.R.E. and Eugene Carpenter, Ph.D., *The Complete Word Study Dictionary Old Testament*, Chattanooga, TN, AMG Publishers, 2003, p 10966 (no. 263 Lucifer). My memory from my high school Latin classes proved to be correct. (Google translate lux and ferre) accessed 3/3/20.

[24] https://explainingscience.org/2015/11/10/the-morning-star-venus/ accessed 3/8/23

[25] Strong's *Hebrew*, p 34, 35 (morning star no. 1966 *heylel* and its root no. 1984 *halal*).

[26] Kay Arthur, *Lord Is It Warfare? Teach Me To Stand*, Colorado Springs, CO, Waterbrook Press, 2000, p 48.

[27] Isaiah 25:4-6 was on my heart as I prayed for you.

Chapter 8: *Levels of Demonic Activity*

[1] Strong's Greek, p 71 (no. 4105 *planao* = seduce).

[2] Zodhiates, p 499 (no. 1465 hinder).

[3] Zodhiates, p 902 (no.2967 forbidden).

[4] Zodhiates, p 494 (no. 1439 did not permit).

[5] Zodhiates, p 874 (no. 2852, *kolaphizo*, to strike with the fist, to buffet).

[6] Zodhiates, p 1390 (no.5117 *topos* = place).

[7] Zodhiates, p 452 (no. 1352 give).

[8] Zodhiates, p 995 (no. 345 *mone* = abode).

[9] Zodhiates, p 851 (no. 2730 dwell).

[10] Li, *Triumph of Surrender*, p 294-295.

[11] Dr. Karl I. Payne, *Spiritual Warfare: Christians, Demonization, and Deliverance*, Washington, D.C.,WND Books, 2011, p 152-153.

[12] Payne, p 153-156.

[13] Zodhiates, p 932 (no. 930, *basanistes*, torturers).

[14] https://www.merriam-webster.com/dictionary/oppression, accessed 1/24/24.

[15] Frangipane, p 24-25.

[16] Joni Eareckson Tada, *When God Weeps*, Grand Rapids, MI, Zondervan, 1997, p 152.

[17] https://www.merriam-webster.com/dictionary/dominion#:~:text=%3A%20the%20 power%20(as%20authority),donor's%20dominion%20and%20control%20W.%20 M, accessed8/12/23.

[18] John Loren Sandford and Mark Sandford, *Deliverance and Inner Healing, Revised Edition*, Grand Rapids, MI, Baker Book House Company, 2008, pp 92-93.

[19] Susie Larson, *Your Beautiful Purpose, Discovering and Enjoying What God Can Do Through You*, Bloomington, MN, Bethany House Publishers, 2013, p 45. This is a paraphrase of what she has written.

Chapter 9: *Authority, Access, and Power*

[1] Frangipane, p 12.

[2] Frangipane, p 12.

[3] This term "delegated authority" I first became familiar with through Watchman Nee's book, *Spiritual Authority*, New York, Christian Fellowship Publishers, 1972. This term is used throughout his book, and we will discuss it in more detail in Chapter 17.

[4] I think I may have heard this many years ago from the videos that accompany Kay

444   Triumph In Warfare

Arthur's Precept Upon Precept study, *Kinsman Redeemer*, Chattanooga, TN, Precept Ministries International, 2002.

5 Zodhiates, p 210 (no. 554 disarmed).

6 Strong's *Greek*, p 10 (no. 554 disarmed).

7 https://www.dictionary.com/browse/divest?s=t accessed 3/4/19.

8 https://www.dictionary.com/browse/despoil?s=t 3/4/19.

9 Zodhiates, p 245 (no. 680 *haptomai* = harm)

10 Zodhiates, p 178 (no. 436 *anthistemi*).

11 Strong's *Hebrew*, p 118 (no. 6635, Lord of Hosts).

12 Li, *Triumph of Surrender*, p 304-309.

13 Zodhiates, p 1375 (no. 5055 *teleo* = perfected).

14 Zodhiates, p271 (no. 769 *astheneia* = weakness).

Chapter 10: *Formation of a Stronghold, Part I*

1 Frangipane, p 31-32.

2 These Scriptures were on my heart as I prayed for you: 1 Kings 8:39, Romans 8:27, Jeremiah 17:10, Proverbs 21:2, Hebrews 4:12, Psalm 139:23, 1 Corinthians 4 4, Psalm 25:14 NIV.

3 Frangipane, p 24, 32, 29, and 23

4 Many freedom and healing ministers agree that a stronghold means demonic activity, for example Neil T. Anderson, *Victory Over Darkness*, Bloomington, MN, Bethany House Publishers, 2013, p 150; Chester and Betsy Kylstra, *Restoring the Foundations: An Integrated Approach to Healing Ministry*, Henderson, NC, Restoring the Foundations Publications, 2001, p 327, John Loren Sandford and Mark Sandford, *Deliverance and Inner Healing*, Grand Rapids, MI, Chosen Books, 2008, p 305.

5 Zodhiates, p 1083 (no. 3794, *ochuroma* = stronghold).

6 Sheets, p 183.

7 Kylstra, *Foundational Problem/Ministry Areas* p 101-318, and Chapter XII, *Demonic Strongholds*, p 327-337, with visual depiction on p 328-329.

8 Cynthia Kubetin and James Mallory, M.D., *Shelter From the Storm Hope for Survivors of Sexual Abuse*, Titusville, FL, Robert S. McGee Publishing, 1995, p 170.

9 https://www.thegospelcoalition.org/reviews/thats-good-recovering-lost-art-discernment/, accessed 4/5/22.

10 Tada, p 85.

11 Frangipane, p 30.

12 Zodhiates, p 923 (no. 3053 *logismos*).

13 Zodhiates, p 1083 (no. 3794, *ochuroma* = stronghold).

Chapter 11: *Formation of a Stronghold, Part II*

1 I had sensed for many years that iniquity was within our hearts under demonic

control, but reading this website helped me to see this more clearly. https://seekingscripture.com/what-is-the-difference-between-sin-iniquity-and-transgressions/#:~:text=Sin%2C%20it%20turns%20out%2C%20is,sin%20by%20transgressing%20God's%20law, accessed 4/18/24.

[2] These Scriptures were on my heart as I prayed for you: John 16:13, James 1:5, Psalm 33:11, Isaiah 55:8-9, Proverbs 3:5-6, Romans 8:38-39, and Psalm 46:1-3.

[3] Warren Baker and Eugene Carpenter, *The Complete Word Study Dictionary Old Testament*, Chattanooga, TN, AMG Publishers, 2003, p 814 (no. 5771 avon = iniquity). I also read about this word in Derek Prince's *Blessing or Curse, You Can Choose: Freedom From Pressures You Thought You Had to Live With*, Chosen Books, Grand Rapids, MI, 2006, p 192.

[4] Zodhiates, p 84 (no. 96 iniquity).

[5] W.E. Vine, Merril F, Unger, William White, Jr., *Vine's Complete Expository Dictionary of Old and New Testament Words,* Nashville, TN, Thomas Nelson, Inc., 1996, p 326.

[6] Zodhiates, p 84 (no. 96 *adikia* = iniquity).

[7] Zodhiates, p 85 and 130 (no. 266 *hamartia* = sin).

[8] Baker, p 913 (no. 6485 visiting).

[9] Baker, p 913 (no. 6485 visiting).

[10] https://www.aacap.org/AACAP/Families_and_Youth/Facts_for_Families/FFF-Guide/Children-Of-Alcoholics-017.aspx, accessed 9/7/23.

[11] https://www.who.int/news-room/fact-sheets/detail/child-maltreatment#:~:text=Child%20maltreatment%20is%20often%20hidden,one%20generation%20to%20the%20next, accessed 9/7/23.

[12] https://www.apa.org/monitor/2023/07/how-gambling-affects-the-brain#:~:text=Seeing%20parents%2C%20siblings%2C%20or%20other,107460%2C%202022), accessed 9/8/23.

[13] https://www.ncbi.nlm.nih.gov/pmc/articles/PMC2732348, accessed 9/8/23, https://saulandsaul.com/wp-content/uploads/2016/10/Children-of-Workaholics-COWs.pdf, accessed 9/8/23, https://www.ncbi.nlm.nih.gov/pmc/articles/PMC6051714, accessed 9/8/23, https://www.medicalnewstoday.com/articles/319250#Mothers-insomnia-may-influence-childrens, accessed 9/8/23.

[14] Kylstra, p 108, 116.

[15] Zodhiates, p 1433 (no. 5313, *hupsoma*).

[16] Zodhiates, p 611 (no. 1869, raised up).

[17] Rick Warren, *The Purpose Driven Life: What on Earth Am I Here For?*, Grand Rapids, MI, Zondervan, 2002, p 186.

[18] C.S. Lewis, *Mere Christianity*, New York, NY, HarperCollins Publisher, 1952, p 128.

[19] Zodhiates, p 156 (no. 372 rest).

Chapter 12: *Satan Operates in Legalism*

[1] I read this phrase somewhere about God bending His own laws, probably in one of the books in the Resource section.

[2] Zodhiates, p 1107 (no. 3875, *Paracletos*).

[3] Derek Prince, *Blessing or Curse, You Can Choose: Freedom From Pressures You Thought You Had to Live With*, Chosen Books, Grand Rapids, MI, 2006, p 47.

[4] Zodhiates, p 596 (no. 1809, demanded permission).

[5] This "sifting" passage following right after the "who is greatest" passage was brought to my attention in a book or message somewhere, I cannot recall where.

Chapter 13: *The Consequences of Obeying – or Disobeying – God's Laws*

[1] Jack Frost, DVD *Breaking Free*. I heard Jack Frost speak about this many years ago. Other authors have spoken and written about these seasons also.

[2] Timothy Keller, *Loving Your Enemies*, podcast by Gospel in Life, 8/28/23, helped me to understand that it is not Christlike when we refuse to confront injustice, and what it means to stand for truth and justice with humility, forgiveness, and love.

[3] Dr. Henry Cloud & Dr. John Townsend, *Boundaries*, Grand Rapids, MI, Zondervan, 1992, 2017. These teachings are the theme throughout this book.

[4] Li, *Triumph of Surrender*, p 219.

[5] John Loren & Paula Sandford, *Restoring the Christian Family: A Biblical Guide to Love, Marriage, and Parenting in a Christian World*, Lake Mary, FL, Charisma House, 2009, p 146-147.

[6] Kylstra, p 43.

Chapter 14: *Satan's Strategies to Usurp Rule*

[1] Zodhiates, p 1091 (no. 3823, *pale* = wrestle)

[2] Prince, *Blessing or Curse: You Can Choose: Freedom From Pressures You Thought You Had to Live With*, p 55.

[3] Frangipane, p 23,24,26.

[4] These Scriptures were on my heart as I prayed for you: Psalm 139:3,23, Psalm 40:2, Romans 2:4, Psalm 34:1-4, Ephesians 2:4, Psalm 9:1.

Contributors Volume I

www.ingramcontent.com/pod-product-compliance
Lightning Source LLC
Chambersburg PA
CBHW021037090426
42738CB00006B/126